Avenging the People

Avenging the People

Andrew Jackson, the Rule of Law, and the American Nation

J. M. Opal

OXFORD
UNIVERSITY PRESS

Oxford University Press is a department of the University of Oxford. It furthers the University's objective of excellence in research, scholarship, and education by publishing worldwide. Oxford is a registered trade mark of Oxford University Press in the UK and certain other countries.

Published in the United States of America by Oxford University Press
198 Madison Avenue, New York, NY 10016, United States of America.

Library of Congress Cataloging-in-Publication Data
Names: Opal, J. M., author.
Title: Avenging the people : Andrew Jackson,
the rule of law, and the American nation / J.M. Opal.
Description: Oxford [UK] ; New York : Oxford University Press, 2017. | Includes index.
Identifiers: LCCN 2016044301 (print) | LCCN 2017000057 (ebook) |
ISBN 9780199751709 (hardback) | ISBN 9780190660253 (Updf) |
ISBN 9780190660260 (Epub)
Subjects: LCSH: Jackson, Andrew, 1767–1845. | Lawyers—United States—Biography. |
Presidents—United States—Biography. |
Rule of law—United States—History—19th century. | Law—United
States—History—19th century. | United States—Politics and
government—1829–1837. | Democratic Party (U.S.)—History—19th century. |
BISAC: BIOGRAPHY & AUTOBIOGRAPHY / Presidents & Heads of State. |
HISTORY / United States / Revolutionary Period (1775–1800).
Classification: LCC KF368.J33 O63 2017 (print) | LCC KF368.J33 (ebook) |
DDC 973.5/6092 [B] —dc23
LC record available at https://lccn.loc.gov/2016044301

1 3 5 7 9 8 6 4 2

Printed by Sheridan Books, Inc., United States of America

If I whet my glittering sword, and my hand take hold on judgment, I will execute vengeance on mine enemies, and will reward them that hate me. I will make mine arrows drunk with blood, (and my sword shall eat flesh) for the blood of the slain, and of the captives, when I begin to take vengeance of the enemy. Ye nations, praise his people; for he will avenge the blood of his servants, and will execute vengeance upon his adversaries, and will be merciful unto his land, and to his people.

Deuteronomy 32:41–43.

CONTENTS

ACKNOWLEDGMENTS

I would first like to thank the editors of *The Papers of Andrew Jackson* at the University of Tennessee, most of whom I have never met. With extraordinary precision, they have collected and explained a huge range of documents while also directing the researcher to the still more massive stores of Jackson papers at the Library of Congress and other repositories. Their work gave my investigations a method, a center, an evidentiary base. I have had the pleasure of working with the director of the *Papers*, Daniel Feller, who has been one of my project's most helpful readers and engaged critics since the beginning. Dan even shared with me the latest volume of the *Papers*, covering 1832, just before its release. In the late stages of writing I also profited from the expertise of Thomas Coens. I owe an equal debt to my editor at Oxford University Press, Susan Ferber, who believed in the project from the outset and handled it (and me) perfectly for longer than I care to remember. Among many other things, Susan put me in touch with Nicole Eustace, who greatly helped with a drafty first draft.

I began this book while teaching at Colby College, where I benefited not only from the financial support of the Harriet S. and George C. Wiswell Jr. Chair but also from colleagues and friends Elizabeth Leonard, Margaret McFadden, Gil Frank, Rob Weisbrot, David Lewis-Colman, Peter Ditmanson, David Paul Josephson, Raffael Scheck, Jim Webb, Larissa Taylor, and John Turner. Jason and Heidi Long were my friends and supporters throughout my years in Maine. At Bowdoin College, Matt Klingle, Connie Chiang, and Patrick Rael helped me get things off the ground. Jeffrey Selinger, Jayanthi Selinger, and Nick Touloudis carefully read early offerings, gently suggested big changes, and encouraged me to keep digging. Also in Maine, Ruquaia Abdalhossein and her three children, Zainab, Mohammed, and Ahmed, taught me about the more relevant forms of courage.

At McGill, I was lucky to have a grant from the Social Sciences and Humanities Research Council of Canada. This allowed me to make many trips to the Tennessee State Library and Archives, where I turned again and again to Tom Kanon and his colleagues. Marsha Mullin, vice president of

Museum Services and chief curator at the Hermitage, helped me with some last-minute puzzles. My fellowship also connected me to an extraordinary group of students. Melissa Gismondi helped me with a list of sources, databases, and edits too long to recall. Suffice it to say that it was a great privilege to work with her, and an even greater joy to learn from her now as a colleague. Jonathon Booth was every bit as impressive as a research assistant as he was in seminar. Eliza Wood poured through secondary sources and helped me to review relevant historiographies, while Katherine Wilson chased down old newspapers and read several chapters. Ariane Jacques-Côté, Margaret Carlyle, Raminder Saini, Matthew Wyman-McCarthy, Nadir Khan, Lauren Konken, Graeme Mack, Kate Bauer, Lauren DuVal, G. Patrick O'Brien, Nicolas Magnien, and Andrew Dial all helped with the revision of various sections. Sarah Eastly read the penultimate draft and made it much better. And C. L. Aber was an extraordinary editor and fact checker, working through draft after draft and keeping me sharp right to the end.

McGill has been no less generous in terms of faculty colleagues. Len Moore, Laila Parsons, and Rob Wisnovsky welcomed me to campus and listened to my half-baked ideas about what the book would eventually become. Elizabeth Elbourne, Daviken Studnicki-Gizbert, Catherine Desbarats, Tom Jundt, Malek Abisaab, Rula Abisaab, Jarrett Rudy, and Johanna Ransmeier offered crucial insights. Mitali Das helped me to advise and (hopefully) to help our graduate students. Lorenz Lüthi and Catherine Lu were mentors in all things relating to McGill and Montreal. Michael Fronda and Hans Beck fielded questions about classical allusions, and Allan Greer enabled me to make sense of land laws. Arash Abizadeh, Tassos Anastassiadis, Brian Lewis, and Brian Cowan all helped me to think through some important pieces. François Furstenberg and Julien Mauduit offered critical insights at multiple phases while also welcoming me into a francophone environment. Gavin Walker, Rachel Sandwell, and my old friend from Brandeis, Anthony Smith, have all been wonderful listeners and tireless supporters.

I first presented bits of this project at the annual meeting of the Society for Historians of the Early American Republic in 2008, and SHEAR has remained an invaluable venue for advancing and exchanging ideas. Jane Kamensky, Catherine E. Kelly, Jessica Lepler, Dan Richter, Brian Rouleau, Beth Shaler, Toby L. Ditz, Benjamin Carp, Alan Taylor, David Waldstreicher, Eric Schlereth, Max Dagenais, Marjoleine Kars, John Fea, Woody Holton, Jessica Choppin Roney, and Brandon Mills all made comments and posed questions that stayed with me. I was also lucky to take part in the 2011 Chicago Conference on the American Revolution, organized by Jane Kamensky and Edward G. Gray. Their comments along with those of Eliga Gould, Rosemarie Zagarri, and Benjamin Irvin helped enormously. I was also privileged to meet Stephen Aron, Reeve Huston, and the late Drew Cayton at a conference that Drew helped to organize in Montreal. Andrew Shankman generously invited me to write an essay about some of the economic and legal themes of the project, on which both he and Daniel Walker Howe offered key feedback.

I also owe a great deal to the Gilder-Lehrman Institute of American History for giving me many forums at which to present parts of the book. I was delighted to work with Tim Bailey while doing workshops in Georgia, Massachusetts, Rhode Island, New York, and Wisconsin and with Sean Enos-Robertson during a week-long seminar in Montreal in August 2015. The exceptional educators in that seminar were an enormous help as I tried to bring this unruly project to a close.

My family is the center of my world, no matter how much this book encroached from time to time. My parents, Katherine Ann Opal and Steven Michael Opal, have always stood by me, and their profound benevolence is a constant wonder. My brother, Michael Oscar Opal, is everything an elder sibling should be, and also a super smart guy. My aunt, Mary Jane Weeks, is one of the finest writers I know, and a kindred spirit who is never more than a witty email away. I hope she will see her contributions throughout this book.

Holly Stuart Buss is my best friend and soulmate, and I don't know how to thank her enough for making me a better person. More than anyone, she has lived with this book for a bit too long, and I hope it makes her proud. I would like to dedicate *Avenging the People* to our daughter, Anya Joss Opal, who came along just as I started writing. I thank her for letting me work even when it cost us Harry Potter reading time and for knowing when to smile, laugh, or say something profound. *Je t'aime, ma rebelle*. Luke, my dear son, the next one is for you.

J.M.O.
October 2016
Montreal, QC

Avenging the People

Introduction

In Our Blood

Sometime after rising to international fame in 1815, Andrew Jackson lamented that his critics had him all wrong. Whether from ignorance or malice, they spread rumors and lies about his actions and motives. They also smeared his wife, Rachel, with whom he often shared his sense of persecution. Although most Americans seemed to worship him, these attacks were still painful, for they hit core parts of the general's self-image. His "settled course" in life, he told a trusted friend, was to honor the rigid code of behavior with which his mother had once entrusted him. He was, he believed, completely devoted to just dealings and always careful to avoid insults. He was, he insisted, especially loyal to the US Constitution. Yet his enemies said that he was "a most ferocious animal, insensible to moral duty, and regardless of the laws both of God and man." Since these foes were too numerous and cowardly to confront in person, Jackson could only hope that the biography his friend was preparing would set the record straight.[1]

This book takes issue with many things that Jackson wanted people to think about him. In particular, it questions his place in America's democratic tradition, drawing attention to the popular efforts and egalitarian ideas that he and his allies helped to bury. It tries to avoid the strong pull of his personal legend and the historical narratives that bear his name, often moving him off the center of analysis to better see the people, places, conflicts, and choices that made him. In telling the story as Jackson and his devotees would not have done, the book is critical and "revisionist." But it does not doubt the sincerity of Jackson's belief in his own lawfulness, nor even the accuracy of that belief. He really did believe in the law. He certainly wanted justice. And his efforts to inflict his versions of both defined his life and career in ways that his other roles and identities—an Irishman, a southerner, a westerner, a soldier, a slave owner, a Democrat—cannot explain. His life was a mission, the mission was just, and its enemies would be judged.

Jackson was sure that his duties were authorized at the highest levels, and for good reason. His views on civil order and property rights often aligned with those of America's first national leaders, who were also keen to draw the new republic into a larger society of "civilized" states. In this sense he was a proper nationalist. On the other hand, Jackson took an oath to a European monarch, was implicated in two secessionist plots, accused the federal government of suicidal cowardice, and threatened to incinerate a US government building and official. He chafed at the national terms of the rule of law and had little use for competing forms of American fellowship and sovereignty. A long series of regional traumas and global crises made him a particular kind of hero in 1814–15 and again in 1818–19, a larger-than-life "avenger" with a passionate bond to the American "nation." His very name evoked a set of feelings and stories that marked Americans in some essential way—in their very blood, as the saying quite appropriately goes. The purpose of this book is to show how that happened and to explore the implications for the man and his nation.

PAPER AND CIVILIZATION

Jackson never studied at one of British North America's nine colleges, but he had all the education he needed to transcend his modest origins. Tales of his backwoods simplicity are much exaggerated. Born along the seams of the two Carolinas in the spring of 1767, he was by all accounts a promising boy who could recite Bible verses, relay stories, and write a good hand. He also grew up near one of the largest Presbyterian churches in the western settlements. With the support of his pious mother and a prominent relative, the young man studied with clergymen who impressed upon him the special importance of their knowledge along the far corners of British civilization. Later in life one of them proudly recalled that he had taught Jackson the stern truths of Calvinist Christianity, and also that his own wife had fought the fiendish Indians during an attack on her Pennsylvania settlement. All that terrible Sunday, she had supplied the defenders with ammunition, "though her father was lying a corpse." Jackson heard many stories like this.[2]

Accustomed to think well of his mind, "Andy" tended to force new information into prior convictions. He thought and read intensively, not broadly. Among his favored books were the Bible and the Westminster Catechism, the latter of which reduced the moral complexity of the world to 107 queries with 107 replies. (Question: "What is the chief end of man?" Answer: "Man's chief end is to glorify God and to enjoy Him forever.") In his own way Jackson would remain a fervent believer in the inflexible rules that God had given to his ungrateful children. But after the Revolution took almost everything, he turned from revealed religion to another source of authoritative knowledge, the law. Here, too, he relied on a few titles. None were more important than Sir William Blackstone's *Commentaries on the Laws of England* (1765–69) and Emer de Vattel's *The Law of Nations* (1758), the combined influence of which is hard to overstate. Together these super-texts offered a universalizing vision of the rule of law within and between nations, a call to order in which Jackson's life was deeply embedded.[3]

Blackstone's goal was to bring order to the vast heap of rulings and statutes that made up common law. To this end he routinely cited Scripture as the original source of truth and assumed, with most European theorists, that he who enforced rather than obeyed the law—the sovereign—was very much like God, at least until he died and was judged himself. The law according to Blackstone remained "a terror to evil-doers," the latest versions of Deuteronomy 32:35 ("Vengeance and recompense are mine"), Exodus 32:34 ("I will visit their sin upon them"), and other warnings of divine justice. In the *Commentaries* as at the gallows, sovereignty was about judgment and punishment, about physical and moral assertion over the lowly and guilty. But what really accounted for the growing power of lawyers and courts was their command of the new, more fluid notions of property that had been spreading around the Atlantic world for decades. Blackstone tried to explain with some stories about where "things" came from.[4]

Everyone could agree that someone who cut down a tree and then made fence posts from the wood "owned" those posts. (One legend says that Jackson's father died after straining to move a log.) At first, Blackstone suggested, the tree cutter's exclusive claim ended as soon as he stopped using the wood. Labor and use were still "the fairest and most reasonable title" to property. As society advanced, though, it granted ongoing rights of possession, so that "the very *substance* of the thing to be used" could be monopolized. This, too, was common sense. When the hypothetical man arranged the fence posts around a given plot, his claims upon nature grew more complicated. Blackstone spent many tedious chapters explaining how pieces of contemporary England could be bought, leased, entailed, rented, forfeited, seized, and otherwise named by official-looking pieces of paper. The most recent innovation in property was "commercial traffic," which made such documents much more than paper. The debts and investments described by the right documents were "things in action" (often rendered in the French, *choses*) rather than "things in possession," but things all the same.[5]

Blackstone did not know when property had taken leave of its self-evident origins. He could not say when a bit of parchment bearing signatures and interest had become more valuable than the tree from which it had been made. What mattered was that these latest property forms, paper-thin as they were, *remained* property, and that society treated them as such. Indeed, he stressed the social and conditional rather than the natural or absolute basis of property rights. The changing rules of a commercial society were "a kind of secondary law of nature," and they had to be enforced by the sovereign, as by returning paper investments in gold or silver and, if need be, by repossessing more visible *choses* to satisfy creditors. A merchant who held a promissory note (an interest-bearing IOU) was just as entitled to the sums described as the fence maker was to his posts. An investor who held a note of hand (a formal request by one party to pay another) held a "chose in action" that courts and judges had to protect just like a "chose in possession."[6]

All of the paper instruments "now introduced into all sorts of civil life" were, in the final analysis, contracts. And contracts, in terms that again brought bench and pulpit together, were "sacred." This bore repeating, for never had so much property taken so many forms that required so much imagination. Never had so many commodities drawn from the fertile soils and whipped backs of distant plantations circulated through European markets, financing more and more "choses in action." Never had empires spent so much to protect those plantations from their rivals, creating in turn new bonds and securities to pay for more ships and soldiers. The eighteenth century was the Age of Paper before it became the Age of Revolution, and at least one American from Andrew Jackson's home state saw the "astonishing" growth of "commercial capital" as the real break with the past. In "modern times," Senator Robert Y. Hayne of South Carolina noted, "there is scarcely a particle of visible property, which is not represented by an equal amount of invisible property."[7]

Wherever governments made sure that property in all its proliferating forms was protected, Blackstone saw "the grand ends of civil society" at work. New volumes of exchange had spread "a vast variety of obligations" around the globe, and the law was there to enforce them. Call it commercial

Figure 0.1 Sir William Blackstone (1723–80). His four-volume compilation of English and British law was the dominant source of legal expertise in the Anglo-American world of the late 1700s and early 1800s.
National Portrait Gallery, London.

order: a legal regime in which property could be represented on paper, exchanged for more paper far away and much later, and still collected to the satisfaction of the holder. Blackstone saw it as the starting point for a better, more enlightened world. In this he echoed Emer de Vattel, the Swiss diplomat whose *Law of Nations* saw happiness and not mere survival as "the great end of the law of nature." If nations were still akin to individuals in nature, Vattel argued, recent history had lifted their rights and duties beyond the brute laws of tooth and claw, enabling at least some people to coexist. "A dwarf is as much a man as a giant; a small republic is no less a sovereign state than the most powerful kingdom." Since "men are naturally equal," Vattel reasoned, "nations composed of men" were as well.[8]

The "civilized nations" had more and more reasons to respect each other, Vattel believed, especially as "*exchange*, or the traffic of bankers" pushed huge sums of paper wealth across political boundaries. Every government had to secure the private investments of those within its domain, "whether citizen or foreigner," or lose the trust of future investors and other governments. Treaties, too, were like contracts, and they made up a kind of common law for the civilized world. Taken individually, treaties were "mere conventional acts between the contracting parties," argued William R. Davie, a North Carolina lawyer and soldier whom a young Andrew Jackson much admired. "Yet by the law of nations they are the supreme law of the land to their respective citizens or subjects." By respecting those agreements, Davie argued, modern states fostered "that commercial intercourse, which founded on the universal protection of private property, has in a measure made the world one nation." In legal terms they recognized the transitory rather than local rights of men with choses in action, enabling those men to move around the world with all the wealth their paper could describe.[9]

Beyond Blackstone and Vattel, such visions relied on the theory of the social contract as described in Jean-Jacques Rousseau's 1762 book of the same name. Also important in the Anglophone world was Henry Home, the Lord Kames, whose *Historical Law-Tracts* (1758) had none of Rousseau's nostalgia for the woods. At some crucial moment in history, Kames declared, civilized people had given up their natural right to recover their debts and avenge their injuries. They had entrusted revenge, "the darling privilege of human nature," to their sovereign, who then offered security to everyone living under his laws. "There, perhaps, never was in government a revolution of greater importance than this," for it enabled people who did not share family or religious ties to live in peace. "Under civil government," one philosopher typically declared, "subjects ought not to continue violence after they are secured from present danger." Unless their lives hung in the balance, they should contain their "hot" and partial passions, trusting the cool and even-handed law to do them justice. The man who instead took retribution out of "hatred of the person, and joy in his misery" was guilty of "that criminal *revenge*, which is condemned both by the natural and christian laws."[10]

Of course, European sovereigns had always tried to monopolize vengeance. English armies had long disarmed Scottish clans while waging war without mercy on Jacobite rebels. French rulers since the "Sun King," Louis XIV, had built vast armies while cracking down on the aristocratic custom of dueling. Imposing the rule of law was ultimately a matter of force, of granting security and demanding allegiance. Such was the "protection covenant," and it was nothing new. The good news from Blackstone and Vattel during the 1760s and 1770s was that the job was nearly done. Enlightenment Europe was emerging from clannish feuds and religious hatreds. Pacified within their boundaries, the "civilized nations" were learning to get along and move ahead, to foster civil society and secure commercial order.[11]

Every nation, Vattel insisted, should "labour at its own perfection and that of its state," pursuing its own self-interest until it ran into that of other civilized peoples. Exactly what that meant occupied much of *The Law of Nations*. In a commercial age, each nation should follow England's example and "trade together for the common benefit of the human race." Because the sovereign's first duty was to his own nation, however, he could also protect domestic manufactures through import duties, foster literacy through public education, and enhance the value of lands via roads and canals. More than free trade theorists like Adam Smith, Vattel thought that governments should direct and promote progress. He could never have guessed how important such ideas would be in the North American states that emerged shortly after his death (and Jackson's birth) in 1767.[12]

Civilized states made up an international society, not a coherent nation, and they retained the sovereign power to defend their rights by force. But even in war they no longer targeted the *existence* of their enemies, as by burning farmlands or enslaving prisoners. To treat enemy soldiers with such ferocity was a "disgrace to humanity," Vattel reported, and it was "happily banished" from Europe, a relic of the continent's total wars and a new boundary line between the progress within and the savagery beyond. The pale of civilization he described made violence anywhere else terrifyingly normal. His ignorance of the native peoples of Africa and the Americas was especially lethal. Since aboriginals did not farm, Vattel asserted, they did not own anything. Since they did not respect laws or treaties, they preyed upon each other in prehistorical cycles of retributory violence. Only lawful, peaceful states could secure liberty and safety.[13]

Blackstone said much the same thing even before his colleague at the bar, Lord Mansfield, famously decreed in 1772 that a black slave could not be held in irons for retransport across the Atlantic. British soil was free ground and civilized space: anyone who put his feet upon it enjoyed the protection of its laws. Was this true of the "more distant plantations in America"? Writing while Andrew Jackson's parents left for the colonies, Blackstone could not really say. As early as 1720, one authority had declared that "the common law of England is the common Law of the plantations," and later statutes empowered metropolitan creditors to take land and slaves from colonial debtors. Some provincials from the Anglican colony of South Carolina were even studying at the Inns of Court. Yet New England and Pennsylvania still bore traces of their Puritan and Quaker origins. The Delaware River Valley was home to what William Penn had called a "Collection of divers Nations," including large numbers of German speakers. Maryland had once been run by Catholics, New York by the Dutch. And throughout the semitropical provinces whose staple crops financed the Age of Paper, slavery ruled.[14]

Blackstone could only conclude that the colonies were "conquered or ceded countries" that were not ready for self-government; in Parliament during the 1760s, he showed little sympathy for American protests. Vattel took the same premise—that the colonists lived closer to war and nature than to peace and society—and used it to authorize extreme violence upon the "savages of North America." Much like pirates, Indians "infested" certain places, took shelter in "haunts," and acted like "monsters." They were in need of a brutal lesson. "When we are at war with a savage nation . . . we may punish them in the persons of any of their people whom we take (these belonging to the number of the guilty), and endeavor, by this rigorous proceeding, to force them to respect the laws of humanity. But wherever severity is not absolutely necessary, clemency becomes a duty." Lawful people in lawless places could even "suppose" what the sovereign wanted and then do what had to be done, becoming in effect their own sovereigns.[15]

BLOOD AND NATURE

"We have now the Pleasure Sir," reported the commander of a South Carolina fort to the royal governor in 1760, "to fatten our Dogs with their Carcases, and to display their Scalps, neatly ornamented on the Tops of our Bastions." The carcasses in question were Cherokees, whose bodies enjoyed none of the protections due to white soldiers. Three years later and six hundred miles north on the Great Wagon Road, fifty men from Paxton and other towns rode into Lancaster, Pennsylvania, targeting a workhouse where some Conestoga Indians had taken shelter. The whites broke in, murdered three couples and eight children, and rode away. It is unclear who first called the Paxton killers "Boys," but they soon appropriated the name. If men had to give up their natural rights to kill and rampage upon entering society, then they preferred to remain boys.[16]

Such ideas had long disturbed Quaker authorities in Pennsylvania, for whom peace was required by God rather than recommended by Vattel. Vigilante violence also appalled the Moravians, a group of German pietists who settled in western Pennsylvania and North Carolina, not far from Andrew Jackson's kin. (More discerning than the white invaders, native warriors often exempted such groups from attacks.) What makes the response to the Conestoga massacre unusual is the extent to which more cosmopolitan elites like Benjamin Franklin denounced the "Boys." The poor Conestogas, Franklin charged, would have been better treated by Turks, Saracens, Spaniards, and even "*Pagan Negroe[s]*" than by these "CHRISTIAN WHITE SAVAGES." Those natives had been living peacefully within Pennsylvania's boundaries and were thus entitled to the protection of its laws. Now the law should do the next best thing and punish the guilty. Otherwise, Franklin warned, "THE BLOOD OF THE INNOCENT WILL CRY TO HEAVEN FOR VENGEANCE."[17]

In North America, blood revenge and total war were at least as old as European settlement. "Wheras we are advised by you to observe rules of Justice with these barberous and perfidious enemys," Virginia colonists had told their English sponsors in 1623, "wee hold nothinge injuste, that may tende to theire ruine, (except breach of faith)." All of the Indians had to be wiped out, not just those who had nearly annihilated Jamestown the year before. White militiamen thus marched to the nearest villages and cornfields, targeting the crops and homes whose very existence belied the rationale for displacing "savages." The following decade, Puritans and their native allies cooperated to avenge "the innocent blood of the English" shed by the Pequots, killing some four hundred people in a single village. Such was the "work of the Lords revenge." All-out violence resumed in New England and Virginia in the 1670s, followed by another round in the Carolinas in the 1710s. "What spectacle can strike a man with more horror and stir [him] up more to revenge?" asked one witness of the 130 men, women, and children whom Tuscarora attackers left in pieces along a North Carolina river. After that nation, too, had been destroyed, a grim truce mostly held until the renewed bloodshed of the 1750s and 1760s that shaped Andrew Jackson's youth.[18]

Europeans were right to see retribution as central to native ideas of justice and sovereignty, but they misunderstood its rules and goals. Most Indian peoples of the eastern woodlands were organized by matrilineal clans and village centers, and it was generally up to the male relatives of a murder victim to take revenge as women and other kin saw fit. Satisfaction might come in the form of the dead or captured murderer, a dead or captured enemy, or suitable gifts and apologies to calm troubled spirits and "screaming blood." Creeks and Cherokees designated certain places where vengeance could be taken, thereby preserving "peace" towns where no living thing could be killed. To avenge murders committed by other nations, young men also waged "mourning wars" beyond these literal and cultural boundaries, returning with enough scalps or captives to satisfy their sisters, aunts, and elders. Ideally, vengeance ended there. And it often did, for natives had no sovereigns to compel longer wars for more abstract causes.[19]

Still, bloodshed was hard to contain, especially as white traders, hunters, and settlers pressed for native lands, loyalty, and resources. The English and French nations were much larger than natives ones, and the bloodlines they avenged stretched all the way across the Atlantic. Their protection covenants with distant sovereigns, no less than their guns, pigs, and pathogens, made them dangerous foes. So while Cherokee women and men clamored for revenge on the South Carolinians who fed their kin to dogs in 1760, the clans and villages most vulnerable to white invasion sought a bitter peace. "Ruin and Destruction hangs over your whole Nation," one British officer had warned. His Majesty's armies would take "the most Exemplary Vengeance" for Indian atrocities, another resolved.[20]

Of course, imperial authorities did not protect or avenge all their people all the time. The French monarchy had more or less abandoned the Acadian settlers of Nova Scotia before the British deported them in 1755. British authorities wanted little to do with their wayward subjects along the Mosquito Coast, focusing instead on the Caribbean islands. After their great victory over France in 1763, they also drew new lines around the mainland empire, prohibiting colonists from purchasing Indian land or trespassing upon it. Anyone who violated the Royal Proclamation line and subsequent surveys, Virginia's governor declared, "must expect no protection or mercy from Government." Instead, they would face "the revenge of the exasperated *Indians*" on their own. His Majesty's officials had tired of North American violence, not least because several colonies had funded their wars by printing their own money. That kind of paper did *not* count as property, for it enabled debtors to "pay" their creditors in bills that no one in London would accept.[21]

As British power, English common law, and the law of nations came together in the minds of imperial officials after 1763, North American savagery became a new way to measure European civility. Disgust with the Indians' "law of blood" became a more secular way to assert Christian superiority. If the natives were dying out, it was their fault for not having imposed the rule of law over themselves. The "Canadian nations" had failed to give up the "right of redressing and punishing [their] own wrongs," one philosopher argued. They remained captives to "the evils arising from ungoverned resentment," slaves to past injuries and baser needs. "Revenge is the darling passion of savages," commented a British historian of the early colonies. Much like the African nations whose endless wars sent the walking dead toward the slave ships, Indian nations were unable to form their own pales of civilization. Every clan and warrior clung to the most brutal kinds of sovereignty. "Revenge takes an entire possession of his soul," a Vermont naturalist later commented of the Indian male at war. His "diabolical" anger was terrible to see, a "fierce, brutal, horrid, bloody, and implacable" spell. Revenge was savage, and savages took revenge.[22]

Hence the strong reaction to the Paxton Boys. Increasing tensions between colonial leaders and imperial officials over the scope of British sovereignty initially reinforced the need to impose law over the "white savages" of western Pennsylvania, Virginia, and the Carolinas. In the 1760s and early 1770s, that is, both Whig and Tory elites condemned borderlands avengers, for they both wanted to make North America more British and European. They both wanted to draw the provinces more closely into the domains of common law and the law of nations, of Blackstone and Vattel. They differed over whether that should mean more or less autonomy for the colonies. They split over who should oversee the ascendant rule of law: the Whig-dominated assemblies or the Crown-appointed governors.[23]

One of the most radical Whigs, Thomas Jefferson, turned both Blackstone and Vattel to new purposes in his 1774 *Summary View of the Rights of British America.* White Virginians and other provincials had carried the rights of preconquest Saxons across the Atlantic, he theorized. "Their own blood was spilt in acquiring lands for their settlement." Their rights came from nature and their own suffering, as well as from their English birthright, and they remained entirely free to take those rights to greener pastures. Only their affection for the king still tethered them to their homeland. And yet British authorities denied them both free trade and domestic manufacturing, not to mention political representation. Already Jefferson was redeploying Vattel's principle of national equality in service to American independence, even though the colonial population hardly qualified as a nation. Meantime he joined other provincial elites in denouncing the frontier raiders who murdered Delawares, Shawnees, and Mingos in 1774–75.[24]

Everything changed as imperial rule collapsed. In early 1774, the empire cracked down on troublesome Massachusetts; later that year an alliance between New England and Virginia took form at the First Continental Congress; the following spring fighting broke out between provincial militia and British regulars around Boston. Within weeks, panic over slave uprisings spread through the southern provinces, even before the king declared the colonies in rebellion (August 1775) and the royal governor of Virginia invited loyal slaves to help put down rebel masters (November 1775). That winter, Benjamin Franklin requested copies of Vattel's *Law of Nations* for delegates to the Continental Congress while the British expatriate Tom Paine accused the empire of plundering south Asia, west Africa, and now North America. Paine thereby inverted the usual geographies of civilization and savagery and encouraged colonials to see themselves as a last best hope. After dozens of towns and associations renounced Britain on their own and stories of native barbarity arrived from Quebec and Carolina, Jefferson once more took up his pen on behalf of white Americans.[25]

Jefferson made the Declaration of Independence an indictment of imperial misrule along with a proposal for American self-rule. After his famous paragraphs about natural equality and inalienable rights, he made a long list of charges against the king, all but one of which—about the roots of slavery—made it into the final draft. Far from protecting his subjects, George III had ignored and injured them. He had violated common law, the law of nations, the protection covenant, and "our common blood." Jefferson's disgust with British power culminated in this shocking charge: "He has excited domestic insurrection among us, and has endeavored to bring on the inhabitants of our frontiers, the merciless Indian Savages, whose known rule of warfare is an undistinguished destruction of all ages, sexes, and conditions." Put simply, the king had turned savage. He had *knowingly* set Indian and black enemies to kill white subjects in their very homes.[26]

Cast out of the civilized world, Americans had little choice but to think critically about the rule of law and its relation to natural rights. The king and his minions were waging a "most cruel and unjust war," the first constitutions of Vermont and Pennsylvania declared. They were pursuing the good people with "unabated vengeance." South Carolina's new charter accused the British of conduct that would "disgrace even savage nations," while New Jersey's deplored a "cruel and unnatural" hostility that left the people exposed to "the fury of a cruel and relentless enemy." The king had not just withdrawn his protection, North Carolina reported, but had also declared open season on American persons and property, risking "anarchy and confusion." Seeking allies in Europe, Benjamin Franklin stunned his British counterparts by accusing the empire of "Barbarities" once associated with frontier scalp hunters.[27]

Stories of imperial savagery lent narrative form and moral purpose to eight years of war, during which some 40% of the free male population over sixteen served in either a Patriot militia or the Continental Army. The larger theme of existential peril reappeared for the next fifty years, framing the life of Andrew Jackson, among many others, and shaping almost everything they said about virtue and republics, society and sovereignty, nation and allegiance. Unsure if the British Empire would let them live,

Figure 0.2 *The Murder of Miss Jane McCrea*. One of many depictions of the 1777 killing of a Loyalist woman in New York, this image captures the larger sense of white victimization that emerged from the Revolution.

Courtesy of the Library of Congress, Prints and Photographs Division, LC-USZ62-22947.

they wondered if the rule of law would ever replace the state of nature. Unsure if the law of nations constrained any of the "civilized nations," especially after the French and Haitian Revolutions set the world aflame, they argued over how and if they should respect the same standard. In so doing they also debated how and if they were a "nation," as well as a republic or union.[28]

When and where was vengeance just and lawful, and when and where was it cruel and criminal? Who had the right to take it on behalf of the reinvented people? On such questions Americans consulted Vattel again and again, not at all in the same ways. For Jackson they evoked memories so awful that the usual terms of law and politics did not apply, demanding new bonds of holy wrath and redeeming blood. His arguments thrilled many Americans and disgusted others. Decades of economic turmoil also revived some of the questions that Blackstone had tried to resolve. What made property real? What was money and what was just paper? Were the revolutionary states still bound by the emergent rules of international finance? If they valued "independence," should they try to secure it for their households, even if that put limits on the commercial freedoms of enterprising individuals? What, after all, did the sovereignty of the people enable them to do as a nation? Here especially, Jackson's beliefs were often more vehement than popular, and though he never hid them he also learned how to change the conversation.

Using Jackson more as its main character than its subject, *Avenging the People* explores the times and places that shaped and were shaped by him from the 1760s to his election as president in 1828: the Carolina borderlands, the Cumberland settlements, Tennessee and the Gulf Coast, and finally the United States as it emerged from its postcolonial phases. I focus on what Jackson and his peers meant by the "rule of law" in its biblical, natural, commercial, constitutional, and international forms, and on how those meanings mapped onto different visions of an "American nation." I consider how various notions of sovereignty developed in revolutionary and postrevolutionary contexts, and study vengeance—the last full measure of sovereignty—as a moral, political, religious, and military problem for the new states. Ultimately, I suggest that the sort of nationhood Jackson came to embody left Americans with a diminished sense of the law and their right to make it, indeed with less power, to be the nation they wanted to be.

CHAPTER 1

States of Nature

Andrew Jackson told a few stories about his childhood in the western reaches of North and South Carolina, but there was much he preferred to forget. Perhaps there was little to say. Fatherless at birth in the spring of 1767, he grew up in the household of his mother's brother-in-law, James Crawford, and of James's more prominent brother, Robert. Both lived along small creeks that fed into the Catawba River, some two hundred miles northwest of Charles Town. Their settlement was known as the Waxhaws, after a tribe that had long since fled. A Catawba chief known as King Haiglar claimed some of the area at midcentury, but rival Shawnees killed him shortly before Jackson was born. Catawba warriors retaliated, and according to an early history they tortured a group of captives "until revenge was satiated; and savage fury lost its force." By the 1760s, after a brutal war between the Carolinas and the region's dominant nation, the Cherokee, the Waxhaws were well settled with north Irish Presbyterians. The little colony was best known for its minister, the Reverend William Richardson, who was found dead in 1771 leaning against a chair, a bridle around his neck and his hands raised as if in prayer.[1]

No one of consequence was impressed by the Waxhaws, nor indeed by any part of the Carolina borderlands. "A mix'd Medley from all Countries and the Off Scouring of America" was how the Anglican minister Charles Woodmason described the regional population. A good many were "the lowest vilest Scum of Mankind," he reported, and the rest were bigoted Presbyterians. Most had not bothered to organize townships around their cabins, barns, and fields, making property claims in advance of civil order. None of them knew "the Bands of Society and Government" or the protections of "Civil Police." The few and poor roads did not so much open the dark forests as draw the traveler deeper into them. The land itself was "broken" and "impenetrable," a "Shocking" anti-landscape without vantage points or meeting places. It was not clear where one Carolina began and the other ended, where white settlements gave way to native grounds, or where pigs, cows, and dogs ceded to deer, bison, and wolves. The people lived "in a State of Nature," indeed "in a State of War."[2]

Woodmason's arrival was part of a concerted effort to bring Anglican clerics to the far corners of South Carolina, thereby reminding the people of the close link between God and king in that distant but wealthy province. Despite their more modest resources, North Carolina authorities had also begun to settle university-educated clergy and build county-level governments. Both provinces tried to clarify their boundaries as the British Empire reorganized after 1763, in part to satisfy the metropolitan creditors and provincial elites who wanted to contain the settlements. From the perspective of many residents, in fact, places like the Waxhaws were already *too* lawful, prematurely weighed down by people like Woodmason and his secular equivalent, the lawyer.[3]

For all their differences, most Carolina settlers wanted landed property and lawful titles. They also sought physical safety from their many enemies. Otherwise, their political loyalties were fluid, for they were not sure if their sovereigns shared their priorities. On the one hand, the British Empire enabled them to claim "natural" rights to freehold lands; on the other, it required them to surrender those rights to the unnatural demands of creditors and landlords. Just north of the Waxhaws, large numbers of people rebelled against the emerging rules of property, embracing a fundamentally Christian view of just desserts. Just to the south, a critical mass of settlers instead raged at the failure of those rules. Up to the Revolution, the Jacksons and Crawfords lived quietly in between, taking in something of both Carolinas and enabling "Andy" to envision bigger things within the little world that his mother and kin had made for him.

ENEMY COUNTRY

The common folk of North Britain, scoffed one observer on the eve of the Revolution, were bound for North America on the belief that "they can still obtain land for themselves and their flocks of cattle at a trifling rate or [by] conquering it from the Indians with the sword." Rather than sell their labor in Scotland or northern Ireland, they hoped to seize land beyond the sea, outrunning the rule of law as it continued to drive poor people out of common lands and punish anyone who remained as vagrants. Since the early 1600s, Scottish Presbyterians had escaped Anglican authorities by crossing the Irish Sea and settling in Ulster, where they secured longer leases, better wages, and the occasional protection of British authorities against displaced natives. And yet they remained subordinate to English landlords while becoming dependent on the English linen industry. Andrew Jackson's mother, Betty, came from a family of wool and flax spinners, and if it was not her place to discuss imperial policy with her husband, Andrew, she certainly told her sons about the hardships that Englishmen had wrought on their people.[4]

Betty Hutchinson Jackson had five sisters, and by 1765, when she and her husband and their two older children left Ulster, the whole family had joined the roughly fifty-five thousand Protestant Irish who came to North America between the Seven Years' War and the Revolution. They expected more than better rents on the far side of the Atlantic. They wanted land in "fee simple," without liens or lords, so that they could produce their own food and clothes, sell surplus goods at market, and give their children nearby farms. First they had moved to the hill country of central New England and the hinterlands of Philadelphia. Then, around midcentury, they began to descend the Great Wagon Road along the Appalachian ridge, forming an archipelago of "Irish settlements" from Pennsylvania to Georgia. Betty and Andrew probably sailed directly to Charles Town, part of a last major wave before British authorities tried to stem the tide in 1773.[5]

The Carolinas emerged as major destinations as Pennsylvania and Virginia grew more expensive and royal governors of Scottish origin tried to populate the deep southern colonies. North Carolina's governors, in particular, found their province undersettled, its common folk spoiled by plentiful lands that too easily yielded a bare subsistence. "Poor Carolina" was attracting too many rejects from Virginia, too many ex-servants who wanted to sleep late and drink early. Royal governors around 1750 thus cooperated with promoters in Belfast and London to recruit the industrious poor. In return for land, the newcomers would drain swamps, cut forests, and pay a yearly tax, known as a quit-rent. The Earl of Granville, who held claims to the entire northern half of the province, also granted family farms along with one hundred thousand ill-defined acres to the Moravians, German-speaking pacifists who settled some seventy miles north of the Waxhaws.[6]

The rulers of South Carolina were also eager to recruit white families. In its early decades, the labor-starved colony had preyed upon the neighboring Yamasee, but a desperate attack by the natives in 1715 ended in the destruction of that nation. The Carolinians then shifted to West African and Afro-Caribbean slaves, who were made to grow black rice on coastal plantations. Along with indigo, rice made the low country around Charles Town one of the most lucrative parts of North America. "History may be resorted to, but in vain," boasted one early historian, "to find colonies so soon emerging from insignificance and dependency, to wealth and prosperity." The vast profits from "black gold" built fine homes and churches, a fleet of ships, and a network of slave-built roads and waterways. Of course, the "hands" might also turn their axes and hoes against their tormentors. In 1741, two years after an insurrection, the assembly noted their "peculiar Case" within the empire: they required protection *from* their property, not just *for* their property.[7]

The new province just to the south, Georgia, was initially no help, since its founder, James Oglethorpe, wanted a sober, industrious colony without slaves, rum, or lawyers. This in turn magnified the threat from the Spanish in Florida, whose Catholic priests and officials sometimes sheltered escapees. South Carolina thus resolved to whiten the province by granting lands to those who could afford the Atlantic passage. Otherwise, the colony relied on a harrowing system of slave patrols brought from Barbados and Jamaica and on periodic acts "for the better regulation of negroes." Once an owner gave up on a runaway, for instance, he could declare the slave "outlawed," announcing that every white person should kill on sight and present the body parts for a reward. While on his way to dine with a low-country planter around the time of the Revolution, the French immigrant J. Hector St. John de Crèvecoeur found a half-dead slave rotting in a cage. The planter explained that this slave had killed an overseer, and that "the laws of self-preservation" required retribution. The horrified Frenchman agreed insofar as he noted that the slaves nursed "a wish of perpetual revenge."[8]

For emigrants like the Jacksons, North America's cheap lands and high wages outweighed its exotic perils. North Carolina was "the most temperate part of the earth on the north side of the equator," one promotional tract enthused. "The whole country is in a manner one forest, where our planters have not cleared it." Ordinary people rode horses, carried weapons, and took whatever fish and game they needed. Five "healthy negroes" could do the hardest work, "so as you shall have every thing in abundance for your family, with little trouble to yourself." In this "country of Freedom," wrote one Georgia planter in a letter reprinted in Belfast, "I keep as plentiful a table as most gentlemen in Ireland." Oglethorpe's vision quickly vanished, leaving Georgians as free as Carolinians to hold slaves. "If any person that comes here can bring money to purchase a slave or two," the letter noted, "they may live very easy and well." Headright policies encouraged slave buying: each slave, like each child or other dependent, brought an additional fifty acres to the head of household, who could claim one hundred acres by himself.[9]

The Ulstermen who arrived in the 1760s and 1770s thus had good reason to think that they could "still" obtain land "at a trifling rate" somewhere down the Great Wagon Road. In one Georgia township peopled by ships from Belfast, thirty-three of thirty-nine settlers who had been offered land

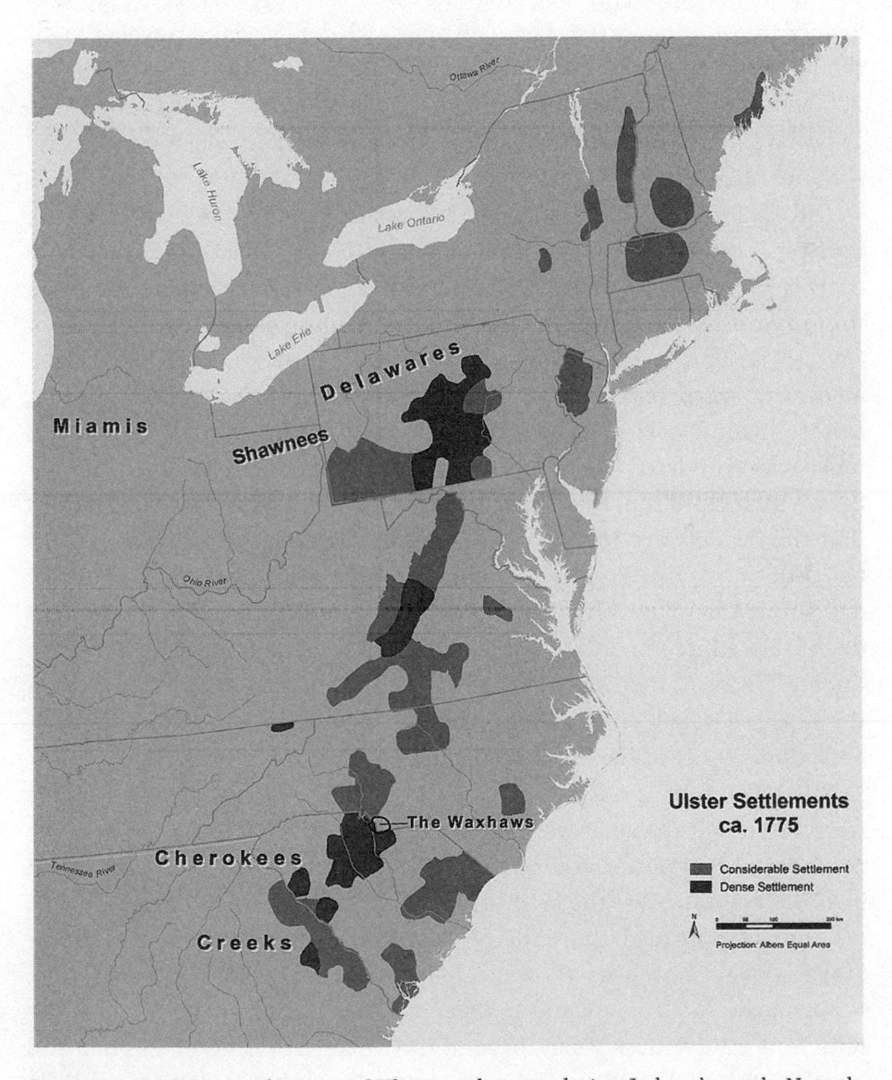

Figure 1.1 Approximate location of Ulster settlements during Jackson's youth. Note the heavy concentrations in Pennsylvania and on the South Carolina side of the Waxhaws. Based on *Atlas of Early American History: The Revolutionary Era, 1760–1790*, ed. Lester J. Cappon et al. (Princeton, NJ: Princeton University Press, 1976). Ruilan Shi, Geographic Information Centre, McGill University.

completed their grants, becoming "yeomen" or "husbandmen" and landing, for the moment, on the right side of the law. South Carolina offered especially generous terms in 1761, resulting in a new influx of "bounty Irish" into places like the Waxhaws. With his wife and two sons, Andrew Jackson the elder might have claimed 250 acres there, a few miles south of where his wife's sisters and their husbands had started farms. Disembarking at Charles Town, they would have ridden and walked north before crossing the Santee, gasping at the heat and taking in the strange new sights and sounds: black slaves speaking Wolof and Bambara, cypress trees draped in Spanish moss, pine forests where no one settled. Four days' travel brought them to their new home. Instead of putting in for a bounty, Jackson bought 200 acres of land on the northern end of the Waxhaws, just south of the Catawba Nation, a block of land fifteen miles square in which surveys and settlements were prohibited.[10]

Did Ulstermen also think that they could simply take land from the natives, "conquering it from the Indians with the sword"? Did they hate natives upon arrival? One group of north Irish in Pennsylvania denounced the very concept of treaty-certified Indian country as "against the laws of God and nature." It denied would-be freeholders the status they had crossed an ocean to earn, imposing North British hierarchies over North American forests. Living next to one such territory, Andrew and Betty Jackson must have wondered where future emigrants would find a home. The year before their third son, Andy, was born, North Carolina authorities worried that the residents of Mecklenburg County, abutting the Waxhaws, might be "shut out of this Province" by a new treaty with the depleted but still dangerous Cherokee. Mecklenburg settlers decried any policy that might discourage white immigration into countries forever in range of "A Savage Enemy." South Carolinians, for their part, knew that the 1758–61 war with the Cherokees had left many unavenged deaths among their proud neighbors. Some white leaders spoke of exterminating the natives.[11]

Still, Ulstermen preferred legitimate titles in peaceful areas, and they were perfectly capable of working out "middle grounds" with their native neighbors. Most westerners, the royal governor of North Carolina reported in 1767, did not have "the least inclination to abuse the Indians." Chronic violence was instead the fault of "some stragling Hunters and Horse Stealers" who moved north–south between the Carolinas and east–west between the settlements and Indians, eluding justice on all sides. In the remote Watauga River Valley, beyond the western reaches of Virginia and North Carolina, Ulster settlers eager to evade both jurisdictions actually leased land from the Cherokee during the early 1770s. Although the settlement violated both the Royal Proclamation Line of 1763 and the Treaty of Hard Labor of 1768, the natives tolerated the Wataugans as a source of trade goods. As for the Jacksons, the Crawfords, and other Ulstermen in the Waxhaws, they managed to live with the Catawbas—"the Nation," the whites called it—throughout Andy's boyhood. South Carolina's government even employed Catawbas to "hunt the Negroes."[12]

What set Ulster Presbyterians apart from the Irish Quakers, Welsh Baptists, French Huguenots, and assorted "Virginians" spread over the southern backcountry was less a propensity for anti-native violence than their century-old story about that violence. In this respect they had much in common with earlier settlers of New England. Puritan leaders, after all, had called for holy and total war against the forest "Heathens" during the 1630s and again in the 1670s, noting that "sometimes the Scripture declareth women and children must perish with their parents." The enemies of their New Israel had to be slain, as God willed. During those same decades, Scottish Presbyterians were invading Ireland. A standard narrative of a 1641 rebellion against the newcomers called it "so execrable in itself, so odious to God and the whole World, as no Age, no Kingdom, no People can parallel [its] horrid Cruelties [and] abominable Murders." The Scottish troops and chaplains who finally saved the colonists then organized a Presbytery in Carrickfergus, the ancestral home of Andrew Jackson's parents.[13]

Much like New England captivity narratives, Ulster sermons on the anniversary of the 1641 revolt turned past traumas into an enduring bond. "Must this day still be preserved as an anniversary on which to raise men's passions against the innocent posterity [of the native Irish]?" asked one such sermon. "Yes, it must and it ought." Far enough from king and church, the Ulstermen were still surrounded by those who hated them for having brought law and order to a savage land. "We are really in an enemy's country," Ulstermen were told into the 1760s. A 1751 edition of the standard history of the Irish revolt offered a grisly recital of bodily violation along with bitter promises of supernatural justice. The very land and water had turned on the native Irish, who believed that their victims' blood would not wash off a certain bridge in Armagh County and who saw blanched cadavers bobbing in the waters below at twilight. A female apparition, pale as snow, was said to "stand straight up in the water, often repeating the word, REVENGE! REVENGE! REVENGE!"[14]

In the Calvinist tradition of both New England Puritans and Ulster Presbyterians, bloodshed also signified God's anger with the chosen people with whom he had a special covenant. The backsliding Protestants in Ireland, for example, had "long continued to provoke [God] in this Land," until at length his "fierce Wrath" had broken loose in the form of heathen rebels out for blood. And yet the nonbelievers were simply the tools of

God's passing desires, never the objects of his greater hopes. Rather than for any just cause, the infidel Irish had "*taken vengeance with a despiteful heart, to destroy them for the old hatred.*" They did not know, as the believers did, that vengeance belonged only to God, who mourned for those he punished and forgave them for their sins. Far from simple scripts of Good versus Evil, then, the vengeance stories that people like the Jacksons and Crawfords grew up with were complex dramas of guilt and innocence, blood and tears, fury and mercy.[15]

Little is known about backcountry Presbyterianism, and no doubt many settlers knew little themselves. It is difficult to say how, or even if, north Irish religious beliefs shaped perceptions of settler–native conflict in places like the Waxhaws. At the very least, though, the cultural theme of pious settlers in ungodly lands made Ulster families receptive to what historian Peter Silver has called "the anti-Indian sublime," a vivid way to recount borderlands violence that developed in Pennsylvania during the Seven Years' War. Here is an example:

> O Pensilvania . . . —all ages sex & stations hath no mercy extended to them . . . our tender Infants hath thair brains dashed out our wives big with child hath thair bellies ript open those killed within thair houses is mostly burnt with them . . . if thay flie into the woods or hideth in the hedges the murderers soon finds them & plunges their hatchets either into thair brest or skull . . . their once sweet cheeks & lips now stained with dust & blood & thair bosom filled with clotted gore.

Such accounts focused on the damage done to white people's bodies and homes, rather than on the train of events that had led to those traumas or the particular Indians who might be guilty of them.[16]

Just before the Jacksons came to America, Ulster settlers fleeing Shawnee and Delaware attacks in Pennsylvania began to meet those reeling from Cherokee raids in the southern backcountry. Ulster migrants to the southwest of the Waxhaws, in the Long Canes settlement, bitterly recalled a 1760 assault by mounted Cherokee on a group of women and children. Some of the younger victims had survived, walking a few days later into Savannah, dazed and scalped. Many of the older residents of the Waxhaws were from "Pennsilvanie," others from "Virginny," where the Paxton Boys and their southern counterparts had just turned vigilante. In such dangerous times and places, people were more likely to abide a dissenting minister or a militia captain than a representative of imperial authority. They were just as likely to see themselves as Irishmen or Presbyterians as Carolinians or Britons.[17]

The Reverend Charles Woodmason wanted to change that. "There is an External Enemy near at Hand," he declared to backcountry listeners around 1770. "We have an *Internal* Enemy" as well. "We ought to keep a very watchful Eye" over our slaves, Woodmason intoned, "lest they surprize us" and involve all white people in "one Common Death." (He had done his part in creating this racial dilemma, purchasing eighteen internal enemies to claim more headrights in lands once held by the external ones.) Woodmason could only hope that the terrifying insecurities of North America would convince the settlers to give up their bloody loyalties and natural rights, to join the civilized world by submitting to its laws.[18]

BETWEEN CAROLINAS

Andrew Jackson believed that he had been born in South Carolina, and later studies bear him out. At the time of his birth, however, being "in" one Carolina or another referred less to a location on a map than to the types of land titles that predominated among one's neighbors. In its ideal form, a headright from the government in Charles Town enabled a man to present himself before the surveyor general or another deputy with his wife, children, servants, and slaves, whereupon he made an *entry* for a given quantity of land. He then received a *warrant* that had to be "filled" within a given period, meaning that someone had to render a detailed *survey* of the land. The claimant then returned the survey along with the associated fees. If the plots named did not conflict with any others, he received a *patent* for his little piece of South Carolina. A lively market in land titles had also developed in places like the Waxhaws. For someone like James Crawford, in whose home Jackson was probably born, the way to wealth led through these purchases rather than from grants by the Crown. James's brother Robert owned both slaves and land in North Carolina, while also holding a militia title from South Carolina.[19]

Unlike their counterparts in Virginia, who had exhausted their best lands and thus scrambled for what became Kentucky and Ohio, the low-country elite of South Carolina increasingly looked east and south, toward British and Caribbean markets and suppliers. The deerskin trade with the Cherokee was in decline, while the coastal rice plantations were both profitable and expensive, and in any case impossible to reproduce west of the tidewater. Besides, the colony only claimed a small sliver of western land. So South Carolina's rulers were mostly happy to offer those lands to incoming whites, pushing back the Cherokee while sealing in the slaves. Andrew Jackson's father had purchased his two hundred acres from a low-country family, one of the many ties that his third son would have to the great seaport and its haughty elite.[20]

Since most settlers were headed south on the Wagon Road, travel to South Carolina was more expensive than voyages that ended in Virginia or North Carolina. Along with headright policies that excluded the poorest migrants and bounties that enabled families to gain property before paying taxes or fees, this made for a prosperous population. In 1768, the lieutenant governor reported that "almost every house" in western South Carolina had its own loom, which along with the more common spinning wheels enabled women to produce fabrics and clothing while their husbands and sons turned out beef, tallow, tobacco, and flour for use and sale. They mostly lived in single-story cabins, but more and more two-story log homes and even frame houses were cropping up, and with them silver and glassware along with wooden spoons and pewter bowls.[21]

Such were the households where Andrew Jackson grew up. After her husband's death, Betty Jackson sent her eldest son, Hugh, to live with another relative while she and the younger boys removed to the home of James Crawford. Betty put her spinning skills to use while also keeping the garden, smoking and salting beef and pork, milking cows, and making cheese and butter. Andy and his brothers joined the Crawford boys in working the cornfields, tending livestock, making whiskey, and hunting. His mother made sure that he listened to the temporary pastors who spoke in the Waxhaw meetinghouse, four miles away, and that he paid his respects to the "session" or church elders who tried to instill the fear of God in young sinners. Neighbors and relatives knew him as a Crawford, adopted son of a weighty family. They also recalled him as a slim, prideful boy who could not bear to lose.[22]

Whatever the Crawfords wanted to sell went south, down the "great road" to Camden, across the Santee River, and from there to Charles Town. The Savannah and Pee Dee Rivers connected other parts of South Carolina to the metropolis, where great cargos of rice and indigo awaited transport. The profits that came back turned Charles Town into a kind of mini-London: a voracious consumer of rural produce and luxury goods. By the 1760s, backcountry farmers used the proceeds of their low-country sales to buy their own slaves, imported in hellish ships to Sullivan's Island, just off Charles Town harbor. The huge number of black workers living, as one physician wrote, "in our bowels!" was a chronic emergency, but it also enabled men like Robert Crawford to build stately homes and ride tall horses. "Uncle" Robert was surely one of Andy's first role models.[23]

In 1771, when Andy was four, surveyors finally clarified the line between the Carolinas, making James and Robert Crawford part of the southern province. Otherwise, South Carolina wanted little to do with them. The low-country south of the Santee River was covered by fifteen parishes, a dense web of jurisdictions that enabled the ruling race to buy, sell, pray, sue, marry, and even vote with relative ease. By contrast, the entire region north of the Santee and west of the coast was divided into just a handful of parishes, even though they accounted for most of the white population. In lieu of regular county courts, plaintiffs had to travel all the way to Charles Town to collect debts and settle disputes. They were unlikely to find help among the city's thirty lawyers, whose friends and clients in the assembly mostly concerned themselves with private bills rather than with any kind of public policy. Western settlers also remembered how the low-country elite had ignored refugee families fleeing Cherokee attacks in 1760.[24]

Drawn to South Carolina's markets but left out of its government, people in the Waxhaws and other settlements were not even sure if their marriages were binding unless overseen by an Anglican priest like Rev. Woodmason, who offered to marry cohabitating couples free of charge. Otherwise, he warned, he would come back and prosecute them under His Majesty's 1760 proclamation against vice and immorality. No wonder people hated him. In one case a group of Presbyterian rowdies released fifty-seven dogs ("for I counted them") inside the church where he was preaching. Undaunted, he tried to make sense of the different vices among Presbyterians, Regular Baptists, New Light Baptists, Quakers, Moravians, and the utterly impious. He was disgusted to find 94% (again, he was counting) of the women he married pregnant on their wedding day. He was saddened to see so many orphans wandering about, "expos'd in a State of Nature" rather than cared for by a county court. It never occurred to him that extended kin usually offered such services, as in Andy Jackson's case.[25]

Woodmason was sure that sectarian hatred had played a role in the Reverend Richardson's strange death in the Waxhaws in 1771. The Presbyterians' focus on God's wrath, Woodmason saw, encouraged them to think or hope that they were entirely innocent, and thus to confuse their anger with that of the Lord. But at least the Presbyterians recited hymns and verses during their long, somber meetings. At least they had rules, elders, and bodily shame. One Presbyterian minister on the North Carolina side of the Jacksons owned land in Virginia, as well as slaves and farms in Mecklenburg County. He stipulated that his boys "Shall be kept at Learning till they attain to what learning that can be had in [these] parts." For Presbyterian elders, the word of God was both complicated and non-negotiable, much like the private contracts that they often called "sacred."[26]

Betty Jackson's youngest son had a sharp memory and a winning manner, and his quick mind and hard stare made people listen. He stood out in the "English school" that he attended with his brothers, and it was only natural that his pious, strong-willed mother should have considered him for the ministry. As a close friend of Rev. Richardson's widow and a member of the weighty Crawford family, Betty could reasonably hope to send Andy to the "Latin schools" that Presbyterians had organized from the Waxhaws and Mecklenburg all the way to Pennsylvania. There he would master the arcane languages and the fine points of Scripture, perhaps even studying with the leading Presbyterian cleric in North America, the Reverend John Witherspoon of the College of New Jersey. So Andy's future led through places like Charlotte, North Carolina, the Mecklenburg county seat whose courts were far closer and more accessible for Waxhaw people than those of Charles Town.[27]

The North Carolina imprint on Jackson's world also traced to a borderlands leader named Griffith Rutherford. Another orphaned son of Ulster immigrants, Rutherford had moved into the Waxhaws around 1750, bearing North Carolina patents. Stocky, pious, and cruel, Rutherford marked off lands for clients and patrons back east, threatening anyone in the way. In the Cherokee War of 1758–61, he learned how to muster troops from isolated settlements and to target tiny cornfields hidden in trackless forests. By 1766, he had risen to the provincial assembly, an emergent spokesman for the neglected west. In 1772, he sold one of his plots on the same creek where the Jacksons had settled, and Andy certainly grew up knowing the name Rutherford. Indeed, the career of this obscure strongman not only shaped the young Jackson's world but also anticipated the core tensions of Jackson's life.[28]

Although his bare-knuckles approach to land speculation could be found in other provinces, Griffith Rutherford was very much a product of North Carolina. Besides lumber and pine pitch for the Royal Navy, for which His Majesty paid a bounty, its planters did not have a major export to fund private fortunes or public projects. Nor could they market their beef, flour, and deerskins too far from home. North Carolina was short on good harbors and navigable rivers, and thus on market centers. A handful of hatters, tanners, and shipbuilders had set up shop, Governor William Tryon reported in 1767, but none "of any Note." Political power was more diffuse here than in South Carolina, with the capital itself moving with a trunk of papers between Edenton, Wilmington, and New Bern. All of this appealed to poorer families and religious minorities, but it also led the assembly and governors to outsource the job of peopling the backcountry to an unseemly cast of aristocrats and speculators who gave the law a bad name.[29]

Sometime before his arrival in 1767, Governor Tryon reported, "it became customary" for his predecessors to sell land on their own accord.

The empire's interest in developing its colonies had lost out to more private motives, and not just those of small-time hustlers like Griffith Rutherford. Take the case of Henry McCulloch, a Scottish noble with claims to some 1.2 million acres in the 1750s. McCulloch later entrusted these lands to his imperfect son, Henry E. McCulloch. In a 1766 letter to his friend, the Yale-educated lawyer Edmund Fanning, the younger McCulloch—fresh from his own legal education in England—reported that he was indulging "every gratification" while serving, so to speak, as collector of revenue in Edenton. He invited Fanning to drop by so that he could introduce his new mistress, stripped naked if Fanning preferred, and also offered to deliver to Fanning any woman he wished to have sex with, including married ones "shouldst you lust after [them]." One wonders if the Reverend Woodmason would have found this behavior as degenerate as that of backcountry couples.[30]

With his updated knowledge of property law, the younger McCulloch rejected squatters' rights to the improvements they had made, insisting that his family had an "indefeazible and undoubted right" to every last acre. He also dismissed any interference by His Majesty or any other sovereign "in the decision or direction of disputes concerning private Property." He could do whatever he wanted in North Carolina, where there was no aristocracy to offend and few resources to exploit. "Extent and quantity is not a proper rule by which a judgement can be formed of the value of Landed property in America," he noted. Much of the province was barely worth the paperwork to secure it: pine forests sitting on thin soil, dark swamps filled with alligators, remote hilltops with no access to rivers or roads. Only well-drained locations with good topsoil and the right mixture of clay and sand underneath fit the bill. Only well-surveyed tracts surrounded by other estates made "desirable objects of purchase."[31]

But purchase by whom? Poor settlers saw the farms they had hacked and burned out of the forests to be theirs already, even if they had not paid the fees needed to "ripen" their claims from entry to warrant to survey to patent. Many had received five-year tax waivers from authorities trying to populate the colony. They were not eager for the payments to start, or sure when they would, since titles often changed hands back in London, Glasgow, and Belfast. Taking full advantage of this benign neglect, a probable majority of men in the piedmont counties of North Carolina were able to claim around two hundred acres of land, just like Andrew Jackson the elder. When they did have to pay, or when they tried to buy more land, they often did so in "proclamation money." Printed by the province in times of need, these bills remained in circulation years or even decades later, vexing creditors who wanted final payment in gold or silver specie or "Cash."[32]

Henry E. McCulloch also wanted cash. Having carefully divided his family's vast holdings into several hundred two hundred- to three hundred-acre farms with the right combination of "Wood, Water, and Soil," he wanted to sell these lots to the better kind of immigrant to be found in South Carolina, who "annually migrated with Cash, from the northern and middle colonies." McCulloch gave current settlers the "reasonable indulgence" of a pre-emption claim, or a right of first refusal, before other offers drove prices higher. He later explained that he made these sales "in my character of a private person," for he was charging up to five times more than what his father had collected on behalf of the king. Beginning in 1765, he issued writs of ejectment to those who had not paid their quitrents and patent fees. McCulloch titles covered the lands around Andrew Jackson and his uncles, although their properties were secure.[33]

The incoming governor was much more likely to trust someone like McCulloch than Rutherford while trying to shore up colonial finances after the Seven Years' War. Indeed, Tryon suspected that Rutherford and other westerners were undercounting the sums due to the province, the better to funnel monies toward their own, illicit sales. Most settlers "dread the opening of his Land Office (tho' they want extremely the Land)," Tryon told the Earl of Shelburne, for they had suffered "many Impositions and Abuses" in the name of the law. The answer, the governor thought, was to reclaim the Crown's sovereign right to divide and sell estates in a new, legitimate land office. Betty Jackson certainly wanted her kin on the right side of the law: in 1770, she and James Crawford secured the deed for her late husband's two hundred acres, the title for which he had apparently left in limbo. Since the land in question was in Mecklenburg, this document named Andy and his two brothers as North Carolina residents of that county.[34]

REBELS AND VIGILANTES

As early as the late 1750s, settlers in several North Carolina counties resisted efforts to collect fees and quitrents, noting that they had no specie with which to pay. The following decade, Henry E. McCulloch's efforts to divide and sell his family's estate sparked similar outrage against the "cursed hungry caterpillars" who preyed upon the deserving poor. In Mecklenburg, a small group of men in 1765 painted their faces black and ambushed a surveying party in McCulloch's employ. Farther north from the vague border, large crowds jeered and threatened him as he delivered his terms, although they also offered to pay reduced sums in proclamation money. McCulloch refused to see popular money as anything more than a burlesque on commercial order and swore to uphold "the Principles of Law" against mob rule and "Blockheads."[35]

The British government weighed in here with the Currency Act of 1764, which forbade the colonies from printing their own money. This capped a long struggle by metropolitan creditors to make sure that provincial debtors eventually turned their paper promises into cold, hard specie, on pain of having their goods and then lands sold at auction. Shelburne repeated the order—*no paper money*—in his instructions to Tryon. Carolina debtors, one official complained, had hoped to "overflow this province with paper money," diluting the value of their debts by declaring bills to be money. But no more. Of all the new assertions of imperial sovereignty made during the 1760s and 1770s, the hard-money crackdown may have been the most painful for those who had settled just north of the Jacksons.[36]

Unable to raise revenues on tobacco or rice exports like its wealthier neighbors, North Carolina relied on a crude, regressive poll tax. Every white male from the age of sixteen counted as a poll, along with blacks of whatever sex or status from the age of twelve. These monies paid for the assembly's annual business: gifts for the Cherokees, bounties for wolf and cougar pelts, payments to slave owners whose chattels had been hanged or incinerated in the name of public safety. But the real tax burden could be much higher, because justices of the peace (JPs) and county courts routinely decided when more money was needed and then told their sheriffs to collect it. Everyone knew that many of those sheriffs pocketed said monies in collusion with the JPs, thereby making theft organized if not legal. Anyway, unrepresented westerners with shaky titles were in no position to challenge the courts' decisions.[37]

During the 1750s and 1760s, enterprising merchants began to see the North Carolina backcountry as an emerging market with a favorable tax environment. So they opened stores beyond the coastal plain, extending loans for cash crops and consumer goods and then suing those who failed to repay. The results were stunning. Take, for instance, Orange County, organized in 1752 in the central part of the province, some 120 miles northeast of Mecklenburg and the Waxhaws. In 1755, its magistrates had heard only seven debt cases, none of which involved firms. Just ten years later, Orange County heard 111 such cases, 35 of them involving merchant houses or partnerships. Here, too, the new legal impositions were less jarring in the Waxhaws, with its relatively stable titles and decent access to (South Carolina) markets and (North Carolina) courts.[38]

More litigation attracted more lawyers—forty-five of them, by Governor Tryon's 1767 count, up from just a smattering of lay attorneys a generation earlier. Lacking the potential income of their South Carolina peers, they scrambled to recover fees from a cash-poor population. They also inflated those fees. And while representing merchants, landlords, and other lawyers, they worked hand in glove with the sheriffs who foreclosed property to cover unpaid debts or taxes. Lawyer Edmund Fanning, Henry E. McCulloch's friend in sexual predation, was especially adept at snapping up distressed properties at auction. The key decisions were increasingly made, quite literally, behind the bar: lawyers now sat on designated benches next to the judge and clerk, opposite the jury and the rest of the laity. If he could not obtain a better kind of justice, one westerner swore, "he would burn as bad as Aney Cherokee and would tak it at his own hand."[39]

The depth and scale of North Carolinian misrule enabled aggrieved settlers to call themselves "Regulators" instead of rebels. "[It] is not our mode, or form of Government, nor yet the body of our laws, that we are quarreling with," one western leader announced in a 1765 speech, "but with the malpractices of the Officers of our County Court." Their enemies were neither Parliament nor the king, nor even the provincial assemblies where opposition to British rule was mounting. At first they did not blame Governor Tryon, or even Henry E. McCulloch. Instead they targeted the "Pettyfogging Lawyers" who overcharged and the "Bomb Sheriffs" who overcollected. They denounced the official-sounding orders that came out of inaccessible courthouses. "Are not your lands executed [along with] your negroes, horses, cattle, hogs, corn, beds, and household furniture? Are not these things, I say, taken and sold for one tenth of their value?" The answer was clear to North Carolina rebels who measured value more by the labor they had done than by the papers they carried.[40]

One of their leaders was Herman Husband, who had turned his back on his slave-owning, Anglican parents to become a Baptist and then a Quaker. His "New Light" faith called him to distrust all forms of authority, except the "natural" power of men over women and children. Like many evangelicals, he argued that ordinary people were capable of interpreting God's will without elite guidance and that the Holy Spirit was a living sentiment, not a dead letter. In 1766, Husband helped organize the Sandy Creek Association, which challenged the circulation of power between the assembly, the courts, and the governor by sponsoring its own members for office. They told Governor Tryon of "the unequal Chances [that] the poor and Weak have, in Contentions with the Rich and powerfull" and of the sorry fact that they did not know what laws applied to them, which "may seem strange to them who have it in their Power to consult Lawyers." As loyal subjects, they asked for his protection.[41]

Tryon had no more patience for rural malcontents than Henry E. McCulloch or indeed than the royal governors of New Jersey and

New York in the face of similar protests. He had come to draw North Carolina more firmly into imperial norms and markets, to make it appealing to merchants and planters rather than debtors and dissidents. (He had less need for artisans or manufacturers, since the colonies were supposed to buy their handicrafts from Britain.) So the governor told the sheriffs to keep Sandy Creek members away from office while announcing some new expenses for the good people to pay: £1,000 in presents and surveying fees from a new Cherokee treaty and £12,000 for a new governor's mansion, a sum equal to about one-fifth the total amount of paper currency in circulation in the province. If taxation was ever tyranny, it was in North Carolina, circa 1767.[42]

Over the next two years, as Tryon posted one-page bills to remind squatters on Cherokee lands that they "deprive[d] themselves of the Protection of this Government," full-blown insurgency broke out in the western counties most affected by litigious creditors, corrupt sheriffs, and Henry E. McCulloch. Regulators prepared for open war while still trying to win elections. Drawing from New Jerusalem, the Christian commonwealth described in the Book of Ezekiel, they called for progressive taxation, small-claims courts, and pro-squatter laws. Perhaps influenced by the public loan offices or "land banks" of Pennsylvania, in operation since the 1720s, they also proposed lending notes to small landholders willing to use their freeholds as collateral. More money in circulation would reduce the social power of merchants, landlords, and lawyers, spreading wealth more equally within a civil society built on Christian fellowship rather than commercial order.[43]

Such visions were sullied by Regulator violence that government supporters, with their control of presses and pulpits, made into the official narrative of events. While closing down a county court in the town of Hillsborough, for example, Regulators fired shots at the home of Edmund Fanning, who then had Husband arrested. This set off a spree of jail-breaking riots and two more Regulator takeovers of Hillsborough. According to one of the few accounts of the last incursion in the fall of 1770, the Regulators broke into Fanning's home, beat him up, and then threw stones at him as he ran away. Then they invaded the courtroom. After leaving obscene records of mock trials and defecating in the judges' chairs, they allegedly placed the rotting corpse of a recently executed slave in the lawyer's bar. They thereby "leaped the strong barrier of private property, and audaciously violated the laws of God and man." They "glutted their revenges" and acted like "bloodthirsty and cruel savages." Another attorney overheard Regulators cursing Governor Tryon as "a Friend to the Lawyers" and swearing that they would kill "all the Clerks and Lawyers."[44]

Setting aside their escalating dispute over who should rule the colonies, Tryon and the assembly worked together to both crush and co-opt the rebellion. In 1768 and 1769, legislators promised to reduce taxes, reign in corrupt sheriffs, and provide lawyer-free ways to collect small debts. This was more than enough to satisfy Griffith Rutherford, who fought against the Regulators as of 1768. Meanwhile, Tryon readied a force drawn from the eastern counties and supplied by His Majesty's arsenals. Indeed, the government's clearest advantage was not so much in popular opinion as in heavy artillery. With their brass cannon and swivel guns, Tryon's forces could kill and maim at a safe distance from small arms fire. During the final confrontation near Great Alamance Creek on May 16, 1771, a government force of some 1,100 men easily routed the larger Regulator army.[45]

One "outlawed" Regulator who refused to repent was hanged without trial the very next day. Twelve others were condemned to die in June, of whom six had their necks broken in front of a large crowd while the others received a last-second pardon from their merciful sovereigns, Governor Tryon and King George III. This was a fitting end to what the Reverend George Micklejohn called the "dreadful impiety" of popular revolt. All of the rebels would be punished in this life and the next. All of their victims "will rise up in judgment against them at the last day, and call for tenfold vengeance on their devoted heads." To avoid such judgment and make their peace with the government, some 6,400 North Carolinians—about three-quarters of the free male population of the piedmont counties—signed a loyalty oath in 1771. Others fled north, south, or west, away from the rule of law and its inevitable hostility to natural rights. Among them was Herman Husband, who slipped north under the pseudonym Tuscape Death.[46]

To rebel against the law and its magistrates, Rev. Micklejohn made clear, revealed the "basest ingratitude." The good subject instead recalled Paul's counsel to the Romans: "to obey *Magistrates* . . . to be no *brawlers*, but *gentle*; shewing all *meekness* to *all men*." Obedience to those "*guardians* of the public and general welfare" on whom "God has been pleased to confer a divine authority" was a Christian duty, for "*The powers that be are ordained of* God!" The colony's rulers protected the people from both "foreign Enemies" and "every domestic foe," Micklejohn insisted, granting everyone "all the advantages [of] civil society." In return they deserved allegiance, if not love. Such arguments had special traction among Presbyterians, who emphasized God's law rather than Christ's spirit. In 1768, four Presbyterian clergymen from the backcountry avowed their support for His Majesty's "Sacred Person and Government," and Regulator support in Presbyterian strongholds like Mecklenburg flagged as the conflict intensified.[47]

For a population that was unsure what the rule of law meant for them, this call to order ultimately appealed to its sense of having escaped something worse. In North Carolina, ordinary families could indeed become landowners, thereby qualifying for the protections of common law. They were better off than they would have been in Ulster, or even in Virginia, where Herman Husband saw "great men" with their "tribes of Negroes" displacing poor people. Anyone with an entry or a survey in his hands, with a debt or a slave to his name, had some stake in the standing order—even if that order increasingly recognized property without reference to the labor that had created it. Conservative religion turned these material concerns into moral imperatives. It pushed people to accept a narrative in which law had displaced nature, mooting claims based on honest labor or Christian aspirations and demanding instead that the wicked atone for their rebellion.[48]

The settlers of South Carolina had more reasons to keep this faith. True, the government in Charleston ignored them, but that was not necessarily a bad thing so long as they had their land titles and did not need to defend them against someone like Henry E. McCulloch. The planters, merchants, and lawyers who ran the province paid for it through *ad valorum* taxes and duties on slave-grown rice and indigo. They had no reason to steal pennies from western planters, who in turn had no occasion to protest the sheriffs in their midst. Instead, western planters began as early as the 1750s to clamor for *more* sheriffs, courts, and JPs. Their demands grew as new waves of very poor people and refugees arrived from Europe and the northern colonies. Suddenly, the more established planters felt surrounded by horse thieves, poachers, and bandits. They also worried about hunters who left deer carcasses strewn around, drawing wolves to their very doors.[49]

With so many "Lawless and Idle people" about, the Reverend Woodmason decided, the decent if Presbyterian settlers in places like the Waxhaws were stuck in time. They were "Without Laws or Government Churches Schools or Ministers—No Police established—and all Property quite insecure—Merchants as fearful to venture their Goods as Ministers their Persons." Unable to deploy wealth through promissory notes and bills of exchange, they were caught in the more primitive forms of trade and possession. The primary victims were the "Widows Orphans, Creditors, and Strangers" of western South Carolina: those who relied on legal and civil rather than household or neighborhood protection. Respectable merchants who carried cash were also vulnerable. In the summer of 1766, for example, outlaws mugged a businessman who unwisely went by the name "Ready Money" and then disappeared over the Georgia border. Later that year, one of the Jacksons' neighbors in the Waxhaws was attacked at his home.[50]

Whereas North Carolina rebels were moved to action by auctions and foreclosures, South Carolina vigilantes turned to force against cross-border, sometimes mixed-race gangs. In the fall of 1767, several thousand men signaled their support for direct action on behalf of property, slavery, and the laws necessary to acquire more of both. Almost all of these Regulators held secure titles, and a sizable fraction owned at least one person. Besides planters, their leaders included storekeepers, ferry operators, surveyors, and even manufacturers. They caught, tied, and whipped men who did not provide for their dependents, women who had multiple partners, and anyone who claimed "rights in the woods" instead of working on private enclosures. One group of Regulators in the Pee Dee region, southeast of the Waxhaws, offered to help creditors track down debtors. In the face of "shocking Outrages" and "infernal Gang[s] of Villains," Rev. Woodmason explained, the good folk had no choice but to inflict rather than obey the law.[51]

The leading men of South Carolina defused this Regulation by opening new courts and prisons beyond the coastal plains and issuing a general pardon to those who had used violence in the name of order. In passing what Woodmason called "Coercive Laws fram'd for the Punishment of Idleness and Vice," the low-country elite belatedly invited their up-country counterparts into a legal space that was very different from that described by Blackstone or Vattel. Rather than a civil society that reached out to every corner of the realm, this was more like an owner's club for enemy country, a place where white property owners were not only superior to but also sovereign over everyone else. At the same time they drew the settlements more tightly into trans-Atlantic rules about money, debts, and credit. Now that the dangerous poor could no longer "bid Defiance to their Creditors," Woodmason exulted, the province could "raise Staple Articles for the Foreign Market," a lawful member of a civilized empire.[52]

PANIC AND UNITY

The Waxhaws stayed out of the Carolina Regulations. Andrew Jackson's home colony was a relatively stable place, run by propertied families and Presbyterian elders and divided mainly between older, more prosperous clans along the Catawba River and poorer, more recent settlers along the smaller creeks. Its residents had fewer grievances with the colonial government, at least in terms of land titles. This was also true of neighboring Mecklenburg, which provided two regiments for Tryon's Army during the 1771 crackdown. Petitioners from that county were quick to point this out when complaining about repeated efforts to "seat" an Anglican minister in their midst. As for young Andy, he was raised to be a good boy, to heed and eventually embody the law rather than to rebel against it. Around 1776, the nine-year-old began to live with Uncle Robert while attending Latin school at the Waxhaw meetinghouse. For the better part of two years he studied here, on track to fulfill his mother's wishes.[53]

In 1771, Queen's College had opened in Mecklenburg to train young ministers and other professionals. Jackson might well have gone there from his Latin school, but the Privy Council rejected its application for a charter. For Presbyterians, this was another indication that North Carolina was becoming another pawn of Greater England. Although Mecklenburg planters did not have to worry about paying Henry E. McCulloch, they still used "proclamation money" to buy land, making them vulnerable to the Crown's hard-money dictates. The Privy Council's prohibition of North American grants in 1773 raised fears of an outright ban on emigration and final separation from family back in Ireland. And they wondered if the Crown would side with the Cherokee in the likely event of future conflicts, in effect trapping the settlers between the uncaring coast and the menacing mountains.[54]

In late May 1775, then, the Mecklenburg Committee of Safety declared all British authority "null and void" and any British servant an "Enemy to his Country." They canceled the protection covenant. Nothing better illustrates the instability of political allegiances in young Jackson's world than this county's shift from pro-government stronghold in 1771 to anti-imperial hotbed four years later. Its planters, or at least its leaders, did not understand themselves as perpetually bound to the British sovereign, but rather as deserving of the rights and privileges of British land owners. Both Regulators and anti-Regulators could complain of insufficient regard for the property they had made from nature. Indeed, natural rights were the only ones they still had after George III declared the colonies in rebellion that August. Frightful stories now crashed into Andy's sheltered world: of an English aristocrat named Lord Hook who burned Presbyterian churches, of "York Tories" who gave no quarter, of "heathen" Hessians who took children back to Germany.[55]

In the rest of the Carolinas, the whig-dominated assemblies and their "committees of safety" made accusations rooted more in North American terrors. In July 1775, as North Carolina patriots spread the word that the king had promised a plantation to "every Negro that would murder his Master and family," the Beaufort County Committee described a "deep Laid, Horrid, Tragick Plan" for "distroying the Inhabitants of this Province without respect of persons age or sex." Slaves from several counties, they said, were poised to kill their masters' families and burn their way to the backcountry, "where they were to be received with open arms" by the governor's friends. In response to these incredible charges, this committee tortured some forty slaves, while the Pitt County Committee gave their patrols "Discretionary Power, to shoot any Number of Negroes above four" found off their plantations.[56]

Rumors of British–Indian plans further shook the Carolinas in the summer and fall of 1775. Here again, the committees laid claim to emergency powers for dealing with emergencies they had declared. Ahead of solid information, they cited a "horrible conspiracy" involving Loyalists, Cherokees, and perhaps slaves as well. Tory spies, hidden in plain sight, would gather in frontier forts, enabling scalp hunters to murder everyone still at their homes. Or they would use secret symbols outside their doors to signal their alliance with George III and Dragging Canoe, a charismatic young leader disgusted by older chiefs' land sales. In fact, British agents counseled neutrality to the Cherokee, until a May 1776 visit by Shawnees and Mohawks led angry braves to follow Dragging Canoe to war.[57]

Charges of imperial savagery suddenly tore the Carolinas into hostile, shifting camps of patriots, tories, and neutrals. The great planters of the South Carolina low country, for their part, spoke a vivid dialect of "country Whig" opposition to kingly usurpation, denouncing any government they did not completely control as a mortal threat to liberty. They drew backcountry planters and former Regulators to their standard by including more western seats in a new provincial congress and describing demonic threats to hearth and home. Leading revolutionaries in Virginia and North Carolina followed suit, winning over even such far-flung and troublesome colonies as Watauga. On the other hand, former Regulators from North Carolina were skeptical of the whig leadership. Most of Charles Town's lawyers also sided with the Crown, as did recent arrivals from Scotland. So did the Reverend Charles Woodmason, whose vision of union through fear had backfired.[58]

For the patriots, the most alarming part about British repression was that it named them "rebels" or even "traitors," insurgents who, according to Vattel and Blackstone, were not entitled to any mercy from their sovereign's vengeance. South Carolina planters who were hopelessly outnumbered by the slaves they brutalized could easily imagine what such vengeance would entail. In an April 1776 speech to the legislature, John Rutledge, president under the new state's constitution, detailed British efforts "to engage barbarous nations [and] embrue their hands in the innocent blood of helpless women and children" while also inciting "ignorant domestics" to war upon their fathers. For the deeply conservative Rutledge, this called for "Divine vengeance" along with a new social contract. The arrival of a British fleet off Charles Town and word of a planned uprising among Jamaica's slaves reinforced the awful sense of impending doom, of a near future in which white colonists faced "savage" foes to the west, imperial enemies to the east, and black revolutionaries in their very homes.[59]

With independence declared, "evil reports" spread through even the most isolated settlements. Moravian neutrals in western North Carolina heard that much of New York City was in ashes, that "the Northern Indians" were cutting scalps in Pennsylvania, and that six thousand Indians were encamped at Watauga, ready to strike. The next day the Moravians learned that the figure was closer to six *hundred*. Another rumor had fifty thousand *Russians* bearing down on the colonies. A blizzard of hearsay detailed imminent attack by Cherokees or other "wild men" from the mountains. More plausibly, the Moravians heard that Griffith Rutherford wanted to press them into service, to punish anyone who refused North Carolina or continental money, and to execute tories.[60]

Rutherford's ascent from backcountry ruffian had accelerated during the Regulation, when he sided with the new property regimes while still conveying western grievances about taxes and representation. Now he was an archetypal patriot: a dissenting Protestant with no direct ties to Britain, and a man of influence at the regional and provincial but not the imperial level. He used his place on a committee of safety to relay reports of Indian ambush. In July 1776, he told North Carolina's new Council of Safety that three dozen settlers along the Catawba River, not far from the Jacksons, had been killed by Cherokees. Allied to the Crown, that nation seemed more formidable than ever, a terrifying foil to the dispersed and divided whites. The only answer, Rutherford argued, was the "finel Destruction of the Cherroce Nation."[61]

By early September 1776, Rutherford had mobilized some two thousand men for action, while the Council of Safety coordinated with its equivalents in Virginia and South Carolina to raise even greater forces. The Virginia commander, William Christian, resigned his Continental Army rank to attack the hated Cherokee; his South Carolina counterpart, Andrew Williamson, had nearly seen his family killed by Cherokee attackers in 1760. "They one and all are displeased at [those who give quarter to prisoners]," declared one South Carolinian, "and declare they will grant none either to Indians or white men who join them." At least two volunteers from the Waxhaws also took part, as they had in late 1775 to put down a tory uprising. Still safe at home, Andy Jackson learned that boys and men were supposed to be cool and calm in the face of danger, even when their leaders urged them to holy rage.[62]

"It is expected you make smooth work as you go—that is, you cut up every Indian corn-field, and burn every Indian town," the chief justice of South Carolina wrote to one militia commander, "and that every Indian taken shall be the slave and property of the taker." The assembly later balked at enslaving Indians in this way, but the basic message was clear: the Cherokee nation was to be wiped out by the united armies of the Carolinas and Virginia, and the troops were to be paid in the lands and bodies taken from it. As North Carolina's delegates to the Continental Congress explained, the Cherokees had no "pretension to mercy" because they had violated solemn treaties and killed "our fellow whites on our Frontier." In the name of both policy and "the blood of our Slaughtered Countrymen," Carolina might "extinguish the very race of them." Only Christianity, "the dear Religion of peace and mercy," could stay the hand of vengeance. In this spirit, the Council of Safety hoped that Rutherford would "restrain the Soldiery, from destroying the women and Children," while Col. Christian supposed that Virginia would not want him to "commit [an] act of Barbarity" by wiping out "a whole nation of Enemies."[63]

The white armies surged into Cherokee country during the late summer and fall of 1776. Among the few captives they took were two women and a boy, whom a North Carolina officer wanted to take to his superiors. As the prisoners stood trembling, the rank and file "swore Bloodily" that they would kill and scalp all three unless the officer let them sell the captives "upon the spot." Guided through the forests by Catawba scouts, Rutherford's men saw little action, making war mostly on rich fields and stores of corn, potatoes, beans, and apples. In six weeks his men and their South Carolina counterparts burned some three dozen towns. The Virginians swept down into Cherokee lands later that fall, while the North Carolinians cut a new road, "Rutherford's Trace," so that they could repeat the mission as necessary. Along with the treaties they forced on the survivors in 1777, this road opened what is now southwestern North Carolina and eastern Tennessee to white settlement. Judging by all the marks they left on trees, many of the Virginia and Carolina invaders already saw themselves as the region's first landowners.[64]

A smaller group made larger claims farther west, for the real prize was not the mountainous near frontier but the distant lands watered by the rivers that led, eventually, to the Mississippi. Among these were the bluffs near a bend in the Cumberland River, more than two hundred miles west of the far Carolina settlements. A group of speculators known as the Transylvania Company had "purchased" the spot from some unpopular Cherokees in 1775, and two expeditions converged to form a colony there

Figure 1.2 *General Williamson and Pickens pursuing the Indians*. This is one of the few images of the Rutherford campaign of 1776 and subsequent invasions of Cherokee country by Virginians and South Carolinians.
Caroliniana Library, University of South Carolina.

five years later. One was led by James Robertson, a Watauga veteran who knew how to perforate the skull of a scalp survivor with a shoemaker's awl, enabling scar tissue to form before the raw skin sloughed off. The other was led by John Donelson, the father of Andrew Jackson's future wife, who brought teams of slaves along with his large family. At first they relied on deer and bison, smoking the carcasses around the fort they built on the bluffs. Survivors recall the sound of their dogs barking all night, alerting them to wolves drawn by the smell of fresh meat or, they dared not say, to Cherokees seeking revenge for loved ones killed back east.[65]

MANY BLOODY DEEDS

The destruction of Cherokee country found its northern counterpart in the Finger Lakes region of south-central New York. The Six Nations of the Iroquois Confederacy had broken into warring factions, and those who sided with the Crown joined Loyalist rangers sweeping south into the Wyoming River Valley of northeastern Pennsylvania in July 1778. After the attackers allegedly scalped rebel fighters and burned men, women, and children alive, Pennsylvania patriots bitterly recalled a "Wyoming Massacre": one of many new stains on the land, and a focal point for North American rather than Old World blood loyalties. General George Washington then tasked General John Sullivan to leave no home, field, or cornstalk standing in Iroquoia. More than four thousand Continental troops from several northern states thus laid waste to about forty villages in the summer of 1779. The survivors huddled at British Niagara and started calling Washington *Hanondagonyes*, or "Town Destroyer."[66]

Deeply conscious of his army's image, Washington made clear that the Sullivan Expedition conformed to the rules of war as Vattel described them. The attack was authorized at the highest levels and by the fundamental right of a "civilized" government to "chastise" a foe from beyond the pale. On the same principles, Washington made a point to treat white prisoners—British, Loyalist, and Hessian—with civility. He held to this even after Tom Paine spread reports of British brutality and suggested that Americans send spies to burn down the Bank of England. A proposal in Congress to "reduce to ashes the towns of Great Britain" also went nowhere with the civilian leadership in Philadelphia. The Continentals were trying to win European recognition along with American independence, to convince the "civilized nations" that they belonged too. Massachusetts delegate John Adams further described "Piety, Humanity, and Honesty" as the best policy for an enlightened age.[67]

South and west of Pennsylvania, rebel leaders had a freer hand to make total war but fewer resources to do so. Before launching an Ohio River Valley campaign in 1779, for example, George Rogers Clark told a group of native "Devils" that indiscriminate revenge was "beneath the Character of Americans." Should they ever take up arms against Virginia or other states, though, they could "blame no Person but themselves when their Nation should be given with the English to the Dogs to eat." Yet Rogers could only mobilize about two hundred men for this mission, and most of them wanted to head home before reaching their target. He had to offer "great presents and promises" in return for further service. Even Griffith Rutherford found that his enraged Carolinians did not want revenge too far from home.[68]

As the initial crisis passed and the war moved north, Rutherford helped to push a harsh confiscation act through the North Carolina assembly. Thomas Jefferson did the same in Virginia, although he regretted the "departure from that generosity which so honorably distinguishes the civilized nations of the present age." Jefferson also took the lead in the "sequestration" of private debts owed to British subjects. Under this plan, Virginia debtors could pay those sums into a state fund with state currency. The Old Dominion eventually accepted more than £275,000 in these paper payments, at a sterling value of just £15,000. From a British perspective, Virginia had annulled its debts in the name of revolutionary sovereignty, becoming a rogue state as well as a traitorous colony. Patrick Henry defended such affronts to modern property by citing Vattel's *Law of Nations* and the deeper obligations of *salus populi*, the people's safety, in desperate times. "When you consider injuries done to your country," Henry later insisted, "your political duty tells you of vengeance."[69]

Popular as these measures were, the new legislatures also lost support with their demands for troops and taxes and their unwillingness to leave their own plantations. Interstate cooperation flagged in the absence of a shared, imminent threat. Virginia's governor wanted to show the Indians that "all the American States are one people" and that "an Injury done to one would be resented by the whole of them," yet he also noted that his state had no immediate quarrel with the Chickamaugas, the Cherokee faction led by Dragging Canoe. As such, Virginia would not help the Carolinas with this new campaign. Scrambling to finance their war, patriot legislators made more and more promises to their ambivalent publics. They printed money, auctioned tory estates, and organized slave bounties. Above all, they offered land grants in the Cherokee homelands razed in 1776 and ceded in 1777.[70]

Then the British tried to recapture the southern provinces, transforming the conflict and turning Andy Jackson's world upside down. In late 1779, his oldest brother, Hugh, rode off with a North Carolina unit to defend Georgia; he returned deathly ill and died a few months later. After a large British force seized Charles Town in May 1780, the dreaded cavalry led by Banastre Tarleton followed much the same route that the Jacksons had taken to their new home fifteen years before. On May 30, the villain himself rode near to where Andrew and his cousin were hiding. "I could have shot him," Jackson swore decades later. In early June the fields around the Waxhaws meetinghouse filled with wounded soldiers from Virginia, giving the young Jackson his first taste of war: the sight of amputated legs, the smell of infected wounds, the sounds of a dying man.[71]

On August 16, 1780, patriot forces were routed near Camden, just a day's ride south of the Waxhaws. The enemy at her doorstep, Betty Jackson decided to save her two remaining sons by taking to the roads. They spent the fall and winter of 1780 as refugees in Mecklenburg County, staying with distant relatives and waiting for news. In early 1781, they slipped back over the border, sometimes "lying out" to avoid nighttime raids and sometimes staying with reliable Whigs. At least once Andy fired at some Tories during

Figure 1.3 Sir Banastre Tarleton (1754–1833). Hated embodiment of British cruelty in the South during 1780 and 1781, Tarleton apparently passed within shooting range of a young Andrew Jackson.
National Portrait Gallery, London.

a home invasion. Uncle James was shot during this incident and died later that spring. With their family disintegrating, the two Jackson boys briefly rode with a band of rebels. Ambushed by a company of British dragoons in April, they hid in the woods while the Waxhaws meetinghouse went up in flames. Soon after, the British caught them. When an officer told Andrew to clean his boots, the nervy boy refused, and the man struck with his sword, leaving a deep gash in Jackson's skull. Bandaged and scared, the teenager and his brother were marched off to Camden jail, no doubt wondering if they were to be hanged or shot as traitors.[72]

Jackson's experience during the British invasion was dreadfully typical. After falling prisoner to a tory band, one North Carolina man "well recollects" that he signed on to the nearest patriot company "to take vengeance on them who had cruelly used [me]." Another man said that he had volunteered for a third term of service because he was "much troubled in my mind" after the murder of his father. Besides patriotism, he testified, the "only feeling that fired my bosom" was "revenge" for his family. Another North Carolinian blamed all the traumas of his childhood—the death of his Regulator father and the helpless state of his mother—on the empire, swearing that he would take his rancor to his grave. One Carolinian who had been born in Pennsylvania during the 1757 Indian attacks began his pension application with this remarkable sentence: "Ever since the Revolutionary War, in which I lost many relations and property, being poor, I choose the Western Frontier, wishing more for revenge from the Indians, than a Pension from my country." As one veteran recalled, "many bloody deeds" were done in the Carolinas during 1780 and 1781, mostly by small groups who wanted to kill certain people and burn certain houses.[73]

If anyone could turn all these intimate hatreds into a single campaign, it was Griffith Rutherford. Captured at Camden, he spent ten months in a St. Augustine jail before a prisoner exchange brought him back to North Carolina. There he found his plantation sacked and one of his sons dead. During the summer of 1781, Rutherford again mobilized his own force of militia, irregulars, and volunteers. This time his targets were the Loyalists along the Atlantic coast, whom he called "imps of hell" and "sons of darkness." Rutherford also warned of closet Loyalists and British agents, "Wolves, in sheeps Clothing," who would soon turn on the good folk. Loyalists called him "a perfect savage." Continental Army officers like Nathanael Greene saw him as a loose cannon whose brutality jeopardized "the cause of America and of humanity."[74]

After hearing that Rutherford's men were targeting (white) women and children and destroying property, Greene told Rutherford to stand down. Neither North Carolina nor the United States would benefit from a "narrow spirit of private resentment," the Rhode Island native made clear. Anger on behalf of others could be virtuous, but rage without duty was radically selfish. In the same spirit, a Loyalist officer acknowledged that a full-scale campaign to retake the Carolinas for the Crown would incur the "most calamitous period . . . ever," because "every man exclusive of his attachment to the Common Cause would have a number of private injuries to revenge." Vengeance mobilized people for short bursts of extreme violence, only to alienate them from whatever "Common Cause" they served. It took form in "small murdering parties" rather than well-disciplined armies.[75]

In this first of many disputes between the military and civilian leadership of the United States and the southern and western strongmen of enemy country, Rutherford grumbled that he had made war on a "set of Miscrents" who deserved every bit of it. He had no doubts or regrets, for he came from a world of pitiless extremes: heroes and traitors, brothers and villains, Christians and devils. Unlike their distant kin in the river valleys of Pennsylvania, his men and their families had never been protected by any government or army. So they had avenged themselves. If Greene or other proto-nationalists wanted to pursue the matter, Rutherford warned, "I have the Law of my Country to Protect me." As of 1783, Rutherford's "Country" was revolutionary North Carolina, and his "Law" was whatever it had to do for its safety.[76]

Andrew Jackson spent two awful weeks in Camden jail in April 1781. The sights, sounds, and smells of the prisoners never left him. Many of their faces and hands were covered by smallpox, and the ones in the later phases of the disease gave off an unholy stench as their pustules oozed. The tories "abused us very much" and promised to "hang us all," he recalled. Death was very close and all around; perhaps it did not seem so bad. Mercifully he and his brother were swapped for British prisoners, enabling him and Robin and their mother to head home to the Waxhaws, alone as a family for the last time. This trip was a hazy memory, for Andrew was sick with smallpox. By the time he recovered in May or June, Robin was dead of the disease. Then his mother—brave as a lion, he marveled—announced that she was going to Charles Town to save some of the few relatives they still had in the world from the British prison barges, where conditions were also unspeakable.[77]

Before leaving, Betty Jackson confided some essential truths to her son, as if she knew that she was not coming back. "Her last words have been the law of my life," Jackson insisted. In his words, those last words were:

> In this world you will have to make your own way. To do that you must have friends . . . [to forget a kindness done] is a base crime—not merely a fault or a sin, but an actual crime . . . [avoid conflict] but sustain your manhood always. Never bring a suit in law for assault and battery or for defamation. The law affords no remedy for such outrages that can satisfy the feelings of a true man.

Betty's companions later returned with some of her clothes. She had fallen ill with "ship fever" in Charles Town, they explained. She had died on the side of a road, or perhaps in a Good Samaritan's home. She was gone, and her son would never know where her body rested. The details were mysteries, but Jackson remembered them with fanatical clarity, narrating his own life as a series of devotions to the faith she had put in him.[78]

Andrew was now a fourteen-year-old orphan. His home was in ruins, his loved ones were dead, and his bright future was a bitter memory. One of his best biographers wonders if these losses took away his fear of death, not to mention his faith in the normal course of things. Instead of making his peace with much of anything, though, the young man turned to a radical discontent with his apparent fate. In some ways his moral development halted with his adolescent traumas; he never accepted, as most adults do, that some things have to be accepted. Instead, he raged against the moral chaos of the world, yearning to be a hero and a gentleman and to wield a bit of God's ultimate sovereignty. All of this made Andrew Jackson more insatiable than unscrupulous. It also made him unpredictable, in that he sometimes opened his heart to the suffering around him, even when he was responsible for it.[79]

CHAPTER 2

A Nation of Laws

Tragic as the war had been for Andrew Jackson, he still had a home of sorts at Robert Crawford's plantation, which had become a supply station for patriot troops. Planters, traders, and officers filed in, exchanging beef, whiskey, and other goods in return for IOUs from the new state of South Carolina. Jackson might have been a useful clerk were it not for his thin skin and violent pride. A militia captain, John Galbraith, tried to discipline the youngster for one mishap or another, whereupon Jackson threatened to kill anyone who so mistreated him (or so Jackson recalled). Uncle Crawford wanted to help Andy, but he had no legal obligation to care for his late brother's nephew. So off Jackson went to another relative's home in the Waxhaws, this time to learn the saddler's trade.[1]

Saddling was "honest" work, meaning that the men who did it carried a decent reputation among those they knew and worked around, but not any "honor" in the wider world. It involved stretching and shaping rawhide—possibly prepared by a Cherokee woman—to fit each horse and rider, normally with one or two leather-aproned masters and apprentices in a small workhouse. It meant cutting tree branches to fashion a wooden frame for the leather, along with the secondary work of felling trees and "hewing" stumps. This last labor, in particular, marked those of humble rank and small reputations, the "hewers of wood and drawers of water" described in the Book of Joshua. Jackson could not bear such a future. One day, the story goes, he "threw down his axe and swore that he was never made to hew logs." Other young men in post-Revolutionary America recalled similar moments of aspirational clarity, in which they literally cast aside the tools of honest trades and set out toward the horizon.[2]

Opportunity first led Jackson south and east, not west. At least once and possibly a few times in 1783 and 1784, he went with Robert Crawford to Charleston, which was no longer spelled "Charles Town" in honor of any king. Monarchists were now in flight, packing into British- and Caribbean-bound ships while displaced Whigs and other refugees poured in and called for payback. Uncle Crawford had more literal sums to collect from the new government, likely in the form of certificates and "indents" that he probably wanted in hard coin or legally binding notes. Andy, too, may have gone to the city to claim whatever sums his mother or other relatives back in Ireland had left behind. But the four-day trip revealed how difficult it would be to settle any accounts in the devastated Carolinas.[3]

Everywhere he saw burned-out homes, wandering livestock, and abandoned fields. Especially after the British defeat at Yorktown, Virginia, in October 1781, Whigs had looted Loyalist estates without fear of reprisal, and the passing armies and "small murdering parties" had freely taken food and supplies from the countryside. Depleted households could not produce enough to cover their expenses or to pay for the British goods that now flooded all markets. Rice and indigo lost their imperial bounties and buyers, leading to a sharp decline in both the production and price of these staples. When state governments hiked taxes to pay back "public creditors" like Robert Crawford, they pulled still more currency out of circulation. Lawsuits multiplied as cash evaporated. Even as he advertised "a large assortment of East-India and European GOODS" for sale, one Charleston merchant notified his debtors that he would soon "put their accounts in the hands of a Lawyer." Even this would be difficult, since much of Charleston's prestigious bar had fled.[4]

Jackson spent whatever sums he managed to collect drinking and gambling. Perhaps he gained sexual experience by visiting some of the city's scandalously well-clad prostitutes. By 1784, he was back in the Waxhaws with little to do. Once he drove a few of Uncle Robert's slaves eighty miles to potential buyers, no doubt showing them that he carried a gun and would not hesitate to use it. At some point he learned that his cousin, Will Crawford, had gone to North Carolina to become a lawyer, which was easier to do in that state because of its more dispersed court system. So had William R. Davie, a Whig commander who had caught the young man's eye during the war. After brushing up on his Latin, then, Jackson went off to "read law" in the poorer, more accessible Carolina. In the fall of 1785, he drew up one of his first deeds, transferring an illiterate soldier's indent for £120 to Jackson and a partner in return for £50 in cash. The following spring he made a fitting purchase for his chosen profession: a "quire," a twenty-four-page roll of paper.[5]

In the 1780s as in the 1760s, no one in North Carolina would have called a lawyer's work "honest." Whether it was honorable or not went to the heart of one's ideas about what the Revolution had meant. Had the rule of law returned? If so, what kind of law, and on behalf of which natural and civil rights? Should the new states take aim at the kind of society that great landlords like Henry E. McCulloch had preferred, or simply at individuals like McCulloch for their Loyalism? Especially in the southwestern colonies just taken from the Cherokee and peopled, in part, by former Regulators, the relationship between law and justice remained vexed and unclear. So did the theoretical connection between protection and allegiance. But while many settlers tried to escape the law as they had known it by heading west and even forming their own states, Andrew Jackson tied his fortunes to a new version of that law, and thus to a new kind of nation.

LAWS AND ORDERS

The Battle of Yorktown did not end the fighting in Jackson's world. Whig companies continued to pursue their enemies into British-controlled regions to the east and south, while western strongmen continued to devastate Cherokee country. They literally followed the footsteps of Griffith Rutherford and his Virginia and South Carolina counterparts from the 1776 campaigns. The most important of these regional warlords in Jackson's life was John Sevier, a Virginia native who had routed Loyalists at the Battle of King's Mountain in late 1780. In 1782, he led horsemen deep into the Cherokees' mountain strongholds. Bold and brutal, Sevier chased Cherokee warriors and their families as far south as the Coosa River, in the Creek country of northern Georgia. By 1783, he was the most popular man in the fast-growing settlements around the once-isolated colonies of Watauga and Holston. Settlers called him "Nolichucky Jack" after the river where he had his plantation and slaves. He loved as much as he hated, siring eighteen children over the course of two marriages.[6]

For Sevier as for Rutherford, Creeks and Cherokees were a single, savage enemy that had to be wiped out. He paid no mind to the 1783 Treaty of Paris, which named the United States the sole protector of all lands east of the Mississippi, not its exclusive owner. He preferred the "conquest theory." So did the Georgia legislature, especially after Creek warriors (or Cherokees living with the Creeks) raided some of its settlements. "The Creek Indians shall be considered as without the protection of this state," the 1787 Act for Suppressing the Violences of the Indians stated, "and it shall be lawful for the Government and people of the same, to put to death or capture the said Indians wherever they may be found within the limits of this state." All Creeks were effectively "outlawed," much like the runaway slaves they were accused of harboring. Homicidal ideas like this circulated up and down the old Wagon Road. As the president of Pennsylvania's Supreme Executive Council put it, all Indians had to learn to "depend upon us for their preservation," or else the citizens would "extirpate them from the land."[7]

Loyalists were less vulnerable but just as hated. At least sixty thousand fled the new states during and after the war, chased out of the republic by what Sir Guy Carleton, coordinating the New York evacuation in 1783, called the "barbarous menaces" of radical Whigs. With bodies still turning up in makeshift graves or washing up from prison barges, feelings in that city ran high and raw against the Crown and its subjects. "Flee then while it is in your power," one New York paper warned in 1783, or face "the just vengeance of the collected citizens." Vengeance aside, states like North Carolina needed money, and liquidating enemy estates was much easier than raising taxes. From 1784 to 1787, some five hundred Loyalist properties spread over twenty-nine counties were sold in North Carolina. One of them may well have been the two-acre plot in Salisbury where Andrew Jackson studied law in 1785 and 1786.[8]

Henry E. McCulloch had his lands confiscated in late 1777, whereupon he repaired first to New York and then to England. All those plots he had readied for profitable sale instead passed to the new state of North Carolina, which auctioned them off to small-scale speculators and well-placed farmers in former Regulator hotspots. McCulloch begged to have his property restored, but Griffith Rutherford would have none of it. Now one of the commissioners of confiscated lands, Rutherford longed to punish those who had burned his home and killed his son. "Send for your family if it suits you," he told McCulloch, "and go to Nova Scotia where I understand the Royal Brute of Britain has made provision for all loyalists in North America." McCulloch opted to stay in England, lamenting his fall "from affluence, to the most distressful Circumstances."[9]

The laws that allowed people like Rutherford to pillage people like McCulloch were "narrow and contracted," declared Edenton representative James Iredell in 1783. In fact, they were not laws at all, for in Iredell's mind the whole point of constitutional and civil order was to curb "*Revenge*." Back in 1776, this English-born lawyer, customs officer, and anti-Regulator had been as appalled as anyone by the "more than diabolical" plots by the Crown to incite Indian attack and slave insurrection. The creation of the republic was glorious evidence of divine deliverance from such horrors. But where violence ended, law returned. When war was over, society resumed. Vattel had organized *The Law of Nations* around these temporalities, concluding with an entire "Book" on the reassertion of peace and progress after wartime. And whatever else he was—Iredell's relative and patron, as it happened—Henry E. McCulloch was the subject of a civilized nation with which the republic had made a solemn treaty. So the new states had to secure McCulloch's property just as they did Rutherford's.[10]

Although they liked to say that the Revolution had begun the world anew, Iredell argued, Americans had to honor their obligations and adapt to the standing order of Atlantic civilization. They had to treat Loyalists with "motives of Policy, not of Revenge." Presiding over the Court of General Sessions in Charleston in 1783, the first to sit in four years, Aedanus Burke also invoked the need to "restore harmony under the protection of law" before people resumed killing each other. A hot-tempered man in his own right, Burke nonetheless argued that no society could endure if its members indulged their hatreds at the expense of treaties and properties. "*Private revenge* may be truly called *the demon of discord*," he perceived, "and should be banished from the land as if it were a pestilence."[11]

Along with the "sordid" desire to evade debts and seize property, the chancellor of New York similarly blamed the "violent spirit of persecution" in his state on a "blind spirit of revenge and resentment" that did not bode well for any new country. He shared these concerns with Alexander Hamilton, who urged his fellow citizens to cherish "legal liberty" against the "little vindictive selfish mean passions" of lesser men. To exclude unpopular persons from legal protections, Hamilton argued, was to unravel the social compact and "*enact* a civil war." Besides, any law that kept a Loyalist from his property violated the Treaty of Paris. Disregard for such agreements would make all the states and any union they might form "the scorn of nations." Burke worried that South Carolina confiscations would mostly hurt women and children and wondered if "a numerous democratic Assembly" could ever secure private property. Vindictive measures "would fix disgrace on the very name of a republic." If the confiscations and other treaty violations went on, Iredell warned, "this will not be a country to live in."[12]

In part because they shared these dire concerns, lawyers and judges were able to both check and conflate popular vengeance and radical democracy. Gentlemen of the bar were few but organized, a cohesive "order" with clear priorities. Hamilton, for one, began to defend wealthy Loyalists and British subjects in Manhattan. In 1784, he took heart as the newly reopened mayor's court curtailed an anti-Loyalist statute that ran counter to the law of nations. The code of international society had remained part of New York's laws when it adopted its 1777 constitution, the court decreed, and this voided the rash deeds of the angry masses. (Outraged citizens could not believe that the mere "custom of nations" overruled their express desires.) James Iredell pioneered judicial review in North Carolina, where he sat on its new superior court. Aedanus Burke and other low-country elites managed to head off the feared wave of revenge killings in South Carolina, although in 1790 he almost dueled with none other than Hamilton.[13]

J. Hector St. John de Crèvecoeur found it "surprising!" that lawyers could thrive during the postwar depression. But who else could shepherd a demand for an unpaid debt through the reopening courts? Who else knew how to attach a property, garnish a wage, terminate a partnership, or sort out which liens on estates held *lis pendens* had first claim? And who else, besides the public creditors they often represented, was so invested in the idea that speculative property marked on paper was just as "real" as a farm or a plow? As the depression deepened, courts issued the dreaded *scire facias*, judicial orders to sheriffs and constables to seize a debtor's plows, horses, cows, and even home and land. In some Pennsylvania counties during the 1780s and 1790s, 40% of households faced foreclosure. If the properties taken did not satisfy the debts owed, lawyers could obtain a *capias ad satisfaciendum*, confining the debtor to jail. In lieu of coherent alternatives, gentlemen of the bar imposed ready-made ideas of commercial order over angry but disjointed populations.[14]

The themes of the North Carolina Regulation thus reappeared across the new states, even in places known for good governance and "steady habits." In 1786, for example, a Boston firebrand accused lawyers of turning the law, whose goal was "the safety and good order of society," into "a mere business of traffick." He did not care that "men of enterprise" preferred common law, in part because he did not see why British precedents should linger in American states and in part because he saw no clear link between enterprise and "Justice." Indeed, it was the harsh terms of Anglo-American property law, squeezed out of narrow readings of Blackstone, that most enraged postwar farmers, artisans, and radicals. When state governments levied higher taxes to repay those who had snapped up bonds and certificates for pennies on the dollar, these grievances erupted into a full-scale Regulation in western Massachusetts in the mid-1780s.[15]

Although support for this rebellion was patchy and conditional, antilawyer ideas were widespread and intense. A town in eastern Massachusetts wanted the state to "crush" that "order of Gentlemen denominated Lawyers." Another wanted the order "totally abolished." Large crowds repeatedly targeted courts, lawyers, and sheriffs in Pennsylvania and Virginia during the 1780s, trying desperately to halt the auctions and foreclosures that made a mockery of their independence while their more sympathetic representatives cast about for a simpler, more democratic rule of law. Six state constitutions tried to limit the use of common law to decisions made since the Revolution. One new charter would have banned lawyers from its assembly, and at least one other convention considered as much. If lawyers represented the executive power of the state, radicals argued, they ought to be excluded from its legislative body.[16]

"Yet notwithstanding all this," the young lawyer John Quincy Adams assured his worried mother, a bond speculator in her own right, "the profession is rapidly increasing in numbers." Just ten years after the Loyalist exodus nearly halved the number of Massachusetts lawyers down to 34, more than 110 practiced there. Aedanus Burke of South Carolina heard all sorts of anti-lawyer grumbling "from the Back Country," but only because a blizzard of unpaid debts meant plenty of business for budding attorneys like Andrew Jackson. Everywhere, lawyers filled in the new state assemblies. All factions within the assembly of postwar Georgia, one member and lawyer recalled, "were composed chiefly of lawyers, who could with great facility, with our then scattered population, govern the politics of the State." Few leaders of continental stature seemed to care, except perhaps Thomas Jefferson. He disliked the stubborn authority of English common law and the growing power of a judiciary that was too "independent of the nation."[17]

All of seventeen when he set out to read law in 1784, Andrew Jackson probably did not grasp the political significance of what he was doing. He simply wanted to be a man of means and correctly saw the law as his fast track. His sharp memory and neat writing would enable him to name cases, cite precedents, and "draw" documents of sufficient precision. As important, he was comfortable around elite men, having spent enough time with Presbyterian clerics, Charleston swells, and professional soldiers to know when and how to talk and listen, eat and drink, boast and defer. He also saw no reason why contracts should not be honored. In 1782, his cousin Will had been cheated out of some promised salary by John Galbraith, the captain with whom Jackson quarreled. Perhaps this contributed to his career choice. If becoming a lawyer meant turning against the most egalitarian versions of the Revolution, it also offered a way to protect the widows, orphans, and strangers who, like him, could no longer rely on the informal fellowships of family and neighborhood.[18]

Keen to escape his painful past, Jackson gravitated to men from Virginia or Charleston—anywhere but western Carolina. At first his efforts were more explosive than disciplined, and he sometimes behaved like an upper-class lout. While studying with two other young lawyers in the county seat of Salisbury, for instance, Jackson once made a stir by inviting two women of ill repute to a dance. Evidently he could laugh at those beneath him. The brutal inequalities of his world only troubled him insofar as he was not yet on top, for in his mind he was the one who had been wronged. And yet he longed to be merciful, perhaps telling himself that this was why he first had to claw his way up. The pious example of his sainted mother worked in mysterious ways, compelling him to see life as perpetual struggle and to distrust the self-assured gentlemen whose esteem he craved. He ached for attention but resented the company of those who did not understand how he felt, who he was, and what he needed.[19]

There are indications that Jackson found a new sort of fellowship as early as the mid-1780s in the Freemasons, a secret fraternity with deep Irish roots that flourished in postrevolutionary America. Celebrating the Enlightenment values of universal reason and nonsectarian goodwill, Freemasonry united elite men around a mysterious set of symbols and rituals. It drew them into a world of brotherhood and magic, of sympathy and privilege. Initiates had to swear that they would never reveal its secrets, on pain of having their throats, tongues, and hearts torn out. Here was another "order" to which Jackson could devote himself, a virtual family of up-and-coming men who would never ask him to cut wood or treat leather. Later generations would call Jackson the voice of the western backcountry, but he was no less a product of southern and urban milieus, and indeed of the more cosmopolitan networks of his time and the legal ideologies they supported.[20]

FRANKLAND AND FRANKLIN

Among the weighty men whom Jackson met in the mid-1780s were investors in the old Transylvania Company, who knew that the southern states had just given out land in inverse proportion to their ability to govern. Georgia, for one, had almost ceased to exist as a patriot jurisdiction during the British invasion. Unable to generate revenue, the state paid 0% of what Congress "required" of member states under the Articles of Confederation. Instead, its legislature promised land to those who had "steadfastly done [their] duty" by not abandoning their homes or plundering their neighbors. Anyone who met that modest standard of virtue could ask for 250 acres, with more going to those who had served in a militia or Continental Army unit. A state with a prewar white population of 18,000 thus offered some 4,400 warrants, to be filled in the lands the state was taking from the Creeks. Adding to the confusion, a crowd made off with the first records in the spring of 1784.[21]

North Carolina's fiscal record was not much better—it paid 3% of its Union dues—and its method of giving out land was only slightly less chaotic. The records of the wartime office that had sold land in the new western counties, one of which was named for Griffith Rutherford, were either lost or ambiguous. Noting that this office did not sell anything larger than 640-acre units, one judge later inferred that its goal had been "to discourage large grants" of the kind that British gentlemen had once taken, ensuring that the people were no longer "oppressed with lordly owners of immense quantities unrighteously obtained." But neither did it *prohibit* claimants from consolidating smaller grants into big ones. In North Carolina's new land office, opened at Hillsborough in the fall of 1783, just fifty claims gobbled up over two hundred thousand acres of prime real estate along the Mississippi, far beyond the most remote settlements. More than three-fourths of these entries were for five thousand acres, the largest sold by this office.[22]

Open for less than a year, this office cast a long shadow over the future state of Tennessee, the public life of Andrew Jackson, and their complex rapport with the United States. It was run by John Armstrong, a militia colonel who had bought at least two of Henry E. McCulloch's confiscated plots and who later met Andrew Jackson, possibly as a fellow Mason, just as Jackson was launching his practice. Armstrong had considerable leeway in deciding who could enter claims. He told one small-time speculator that "occupant claims" had first dibs and that buyers had to swear that the locations "were for themselves." One-quarter of the entries he accepted referred to an etching made in a tree, while others cited streams, rocks, and the remains of Cherokee towns they had torched during the invasions led by the likes of Rutherford and Sevier. One man asked for a fifty-acre plot on an island in the French Broad River, "that Col. William Christian marched through in the night when he went to the Cherokee nation in the year 1776." Rutherford himself put in for two tracts covering six thousand acres, and when two of his relatives also asked for five-thousand-acre properties, to be paid for by the general himself, Armstrong did not object.[23]

Armstrong also cooperated with William Blount, a major figure in the postwar borderlands and the early career of Andrew Jackson. A merchant's son from coastal North Carolina, Blount had served as a paymaster during the Revolution. Perhaps it was his insider's view of public finance that made him doubt the long-term viability of his home state, or indeed of any state. He was too prudent for such patriotism. Both he and his brothers looked for commercial opportunities across Europe and the Caribbean, as well as North America. As a member of the North Carolina legislature,

Blount knew that Armstrong's land office was going to open five months before it did. Promising John Donelson, father of Jackson's future wife, that he would attend "very punctually at the day appointed," Blount asked Donelson to send "as many locations as you can." The following year he told Donelson, John Sevier, and another partner to "make use of any Names fictious one[s] will do I suppose." There was no need to worry about the legal claims that these ghost entrants would thereby obtain: "I can find the People to transfer their Rights to [us]." Lawyers, he meant.[24]

In late October 1783, Blount presented himself at Armstrong's office and put in for a five-thousand-acre spot along the Tennessee River, "including an Indian town." Then he gave Armstrong dozens of other locations on behalf of other people, some real and some not. Here again, Armstrong simply added the notation, "paid for by William Blount" alongside each of the no-show applicants. In such ways Blount eventually gained title or claim to some one million acres, a sum equal to one-fourth the amount entered in Armstrong's office and one-eighth the total acreage of all available parts of what became the Southwest Territory and Tennessee. Yet Blount tolerated no such limits, for he could well imagine what other ambitious men were plotting. He was especially drawn to the mid-Tennessee or Cumberland lands that the Donelsons had helped to colonize in 1779–80. Not content with possible buyers from the Carolinas, he tried to plant stories in British newspapers to encourage trans-Atlantic investment in the Cumberland region, taking care that his own name did not appear on such advertisements.[25]

The biggest prize was located some 120 miles south of the Cumberland, where the Tennessee River made a dramatic turn to the north. Just upriver from this "Great Bent," the Tennessee was wide, rocky, and shallow. Whoever controlled this area, known as the Muscle Shoals, could regulate water traffic all the way to the Ohio River, not to mention land portages from the Tennessee to the Mississippi. Convinced that these lands "must surely be the best in the World," Blount wondered which state, nation, or person would eventually claim them. North Carolina? Georgia? The American Congress? Spain? Griffith Rutherford? Any of them might seize the Muscle Shoals and then make their own rules about how, where, and when to buy land. But speculators did not wait for any sovereign. Along the political and legal borderlands where Andrew Jackson rose to power, they made their own schedules, fixing the rules of the game while placing bets on all sides.[26]

To stay ahead of rival claims to the Muscle Shoals region, Blount teamed up with Griffith Rutherford, John Sevier, John Donelson, the governor of North Carolina, and another speculator to form the Muscle Shoals

Company in late 1782 or early 1783. Blount's uncle, several North Carolina legislators, and one of the richest men in South Carolina signed on soon after. First they purchased a claim to the region from a group of pliable Cherokee while making contacts with Spanish officials, who probably knew the area as the site of an old French trading post. Then, in early 1784, Blount tried to strong-arm Georgia into entrusting the company with the region by insisting that he was in charge of the silent masses looking to settle there. "[You] will necessarily keep up a Report of as many [settlers] being about to go as you possibly can," Blount told one of his partners, "whether true or not."[27]

By the summer of 1784, after Armstrong's office had closed, the Muscle Shoals partners readied to open a land office of their own. They thereby assumed a power once reserved to the Crown and long associated with the high forms of sovereignty. But new political projects intervened. In June, the North Carolina assembly ceded all its western lands to the United States, just as Virginia had done in March. The right-thinking leaders of the Old Dominion had thereby snuffed out some of the more outlandish plans of western speculators while creating a national domain from which the United States might fund itself. North Carolina's leaders were not so inclined, and the legislature rescinded the move that fall, reclaiming their jurisdiction over the lands sold in Armstrong's office. It was good to hold warrants that might interfere with other grants, one surveyor inelegantly surmised in 1785, "for the decisions, and people, in this country, varries in some instances, strangely."[28]

Knowing that speculators and lawyers had the upper hand in this bewildering game of musical maps, most of the roughly twenty-five thousand white people in the western reaches of North Carolina had never wanted Armstrong's office to open. So in late August 1784, delegates from its four westernmost counties voted to form a new political territory. It would encompass all the settlements spread along the rivers that rose in the mountains before converging into the Tennessee River: what became eastern Tennessee, along with parts of western Virginia and North Carolina. Citing "the natural and inherent rights of freemen, entering into a social compact," they drew long-standing grievances over land and property into the broader, more liberal idiom of the Revolution. Their relation to the United States was roughly akin to that of the Republic of Vermont (1777–91), whose citizens wished to be rid of absentee land claims from New York, and of other short-lived "republics" across the unstable geographies of postrevolutionary America.[29]

By the fall of 1785, a Maryland paper described "the New society or State called Franklin" as a place where the "genuine Republican" could find "a safe asylum, a comfortable retreat among those modern Franks, the hardy mountain men!" Indeed, the people of that "New society" seem to have preferred the name Frank*land*, possibly a reference to a mythical Anglo-Saxon past of local self-rule. Their farmsteads along the Holston, Nolichucky, and French Broad Rivers made up a hilly and remote country, not the kind that promised big rewards for absentee purchasers. Armstrong's land records confirm as much. In a sample of claims on or near the French Broad, the average size of the grants was 424 acres, or about one-tenth as large as the average claim along the distant Mississippi. More often, the settlers did not have any titles at all. They had simply followed the trails that Rutherford, Sevier, and others had just burned into Cherokee country, hoping to carve property directly out of nature and end up inside a jurisdiction that honored such claims.[30]

Among the few surviving documents from the "Franks" is a provisional constitution drawn up between December 1784 and November 1785. Of its nineteen signatories, six had just bought tracts in Armstrong's office. One likely contributor was the Reverend Samuel Houston, a Presbyterian who called the charter "the sense of a majority of the freemen of Frankland." Another was a free-thinking Virginia judge who had read British radicals' arguments for "the power of *Civil Society*" over privilege and tradition. Sounding much like Herman Husband two decades earlier, they spoke of "secur[ing] the poor and the ruled from being trampled on by the rich and the rulers." Their "*Commonwealth of Frankland*" would be built on small districts of one hundred men, from which three "Registers" would be annually elected. To settle disputes, these Registers would draw up a jury of twenty-four neighbors, who would decide things without common law or its practitioners. Sheriffs and JPs were to be elected rather than appointed, and all intestate properties were to be divided equally among children, with the widow receiving only a child's share. A single-house assembly (again, no lawyers) would be selected by the freemen each year.[31]

The Franks tried to draw legal authority closer to resident-settlers, lifting the local decisions of laboring patriarchs over the political frameworks of speculator-statesmen. At various points they named pelts as good as specie for paying taxes or buying land, declared limits on how many acres anyone could buy, and set up land grant schedules that were far more egalitarian than those of the Continental Army or eastern states. They also proposed to make at least some Cherokees citizens, if only because, as one correspondent put it, the "poor creatures" were now "in our power." In December 1784, they named North Carolina's provocation of the natives as one reason to secede, yet soon after signed the Treaty of Dumplin Creek

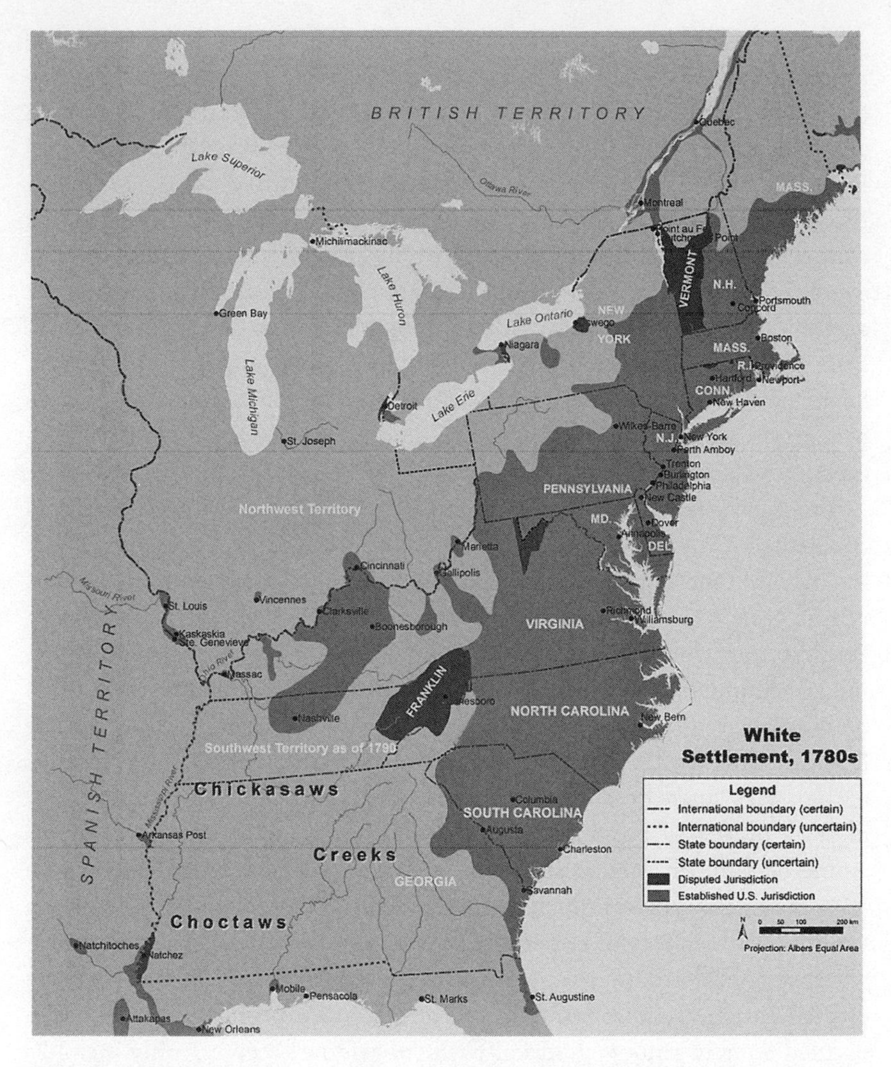

Figure 2.1 Approximate areas of white settlement in the mid-1780s. Note the tiny settlements spread all over the Ohio and Mississippi River Valleys, the large colony reaching from the Nashville area into Kentucky, and the disputed lands of Frankland/Franklin in what became eastern Tennessee.
Based on *Atlas of Early American History: The Revolutionary Era, 1760–1790*, ed. Lester J. Cappon et al. (Princeton, NJ: Princeton University Press, 1976). Ruilan Shi, Geographic Information Centre, McGill University.

to legitimize white encroachments south of the French Broad. United in their desire for freeholds, the Franks could not decide whether to expel or annex the resident nation. They also divided over how to pay for their "New society or State," with some calling for taxes on cash crops to foster internal self-sufficiency and others favoring the conventional, export-driven way to wealth.[32]

At a November 1785 convention, more conservative elements with closer ties to both North Carolina and the Muscle Shoals Company killed the provisional constitution. According to Rev. Houston, they took out the "most important points" and imposed the North Carolina Constitution as a better model. They also began calling the state Franklin, although the namesake founder withheld his endorsement. Among the key figures here was Stockley Donelson, another prolific speculator and future relative of Andrew Jackson. John Sevier was even more important in turning Frankland into Franklin. A speculator no less than a strongman, Nolichucky Jack knew that the reckless entries made in Armstrong's office would move some of the "Chickamoggy" to resist. He preferred to make war for North Carolina, but his would-be soldiers wanted to break away from the old state. As such he was "Dragged into the franklin measures" sometime in 1784, reluctantly serving as governor from 1785 to 1788.[33]

Whether in his capacity as a Muscle Shoals member, as a commissioner of Georgia, or as the governor of Franklin, Sevier descended the Tennessee River in the fall of 1785 to explore and survey the "Great Bend." He and his partners issued "warrants of survey" to interested buyers, further confusing the conventional link between political sovereignty and land sales. Alas, four American commissioners (including a Muscle Shoals member) signed the Treaty of Hopewell later that same year. In the name of the United States rather than North Carolina, this treaty reset the white–native boundary well up the Tennessee River. For the moment, and on paper, it restored native control over the more far-flung grants made in Armstrong's office and much of the territory that the Franks had just claimed. This treaty left many settlers near the French Broad in limbo, promising them only that "the United States in Congress assembled" would attend to their "particular situation" at some later date.[34]

The Treaty of Hopewell also rejected "the punishment of the innocent under the idea of retaliation," and the US signatories saw themselves as imposing law and peace over violent frontiersmen. And yet the Franks had also tried to avoid another war with the Cherokee, both by organizing a more egalitarian jurisdiction and by seeking their own terms with their increasingly desperate neighbors. Watching whites and Indians near the French Broad "exchanging the offices of good neighborhood" in May 1785, one Virginian exclaimed: "What a wonderful alteration since our hostile trip in 1780!" Four years later, a Cherokee leader wondered if those of his nation living along the French Broad and Holston could be "incorporated with the white people and become subjects of the united States, living under the same laws with them." But by then, a lethal alliance had formed between poor settlers with no regard for Indian country and wealthier men who could not tolerate a small freeholders' state along the Tennessee River.[35]

When it came to organizing violence against the "internal and external enemies to American independency" in the 1780s, John Sevier was as effective as Griffith Rutherford had been in the 1770s. He exchanged threats of open war with North Carolina and rival factions within Franklin, and when bloodshed broke out between Creek warriors and Georgia settlers, he rode south once again. Reeling from attacks by white vigilantes in the early summer of 1787, a contingent of Creeks demanded twelve white persons to still the crying blood of twelve Creek victims. "I think it extraordinary indeed that they should have the insolence to demand any white person as a retaliation," Sevier told Georgia's governor, "when it is notoriously known, they were the first aggressors." Recounting events from a moment of his choosing, Sevier made the oldest case for revenge—*they started it*—while describing the white people of the western woods as a coherent moral and historical whole.[36]

Sevier promised Georgia up to one thousand Franks for action against the Creeks. Georgia's legislature replied in November 1787 by making these would-be Franklin soldiers eligible for land bounties, including fifty-acre tracts in the Muscle Shoals region. Land offices in Franklin also began to offer grants around Chota, one of the "mother towns" of the Cherokee nation. One atrocity, among many, broke the regional tension and released its hatreds. Knowing that the whites would ignore the Hopewell boundary line, a Cherokee war party killed everyone they found inside the household of John Kirk Sr. in the spring of 1788. In retaliation, Sevier's army rampaged along the Hiwassee and Tennessee Rivers, burning one town for the second time in a decade and sending more refugees to the mountains. One party also lured five or six Cherokees into a cabin where John Kirk Jr. was waiting with an axe. With visions of his loved ones' body parts fresh in his mind, the young man killed them all.[37]

Among the victims was Old Tassel, who had long tried to prevent further losses for his diminished nation. "They are not my people that spilt the blood and spoiled the good Talk a little," he had declared at a summer 1786 parlay with Franklin officials. Creek militants were the guilty ones: "*They* have done the murder." Old Tassel's followers were said to shout "Chota," a place of peace, whenever they saw white people. His grisly murder now threatened all-out war. The governor of North Carolina thus issued a warrant for Sevier's arrest in July 1788, although it is not clear for which of several offenses. Indeed, a sheriff acting under one authority or another had seized some of Sevier's lands and slaves earlier that year. Nolichucky Jack was taken into irons that October by a rival leader from Franklin, apparently after a drunken dispute with a tavern keeper who refused to serve Sevier a last drink.[38]

If the alliance between Franklin and Georgia went down with Sevier in late 1788, though, relations between Franklin and North Carolina continued to improve. The assembly of North Carolina had been legislating for the western counties as if they were still in the old state, and since their constitutions were so similar this worked as well as not. In early 1787, Sevier had also arranged for greater cooperation in law enforcement between the two states. Besides, Franklin was bitterly divided over its rival constitutions and land offices, and its assembly could find no replacement as governor when Sevier's term expired. So the state died off by 1789, its partisans demoralized or won over by North Carolina's offer of a blanket pardon and tax relief.[39]

The leading men of North Carolina also forgave Sevier, for they needed him. No one else could command the western settlers whose ideas of justice recoiled from the likes of William Blount much as they had from Henry E. McCulloch. In late 1789, the state finally ceded all its western lands to the new authority created by the Federal Constitution, which promised to honor land grants already made and to tax nonresident owners the same as occupants. All western residents with eastern debts would be "held and deemed liable to pay." Those living south of the French Broad were now squatters on American-protected Indian land rather than residents of Franklin, to say nothing of Frankland. The Act of Cession merely promised that it would "not prevent" them from seeking pre-emption rights "should an office be opened for that purpose." No wonder they were loyal to Nolichucky Jack. If the law was not going to protect their property from other whites, Sevier at least promised to avenge them against their nonwhite enemies.[40]

THE LAW OF THE PEOPLE

Word of places like Franklin and people like Sevier deepened the gloom among the would-be leaders of a more perfect Union. Alexander Hamilton referred to "the revolt of a part of the State of North-Carolina." George Washington read about the "Mr Sevier" who had "occasioned so much trouble in the Western Country." These were deflating echoes of the war years, when states and strongmen had waged war independently and badly, and further evidence that the new confederation was too weak to make policy or honor treaties. On the other hand, the individual states were too strong, defying even the rules of international finance in the name of the sovereign people. If this continued, Washington warned, Americans would lose their "united character" and European recognition, whereupon "we shall be left nearly in a state of nature."[41]

For those who organized as Federalists in 1787, "stay" and "replevin" laws were the worst symptoms of this political pathology. Loosely derived from common law safeguards for distressed property, these either forbade debt prosecutions for a given period or allowed debtors to reclaim estates lost to creditors. They asserted legislative control over legal remedies. North Carolina announced a one-year halt to all debt prosecutions beginning in the spring of 1783. In South Carolina, three consecutive one-year stay laws were followed by the Sheriff Sale Act of 1785, otherwise known as the Pine Barrens Act. It enabled a debtor to pay with whatever assets he chose, provided that its assessed value equaled three-quarters of his debt. Opponents bitterly noted that "artful and designing debtors" used the low-quality pine lands in the middle of the state to (under)pay their "honest and indulgent creditors." Unless a creditor physically confronted his debtors, one low-country planter lamented, "they will put you off."[42]

North Carolina's government also authorized emissions of £100,000 in 1783 and again in 1785, and seven other states tried fiat money during the postwar meltdown. Confusion prevailed as to whether these bills were legal tender. In a time of stay laws and pine barrens acts, however, a creditor might see no choice but to take whatever paper he could get, even as his own creditors demanded gold or silver. Scratch farmers could agree to pretend that North Carolina bills were money, but anyone with out-of-state clients faced more "pernicious Consequences." The "well being of all commercial Countries, in a great Measure depends on the Support of Credit," lectured one group of up-country South Carolinians. Beyond encouraging free trade, that meant "compelling Persons who enter into pecuniary Engagements, Strictly to comply with them." Such arguments had clear roots in the South Carolina Regulation and made perfect sense to the professionals around whom Andrew Jackson remade himself.[43]

"There is no want of Money for Lawsuits, Drunkeness, and . . . foreign Goods," lamented the Reverend Charles Nisbet of Pennsylvania. "Only Debts and Taxes remain unpaid." In a 1786 sermon to the trustees of Dickinson College, this ultra-conservative Presbyterian argued that ordinary people and their demagogues had no sense of "the sanctity of public and private Faith," as evidenced by the shocking new measures to dilute the money supply and "stop the Course of Justice." Such laws would of course hurt salaried men like Nisbet, as well as widows and orphans who relied on income payments. Rising slave owners in western Virginia raged on "recent Invasions" of their "sacred rights of property," condemning liberal reforms in manumission laws along with currency emissions. They deserved better after laboring hard to pay their own debts. Such arguments also took root in some of the distant colonies of Kentucky and mid-Tennessee. The Political Club of Danville, Kentucky's first capital, denounced fiat money and runaway assemblies. "Paper currency is hated as the devil," one member summated. The first owners of the Cumberland settlements, Jackson's future home, quickly established a court "for the recovery of debt or damages."[44]

Yet popular innovations on the rule of law kept coming, and not just in frontier experiments like Frankland. Pennsylvania Republicans had wanted to include a clause in the 1776 Constitution empowering the state to "discourage" inequality. Throughout the 1780s and beyond, they insisted that the people had the right to regulate debt collection and private contracts, no matter what the courts or treaties said. Such ideas drew not only from deep prejudices against speculators and lawyers but also from a particular view of popular sovereignty and revolutionary time. The liberated people were still "in" nature and could therefore decide which rights to retain as individuals and which ones to entrust to law. This had an inflationary effect on rights talk, moving various radicals to argue that man was naturally free *and* independent, and that any good society should restore and perpetuate those rights. Too often, argued James Jackson of Georgia, civil society absorbed the "avarice and ambition" of its most cunning members, depriving the honest masses of their "natural liberty." Revolutionary republics, by contrast, did the "least violence to nature" by securing "as near an equality as possible."[45]

One of the most popular men in his state after the so-called Yazoo land frauds all but overturned its government in 1795, James Jackson made clear that he hated Creeks and abolitionists, as well as capitalists. In this sense he was much like Nolichucky Jack. On the other hand, he saw that a republican society would require the "peaceable possession" of well-defined territory. War was fatal to such hopes, not because it fostered standing armies but because it withered natural rights. Frontier violence swept away plans for greater equality, diminishing *salus populi* to a frantic logic of kill or be killed. Speculators who ran surveys deep into native land therefore betrayed the principle of republican equality while endangering the conditions that made it possible. Their "speculating genius" would not only allow "inequality [to] break in" among the citizens but also move natives to "wreak their vengeance on our defenceless frontiers." To those who shrugged that individuals were free to chase their own interests, the Georgian replied "in the language of Vattel": individuals who only pursued "their own immediate advantage" were "traitors" to both nature and nations.[46]

Federalists also denounced "land jobbers" and squatters for spoiling the public domain and treasury. In this sense they too decried unregulated self-interest. But while James Jackson targeted the "restless, aspiring, and ambitious thoughts" of men like William Blount or indeed Andrew Jackson, Federalists focused on problems of national cohesion and respectability. They worried more about indulgent publics than aggressive individuals. Good states, in the Federalist view, aligned commercial self-interest with national loyalty, securing the paper wealth of individuals in return for their financial and political support. They repaid current holders of government securities with no questions asked and enforced the letter of both treaties and contracts. This was the key to what Hamilton called "national dignity and credit" within a competitive but civilized world.[47]

No one did more for this first draft of American nationhood than James Wilson, whose passage from North Briton to North America had been much easier than that of the Jacksons. He was from Scotland, not Ulster, and his prewar experience in Pennsylvania involved getting rich as a lawyer rather than dreading Indians on the frontier. He was a true believer in commerce, progress, and his profound knowledge of both. Precisely because individuals in modern society had to make good on promises made long ago and far away, Wilson thought, they rose to new moral and economic heights. The commercial self was newly free to make a wider range of choices and equally bound to face the consequences. Indeed, Adam Smith's *Wealth of Nations*, an emerging favorite for innovative conservatives like Wilson, underlined the need for debt collection within nations, as well as the virtues of free trade between them. While leaving supply and demand to the invisible hand, the liberal state was "regularly employed" in enforcing contracts.[48]

Wilson was sure that he could make the American nation a better version of the British hegemon, if only he could get past the American people. After signing the Declaration of Independence, he opposed the Pennsylvania Constitution and denounced price controls and confiscations. At the Great Convention to draft the Federal Constitution in the summer of 1787 he was everywhere, speaking no fewer than 168 times and helping to devise the crucial, late-entry language in Article I, Section 10 that prohibited states from interfering in contracts or issuing bills on their own credit: the so-called contracts clause. (About the only subject Wilson did not mention was slavery, although he later called it "repugnant" to "any social system.") While rushing ratification past strong opposition in Pennsylvania that winter, he said that the contracts clause alone made the Constitution worthy of support, for at present any man who did business across state lines ran into debtors' havens and democratic currency. "How insecure is property!"[49]

As harsh as he wanted it to be against debtors and fiat money, though, government for Wilson was but "the scaffolding of society." Common law and now constitutional law were the starting points of civil society, not the final products. Society developed through time, enabling people and nations to escape war and improve themselves. Peace was "the mild and modest harbinger of felicity," the natural outcome of people living within a shared space of legal reciprocity. Women were confined to and entrusted with the "domestick society" of home and friends, he pontificated, while men were at once household heads, citizens of their state and nation, and members of "the great commonwealth of nations." Wilson also wanted the new government to promote national commerce and society, as by building canals through the hinterlands. Such projects would enhance the price of the western lands in which he had speculated on a Blount-like scale.[50]

After helping to secure ratification along with a revised constitution for Pennsylvania, Wilson gave a series of lectures at the College of Philadelphia in 1790 and 1791. These might qualify as the first course in constitutional law ever taught in the United States. The law was a principle of action, he began, rooted in the will of God but discernible through reason and study. In free societies, its authority traced not to the will of the sovereign, as Blackstone would have it, but to "the consent of those whose obedience the law requires." Wilson favored a wide suffrage to draw as many men as possible under these terms. Once given, their consent permanently tied them to a state that was itself bound by the larger society of nations. As he had noted during the 1787 convention, the United States should not pretend to "*define* the law of nations," since that law "depended on the authority of all the civilized nations of the world." National sovereignty grew with international norms, not against them.[51]

"How far, on the principles of [the Constitution], does the law of nations become the municipal law of the United States?" Wilson devoted an entire lecture to his answer. Too often, he intoned, people noted that the law of nations could not enforce the consent it required. As such, it was not really law. And yet the law of nations was the foundation of all moral action by states, just as the law of nature was for individuals. "Universal, indispensable, and unchangeable is the obligation of both." Since both states and people improved after forming social compacts, they had both moved beyond the brutal rights of mere survival. This was especially the case when the people were still in charge of those compacts—where they were, in a sense, sovereign. In a republic like the United States, Wilson ventured to say, "the law of nations is the law of the people."[52]

Knowing how badly that sound bite could be misapplied, Wilson launched into a remarkable clarification. He did *not* mean that Americans could ignore the treaties that their representatives had made or otherwise betray the sacred trust of "the civilized and commercial part of the world." Rather:

> I mean that, as the law of nature, in other words, as the will of nature's God, [the law of nations] is indispensably binding upon the people, in whom the sovereign power resides; and who are, consequently, under the most sacred obligations to exercise that power, or to delegate it to such as will exercise it. . . . How vast—how important—how interesting are these truths! They announce to a free people how exalted their rights; but, at the same time, they announce to a free people how solemn their duties are.

In consenting to the Constitution, the people had formed a nation of laws that would honor the law of nations. "By adopting this system," Wilson had said while urging ratification, "we become a NATION." Americans had transferred their original sovereignty to that "system," installing a new kind of fundamental law beneath and beyond their local and passing desires. As optimistic as he was elitist, he was sure that Americans would now surpass all others in "the stability of their laws" and ascend to the very top of "the globe of credit."[53]

Wilson congratulated himself and the other framers for having given "minute attention to the interest of all the parts" while following "a predominating regard to the superior interests of the whole." From the newspapers and pulpits they dominated, the Federalists summarized this talent with the word "liberality." The delegates to the convention had revealed a "well conducted liberality," enthused one editor. Now it was up to the state conventions to lay aside "every narrow, contracted idea" in favor of the "diffusive liberality of sentiment" necessary to form a civil society over vast geographies. Long associated with the genteel capacity to tolerate difference, liberality now meant a willingness to sympathize with leading men from other states and to welcome back those from abroad. It assigned a moral quality to modern property rights and the enlightened laws that protected them, embracing "the broad basis of nation union" over the particular needs and feelings of certain places.[54]

Setting "liberal sentiments" against "local prejudices," the Federalists appealed to the broad horizons of a national public while also narrowing its effective range. It was liberal for southern representatives to suffer those from New England; it was divisive for people within those states to shift tax burdens to bond speculators. It was virtuous for North Carolina to cede its western lands to the general government; it was unjust for that state to seek middle grounds between its debtors and creditors. As Madison famously explained in *The Federalist*, the deepest divisions in modern life followed from property relations and economic changes. "Those who are creditors, and those who are debtors" would never agree. National politics would thus transcend these matters while seeking compromise about everything else. (Madison did prefer the "liberal" repayment of the war debt so that original holders and current ones would share the bounty, one of his early breaks with Hamilton and the Federalists.) Public debates over debts and contracts thus became a kind of shadow politics, especially in Andrew Jackson's home regions.[55]

If liberality was the new virtue, then even William Blount could count as virtuous. Certainly he was not local-minded. In the summer of 1787, he was looking for a national state strong enough to secure his western investments but weak enough to enable him to ignore boundary lines. He served in both the Continental Congress and the Great Convention, where, like Washington, he kept his mouth shut. Blount had his doubts about the national charter, but in the end he told his colleagues that he would, "without committing himself," return to North Carolina and present the Constitution as their unanimous choice. Privately he guessed that the many and future states of North America would eventually become "perfectly independent of each other." With nations as with investments, he would keep his options open.[56]

GENUINE AMERICANS

Andrew Jackson received his licence to practice law in North Carolina on September 26, 1787, just as word of the new Constitution began to spread over the largely Anti-Federalist state. One of Jackson's first idols, William R. Davie, was among the Constitution's outnumbered friends at the state's first ratifying convention. A soldier and lawyer, Davie called the hard money, anti-relief rules of Article I, Section 10 "the Best" part of the national charter. They reflected "the strongest principles of justice" in the modern world. Radical opponents of Davie countered that North Carolinians still had no money, paper or otherwise, and that the Constitution would tighten the screws still further. "In land affairs particularly," one westerner noted, "the wealthy suitor will prevail." Yet the Anti-Federalists also included the largest slave owner in an eastern county, who hated the "damned Confiscation laws" and the "Saints of the Backcountry." Griffith Rutherford also shook his fist at this new assertion of national power, but not on behalf of squatters and debtors.[57]

By the time a second convention in November 1789 dragged North Carolina into the federal Union, the national state was up and running.

Hopes were high and varied as to what it would do first. Trying to stop the inflow of better, cheaper British goods, most states had imposed tariffs during the depression, and mainstream thinkers now called for something similar on a national scale. For urban workers and manufacturers, especially, Congress's new power to regulate trade promised more economic self-determination. During the "Grand Federal Procession" of July 4, 1788, tradesmen marched through Philadelphia to fete Revolution, ratification, and their livelihoods. The whip and cane makers, who presumably had a market in southern states, carried a banner that read: "Let Us Encourage Our Own Manufactures." In their view, the ability to produce finished goods was what separated independent nations from mere colonies, and it marked their labors as something more than honest. But Federalists like James Wilson, who gave the keynote that day, insisted that Americans first rejoin the civilized world by honoring their treaty with Britain and their debts to Britons.[58]

Wilson was one of the first six members of the US Supreme Court, created along with three circuit courts and thirteen district courts by the Judiciary Act of 1789. Among the early court's cases was a suit brought by a British subject damaged by confiscation laws from Georgia and South Carolina. "The state is composed of *all its inhabitants*, not *of the majority merely*," argued James Iredell, another early justice, on behalf of the plaintiff. Riding circuit and scrambling to pay his own debts in 1796, Wilson went further in condemning Virginia's wartime efforts to protect its debtors. The moment the states had declared their independence, he intoned, they were automatically "bound to receive the law of nations, in its modern state of purity and refinement." Since that law increasingly saw the confiscation of debts as "disreputable," Virginia should have protected its enemy aliens and foreign investors. In 1792, a federal district court annulled a stay law from Rhode Island, the notoriously pro-debtor state that had held out the longest against the federal compact.[59]

Such conflicts between courts and assemblies were central to Andrew Jackson's world and to the wider Federalist effort to turn international norms into national rules. Just as he joined the bench and bar of North Carolina, in fact, state legislators were trying to remove the three judges of its superior court, which had struck down a recent statute. Federalists knew how fragile their legal "nation" was and assumed, as Loyalists did, that anyone worthy of citizenship would not tolerate lawlessness for long. Just across the Great Lakes, the British were organizing the counterrevolutionary province of Upper Canada, whose governor boasted that its subjects enjoyed all the liberty compatible with "the subordination necessary to civilized society." Surely Americans would come back to the gracious sovereign who was now offering secure land grants just north of the democratic chaos.[60]

The Spanish domains to the south and west were less intimidating, but the prospects for law and order were even dimmer in the nearest American territories. While control over the Ohio Country had passed to the central government via the Northwest Ordinances of 1785 and 1787, the new administration in Philadelphia was more than a decade behind Blount, Sevier, the Donelson family, and other claimants to early Tennessee. Normally the Federalists were eager to support absentee claims; Secretary of War Henry Knox, for one, had leveraged holdings from Ohio to Maine. But in the Southwest, the rules of commercial order were especially misaligned with the terms of national sovereignty, inviting all kinds of illicit ties between regional elites and other empires.[61]

Despite the quick demise of Franklin, Secretary Knox had little faith in the national faith of the white people south of the Ohio. He accused them of shunning "civil power," of huddling together with kin or clan so that they could indulge their "angry passions." The results were positively Hobbesian: "There can be neither Justice or observance of treaties, where every man claims to be the sole Judge in his own cause, and the avenger of his own supposed wrongs." Knox sometimes conveyed more respect for the powerful Creeks of Georgia and the Gulf Coast, who at least had a clear leader in the multilingual and mixed-race Alexander McGillivray. Like many Federalists, the secretary tended to blame frontier violence on poor whites and to associate violence in general with places they did not yet control. And yet Knox and Washington continued wartime patterns by focusing the government's resources on the north side of the Ohio River, spreading deep and wide roots of anti-government anger to the south.[62]

Instead of troops, the administration sent surveyors such as Andrew Ellicott, a Pennsylvania Quaker who tried to distinguish US from Spanish claims in what became the Mississippi Territory. He described three kinds of southwestern migrants. First there were ambitious men like Andrew Jackson, too impatient for the sponsored kinds of mobility that Federalists preferred. Then there were large numbers of poor people who could not pay their debts back east. If they ever had "the sovereign power of legislating for themselves," Ellicott warned, "the creditors would certainly be much injured, if not ruined." Finally there were more serious criminals, wanted in southern states for all sorts of depravities. Even the propertied migrants worried him, for they brought along slavery, which was bad for civil society. In such a context, Ellicott confided, "the less the people have to do with the government, the better." The Southwest should be run by strong governors and judges, all manned by those "genuine americans" who were "enthusiastically attached to our national government."[63]

Beginning in 1790, Congress forbade private traders from selling to Indians and private investors from buying their lands. President Washington had copies of the new rules spread through the Southwest and warned everyone to "govern themselves" accordingly. Subsequent "Intercourse Acts" set up government-run trading posts where agents would sell civilization-inducing plows, seeds, and spinning wheels at regulated prices. They also prohibited whites from entering native lands south of the Ohio River without a passport. A new treaty with the Creeks in 1790 further marginalized regional strong men like John Sevier and his Georgia counterparts. Signed in New York, it charged joint American–native surveying parties to form a clear border between the Creek Nation and the United States: a twenty-foot-wide line of felled trees through the forests.[64]

The 1790 treaty specified that "neither retaliation nor reprisal" would be tolerated by any party. Whites who launched raids into the Creek Nation would do so as criminals rather than citizens. Those who crossed the line with the intention of settling would also "forfeit the protection of the United States." The Creeks could punish those trespassers "or not, as they please," effectively policing the borders of an American protection covenant as US soldiers did on the north side of the Ohio. Put another way, this treaty announced a new rule of law on both sides of the line it drew, declaring that entire part of North America to be peaceful if not civilized. It conveyed the sovereign power of the federal state to keep the peace over a mixed population while suggesting that sovereignty itself was evolving into the more refined process of administration—and all without providing the means to enforce much of anything.[65]

Knox handled the 1790 treaty as the personal representative of President Washington. The next year, the administration tried to extend the domain of law northward, to the white settlements and Cherokee villages along the Tennessee River. The so-called Treaty of Holston once again specified boundaries and renounced "retaliation." Once again the United States forsook white invaders of Indian country, entrusting the Cherokees, whom Knox saw as the victims of "many unprovoked outrages" by Franks and Carolinians, to punish squatters, surveyors, hunters, and anyone else without a passport. The 1791 treaty also reduced the number of illegal settlers by incorporating the region south of the French Broad to the United States. This time, the US delegate was not a confidante of George Washington but the governor of the new federal territory just organized from North Carolina's old western lands.[66]

Who was enough of a "genuine American" to fill that role? Who was familiar enough with the region's lands and leaders, and also unsullied by illicit violence (John Sevier), anti-Federalism (Griffith Rutherford), and agrarian radicalism (any Frank)? The administration had few options here. Western Carolina had no Continental Army veterans, no trusted Virginians, no northern businessmen who had literally invested in the United States. The only possibility was William Blount, who had been present at the Constitution's creation. Blount also came from a fine family, always important for Federalists. Without irony, President Washington's June 8, 1790, letter of appointment cited the "patriotism, integrity, and abilities" of his new man in the Southwest. Blount was more candid. "I rejoice at [my appointment]," he told his brother, "for I think it of great Importance to our Western Speculations."[67]

Figure 2.2 William Blount (1749–1800). North Carolina statesman and speculator, governor of the Southwest Territory, and key patron of Andrew Jackson.
Courtesy of Tennessee State Library and Archives.

MR. JACKSON

After declaring all posts held under North Carolina authority to be "void and of no effect," Blount began to appoint the "proper magistrates, courts, and registers" for planting the law across the long, rectangular space now called the Territory of the United States of America South of the River Ohio, or Southwest Territory. Inside there were two, roughly triangular areas of settlements: the old Franklin counties to the east, whose base abutted the North Carolina line, and the distant Cumberland colony, whose base stretched along one part of Kentucky's southern line. Also inside were the lands that Blount coveted as an investor rather than a governor: the northern part of the Muscle Shoals region and the Mississippi riverfront. While setting up the new capital at Knoxville in the fall of 1790, the governor appointed eighteen justices of the peace for the eastern counties. In December he did the same for the Cumberland settlements, at which point the twenty-three-year-old Andrew Jackson came to his attention.[68]

Jackson's ascent since obtaining his license three years earlier had been fast, if not always smooth. The young man knew enough about the law's technicalities and never doubted its foundational texts. He had studied Blackstone's *Commentaries*, of course, probably encountering the rudiments of the law of nations in the citations. He had also acquired a 1773 appendix to Blackstone that explored the political union between the English and Scottish "nations." Supposedly he also carried a pocket edition of Matthew Bacon's *Abridgment of the Law*, a kind of A–Z guide to English legal terms and codes, and later acquired more collections of British (not American) casework. As Jackson biographer Hendrik Booraem notes, the form and structure of such books agreed with Andrew's quick yet uncurious mind. In legal compendiums no less than Presbyterian sermons, the truth was already known. It had only to be applied.[69]

Then again, that truth had rarely been so questioned, and nowhere more so than in western North Carolina. Jackson heard some of his first cases in a region that had just tried to exclude common law and attorneys from its boundaries. He might have wondered if his first licence, which gave him the right to practice in "the several County Courts" of the state, was meant to include the Franklin region. Indeed, the English common law in which he had been trained was enough in doubt that North Carolina legislators had to pass a special statute declaring it to be in effect. Wherever he went during his long, solitary rides, Jackson had to cope with the latent hostility of a strongly anti-Federalist if not secessionist population. He had to embody the law he meant to impose, relying not on "liberal" arguments or military force but on the art of intimidation.[70]

His leather apron long behind him, Jackson spent much of his early fees on clothes. He dressed in riding boots and waist coats with ruffled shirts underneath, sitting up high on his horse to accentuate his six-foot-one-inch frame. People remembered him for his "straight" bearing and intense eyes, behind which seethed an angry young man with chilling desires. Incapable of resting easy with who and where he was, Jackson obsessed over what distant strangers might say about him. This made him exceptionally sensitive, even compared to other young "blades" who carried cane swords and horse pistols. Yet the young lawyer was polite to white people. He gave out just enough of the frightening signals to make everyone appreciate his composure, and he had a way of earning the trust of people who mattered. Within months of obtaining his license, the justices of Randolph County, not far from the Waxhaws, named Jackson a state's attorney. Around Christmas 1787, his friend John McNairy secured an appointment as a judge in the Superior Court of Davidson County, just organized for the Cumberland settlements. McNairy asked Jackson and another lawyer to join him, presumably with the promise of good appointments.[71]

Jackson spent the summer of 1788 in the old Franklin counties, making two new bids for elite status. First, he challenged an older, more established attorney, Waightstill Avery, to a duel after Avery mocked him in court. "When amans feeling & charector are injured [he] ought to Seek aspeedy redress," Jackson wrote in his August 12, 1788, challenge. "My charetor you have Injured; and further you have Insulted me in the presence of a court and a larg audiac." Duels were illegal by common law and "repugnant to the ends of civil society," as Vattel declaimed. They were also an emerging problem in the new states, the violent epitome of the mad rush for superiority that followed the Revolution along with all the plans for equality. By challenging Avery, Jackson declared himself a gentleman who deserved to be treated "honorably." They met the next day, and they both deliberately missed. Soon after the twenty-one-year-old Jackson bought his first person, an eighteen-year-old named Nancy. She trudged alongside as he rode about, a perfect foil to her prideful master.[72]

Jackson then made his biggest move, heading west through the Cumberland mountain range and arriving at the bluffs at Nashville in late October 1788. This country had grown quickly since its early years of all-out war with Cherokees and Shawnees. The Continental line of North Carolina had selected the region for its military bounties, some of which went in large tracts to weighty men like General Nathanael Greene (whose claims pushed out some of those made by Griffith Rutherford) and Col. Francis Nash (who had helped to crush the Regulation). Fearing that it might lose this colony along with Franklin, the North Carolina legislature gave the Cumberland whatever it wanted, including its own court. This attracted a small group of elite young men who shared the Federalists' vision of order, if not of loyalty.[73]

On December 21, 1789, one month after North Carolina at last joined the Union, the legislature named Jackson attorney general for the Mero District, its term for the Cumberland region. The very next day it deeded the western lands to the new national government. This ended Jackson's brief career as a mere servant of North Carolina and put him directly under the authority of William Blount, who was clever enough to know that lawyers and judges had to be coopted rather than coerced. In December 1790, Blount therefore relicensed Jackson and six others as attorneys in the Southwest Territory. Two months later, Blount reappointed Jackson as attorney general for the Mero District. As of early 1791, then, the young man was one of the governor's key lieutenants, as well as a lawyer with his own clients.[74]

Jackson quickly became a favorite of Nashville's merchants, who had long struggled to recover their debts from the dispersed population. He spent more time than any other lawyer in the Cumberland courthouse, pushing out the lay attorney who had practiced there during the mid-1780s. As attorney general, he also initiated over thirty *scire facias* proceedings on those who had disrespected the court by failing to respond to a subpoena or pay a fee. Such judgments were "contract[s] of the highest nature," Blackstone intoned, and upon their enforcement hinged civil authority itself. Day by day and case by case, Jackson built his reputation and that of the judicial power of the United States. No wonder that one account names him as the man who brought news of the Constitution's ratification to Nashville. Given the career choices and personal ties he had made, it is entirely plausible that Jackson literally announced the arrival of "the New Government" in this distant colony.[75]

Jackson's association with the Southwest Territory also tied him to the US–Cherokee boundary lines that Governor Blount managed at the July 1791 Treaty of Holston. In a frontier context such treaties empowered the national state at the expense of the local population, even as Blount continued to violate its terms through his own speculations. "It will be the Duty of the Attorney of the District Mr. Jackson to prosecute on Information in all such cases," Blount noted of illegal squatters in early 1792. "I have no doubt but that he will readily do it." Legend has it that Jackson came west with "a great ambition for encounters with the savages," but his official duties obliged him to make his peace with Indian country. And Andrew Jackson took his duties almost as seriously as he took himself. "I am required to remove all white men found on the cherokee land," he told squatters a generation later. Anyone who did not submit to "the civil authority of the United States" would have his crops, homes, and fences destroyed in the name of the law.[76]

CHAPTER 3

Extreme Frontiers

Federalist plans for western order and peace quickly ran into the United Indian Nations, an alliance of Miamis, Shawnees, Delawares, and other tribes whose political and diplomatic ties were every bit as new and complex as those of the United States. On November 4, 1791, warriors led by the Miami chief Little Turtle devastated a US Army near the headwaters of the Wabash River. When the smoke lifted, over six hundred regulars and militiamen lay dead, their mouths stuffed with dirt to mock the white man's greed for land. "God knows what shall next be done!" the *National Gazette* of Philadelphia declared. With no regular army left between Little Turtle and the heart of Pennsylvania, and with memories of the Wyoming Massacre still vivid, the article proposed a "scalping plan," whereby frontier whites would be paid to "kill and burn without distinction." Raised along the Pennsylvania borders during the midcentury carnage, the novelist Hugh Henry Brackenridge made the same case in a series of 1792 articles. Indians played on the government's respect for the law of nations, he insisted. Those who imagined natives to be noble were like "young women who have read romances," only far more dangerous for the new nation.[1]

Trying to align the power to avenge with the authority to govern, federal officials reorganized the army while also trying to pay the western tribes for lands seized under the right of conquest. For Secretary of War Knox and President Washington, after all, Pennsylvania and Georgia had never had that right. Now the national state would buy a new peace. "Money, to us, is of no value," a skeptical council of natives noted in the summer of 1793. The invading settlers, on the other hand, clearly wanted for cash, "or they would never have ventured to live in a country which has been in continual trouble." The tribes suggested redirecting the funds so that those settlers could afford to live inside the United States. Herman Husband, the former Regulator from North Carolina, had another plan. Since the "God of nature" had given the Indians first claim to the continent, he proposed paying them yearly rent in corn, tools, and blankets as the lands filled with white families. In that way the Ohio Valley would gradually pass to small farmers rather than to distant speculators or "lazy, bad" hunters.[2]

The administration opted for war, sending a new expeditionary force under the command of General Anthony Wayne into the Northwest. In August 1794, this "Legion of the United States" bested the northern tribes at the Battle of Fallen Timbers, near present-day Toledo, Ohio. The ensuing treaty secured millions of acres between the Ohio River and the Great Lakes for white settlement while also establishing a strong federal presence in the region. With the regular army thus occupied, the Federalist leadership called on state militias to put down the latest outbreak of agrarian protest. This one was all the more serious because it was in Pennsylvania and because its leaders were reaching out to hard-pressed farmers in other states, again raising the specter of radical democracy on a continental scale. In the fall of 1794, more than ten thousand federalized militiamen overawed the insurgents and marched Herman Husband to Philadelphia. The government later dropped the charges on the aging rebel, but he died on his way home. Alexander Hamilton then belittled the memory of it all with the name "Whiskey Rebellion."[3]

These new assertions of federal power were not lost on Governor William Blount of the Southwest Territory, who offered to share the details of Fallen Timbers with some Cherokee delegates at a late 1794 meeting. They declined, instead asking whether the Cumberland region of mid-Tennessee was "under the Protection of the United States" or not. To this fair question, Blount shot back: "all Citizens of the U.S. (of which Cumberland People are a part) are under the Protection of their Government." The white people of that settlement were "as much the care of the President as the people of Philadelphia are," a point he also made to those whites. Addressing a group of immigrants in the fall of 1795, Blount reminded them that killing Indians for past atrocities "will not restore their friends to life" and that all citizens were bound to the peace that the government had made.[4]

Blount insisted upon the rule of law because two years of terrifying violence had exposed its shortcomings. Besieged by elusive war parties and imposing armies between 1792 and 1794, white Tennesseans posed some basic questions about their natural rights and national duties. In what sense were they Americans, if their government failed to protect them? Did they really share laws or "blood" with the United States if its armies refused to avenge them? Such questions were especially painful in the Cumberland settlements around Nashville, where Andrew Jackson wanted to serve the new government. The extreme pressures of an undeclared war shaped his career and ideology much as the traumas of the Revolutionary War had scarred his mind and body, alienating him from Federalist models of civil order and teaching him to narrate vengeance as legal, just, and even holy, if not exactly American.

BETWEEN MIRÓ AND WASHINGTON

Being a lawyer in a commercial outpost like Nashville gave Jackson access to valuable information. His many clients gave him all sorts of ideas and contacts, revealing a world of opportunity that flowed west along the Cumberland River, turning north over the Kentucky border before emptying into the Ohio. From there the current pushed another seventy miles west to the Mississippi. All along the descent to New Orleans, various non-Americans—French, Spanish, Chickasaws, Choctaws, Acadians—were eager to trade with anyone with enough "enterprise" and capital. Jackson had plenty of both, especially as his clients began paying him in land titles and promissory notes that held their values wherever courts and common law prevailed.[5]

As early as 1789, Jackson sought new trade connections between Nashville and Natchez, some two-thirds of the way down the Mississippi. Settled by French traders and nearly wiped out by the namesake tribe in 1729, Natchez was essentially a fort around which plantations had grown up within the British jurisdiction of West Florida. Patriots targeted the region during the Revolution, for it was full of Loyalists and neutrals. Natchez quickly recovered once the Spanish took over in 1783. From its bluff, the mostly Anglophone population watched tobacco, pelts, and livestock drift south on flatboats. They hoped in turn to draw some of the Mexican silver circulating in New Orleans upstream by selling liquor, wine, books, buckles, watches, coffee, and spices to the valley's new customers. These were some of Andrew Jackson's first business partners, and they tied him to the northern fringes of the Spanish Empire no less than to the western edges of the United States.[6]

Men like Manuel Gayoso de Lemos, the district governor of Natchez, and Esteban Miró, the governor of Louisiana, saw themselves as enlightened servants of a recovering empire. They envisioned a new Iberian age built on strong native alliances and mixed-race militias, on *presidios* and missions stretching from California to Cuba. Alarmed by the "plague of locusts" streaming into their lands from the American states, they first tried to exclude the new republic from New Orleans. Yet they also wanted new trade and more settlers, and so changed course in 1788, just as Jackson arrived in the Cumberland. Late that year, Miró announced that upriver settlers from the states could bring their goods to New Orleans, subject only to a modest impost. In return for an oath to obey Spanish laws, alert officials to anti-Spanish plots, and raise their children as Catholics, the newcomers could also receive full property rights in Louisiana, the Floridas, and the disputed Mississippi lands in between.[7]

Standing before de Lemos and his secretary in Natchez, Jackson and seventeen others took this oath in July 1789. He thereby joined several thousand American-born migrants who paid their respects to Spanish officials in Natchez, Nogales, Baton Rouge, and Biloxi in the 1780s and 1790s. Some migrants reported that they were "Americans by birth but not sentiment," but most were more pragmatist than Loyalist. "To acquire and retain subjects appeared to be the object of the Spanish government," noted a later petition from Louisiana. "In *consideration* of which they gave lands, so soon as a claim was shaped into a grant, warrant of survey, or improvement." The king offered about five hundred acres each to ordinary settlers, along with rights to store grain in government silos. As in Upper Canada, the Crown monopolized the land market, so that people like William Blount were unable to game the system. This frustrated such men but pleased those who had tired of corrupt land offices and unforgiving courts.[8]

Miró boasted that his sovereign offered protection without "molesting [settlers] in their domestic operations." In Spanish domains they could pray and marry as they wished, paying nothing but a small quitrent for their lands. As important, Spanish law sheltered lands and tools from seizure by creditors. This too compared well with the American states, where the best settlers could hope for were pre-emption rights to lands that they could always lose in hard times. "Spanish *Customs*" regarding land tenure, one American official regretted, seemed to most settlers "very strong in an Equitable point of view." By "the sweat of their brows," over three hundred Mississippi settlers recounted, they had "reclaimed from a state of nature" certain "pittances of landed property." They had earned what nature intended for them, only to find that "a neighboring despotic government" was more amenable to their goals than the new republic.[9]

Wealthier settlers also saw benefits on the Spanish side. The servants of King Carlos III had made formal alliances with the Creeks, Chickasaws, and others in 1784 and 1785, welcome news for slave owners obsessed with personal safety. Masters also worried about governmental interventions into their peculiar needs, such as the 1787 Northwest Ordinance that barred slavery from the Ohio lands. Subsequent efforts by federal authorities to restrict the importation of slaves from non-US lands drew outraged protest from southwestern masters who wanted to move their slaves from one jurisdiction to another as their credit and labor needs dictated. While scouting for lands in the Illinois country, Jackson's close friend and fellow lawyer John Overton learned that all the slave owners "have gone to the Spanish side," leaving only poor whites on the eastern bank of the Mississippi.[10]

Between ten thousand and twenty thousand Anglo-Americans took the Spanish option in the twenty years after the Treaty of Paris, another reminder to American states that their people saw "quitting the country" as a natural right in revolutionary times. This is why the government of North Carolina tried so hard to keep the Cumberland region in its fold, offering outright land grants to the initial settlers from 1780 and also to the armed escorts who shuttled families back and forth through Indian country. Together with the Continental Army grants given in the region, these policies fostered an unusually stable property base for this distant but valuable colony. By the mid-1780s, the Cumberland was drawing what an early historian called "immense numbers of the more wealthy people of the Atlantic sections." They spread out from each other in a long, thin line: some eighty-five miles from east to west, normally within five or ten miles of the Cumberland River. Governor Blount called it an "extreme frontier."[11]

For natives, the Cumberland was a larger and more threatening version of the white colonies that James Robertson, John Donelson, and others had already planted west of the mountains. Its existence traced to the betrayal of 1775, when a few chiefs had sold the entire area to the Transylvania Company. Subsequent treaties had affirmed these claims, but the actual shape of settlement changed in advance of the maps that described them. Arriving at Nashville by land or water, the colonists left their families at its fort and then rushed into the dense woods and cane. They marked up all the best land, driving away the deer, bear, and bison as they cut and burned the trees. After several years of quiet, then, small teams of Indian men began hitting the settlements in the summer of 1787, killing at least twenty-four people over the span of a few months. Most of the attackers were Chickamaugas: Cherokee refugees from the Revolution who were building new villages down the Tennessee River.[12]

Native sources told James Robertson, now the military leader of the Cumberland, that a huge force was on its way to wipe out the colony. First he and his lieutenants begged John Sevier and the State of Franklin to "revenge the blood" of the settlers. But Sevier was then focused on the Creeks, whom he planned to destroy in alliance with the Georgians.

Accustomed to choosing between governments whose laws did not reach him, Robertson turned to Kentucky and the Spanish. "Cumberland and Kentucky were determined to free themselves from a dependence on Congress," he announced in the spring of 1788. Since the United States had failed to "protect their persons and property" and to "encourage their commerce," Robertson considered becoming a Spanish subject and a Creek ally. Some of his people had already fled to New Orleans, where they received Spanish rights to build a new settlement north of Mobile.[13]

The all-out siege on Nashville never came, but then neither did any help. Robertson thus remained in contact with Miró, noting in the fall of 1789 that his people would "insist on being Seperated from North Carolina" and ally with "the New Congress of the United States," while still seeking "a more interesting Connection" for their remote estates. The Cumberland followed its own path, a kind of rich man's Franklin spread along the far western waters. Slaves poured in after the terror of 1787, and within a few years some 20% of the population was enslaved, against about 5% in the poorest parts of east Tennessee. Its leaders did not hide the fact that their loyalties were flexible, for their needs were extreme. While the eastern counties were organized as the Washington District, with its capital at Knoxville, the three counties of the Cumberland preferred Spanish place names. They became the Mero District, Anglicized flattery to the Louisiana governor.[14]

Jackson took his oath to the Bourbons just after the threat to break away began to recede and just before William Blount and federal authority arrived. Probably Jackson saw it as nothing more than a business expense, or rather as a way to avoid business expenses. Certainly his new superior would not have objected. Blount was eager to enhance the value of the territory, and that required more trade to the west and south rather than to the east. Indeed, one of the biggest appeals of the Constitution to which Blount had more or less committed was its pledge to honor international trade and investment, to secure property no matter what its form or nationality. By 1790, Jackson was corresponding with one of Miró's relatives about possible business with the Choctaws, who wanted more trade with Spanish officials or British firms. He also used his Spanish privileges for more intimate concerns.[15]

PROTECTING RACHEL

The white invaders of early Tennessee lived with the waking nightmare of native ambush. Farmers took turns on guard while working their fields. Merchants put armed men on their flatboats and keelboats. Small parties taking water from a spring formed a circle, "watching, in all directions, for a lurking or creeping enemy." And women like Rachel Donelson offered free board to men who doubled as body guards. Her husband, John Donelson, had disappeared during a 1786 trip to deliver western land claims to North Carolina. Word later arrived that his party had been attacked by unknown natives, and that the sixty-eight-year-old had asked a survivor to hold his entrails in place while he enjoyed a final meal of buffalo tongue. This may have been a targeted killing: Donelson and his sons had purchased at least twenty plots in Armstrong's office and were deeply involved in the Muscle Shoals speculation, always a point of bitter native protest. Warriors expressed regret for having killed another man that year, but not John Donelson.[16]

A day's ride northeast of Nashville, the Donelson compound was a natural meeting place for the scattered families of the Mero. There were eleven Donelson children, and they came and went along with a steady stream of guests and boarders, including, by the end of 1788, the young lawyers Andrew Jackson and John Overton. In many ways the Donelson home was a wealthier version of the Waxhaws households where Jackson had grown up: a world of cousins, aunts, uncles, wards, and widows, as well as parents and children. Courteous as usual, Jackson quickly became a trusted insider. To widow Donelson he was a surrogate son. "My good old Mother," Andrew later called her. As for his slave Nancy, she was surely put to work with the family's other chattels.[17]

Here Jackson also met Rachel Donelson Robards. In 1785, shortly before her father's murder, the seventeen-year-old had married Lewis Robards of Kentucky, whose family pedigree was better than his business record. Everyone agrees that this was a mistake. As John Overton would tell it decades later, Robards was a jealous and bitter man who disappointed his mother and frightened his bride. Perhaps he felt threatened by his assertive and attractive wife. In any case, Rachel left Kentucky in the summer of 1788 and returned to her widowed mother. This qualified as divorce *a mensa et thoro*, from bed and board, which did not allow either party to remarry. But Lewis Robards was not ready to end things, and he reunited with Rachel at the Donelson compound that fall.[18]

Jackson and Overton slept in a cabin adjacent to the main house, all too close to the unhappy couple. No doubt they heard about the Donelsons' dramatic escape from the Cumberland in 1780. Perhaps the twenty-one-year-old Jackson shared his own war stories from that time, or even the painful fact that he too would never know where his loved one was buried. He found the pretty, dark-eyed Rachel lively and genteel, passionate and vulnerable. She could push the boundaries by dancing, smoking, and riding, and yet she did not defy patriarchal order on Heaven or Earth. She was pious but not shy, and her sadness gave her a mercurial depth. Rachel was clearly drawn to the ambitious young lawyer, yet she remained the wife of an unremarkable bully. Jackson wanted to save and protect her, to take her affection and give her a home.[19]

Meeting Rachel seems to have recalled Jackson to the good behavior his mother had expected of him. We hear no more stories of binge drinking or womanizing. He benefited here from an ancient double standard, whereby a man's dalliances were not fatal to his "honor" so long as they did not involve a married woman's bed or result in out-of-wedlock children. Especially if his sexual past concerned women of low status, he was free to turn the page on them. No such absolution was available for Rachel. A woman's honor was her chastity and fidelity, her innocence of sexual contact out of wedlock. So important was this public recognition of her intimate moments that both legal authorities and popular literature valorized women who preferred death to "dishonor." A heroic woman, in other words, would ask a rapist to kill her instead.[20]

Although courts in Davidson County sometimes cited people for fornicating, they were more interested in property disputes than sexual morality. Couples all over the new states faced few barriers to getting married, even if their parents disapproved or a child was already on the way. In some respects the Revolution had loosened patriarchal morality, which was already weaker in newer settlements. Once made, however, marriages remained difficult to undo. Full divorce *a vinculo*, with rights to remarry, was particularly rare in the South, where it required a special bill from the legislature. Barring the discovery of a serious preexisting condition—a prior marriage, for example—marriage was as permanent as the masculine rule it consecrated, especially for families of property and standing.[21]

Instead of simply running off with his sweetheart, then, Jackson left the Donelson compound sometime in 1789 while Rachel stayed with her mother and one of her sisters. Robards sulked and returned to Kentucky, leaving his wife in a legal and social bind. To obtain a bill of divorce, she would have to expose herself to charges of infidelity from the ruling men of Virginia and Kentucky. To remain Robards' wife was equally unbearable. Since she had signed no marriage settlement, anything she kept at her mother's or sister's home still belonged to him. Robards could claim some of that property to answer his debts. If the Donelsons failed to pay, the Kentucky courts could have asked those in Davidson County to seize the property—a duty that would have presumably fallen to its unpaid attorney general, Andrew Jackson. Robards also retained sexual rights to Rachel, for marriage implied lifelong consent. "The husband hath, by law, power and dominion over his wife," intoned a standard legal text that Jackson often cited, "and may keep her by force within the bounds of duty."[22]

Andrew Jackson would build his legend by breaking certain rules in the name of natural rights and aching passions. He was especially adept at naming his particular interests as fundamental law and then raging against its political corruption. But here, the laws that stood in his way came from the very hierarchies he took to be natural or divine: husband over wife, family over society, honor over technicality. His desire for a married woman imperiled his reputation and that of her family. As such, he did not launch a frontal attack on Robards. Instead, he marshalled all his self-control and worked with Rachel, her family, and possibly even with Robards to dissolve one marriage and declare another. That no one beyond his inner circle appreciated that self-control fed his angry pride.[23]

In late 1789 or early 1790, Jackson accompanied Rachel and some family friends down to Natchez. There she stayed while he moved back and forth to Nashville, representing clients and serving Governor Blount. It is possible that they married in Natchez and probable that Rachel's long absence convinced people in Nashville that her first marriage was over. In December 1790, Lewis Robards sought and received permission from the Virginia legislature to sue for divorce, on the grounds of his wife's desertion and adultery. One historian wonders if the Donelson family had made a deal with Robards, perhaps paying him off so that they could lawfully recognize Andrew Jackson as his successor. In any case, the family named Rachel *Jackson* in a January 1791 inventory of her late father's estate, and upon her return to Nashville that spring she and Andrew lived together as husband and wife. Among other income and property from the estate, Rachel received two slaves, whose marriage had no legal standing at all.[24]

The young couple bought a home from Rachel's brother in early 1792, just over the Cumberland from her mother. And yet the Virginia burgesses only granted Lewis Robards his divorce in the fall of 1793. This gap might make people wonder if she had been Jackson's wife or concubine during that time. So at the urging of John Overton, who knew the whole story, Andrew Jackson decisively married "Rachel Donelson Alias Rachel Roberts" in Nashville in January 1794. (The ceremony was overseen by Rachel's brother-in-law, one of Cumberland's justices of the peace.) He never wanted to talk about it again. He and Rachel were entirely innocent, he believed, having followed every rule until finally allowed to follow their hearts. Besides, their first years together had been marred by something far worse than gossip.[25]

Delenda est Carthage

As early as the summer of 1789, Jackson is said to have taken part in a sixty- to seventy-man mission against the natives who had just attacked James Robertson's station house. Two years later he was a trusted messenger between Blount and Robertson and privy to their military planning. But the territory's foreign policy was decided in Philadelphia, not in Nashville or Knoxville. It was made by Henry Knox and George Washington, not James Robertson or William Blount. And the goal of that policy, Knox made clear, was to preserve "a general tranquility in the Southern quarter." The government was preoccupied with events on the north side of the Ohio and the eastern end of the Atlantic. It had no soldiers to spare. Militiamen were therefore to engage in defensive measures only, staying out of Indian lands south of the Tennessee River and the Mero District unless in active pursuit of red-handed attackers. In letters to Governor Blount, Knox framed these rules in terms of the nation's power to "enforce the approbation of the dispassionate and enlightened part of mankind."[26]

Blount did not much care about such approbation, but as of the summer of 1791, when he made a new treaty with the Cherokee, he was no less inclined toward peace. War held back emigration, and thus the value of the territory's potential estates. It halted the digging of iron mines, the manufacture of nails, the construction of wharves, and a host of other projects in which the governor and his brothers were involved. The Indians would go away in good time, and for now it was best not to stir their proverbial lust for vengeance—especially since men like him and the surveyors they employed posed a more immediate threat to natives then mere settlers. On the opposite end of the social spectrum were hunters, who violated Blount's treaty by taking game deep inside native lands. Cherokees repeatedly cited the misdeeds of speculators, surveyors, and hunters as their *casus belli,* first threatening, then assaulting, and finally killing the invaders.[27]

In 1791, Creek and Shawnee men joined the Chickamauga refugees to hit the Mero District at least seventeen times, killing nineteen people. Only a few of these attacks definitely targeted a household, while two others struck one of the district's semifortified stations. All of the dead seem to have been men, just like the great majority of victims during the 1780s. The violence worsened in the spring and summer of 1792. Through October, the district was hit at least thirty times, resulting in forty-four deaths. Of these, one-quarter were women and children. Still, war parties kept certain rules of engagement: of the twenty-one captives they took over those nine months, almost all were women and children, including four slaves.

Figure 3.1 This image from Thomas Anburey, *Travels Through the Interior Parts of America*, captures the terror that native men inspired in the 1790s. Native attackers seemed to emerge from any wooded area, ready to violate the bodies and strip the heads of white invaders.
Virginia Historical Society.

Encountering a group of Indians while traveling to the Cumberland in November 1791, seven white men rode off in panic, leaving behind four women who were "so terrified that they were unable to proceed." The natives simply made them a camp fire. "He is not like you are, for you kill women and children, and he does not," the Bloody Fellow declared. If women and children died in the sting of battle, he warned, "you began it, and this is what you get for it."[28]

While threatening white men they met along roads and rivers, Chickamaugas also stole horses. Riding bareback, a single brave could drive along two of the coveted animals, selling or trading them to French, Spanish, or native buyers to the south and west. This was an easy way to enrich the fragile new colonies they were building down the Tennessee River. In the first four months of 1792, Blount reported two hundred horses stolen from the Mero and Washington Districts, a serious blow to the territory's economy and sense of security. "The only thing I can do is to give passports to the Sufferers to go into the nation in Search of their horses," he told Knox. Denied justice, "the whites" could barely "restrain themselves from taking what they call Satisfaction that is from killing Some of the Indians." In other words, settlers routinely rode into the woods and murdered the first Indians they found because some other Indians had stolen their horses. Judging by accounts in the *Knoxville Gazette*, the territory's only paper, the victims were often small parties of women and children gathering food. White avengers killed women "by mistake" or "by accident," preferring instead to take children and "squaws" as captives.[29]

Throughout the summer of 1792, the Cherokee near Chota and their more militant Chickamauga cousins held talks about all the "crying blood" that white marauders were leaving behind. Should they continue to harass the intruders? Should they avenge their loved ones in the traditional way? Or should they commit to all-out war as the "nation" that whites said they were? Besides grieving mothers, wives, and sisters, the most militant voices belonged to the Creeks and Cherokees whose villages had been devastated by Franks and Georgians as recently as 1788. "[They] openly avow their intention to kill every white man they meet," reported one US attendee of Creek militants, who also confirmed that the Spanish were arming the braves. Fighting for survival and vengeance, native men formed new and unstable alliances to prevent another calamity like the 1776 invasions.[30]

In the late summer, James Robertson held last-ditch talks with various Cherokees at Nashville. A grim, determined man, Robertson was well aware of the Cumberland's unique vulnerability. Four years earlier he had considered an alliance with the Creeks against the Chickamaugas, but two personal traumas since then had simplified his world view. First, a war party hit his station house in the summer of 1789, wounding him. Then, in June 1792, natives fired on him and his son while they were in their fields. Robertson was shot through both arms, while his son took a ball through the thigh. No doubt wondering if the shooters were among those he was addressing, he let his hatred do the talking. "There had been a great deal of blood spilt in his settlement, and [now] he would come and sweep it clean with [Indian] blood." The warriors rode off to the southeast, overruling the more cautious leaders who had seen what white armies could do and who at least wanted to wait until the summer corn was safely harvested. The five Chickamauga towns declared war in early September 1792.[31]

One of Blount's informants, James Ore, warned that some five hundred Chickamaugas and Creeks were on their way, seeking "hair and horses" on a huge scale. And yet the governor was under express orders to keep all militia companies within the limits described by the 1791 treaty. Blount noted that infantry companies made up of poorer men with no horses turned out with "great tardiness and reluctance," unless in hot pursuit of Indians who had killed their own kin. They were hard to mobilize for action and even harder to control in action. Thrust into the role of wartime commander, Blount first put his faith in the small contingent of US troops who had finally arrived that summer. He told one of their commanders to "cordially co-operate" with militia captains while also empowering this officer to court-martial those who failed to turn out enough men or to respect the treaty lines. This was a tall order. It required more local knowledge and repute than a newly arrived officer ranging all over the Southwest Territory could command.[32]

And so, on September 10, 1792, just hours before he received word of the declaration of war late that night, Governor Blount appointed Andrew Jackson to the post of judge advocate of Davidson County, the heart of the Mero District. The twenty-five-year-old lawyer was thereby empowered to bring and hear court martials against negligent or overzealous captains, to judge local performance by territorial and thus federal standards. He was to serve as the government's counsel during such proceedings, swearing in all witnesses and holding them to their words. In the absence of coercive mechanisms or obedient habits, these oaths *were* Jackson's authority, and he came to see them as even more sacred than other contracts. Here again he embodied the law at the far ends of its effective reach.[33]

His first test came on September 30, 1792, when a powerful native army hit Buchanan's Station, just four miles south of Nashville. Unable to set fire to the blockhouses after several harrowing hours of nighttime combat, the braves dispersed into smaller parties. A quiet dread set in as the attackers hid in the dense cane and tall forests that dominated the meager line of settlements. Two weeks of mayhem began in early October, as elusive braves struck on both sides of the Cumberland River. On October 8, a war party burned a distillery and killed a man near Nashville. The next day, the attackers burned four houses and "a large quantity of corn." They stole horses and shot hogs. Desperate to track the enemy, Blount wanted to hire native spies and look-outs. Robertson had found another way to keep track of the "Bodys Coming in": $100 scalp bounties for those willing to reconnoiter the hostile woods and kill anyone with black hair. Jackson did not object.[34]

The war parties divided still further in late 1792, with some heading east to the Washington District and others remaining to haunt the Mero. The most isolated households made the most inviting targets, but with open war declared and so many warriors looking for scalps and captives, no spot was safe. For every attack there were many false alarms, along with staged attacks to justify killings. The *Knoxville Gazette* filled with chilling reports from all over the borderlands, especially from Georgia, where settlers were still calculating losses from "the late Indian war" of 1788. Now they had new accounts of parents and children found lying together, their heads stripped and their bodies violated. During a single week in January 1793, eastern Tennessee was hit by six attacks that left seven dead. One body had no skin.[35]

One settler recalled this period as "the time of the forts." His parents and siblings spent long weeks at makeshift camps, where families stayed in tents or cabins and huddled into two-story forts whenever Indians were reported nearby. They peered into the woods all around, unable to see anything until it was too late. The daytime was boring, the nighttime unbearable. One man remembered the sight of a young woman who had just been scalped: the moaning, the crying, the amazing amount of blood. Those who left the forts risked ambush, while those who stayed wondered if their homes and barns were still there. Unwilling to venture to salt springs or wells, the refugees drained their supplies of beef and water. They waited, hoped, prayed. Governor Blount visited one such station in eastern Tennessee in April 1793, counting 280 men, women, and children, "living in a miserable manner in small huts." Still he condemned captains who violated the treaty lines, insisting that only a "vigorous national war" could lift the siege.[36]

Through it all, Andrew Jackson served both William Blount and James Robertson. He rode along the Cumberland and through the settlements, imploring and threatening the militia captains to fulfill their natural duties and military orders. He tried to bring salt to his besieged district and continued to bring cases to its courts. Closer to Robertson than Blount, Jackson also raged at national policy as the governor never could. Natives had no concept of "the law of Nations" and only sought to commit "Murder with impunity," he remarked in early 1793. Why treat with a "Savage Tribe" that simply wanted to save their towns from incendiary judgment? That May, a boat he co-owned with one of Rachel's brothers, packed with salt, was taken by a large war party while on its way down the Ohio. Indians struck nine times over a three-week period in the Mero that spring, and

Figure 3.2 This picture of a surviving blockhouse from eastern Tennessee gives some sense of how white colonists took shelter during the worst of the violence from 1792 to 1794. Courtesy of Tennessee State Library and Archives.

large war parties were repeatedly seen not far from Nashville—not far, that is, from Rachel, who was presumably at home with the slaves.[37]

On August 29, 1793, Jackson was some 180 miles from his wife, doing his civic duty at the expense of his family ones. At a fort southwest of Knoxville, he met with militia from the Washington District and with some of the few US soldiers south of the Ohio. Early that morning Jackson and an officer set out from the fort. They rushed back upon hearing gunfire—and straight into an ambush. The officer and one other man were seized, dragged away, and put to death "in a most cruel manner," the *Gazette* reported. Jackson lived to tell the tale. Always a fast runner, Jackson sprinted to the nearby station, "from whence the whole frontier was alarmed." Riders set out in pursuit, but the attackers slipped back across the Tennessee, "beyond which our government restricts our operation against them." There followed two months of abject terror in the white settlements of eastern Tennessee and even worse suffering in the native villages just to the south. During most of this time Governor Blount was in Philadelphia, which gave him some immunity from what was about to happen.[38]

Since June, the following announcement had been appearing in the *Gazette*: "The Creek Nation must be destroyed, or the south western frontiers, from the mouth of St. Mary's to the western extremities of Kentucky and Virginia, will be incessantly harassed by them; and now is the time. *[Delenda est Carthage].*" Taken from the Roman Senator Cato the Elder's appeal to destroy their North African foe, this call to arms was probably an anonymous order from Governor Blount to east Tennessee's leading warlord, John Sevier. As in 1787–88, Sevier's plan was to cross the Tennessee River, march south past Chota, and then drive into the Upper Creek towns. As in 1787–88, he coordinated with county strongmen in northern Georgia, who ignored the new peace worked out between that nation and the United States in 1790. Sevier's forces left Knoxville at the end of September 1793, just as word spread that an army of fifteen hundred Creeks and Chickamaugas was poised to sack the capital. The *Gazette* also reported that Sevier's men were actively chasing a war party that had just left a large family in small pieces. They were determined to "chastise them with exemplary vengeance," to teach them by killing them.[39]

Sevier returned to Knoxville in late October. Once again he had taken his own troops off the map, returning with stories only they could tell. Once again he was brutally effective. By burning every town and cornfield, his army forced native men to leave the war path and find their kin. He condemned parents, aunts, and uncles to watch their children freeze and starve in the woods. He further split the once-mighty Cherokees. Some refugees fled west to the Chickamaugas or south to the Creeks, no doubt radicalizing that nation's views about white people. Others regrouped in southeastern Tennessee and northern Georgia, trying to build the kind of civil order that whites claimed to want for them—and all with John Sevier as their neighbor.[40]

"He was amongst the frontier people who adored him," concluded an early Tennessee historian of Nolichucky Jack. Sevier understood the "substantial power" of the people's love, and he relied on military loyalty and popular gratitude much as William Blount counted on executive authority and good connections. Sevier was friendly and charming, ruthless and fearless. Especially in the Washington District and what became eastern Tennessee, his name carried an "electrical power" rooted in the unique bonds of a collective nightmare. He had done more to avenge the people than anyone since Griffith Rutherford, who had just settled on once-Cherokee land in the territory. Both warlords were named to its new legislative council in

1794, the same year the settlements south of the French Broad were organized as Sevier County.[41]

But the fate of the Mero was still in doubt. With most war parties focused on Knoxville, the attacks had relented around Nashville during the summer and fall of 1793. The few incidents reported that winter involved white hunters trading shots with their Indian counterparts, deep in the woods. Perhaps Andrew and Rachel told themselves that the worst was over as they married that January. Then, in late February 1794,

Figure 3.3 John Sevier (1745–1815). The most powerful warlord in early Tennessee, "Nolichucky Jack" was widely and fervently loved for his violent exploits against Loyalists, Creeks, and Cherokees.
Courtesy of Tennessee State Library and Archives.

a new spate of attacks paralyzed the settlements. Allegedly this was the work of Creeks and Chickamaugas led by the war captain Doublehead, who according to the *Gazette* had "shed as much blood as any man (not a Jacobin) of the age." And yet, the paper seethed, this same killer had just been invited to Philadelphia to parlay with US authorities. Like his white foes, he was waging war in one place while talking peace in another, organizing vengeance along the western waters while renouncing it in eastern capitals.[42]

Over the next eight months, seventy-one whites were reported killed by natives in the Mero, twenty-three of them women or children. In one case, a group of Indians fired on five men "near Andrew Jackson's." A projected cotton factory in Nashville, the brainchild of a British émigré who had smuggled the key technology out of Liverpool, was now shuttered. Perhaps its founder fled because the locals hated him along with his native England, "that throat-cutting kingdom." One memorial reported a "daily" exodus from the district to Spanish lands. The colony was "Discouraged," Andrew Jackson wrote in May 1794. In fact, it was breaking up, "Declining [fast]" and unlikely to survive another round of summer attacks. Many refugees also fled to Kentucky, just as Rachel's family had in 1780. But she knew better than anyone that the roads were no safer than the settlements. Sometimes she startled even her new husband with all the "hatred and revenge" she carried inside.[43]

DEEPER HUES OF BLOOD

According to one careful tally, 126 Cumberland settlers were killed by native attackers from 1792 to 1794. The total body count in this extreme frontier was 435 since 1780, perhaps 5% of the Cumberland's white population during its first fourteen years. A better way to measure the ordeal is to recall that the district's large and often related households were themselves the target for two long years, so that everyone knew family members who had spent time in the forts or whose loved ones had died in horrifying ways. Everyone heard stories of Indians hovering over sleeping babies, of men found with their entrails floating in nearby water, of children whose faces and skulls would never look right. It was one thing to watch men die on the battlefield, James Robertson said. It was quite another to see "a helpless woman or an innocent child tomahawked in their own houses." It was something else to realize that parents could not protect their children, that no one was coming to help, that God and government had left the people to their worst nightmares.[44]

The *Knoxville Gazette* made wider news of each calamity, although not always with a call to revenge attached to it. It was, after all, the mouthpiece of Blount and of the territorial government, and the governor fed the editor, Henry Roulstone, a steady diet of reports from US officials along with frequent notices of runaway slaves. Inevitably, these reflected the official viewpoints of Indian agents, military personnel, and federal judges, all of whom were tied to government policy just as Jackson was. "Sacred laws!" declared one US judge while denouncing new efforts to colonize the Muscle Shoals. "You must regulate our conduct." The paper also praised those "member[s] of civil society" who honored the "civil and organized government" in Philadelphia and Knoxville by respecting the 1791 treaty. In September 1794, with the Mero District still on the brink, the *Gazette* even republished James Iredell's most recent praise of the law of nations. Vattel's code, the North Carolina Federalist and Supreme Court justice declared, was the best way to resolve "all controversies between nations and nation."[45]

The boldest article to this effect appeared in July 1793, when "P. Q.," a pen name for the New England Federalist and dictionary writer, Noah Webster, called for law over revenge. The "arm of society" had put an end to the bloody havoc of distant times and savage places, P. Q. counseled. The Constitution had drawn the American people into that historical process. But the liberty-crazed settlers who "take revenge on the savage murderers" did not respect the resulting obligations. (Importantly, he did not blame speculators.) Under the sway of their unbridled passions, the people of the Southwest Territory might fall back into nature's chaos, unraveling society and leaving only "defenceless individuals" in wild forests. The answer was a "religious observance" of federal treaties, another display of virtuous patience from those who had already shown "moderation and forbearance." The same edition of the paper told readers that a revenge mission in Georgia had just failed, proving that "unsanctioned" warfare was both ineffectual and illegal.[46]

And yet the *Gazette* also set the printed word against itself, exposing the party line as it appeared on one line to bitter condemnation on the next. For example, the paper ran Hugh Henry Brackenridge's acid commentary about credulous officials who blanched at the stakes of frontier violence. "The question is," the Pennsylvanian made clear, "Whether we shall submit ourselves to the savages, or they to us?" As total war set in during late 1792, the paper reproduced letters from US Indian agents swearing to the peaceful intentions of 90% of Creeks, followed by the words: "Only four days [earlier], five hundred Creek Indians were at the attack upon Buchanan's station near Nashville!" The following summer it ran the "*Delenda est*

Carthage" segment. Later that year it again mocked the Indian agents' assurances by naming twenty-two "citizens of the United States," twenty of them women or children, held by the Creeks "and sold from master to master . . . in the same manner as negroes are sold." Did the agents take captivity for peace, the paper scoffed, "or do not these gentlemen consider this Territory as part of the United States?" One woman had been gifted to a chief's son, compelled to share a bed with a man who reeked of her people's blood.[47]

The effect was to draw readers and listeners in Tennessee, Georgia, Kentucky, and Pennsylvania into a sprawling kinship of anti-government rage, although not the kind that Regulators and Franks had conveyed. Rather than foreclosing property and enriching speculators, the national state was forsaking those citizens who wanted to obey the law even as they tested its range—hence the repeated insistence that the attacks happened *inside* treaty lines, where people had "a right to expect protection" from the sovereign who had drawn them. This assertion was true so long as one began the story in late 1792, ignoring questionable treaties and illicit speculation. It created a master sequence that more neatly assigned guilt and innocence while setting up a real-time call to action: the "immediate outrages of savage barbarity" were ongoing, happening just as the reader took in the news that the "*philanthropic Congress*" was giving corn to its Indian friends. Under such circumstances, the people's natural right to self-defense remained in effect.[48]

Andrew Jackson surely took part in a convention held by Mero citizens shortly after P. Q.'s article appeared. It produced a memorial that reads much like his future letters and speeches, in that it swore loyalty to the US government while also demanding the right to "do ourselves justice." Jackson may have also had a hand in the *Gazette*'s August 1793 response to P. Q. Drawing heavily from Vattel's *Law of Nations*, this article denounced P. Q. for misunderstanding the fundamental rules of war. For even as the attacks reached the people of the extreme frontiers in their homes, well inside treaty lines, those lines no longer mattered. The law of nations decreed that war halted the prior obligations of civilized states. If the natives were as organized as their 1792 declaration of war implied, then no US territory was bound to any treaty with them while the bloodshed continued. If they were not so organized, then they were savage and unprotected by any rules. Either way, the people of the territory could "pursue the enemy within their own limits" as the law of nations authorized.[49]

Besides, the article continued, what was the law of nations? What did it signify for people who were not sure what laws or nations applied to them? Directly quoting Vattel, the author described it as "originally no more than the law of nature applied to nations." In forming civil societies and making treaties, men "do not cease to be men." They never gave away their natural right to defend themselves or their male duty to protect women and children. Whereas Vattel and P. Q. knew this as the starting point for civilized progress, however, this article named it the ongoing truth to which all laws had to defer. If the sovereign failed to protect, the people were "absolutely at liberty to provide for their own security and safety." The writer made this point with more examples taken straight from Vattel before closing with an account of the recent murder of a pregnant settler "nearly [at] the center of [Washington] district." She was found strapped to the ground, naked and prone:

> [Her body was left] in a most indecent posture—thus insulting the sex, insulting human nature—but Congress can feel no insult offered to us; they are more favorable to their savage, adopted, and illegitimate, than to us their legitimate children. The stain made by the blood of this innocent babe, which received a deeper hue, by flowing out of the wound indecently and insultingly made in its murdered mother, cannot be washed out, but by the blood of the whole Cherokee nation, unless they deliver up the perpetrators of this horrid act.

If the people had erred in taking action during Governor Blount's absences, the article proclaimed, then let the government send an army to punish them as one. "We had rather fall by the hands of Christians than that of savages—Perhaps they will spare our wives and children!"[50]

By shifting from the terms of law and order to those of blood and faith, the article evoked national themes that were both very old and very new. European thinkers had long described nations in terms of bloodline and language, while in Abrahamic traditions blood signified a crude form of citizenship. The God of Israel punished entire nations for sins that "polluted" or "corrupted" the blood of all its number. "For the life of the flesh is in the blood," commands Leviticus 17:11, "and I have given it to you *to offer* upon the altar, to make an atonement for your souls." Blood could be holy or profane, sacred or disgusting. When loosed from the body's temple, it signaled perfect chaos, an audible scream that called for action and judgment. Running blood had to be contained, and drying blood had to be cleansed—or avenged, as Passion plays insisted. "By his own blood," Christ had redeemed his followers, inspiring forms of sacrifice and fellowship that pagans could never imagine. These religious meanings were enmeshed in a folk criminology in which gushes and stains marked guilty people and places.[51]

Tennessee settlers were of many denominations, but the Presbyterians had a brief monopoly on what passed for religious authority, and they put special emphasis on Christ's suffering on the cross. Jesus had shed *his* blood for *their* salvation, their pastors entreated, drawing those who remembered into a "mystical body" of grief and longing. Presbyterians also revived the "holy fairs" of northern Ireland in the southern borderlands. Days-long prayer meetings culminated in huge communion suppers, served on long tables in the woods. Those who took part in the Eucharist, one pastor exhorted, "shall behold [Jesus] exhibited hanging on the cross, all drenched in blood and tears; while the crimson streams of divine blood flow . . . '*great drops of blood falling down to the ground.*'" To break bread while drinking a reminder of Christ's blood forged bonds that were more meaningful than the formal rules of nationhood, especially during a total war that the nation did not sanction.[52]

As the August 1793 riposte to "P. Q." made clear, "the blood of the whole Cherokee nation" was the only expiate that could clean the ghastly mess found near Knoxville. James Robertson, son-in-law to a Presbyterian minister, had said as much while helping start the war the year before: the innocent blood that fouled the Cumberland could only be "swept clean" by guilty blood. God's sovereignty meant that his justice would not be mocked, even if it might be delayed by frontier conditions. Since Indian marauders could not be punished as individuals—by law, that is—retribution would have to come in a more sweeping form. Here the usual terms of civility and savagery could be reversed. Although the settlers were sometimes said to share "white blood" or "Christian blood," they barely qualified as members of the American nation, which in turn only qualified as a nation in a new and legalistic sense. But those who spilled their blood were nations indeed. Carolinians had named the Cherokees as such during the 1758–61 war, and Griffith Rutherford called them a "Nation of Savages" before his 1776 attack. Virtually every official thereafter described them and other natives as "nations" in treaties, letters, and reports.[53]

"Every Indian nation is divided into families, or clans," Blount explained to Knox as the violence began to spiral. They believed "'that all national honors are acquired by the shedding of blood.'" No longer wandering clans who made war on each other, they only wanted to spill "the blood of white people." They were, in effect, huge yet cohesive families, related by bloodline and the "bloodthirsty" urges of a pagan at communion. Even as he told Indians to respect the chains of political command that led up to him, reporting white misdeeds so that he could mete out targeted punishments, Blount warned that no Cherokee was innocent of what another Cherokee might do. They were only safe if "*none* of the Indians of [their towns] join the five Lower towns in war against the United States." Among Indian nations, that is, unavenged sin circulated interchangeably in the blood, marking every member for sanguinary atonement. The Cherokees were "all your nation," the governor told the Bloody Fellow.[54]

Atrocity narratives had long engrossed the reading publics of North America, and the Ohio disaster and Chickamauga War offered grisly new "scenes" for Americans to imagine. A new collection of frontier horror stories was published in Philadelphia just as Congress discussed the violence in the Southwest Territory in the summer of 1794. One delegate from North Carolina, a veteran of the Rutherford campaign, described fathers and sons dying together in their fields. Only militiamen from the southern states could understand, he said, and so only they could defend themselves through "offensive operations" on Cherokees and Creeks. A Senate proposal to instead deploy US regulars led one Virginian to accuse the Federalists of trying to "*scourge*" rather than protect the frontiers. Thomas P. Carnes of Georgia told his colleagues that "every drop of blood in his heart" boiled when he heard someone blame the settlers or excuse the Indians. US troops were worse than useless against a "savage and faithless tribe" like the Creeks, because they prevented militiamen from "crossing what is called the line" while pursuing war parties.[55]

The congressmen who favored US troops over southern militia—northern Federalists almost to a man—stressed the need for cool-headed peacekeepers rather than passionate avengers. They upheld the legitimacy of "the line" and the treaties that repeatedly drew it. In fact, a new agreement had just been signed in the capital, acknowledging "some misunderstandings" between Tennesseans and Cherokees and pledging that the borders would now be "actually ascertained." By 1794, any new assertion of federal power alarmed the Jeffersonian opposition, and the Senate's proposal was defeated. This may have pleased Carnes, but it did little for the Mero District. Two weeks before the new treaty was signed in June 1794, twelve whites were killed on a boat on the Cumberland River. Their twenty-two slaves disappeared.[56]

As one of at least two attorney generals in the Southwest who had been educated by Presbyterian ministers, Andrew Jackson knew how to parse the legal and religious arguments for collective punishment. By the letter of earlier treaties, he explained in the spring of 1794, all the southern Indians had agreed to stop killing white people. As a lawful citizen he lived by such rules. No longer a "Savage Tribe" but a coherent "Nation," the Cherokees should too. Failure to deliver up the murderers in their midst marked their "Tacit acknowledgement" of each atrocity, Jackson argued. "The whole nation ought to be Scurged," for they were all "Equally guilty." If the authorities in Philadelphia did not realize as much, the people of the Mero might have to find "a protection from some other Source." The

Spanish were still an option, but the settlements over the Kentucky line were far more promising.[57]

By early 1793, James Robertson was in contact with militia colonels in Kentucky about a possible alliance against the Chickamaugas. Governor Blount kept his distance but knew all about it. If riders from Kentucky passed through the Mero District, Blount told Robertson in April 1793, he was to "command [them] in positive terms to desist from [their] object of invading the Cherokee towns . . . this you may do verbally if you please, but you must also do it in writing for your justification." Importantly, Blount did not *order* Robertson to *stop* the attack, and with a nudge and wink he noted that some "chastising" was necessary. Indeed, he had just received "truly alarming" reports of multiple attack groups bound for "your country." Later that year the two men exchanged opaque letters about how to pay for future expeditions and who would take the blame for them.[58]

By the summer of 1794, Robertson and Jackson had mobilized all the men they could around Nashville. Reinforcements from Kentucky made for a force of some five hundred men. They also had a "pilot" to guide them right to their targets. Robertson gave formal command to James Ore, and the troops headed south in early September. Upon reaching the Tennessee River, many of the volunteers turned around, while the others crossed stealthily and caught the inhabitants of Nickajack—apparently named because a slave, "Nigger Jack," was hiding there—by surprise. The attackers killed at least fifty people, took over a dozen prisoners, and then torched the town's two hundred log houses and surrounding fields and orchards. They also burned the nearby town of Running Water, sending huge clouds of smoke into the air and taking vengeance "to the terror of others," as Robertson put it.[59]

Legend says that Andrew Jackson took part in this campaign as a humble private, not as judge advocate. There is no way to verify this claim, although one captain later swore that Jackson "knows as much and more than [anyone]" about "Nickey Jack" and other off-the-record operations. Jackson buried much of what happened deep inside. Clearly he emerged from Tennessee's two-year nightmare as one of its trusted avengers, a man who bore its scars and secrets. In 1795, Robertson took the fall for Nickajack, retiring his post as he and Blount had arranged. Some years later, after Robertson again offered his services, Jackson paid his respects to the old warrior. The men who served under your command, Jackson told Robertson, were a "Corps of Invincibles." They revealed a courage "to be found only in republicks," or a government built on "the Opinion and affections of the people." They embodied a "union of Sentiments and Action" in the face of demonic foes. "My God!" Jackson concluded. "How can I express my sensations!!!"[60]

RIGHTS OF SOIL

Two months after the Nickajack campaign, Blount warned Cherokee leaders that the Kentucky strongman Benjamin Logan might be headed south again. Should his raiders destroy more of their towns, the governor intoned, they were to forbear and wait for the US government to reimburse them. Here again, territorial elites held native communities in deep crisis to the highest standards of national cohesion and self-control, on pain of wild retribution by citizens they would not control. The peace talks that followed also made those nations responsible for any missing slaves. All blacks in Cherokee country, "whether captured or absconded from their Masters," were now prisoners of war for whom all Cherokee were accountable. Where were the twenty-two negroes taken the previous summer by the warrior Unacuta? Did Otter Sister still have a "mulatto boy or man," the property of a Doctor White? What about the five slaves missing from Logan's plantations? Frustrated to learn that most black fugitives were gone "in the woods," the white negotiators—Jackson surely included—used the girls they had taken at Running Water to compel the return of white prisoners. Indian agents also recovered some stolen horses, which were advertised in the *Knoxville Gazette*, once more a mouthpiece of Federalist law and order.[61]

As the newest member of "confederated America," one federal judge advised, the people of the Cumberland now had to "labour to acquire a national character." The burden of political reconciliation with Philadelphia was on them, not on the Federalist leadership. Another official simply told the district in 1796 that it once again owed allegiance to "that government, which extends to you protection." Governor Blount, for one, was ready to listen. Impressed by the government's recent success against Indian rebels in Ohio and agrarian rebels in Pennsylvania, he foresaw better times under federal rule. A new treaty allowing American ships free passage through New Orleans while voiding Spain's military promises to natives made him even more of a Federalist, at least for now. Promotional tracts touting Tennessee's fertility replaced calls for blood vengeance.[62]

With the carnage over, one such tract reported, the Carolinas and Georgia were "emptying themselves" into the Southwest Territory, pushing the population toward the sixty thousand necessary for statehood. Conducting a poll in the summer of 1795, territorial officials found that sixty-five hundred potential voters wanted to live in a new state rather than a federal protectorate. Given the deep distaste for neocolonial arrangements in postrevolutionary North America, this should occasion little surprise. Then again, twenty-five hundred men replied that they did *not* want Tennessee to be a state, a figure that surely undercounts the general sentiment in the Anglo-American enclaves along the Mississippi River and Gulf Coast. Blount had found that people "very generally" avoided the census, because they knew that more courts and laws would shortly follow. Mississippi settlers also balked at statehood. They preferred the first stages of territorial government, in which courts and surveyors were few and the proximity of Spanish lands kept American officials honest.[63]

As usual, the Cumberland was different. Its settlers were comparatively wealthy, their estates threatened not by legal eviction but by native attack. They had faced something worse than death in 1780–82, in 1787–88, and again in 1792–94. The memories of such horrors no less than the contours of the Cumberland ridge united them more with Kentucky than with the rest of Tennessee, while their commercial ties pointed them more to the Gulf of Mexico than to the Atlantic. Besides, the eastern counties far outnumbered the western settlements, meaning that the first governor was sure to be John Sevier. The people of the Cumberland much preferred James Robertson, or even Andrew Jackson. Davidson County was in fact the center of opposition to statehood: a remarkable four-fifths of its voters replied to the 1795 poll, of which the same percentage said no.[64]

Thinking about a seat in the US Senate, Blount forged ahead with plans for statehood. County delegates would be elected in December 1795, he announced, with the convention to follow the next month at Knoxville. Both the timing and location helped to push the twenty-five hundred "no" votes off the political margins, and indeed the fifty-six delegates had a complete draft of a Tennessee constitution ready within a week. Assuming rather than debating statehood, they wrestled over the relevant precedents of North Carolina (the parent state and birthplace of seven members) and Virginia or Pennsylvania (the home states of sixteen and eight delegates, respectively). They mostly divided by personal loyalty. Blount's "friends" favored a more conservative charter in which the governor made key appointments. His opponents generally saw Sevier as their leader, although Nolichucky Jack stayed home while the governor presided.[65]

Much like the Whig leaders of 1776, these pro-Sevier delegates united behind a pared-down version of Regulator reforms, targeting executive corruption instead of the political economy of gentry rule. A two-house assembly, elected by a wide franchise of free men, took the lion's share of powers. The charter secured freedom of speech and assembly, guaranteed jury trials and due process, and set maximum salaries for executive officers.

The delegates further described their Declaration of Rights as "excepted out of the General Powers of Government," a list of liberties that "Shall never be violated on any pretense whatsoever." Among these was the right of "bringing Suit" in the new courts, which along with a ban on laws "impairing the obligation of Contracts" aligned Tennessee's charter with Federalist axioms of debt collection. The constitution also mandated a flat tax on land, as speculators preferred. The most democratic change concerned the militia. Henceforth, the men of each district would elect their captains and field officers, who in turn would elect the brigadier generals: a bit of Pennsylvania-style republicanism for a state cut from Carolina oligarchy.[66]

Andrew Jackson was one of five Davidson County delegates, and there is no reason to think that he opposed statehood as the great majority of his neighbors did. He was, after all, a friend and confidante of the governor's, not to mention a lawyer whose professional status relied on the strong courts that this constitution and its federal counterpart prescribed. Jackson served on the twenty-two-man committee behind the first draft and found the final product good enough. "The people Generally approve of the Constitution," Jackson reported to Blount in late February 1796. "Cesar is rendered his due, and If I may hazard an oppinion your Election [to the US Senate] will be unanimous." In this same letter, Jackson advised Blount of some inquiries made by a New York land speculator and also of the rising value of some of their own investments.[67]

Absentee owners of Tennessee lands, Blount told Jackson just before the convention, were "among our greatest benefactors and best Friends." Their interests had to be consulted. "Justice" for speculators was a matter of "National as well private reputation," and it was up to courts and judges to form a legal framework that would prevent future Franklands and Regulations. Jackson and his close friend, John Overton, had just gotten into the game for themselves, forming a partnership in May 1794 to buy lands "without as within" treaty lines. To Blount, Jackson mused that a "good Judiciary" was impartially committed to both the state and federal constitutions, and thus to property owners no matter where they lived. Overton certainly agreed. As early as May 1787, a "Political Club" to which he belonged had endorsed judicial review, and he was especially keen on the part of the new constitution that gave judges the power to declare the law, leaving the mere facts to the jury. Shortly after he partnered with Jackson, Overton became supervisor of federal revenue in Tennessee, an appointee of the president himself.[68]

In short, the twenty-nine-year-old Andrew Jackson and his close allies lined up as frontier Federalists against the more populist figures from the eastern hills. One week into the convention, however, Jackson announced himself as a different kind of rebel against the national Federalists. Describing the boundaries of the new state, the new Declaration of Rights also declared that the people held "sovereignty" over what had once been the charter lands of North Carolina. Jackson moved to add the words "and the right of soil" to this line. By this he meant the power to open land offices, affirm or annul grants, and otherwise turn public domains into private estates. At one level this was a further declaration of independence from the parent state, whose courts continued to rule on the legitimacy of western titles. It also cast doubt on the federal government's power to name certain parts of Tennessee off-limits for sale, such as the Cherokee lands south of the Tennessee and the Chickasaw lands south and west of the Cumberland.[69]

As a challenge to the government they had gathered to join, Jackson's motion sparked one of the few debates of the convention. Ultimately, his peers kept the phrase "right of soil" while loading it with qualifiers. Yet Jackson had tied his name to those words, and thus to a range of memories and interests that promised to unite the white populations of the southern borderlands as no constitution ever could. The ongoing fact of "Indian Country" within state boundaries was a constant reminder of both unrevenged atrocities and unrealized investments, a barrier to poor settlers and wealthy speculators alike. "Right of soil" was an implicit denial that any non-American could hold American territory and an angry demand to empower the state governments that understood this. Tennessee leaders repeatedly employed this threat and tried for years to compensate citizens for losses endured during their unofficial war of survival.[70]

During the summer of 1796, after some Federalists tried to block Tennessee statehood, Blount recommended Jackson as its first representative in the US Congress. The young man from the Waxhaws was too earnest and moralistic to share all of Blount's secrets. He had never learned that elite men did not need to justify what they did or to pretend that all the laws of God and man applied to them like everyone else. He was a true believer in gentry categories of honor and justice that most gentry used and ignored as needed. Still, Andrew Jackson was a safe choice who had served well during the most trying times. So the governor and his friends made it known that Jackson would "hold a pole," and the young man's reputation with militia captains did the rest. "[You] will be most certainly elected," one federal judge assured Jackson. He ran unopposed in the West, winning all 795 votes cast, and was nearly as strong in the East.[71]

In late 1796, he again said goodbye to Rachel and set out for the city that had forsaken the extreme frontiers in their darkest hour. Other congressmen had endured borderlands violence, of course, and more and more arrived with western resentments that echoed late colonial ones. They denounced distant centers of power, culture, and credit and demanded that the American state deliver what John C. Calhoun, another Presbyterian from western Carolina, called "the real spirit of union": the physical protection of "every citizen in the lawful pursuit of his business." "Protection and patriotism are reciprocal," Calhoun reasoned. "This is the way which has led nations to greatness." Yet it would be difficult to find a congressman in the late 1790s who carried more intense grievances than Andrew Jackson. His nationalist roots made his regional traumas all the more vivid. He felt not only abandoned but also *betrayed* by the distant government to which he had tied his fortunes and for which he had risked everything, even Rachel.[72]

Jay's Treaty was a "Cringing" capitulation to the treacherous empire, Jackson wrote in the fall of 1795. The "aristocratic Secracy" in which it had been made was a further insult to "the Grand republick of the United States." But while the Anti-Federalist to whom he addressed this letter drew from "old republican" and states' rights beliefs, Jackson based his dissent on the law of nations: "Vatel B[ook] 2, P[aragraph] 242, S[ection] 325 Says that the rights of Nations are benefits, of which the Sovereign is only the administrator." In dangerous (but not revolutionary) times and places, Jackson began to argue, nations kept that sovereignty rather than entrusting it to their governments. The treaty was void because "the Nation of america," still under British threat, hated it. In this, his first known reference to such a "Nation," Jackson took the legal and civic definition devised in Philadelphia in 1787 and applied it to the Cumberland households he had served from 1792 to 1794. He also likened the American people to the native nations he wanted to burn and bleed, imagining the United States as a proud family that never forgot an injury to one of its own.[73]

CHAPTER 4

I Love My Country and Government

When Jackson traveled east to serve in the US House of Representatives in late 1796, he had already been to Philadelphia twice over the past year and a half, looking to buy goods for a new store in Nashville. He also carried a portfolio of land titles and a shopping list from his friend and partner, John Overton. Among the items to buy was a "likely Negroe Boy." In searching for such a servant, Overton told Jackson, be careful "not to subject yourself to the penal Laws" of Pennsylvania, which had been cracking down on the buying and selling of people since passing its gradual emancipation act during the Revolution. For the most part, though, the two men were looking to sell western lands—either titles to plots within treaty boundaries or first claims to Indian country. One promotional tract reported that a land office in the nation's capitol would soon "give a person in Philadelphia the same opportunity of confirming and completing a title to the lands . . . that the people resident [there] have." In the meantime they could call on Jackson.[1]

Congressman Jackson's other priority was to make the government pay for the horrors he had just survived. "The knife and the tomahawk were held over the heads of women and children," he declared in his first speech to the House, "[and] peaceable citizens were murdered." During such prolonged emergencies, the natural rights of self-defense overruled both civil society and national authority. The new nation was therefore bound to reimburse the newest state for those campaigns, not least so that it could make good on the IOUs it had given to its volunteer avengers. (Overton had speculated heavily in those certificates, a practice that George Washington found "most disgraceful.") Although Representative

Figure 4.1 Philadelphia as it would have appeared to Andrew Jackson in the late 1790s. Jackson traveled to the metropolis as both an elected official from Tennessee and a private businessman with trans-Atlantic interests.
From *History of Philadelphia*, 1884. Courtesy of the Library of Congress, Prints and Photographs Division, LC-USZ62-56347.

Jackson did not impress anyone with his eyewitness *pathos*, most delegates were happy to buy some western goodwill for the modest sums demanded. In securing these funds, Jackson simultaneously saved his partner, legitimized Tennessee's wars, and earned what one observer called a "permanent interest" among its militiamen.[2]

But Jackson could not convince anyone of Tennessee's "right of soil." Just as he was taking his seat, in fact, federal troops were removing squatters in Powell's Valley, a sliver of land in northeastern Tennessee. In early 1798, the Senate made clear that the United States was under no obligation to extinguish Indian titles in that state or North Carolina. The Adams administration also secured a new treaty that ceded Powell's Valley while promising what remained of Cherokee lands to the Cherokee. Outraged petitions from Tennessee cited the people's right to improve the lands watered by their blood and marveled that US soldiers had only arrived in force *after* the carnage, on behalf of the *natives*. These protests joined the older grievances of those who had bought far western claims at Armstrong's land office back in 1783–84, only to find those lands "surrendered to the Indians."

Jackson told John Sevier, now the governor, that Adams was "Grasping after power" at the expense of the states. Sevier angrily concurred, accusing the administration of so favoring the "diabolical" Indians that their Tennessee victims were again taking the Spanish option. In lieu of some dramatic change, Sevier wrote, "I fear one half our citizens will flock over into another government."[3]

William Blount tried to make such a change happen. Although he now sat in the US Senate, Jackson's long-time patron had fallen on hard times, in part because he had cosigned the three promissory notes that Jackson had received in payment for western lands. Such notes were the next best thing to specie, but only insofar as the debtor could pay. And the debtor in question, David Allison, was spectacularly overleveraged. His creditors had every commercial right to come after Blount or even Jackson if Allison defaulted. So early in 1797, Blount slipped out of Philadelphia and approached British officials about a possible invasion of the Spanish territory standing between Tennessee and the Gulf Coast. This filibuster would culminate in a new state or republic friendly to London and led, presumably, by William Blount. When these half-baked plans fell into the president's hands, the House impeached Blount and the Senate expelled him in July 1797. That same month, Allison went to Philadelphia's grim debtor's jail.[4]

Upon learning that he had endorsed the notes of a drowning man, Jackson had rushed to buy and sell more titles. Blount initially bailed him out by cosigning those notes, amplifying the tension between Jackson's personal loyalties and his US duties. He voted against serving a summons on his former boss in early 1798 and left Philadelphia that April, three months before the end of session. By then, a Federalist-led war fever against France was spreading over the republic. In the face of such outrages as the XYZ Affair, President Adams declared, war might be "a less evil than National Dishonour." Jackson, too, fumed at foreign insults, but he also admired Napoleon's "energy" and hated the administration for its "Military Tyranny" and disregard for "the Sovereignty of the State of Tennessee." As such he withdrew from national politics without burning bridges as Blount had.[5]

The relative patience that Jackson and most Tennessee leaders showed with the United States paid off in 1801, when Thomas Jefferson took his place in the new Executive Mansion along the Potomac. At the very least Jefferson was the enemy of their enemies in Philadelphia and London, a southern planter with western affinities. He was also a true believer in natural rights, although not in the way that Jackson was. For Jefferson, nature evoked life and liberty, not blood and vengeance. As a Virginia legislator during and just after the Revolution, he had proposed headright grants to western settlers and seventy-five acres each to landless Virginians entering adulthood. Independence was one of their natural rights, he reasoned, so the political society that had taken some of those rights should grant them the economic autonomy necessary for active citizenship. His plans for public education followed the same logic. In peaceful and enlightened times, Jefferson believed, a republican government should promote the happiness of the society it represented by returning some of nature's bounty to its members.[6]

Of course, the national political system formed by the Constitution limited such efforts, and Jefferson built his opposition by swearing loyalty to that document. He promised to restore the nation's charter rather than the people's natural rights. As president he thus turned to the western future, trying to superimpose an "empire of liberty" upon a nation of laws. In the process he redefined the "genuine American," insisting less on loyalty to his administration than on a love of freedom so accommodating that it also allowed slavery. His administration also put new emphasis on expanding western settlements, not only with the Louisiana Purchase but also by pressing Indian peoples in Tennessee and elsewhere to cede lands in satisfaction for debts. John Overton and Andrew Jackson thus became perfunctory Jeffersonians within a more stable and flexible political milieu, at least until the rule of law fell apart once again, this time on a much larger scale.[7]

POOR PITIFULL PETTY FOGGING LAWYER

The spring of 1797 brought the first militia and cavalry elections under Tennessee's new constitution. The men of each district would now vote for their captains, who in turn would select the higher officers. Predictably, this new grant of power to "the Citizens" (as Jackson called them) did not go smoothly. Among several disputed outcomes was the one for Davidson County's cavalry regiment, which Jackson, keen as always for military honors, observed upon returning from his time in the House. As the election turned into an argument, one of Sevier's favorites produced a letter from the governor. Jackson was appalled. Any interference by the Executive in such a contest was "an unconstitutional act" and a "precedent dangerous to the rights of the people," not to mention an imposition by eastern Tennessee over the Mero. It was a rude taste of life under the state management of John Sevier rather than the federal patronage of William Blount.[8]

Jackson got wind of Sevier's harsh reaction to these comments in early May 1797, just as he was dealing with an aggrieved letter from an old friend, John McNairy. His various replies say something about his political ascent. A decade earlier, McNairy had given Jackson his big break as a Mero attorney. Now seeking a new appointment as a federal judge, McNairy felt that Jackson owed him—and was upset to learn that the congressman had recommended someone else. Deeply offended, Jackson still reminded McNairy that they were both "members of civilized Society" and subject to "those rules and forms of politeness which such a state ought to impose upon every man." With his star on the rise, he could suffer McNairy's ego and abide the rule of law as it was imposed "upon every man." Sevier's pride was another matter. Upon hearing that Jackson had condemned his part in the Mero election, the governor dismissed "the Scurrilous Expressions of a poor pitifull petty fogging Lawyer." In responding to this insult, Jackson did not feel so bound by society's rules.[9]

Before challenging Tennessee's leading man to a duel, Jackson knew to ask Sevier to explain himself. The code of honor required a sequential exchange of evasions and clarifications, the better to reveal the genteel self-possession of the two parties and limit the chances that they would actually shoot each other. Jackson surely hated the long, alliterative insult to his person above all else, but in his letter to the governor he instead focused on the adjective "scurrilous." To contest the word, Jackson was content to "State facts" supporting his view of what had happened. He framed the dispute around the nature of things said, not the caliber of persons involved. Never had he doubted Sevier's "Charector," Jackson made clear. Nor did he question it now, other than to wonder why the governor had not come to him directly. The thirty-year-old Jackson thereby offered the fifty-one-year-old Sevier a way out of a duel while still arguing that they were near enough equals to fight one.[10]

Sevier replied that he had sent blank commissions for the cavalry officers to prepare for the next Indian war. If in so doing he had violated the Tennessee Constitution, "to the proper authority I am accountable." (Translation: Do you actually think the legislature will impeach me for this?) He did not deny that he had been angry at Jackson, for "like yourself when passion agitates my Breast I cannot view things in the calm light of mild philosophy." Anger was a gentleman's right when his honor was questioned, and this emotional prerogative made them equally different from those who brawled on a whim and those who suffered in silence. By definition their indignation was justified, for by definition they were in charge of their passions. Gentlemen knew this about each other and regulated their words and deeds accordingly. Surely the younger man could understand? Jackson said that he did, and he and Sevier remained "friends."[11]

Their truce held in part because Jackson left again for Philadelphia in late 1797 and in part because of what he briefly did there as a US senator.

Shortly after news of the so-called Yazoo land frauds brought radical Jeffersonians to power in Georgia, Jackson heard of a similar scheme from the parent state. Sometime in the mid-1790s, a group of morally flexible men had conspired with North Carolina's secretary of state, James Glasgow, to print land certificates for Revolutionary War veterans and then distribute them to nonveterans. These could be used to claim land across Tennessee, for no one could say which certificates had already been filled, which ones transferred, and which ones lost. Making the certificates "official" required signatures from two military officers, which a party of conspirators in Nashville obtained by getting said officers drunk on peach brandy. One besotted captain apparently signed over five hundred certificates at a single sitting, and the participants eventually claimed about four million acres. Their business model mainly differed from those of other land companies in its indifference to both white and native claims.[12]

Jackson had already warned of the need to take the right of soil from North Carolina. The involvement of his brother-in-law, Stockley Donelson, was also predictable. Rachel's brother had frequently called on Jackson to defend his many titles against legal challenges, in one case telling Jackson that he held something called "early Special Entries" from Armstrong's office. Torn again between family and civic duties, Senator Jackson told the governor of North Carolina what he knew. He thus gave new proof of his integrity while also protecting one state from fraud and the other from more confusion. Exposing the "Glasgow land frauds" helped to draw a line between legal speculation and fraudulent "land jobbing," and thus to legitimize the claims that he and Overton were making on lands they did not work. Indeed, Jackson worried that this scandal might move Congress to annul *all* titles granted by North Carolina, such as the one on which his new home of Hunter's Hill sat. Any such interference by the legislature on a purely "Judicial question" would of course violate "the rights of individuals" under modern property regimes.[13]

Upon his rushed return to Tennessee in 1798, the legislature appointed Jackson as one of three judges of the Superior Court of Law and Equity. To Rachel he promised a better future in which he would not be gone so often. "I am truly Sorry to read from [your] letter, that you are not well," he wrote from Knoxville. "Rest assured My love, that [I will] Stay not a moment longer, than the business of Court requires." He was done with public life and wanted only to live quietly at his plantation. This was a common refrain for Anglo-American men of the "country" tradition, and in Jackson's case it was manifestly untrue but not entirely dishonest. His frantic quest for the world's esteem periodically exhausted him, leaving him in need of repose among dependents and inferiors. He did not like politics in the sense that it offered no clear victories or final vindications, only relentless jockeying with peers and rivals. As a Tennessee judge, on the other hand, Jackson was the master of a safe, familiar space. The post also carried a steady salary, all the more welcome as he assumed custody of several of Rachel's relatives.[14]

As Jefferson's election drew their state more fully into the Union, the Jacksons briefly settled into the role of Nashville gentry. Rachel was a devoted member of its first Presbyterian church, whose pastor, the Reverend Thomas Craighead, may well have written his sermons with paper and ink that Jackson had sold him. Craighead welcomed the revivals sweeping through the region. If camp meetings and mass conversions brought piety and order to the frontiers, then Presbyterian clergymen were in support, although they always stressed God's sovereignty rather than human agency in deciding who would be saved and who would be damned. Indeed, Rachel preferred a more traditional Calvinism that made no promises besides awful punishment for Zion's enemies. For her husband, religion was less a matter of daily behavior than of deeper convictions about good and evil, struggle and virtue, innocence and retribution. In peacetime, at least, this made him more of a Freemason than a Presbyterian. In 1801, shortly after his old patron, William Blount, succumbed to a fever, Jackson helped organize a new lodge in Nashville. He also served as a trustee of Davidson Academy, founded by Rev. Craighead and others as a beachhead of high learning and sound ethics.[15]

If Jackson had a single goal in this period, it was to be major general of the Tennessee militia, the basic civil and political institution of the state. The head officer of those companies was in a sense the commander-in-chief of the citizenry. Jackson had built his reputation with the militia captains during Tennessee's total war and then secured it by convincing Congress to repay them. He knew how to muster volunteers, traverse hostile country, and prepare a forward camp. In action he could channel his hatreds so that fear no longer mattered. For all these reasons he emerged by 1802 as the favorite among the captains and colonels of the old Mero District. He forswore any personal desire for the post, as any gentleman would. But, he told Sevier, the officers had reminded him that "'in a republican Government, when the services of any individual was called upon, his services belonged to the republick, and he ought to obay the Publick will.'" He would do no less than James Robertson had during the darkest hours of 1794.[16]

Alas, the governor heard the same call. Barred by the state constitution from serving a fourth consecutive term, Sevier felt that he had earned his place at the head of Tennessee's armed forces. He was astonished when both he and Jackson received seventeen votes from the field officers. Even worse, the new governor cast the deciding vote for the younger man and commissioned Jackson as major general in April 1802. Over the course of the next year, Sevier and Jackson quarreled by proxy. Jackson told the new *Tennessee Gazette* about Sevier's role in the Glasgow land frauds. Sevier furiously denied these charges and easily won re-election in the fall of 1803. Soon after, the legislature divided the state's militia by region, in effect demoting Jackson to major general of the *West* Tennessee militia. Governor Sevier was so "governed by selfish motives," Jackson seethed, that he would risk the people's safety to glorify himself.[17]

When the two men happened upon each other in front of the Knox county courthouse on October 1, 1803, things quickly escalated. After trading accusations of land fraud and electoral tampering, the governor compared his record of service to that of Jackson. Sevier had been making war on fiendish foes for over twenty years, risking his own scalp and losing seven family members in the process. And what had Jackson ever done? In this full-throttle yelling match over who deserved what honors, Jackson started naming his achievements: his help defending forts, his service as judge advocate, his part in the Nickajack expedition. Unable once more to view things in the calm light of mild philosophy, Sevier scoffed that Jackson had done little more than take someone's wife down to Natchez. In the ensuing melee, both men went for their weapons.[18]

Jackson clearly wanted to kill Sevier, or, better still, to watch him crawl and beg forgiveness in front of the whole town, the whole state, the whole world. Otherwise, those unbearable words about military and marital records would continue to float around, mocking him. He was seized by what early critics of dueling called "the anguish of wounded pride," brimming with "a spirit of frantic rage." In fact, Jackson had already forgotten the *code duello* by attacking the governor on the spot. Your "ungentlemany Expressions, and gasgonading conduct" make you unworthy of righteous anger, Jackson wrote the next day. "But sir the Voice of the people has made you a Governor." Out of respect to that voice, Jackson would meet Sevier on the field of honor and put a hole through his chest. Sevier scoffed that Jackson, too, was well beneath a bullet's dignity, and that "the World" knew it. But since "The Voice of the Assembly had made you a Judge," the governor would deign to duel.[19]

The only problem was that Tennessee had just passed an anti-dueling statute to combat this "Evil Practice." The 1801 law imposed a fine and jail time for anyone who issued or accepted a challenge and named those who killed on the field of honor guilty of murder. "I have some regard to the laws of the State over which I have the honor to preside," Sevier told Jackson, "Altho you a Judge Appear to have none." So the governor asked Jackson to name a place outside the state. "Your attack was in the Town of Knoxville

[and] in the Town of Knoxville did you Take the name of a lady into your poluted lips," Jackson shot back. "And now Sir in the Neighborhood of Knoxville you shall attone for it or I will Publish you as a coward and a paltroon." The sin would be punished on the spot it had fouled. Jackson taunted the governor's "Squemesh fears" of prosecution and boasted that he, a real man, would take "no advantage of the law" while setting things right. Jackson even suggested that they fight on Indian lands, where, they both knew, the laws of Tennessee did not extend.[20]

Sevier's respect for the rule of law was no less complicated than Jackson's, but his reputation was more powerful. Nolichucky Jack also knew how to deploy his honor with democratic panache, bowing to the people's laws while Jackson answered to the selfish passions. He was, quite simply, too much for the younger man to handle in 1803. When the two again crossed paths on October 16 outside of Knoxville, the high-wire act continued, with both men pulling weapons and trading insults before hustling away with their respective entourages—and accounts. The governor's friends called it an ambush by "the head of a faction." Far from a public-spirited gentleman, Jackson was presented here as the most antisocial kind of criminal: an *assassin*, hired to kill the people's favorite. Jackson so wanted to know who wrote this piece that he accosted the secretary of state who had delivered it to the printer. His meteoric rise on hold, Jackson was coming apart.[21]

A TALE OF TWO PARTNERS

As much as they hated each other, Sevier and Jackson shared an elite consensus about public policy for a Jeffersonian Tennessee. The Great Seal of the state, approved in 1802, captured the working alliance between planters and merchants that would dominate for decades. It gave pride of place to "AGRICULTURE," symbolized by a plow, a sheaf of wheat, and a cotton plant. Directly beneath was "COMMERCE," pictured by a boat on its way west, presumably down the Tennessee and Cumberland to the Ohio and Mississippi. Free navigation on all "exportable rivers" was "the natural and inherent right of this state," Sevier told the legislature. During his long run in office between 1803 and 1809, he also called for cooperation with other states to build new roads to Atlantic and Gulf markets. The governing idea was to open more lands and markets to the property rules of the Age of Paper.[22]

Andrew Jackson and John Overton knew the risks that came with those rules. In 1797–98, Jackson had saved Overton by securing congressional repayment for the military pay given to Tennessee's militiamen. Then Overton

Figure 4.2 Great Seal of the State of Tennessee. Leading men like Jackson used "Agriculture" and "Commerce" as shorthands for the major economic interests of early Tennessee. Courtesy of Tennessee State Library and Archives.

handled the tangled claims held by the many creditors of David Allison, who had expired in a Philadelphia debtor's jail in 1798. (Among Allison's *debtors* was James Wilson, Supreme Court justice and founding jurist, who also died that year while hiding from creditors.) The case was brought in October 1801 in a federal district court, and Overton prevailed: six months later Allison's eighty-five-thousand-acre estate went to auction. Acting as an agent for another creditor, Jackson snapped up ten thousand acres at less than $0.02 per acre. He paid Overton with half that amount, granting one thousand acres to his friend and selling the other four thousand at $0.33 per acre. Jackson then divvied up and sold off the remaining five thousand acres in "warranted grants," whose value he agreed to pay if the titles later failed. Their credit restored, he and Overton then set out on different paths.[23]

Overton began from a better spot. His Virginia family counted large tobacco planters, Continental Army officers, and federal revenue collectors, and in 1802 he convinced one of his brothers to move to Nashville with thirty-one slaves in tow. Besides the titles he held with Jackson, Overton had been buying town lots in Nashville, sometimes at the sheriff's auctions he helped to organize. At "Traveler's Rest" the long-time bachelor hosted clients and friends. Over brandy and cigars they talked law, politics, and "the land business." The rules regarding when and how a person or government could claim real estate in places where the right of soil was in dispute were "extremely laborious," he once told Governor Sevier. The fine print was technically complex and politically arid, demanding a close attention to detail and a total suspension of curiosity. No one in Tennessee knew it better than Overton—and he knew it.[24]

From 1803 to 1806, Overton worked on a new transfer of the right of soil from North Carolina to Tennessee. The consummate insider, he held what he called "out of doors" discussions with delegates from both states, all while feeding talking points to representatives in the state assemblies and the US Congress. In Raleigh he insisted that the 1789 Act of Cession left North Carolina with no legal rights over any lands in Tennessee. In Knoxville he urged more conciliatory letters, although he confided that he would not support those same documents in public. "Appearances are necessary to be kept up," he noted. Meanwhile, Overton pored over British and American cases and treatises, trying to figure out how one state could take custody of titles granted by another without betraying "every principle of national faith." In an early American context, after all, "national faith" often meant full faith and credit between *states*, and Overton was deeply committed to that kind of national union. His solutions found their way into bills that he patiently explained to the men who passed them. One such meeting in Raleigh lasted well past midnight. "I am not aware that a majority of the Legislature knew [the bill's] meaning or construction," he noted with satisfaction.[25]

The upshot of the so-called Compact of 1806 was that the newer state took from its parent the sole right to perfect titles inside its borders, except for the far western lands between the Tennessee and Mississippi Rivers and a small section south of the Duck River, which remained US-recognized Chickasaw land. This transfer was necessary, Overton noted, because North Carolina had made too many undocumented promises. Not that he disliked North Carolina's land laws per se. To the contrary, he preferred them to the more meddlesome statutes of Virginia and Kentucky, which on paper offered settlers pre-emption rights and payments for the improvements they made. Distinguishing settlers from speculators proved far more difficult in practice, so Kentucky courts tried to decide on the basis of "notoriety." This brought too much uncertainty, Overton thought. It was better to defer to the "ordinary principles of contracts" and to keep a "strict adherence" to law than to chase after "the fluctuating passions and interests of society."[26]

Wherever squatters held lands but no papers, Overton made clear that they had to go. The "bare possessor of land" had no claim against the holder of "any title good on the face of it." Whenever juries tried to import popular notions of fairness into interpersonal disputes, Overton was equally clear: only judges could determine the law. Courts were "particularly" authorized to handle debt prosecutions, he noted, for the assembly had wisely ceded that power to the judiciary. The law was both inflexible and minimalist, holding everyone to its letter and asking nothing more. Just because Armstrong's land office had not sold plots of more than five thousand acres did not mean that anyone had been forbidden from amassing many entries into larger estates. Just because an entry might be read to describe a smaller space did not mean that the court should impose such modesty. The law assumed that every person sought every "exemption from restraint" while pursuing his own interest. Anything else was "manifestly repugnant to the spirit of our laws" and to the "law of nature."[27]

In making such decisions and then organizing them as the *Tennessee Reports*, Judge Overton continued the work of sheltering the rule of law from the sovereignty of the people. "It is not our own ideas of right, or wrong that constitute law," he concluded in 1814. "It is only found in adhering to the settled opinions of judges who have preceded us." In this he fit squarely within a new generation of conservative justices who knew how to pick their battles with their democratic surroundings. When it came to those "obvious principles" that marked "every Government of the Civilized World," he was unyielding. Otherwise, he was pragmatic. Long-time residents with shaky titles should be "safe in their pre-emptions," he mused, for expelling them would also derange property values. In adapting to the conditions that self-interested individuals created, the law found its real strength. It governed quietly, its new and often unpopular ideas hidden behind claims to inescapable truth.[28]

Compared to the more shameless lawyers of the 1760s and the more grandiose speculators of the 1780s, Overton worked within the political frameworks he helped to form. He sent agents into the Illinois Country, the Gulf Coast, and central Tennessee to find relatively small tracts where the soil was good, the titles sound, and the markets promising. Then he held on to the titles until the time and price were right. While building wealth from what others would pay for these lands, Overton also extracted profits from the soils and slaves of Traveler's Rest. With his neighbors he bought a cotton gin and sold the final product to merchants and factors around Nashville. These men then took on the costs of transportation, the uncertainties of price, and the other hazards of dealing with "the market" as a global phenomenon rather than a discrete transaction.[29]

Overton had taken his seat on the superior court in 1804 to replace Jackson, who may well have accepted the post back in 1798 for the security it offered from David Allison's creditors. Did the Allison affair also sour Jackson on the risky world of commerce? The antebellum historian James Parton made much of this in his *Life of Andrew Jackson*, published on the eve of the Civil War. Parton's sources were then eager to contrast the traditional South with the pitiless modernity of the North. His book turned the Allison notes into a kind of conversion experience, after which Jackson tried to protect himself and the people from bank notes and credit instruments. Jackson was a simple man, Parton insisted, and so disliked the complex world of law and business. "He *hated* debt." Many interpretations of Jacksonian politics trace back to this tale.[30]

It is hard to tell how much of Jackson's frantic business activity around 1802 was designed to pay off debts and how much was meant to make new fortunes. In practice these goals blended together, for capital was always restless. It moved from person to person and ledger to ledger through the bills and notes in which it was counted, pausing only when one party cried foul and tried to collect in nonpaper form. Jackson did change his funding strategy after the Allison affair, if only because Tennessee land had not sold well in Philadelphia. Thereafter he used export crops rather than land titles to jump-start his "Mercantile Business." Yet the scale of that business only grew. He and three different partners operated five different stores on their plantations and on roads and rivers leading to Nashville between 1802 and 1807. He paid a state tax as a "Merchant" and spent much of his thirties trying to bring linens, silks, shawls, shoes, combs, umbrellas, and candlesticks to central Tennessee. That meant more business, not less, with the moneyed men of Atlantic seaports.[31]

Cotton was "an object of great importance to this state, and in all probability, an article upon which the riches of the country will depend," so declared a committee of Mero planters chaired by Jackson in July 1802. On behalf of "the agricultural and commercial interest of this state," they called on the legislature to purchase the patent right that Eli Whitney and another man held on their cotton gin. He and his partners did not wait, using their own gin from 1802 and buying about $10,000 worth of start-up goods. Jackson had been busy selling land in eastern Tennessee over the past two years, dumping almost twenty thousand acres in thirty-six transactions, while buying the same amount back closer to Nashville, mostly at auctions. At the same time he sought "Prime young fellows and wenches" to work his plantations. "[Put] your Negros Under him and as Many Horses and Tools as he wonts and Keep Out of the field your Self," Jackson had earlier been told of an overseer, "and you may Depend On a crop." In short, he and his partners were trying to amass cotton on their own lands, send it to New Orleans, and then use the proceeds to buy goods in Philadelphia.[32]

Jackson was hoping to sell some fifty thousand pounds of cotton at between $0.25 and $0.30 per pound. Even before the bales left Tennessee in March 1803, however, one of his new partners reported that they would "fall Short of our calculations." Now they had to ensure that every last bale made it to New Orleans. Jackson waited two months for news to arrive, no doubt agreeing with one promotional tract that the Mississippi was "more than double the necessary length" and ought to be shortened by ditches and canals. When one partner finally inspected their cargo in early June, he found much of the cotton "So rotten that it all falls apart on moving." Someone had packed it incorrectly into the bottom of the boats, and the muddy water had seeped in somewhere along the Cumberland, Ohio, or Mississippi Rivers. Only about forty thousand pounds shipped to England, where prices had dipped to around $0.15 per pound.[33]

Along with the physical difficulties of bringing cotton to market, Jackson was discovering the cost of doing business in places where the rule of law was more ambiguous and less commercial than he thought it should be. In the fall of 1803, for example, he learned that his partner Thomas Watson had been lax with some of their debtors, "alledging that He felt a reluctance to sue his customers and that some had deceived him, although they were solvent." Jackson had no way to compel Watson to collect what was due or to determine whether their debtors could actually pay. Once more he was at the mercy of debtors. Another man who owed the partners was untouchable because he was "in the Spanish Territory and of course beyond the reach of our process." So Jackson replaced Watson and put his faith in the next season. This time they would not risk sending their goods to the most favorable markets, looking instead to "sell at any markett where we can sell to save ourselves." Wizened to the fragility of cotton, they also sent iron (purchased in Virginia) and deer and bear skins (taken near Nashville) downriver.[34]

Once again, water and distance betrayed them. One of their boats sank, obliging Jackson's partner to spend two days drying the wet bales before overloading another boat. Perhaps we could send more iron to market? Jackson asked. Good idea, his partner replied, but "god only knows how the mony is to be Raist for Carr[iages]." Meanwhile, Jackson had to pay drivers to take the heavy boxes of goods he was buying in Philadelphia to Pittsburgh, where they were loaded onto boats for the trip down the Ohio and then up the Cumberland. Overland transport alone cost more than $600 that season, about the same as his salary as judge. Once they reached Nashville, those goods fetched a good profit. Even as the boxes of goods came in from the North, though, more bad news arrived from the South: their cotton had once again arrived in New Orleans in "very bad order," with only 40 of their 170 bales undamaged. These sold at just over $0.17 per pound.[35]

All he wanted, Jackson told Rachel in April 1804, was to "return to your arms" and "retire to some peacefull grove to spend our days in solitude and domestic quiet." And he (or, rather, his slaves) had done his part, producing small mountains of cotton for sale. But high costs and low prices threatened to "involve us in all the calamity of poverty—an event that brings every horror to my mind." If he and his partners went down, he knew, Rachel and many of her family members would sink too, and that would be too much to bear. Still he refused any easy way out. He sold Hunter's Hill that summer for $10,000, a sacrifice that he and his partner made from "the principles of Justice to my credittors in Philadelphia." Unlike the scoundrels upon whom he had to rely, Jackson told himself and others, he would honor the inflexible terms of his contracts. He called his new plantation "Rural Retreat" and then the Hermitage, pining once more for the quiet life he could never endure.[36]

HONEST CREDITORS AND RUNAWAY CHATTELS

Despite their setbacks, Jackson told his partner in the spring of 1804 that "resolution and industry with oeconomy will remove mountains." They could draw agriculture and commerce into a single enterprise that spanned eastern North America and crossed the Atlantic. In hindsight, they were ahead of their times. After Eli Whitney's invention, the next breakthrough in cotton horticulture did not come until 1820, when Mississippi planters created a new strain of superior "pickability." Until then, yields and profits were often disappointing for those who used the crop to finance other investments. Transportation costs fell wherever new roads and settlements appeared, and the first steamboat appeared on the Mississippi in 1811, but not until the 1820s and 1830s did these dangerous wonders revolutionize transport up and down the great valley.[37]

In another sense, Jackson was behind the curve, having just missed the boom times brought on by the stunning conflagration in Europe. The French Revolution had been revolutionary enough when the new, lawyer-dominated governments confiscated church and *émigré* properties between 1789 and 1792. After the revolutionary *nation* decapitated Louis XVI and declared war on Great Britain in early 1793, American conservatives began to echo their English and Scottish counterparts: this was no ordinary conflict, but a war for civilization itself, a crusade to save the law of nations from democratic violence. On the other hand, general war in Europe meant windfall profits for American shipowners. They exported wheat, corn, flour, and pork from American farms while re-exporting sugar and coffee from the Caribbean, protected—for the moment—by the much-maligned Jay's Treaty. The coin and credit they brought home funded new wharves, homes, and shops from Boston to Baltimore, as well as good wages for sailors, artisans, and laborers. The Bank of England's suspension of specie payments in 1797 disrupted credit lines, but by 1801 exports were booming again.[38]

Then, just as Jackson and his partners prepared for launch in early 1802, the Peace of Amiens broke out. For fourteen months the superpowers held their fire, reducing demand for American staples and carriers. One contact in Natchez told Jackson that prices for flour, corn, and bacon would remain "quite low" during the truce. By contrast, cotton prices had surged throughout the 1790s, reaching a high of $0.44 in 1798. So the smart merchant should go with cotton monoculture. Jackson took this advice with a vengeance, but by the time his undamaged bales finally made it to England in the fall of 1803, war had resumed with even greater vengeance. Due to Napoleon's clamp-down on British citizens and imports, his creditors noted in October, "all business in England wears a most gloomy and discouraging aspect." English demand was set to decline, making cotton exportation "a desperate adventure." All of this bad news arrived while his name and pride took a beating at the hands of Governor Sevier.[39]

Like most people, Jackson made sense of what we now call "economic forces" by naming bad actors, although his way of doing so was characteristically extreme. (He had been "more cruelly treated" by one partner "than ever a christian was by a Turk.") More significant is *who* and *what* he blamed. After all, the chronic shortage of money might have led him to call for more of it, as so many people across North America had for decades and as western leaders increasingly demanded for their undercapitalized voters. The harsh consequences of defaulting on the various IOUs that filled the currency void might have led him to condemn creditors as unfeeling or unpatriotic, as so many debtors did when they were not collecting their own sums. The ongoing reliance on British goods and credit might have led him to consider high tariffs and domestic manufacturing, as northern Jeffersonians were beginning to insist. He experimented with salt-making in 1802 and offered a toast to "American manufactures" in 1805.[40]

For the most part, though, Jackson accepted the rules of both liberal trade and commercial order. More aggrieved businessman than chastened gambler, he told his Philadelphia suppliers that he was "truly sorry" not to be able to pay in good bills. Like them he had suffered at the hands of unreliable paper and shameless debtors. He pledged to do "equal Justice to our credittors" and to honor the "principals of Justice to our Creditors." When the planter who had purchased Hunter's Hill asked to pay in slaves or other property in 1805, Jackson admonished him: "If my Creditors would receive their debts thus, I would meet every demand in four hours, this not being the case, makes cash the object." While serving writs on delinquent debtors three years later, he was appalled to learn that collection agents in Louisiana were entitled to 5% of sums remitted. "[It] is such a practice as prevails no where else, and never ought to prevail anywhere," Jackson wrote. "[It] is buying Justice at two high a premium—it is Taxing the honest creditor too dear." At the same time he often preferred patience with the Nashville customers who bought on credit at his stores.[41]

In the sense that such credit became a new source of currency for him, Jackson's stores were a success, and he briefly did better with a new partner, John Coffee. But neither cotton, nor iron, nor furs sufficiently overcame their transport and transfer costs, especially as competing merchants and grocers arrived in Nashville, including several from Pennsylvania. The only commodities that were always mobile and usually valuable were horses and slaves, and in Jackson's correspondence they often appeared together. He usually wanted to acquire slaves, not sell them. As a merchant and a planter, though, he saw slaves as currency and credit, as well as "hands" and dependents. In 1803, Jackson (through a partner) sold a fourteen-year-old girl for $300 and agreed to settle a $500 debt he held through another slave's sale. His partner made at least one trip to the downriver slave markets in the spring of 1804, looking to "carry on negroes to exchange for groceries," as Jackson put it.[42]

When the master returned to Hunter's Hill after a long business trip in June of that year, he probably broke the news that he had agreed to sell it. Everyone was about to move—everyone whom Jackson did not sell first, that is. One week later a thirty-year-old slave named Tom Gid ran away. A second slave, George, who had lived with his wife under Jackson for over a decade, also escaped around this time. They hit Jackson at one of his most vulnerable moments, exposing his perverse dependence on the value of their bodies. Jackson pursued George for years, sending letters to friends and officials who could handle things discreetly. As for Tom Gid, Jackson printed the following advertisement in the fall of 1804:

> Eloped from the subscriber, living near Nashville . . . a Mulatto Man Slave, about thirty years old, six feet and an inch high, stout made and active, talks sensible, stoops in his walk . . . will pass for a free man, as i am informed he has obtained by some means, certificates as such. . . . He will make for Detroit, through the states of Kentucky and Ohio, or the upper part of Louisiana. [$50] will be given any person that will take him, and deliver him to me, or secure him in jail, so that I can get him. If taken out of the state, the above reward, and all reasonable expenses paid—and ten dollars extra, for every hundred lashes any person will give him, to the amount of three hundred.

As a judge, Jackson had once approved thirty lashes for petty theft. Here he wanted *three hundred* stripes for a man who had defied his rule. Because he categorized people in such stark terms without questioning where those categories came from, Jackson the slave owner only compared himself to the most depraved masters and dealers. He only sold slaves to do his creditors justice, he insisted. He only wanted people to honor him as the gentle patriarch they could not see.[43]

Two years after Jackson published his extraordinary notice, Tennessee organized a more regular system of slave patrols. All militia captains were to form these watches as needed, and any slave who used "insulting or provoking" words with any white person could be whipped. The year after that, Judge Overton further clarified how sovereignty should work in a racial police state. In the 1807 case at hand, three white men had gone to "a house [in Nashville] where there were negroes." Returning to his home as night fell, one of the men happened upon a woman who was probably carrying a bucket of water for her owner. He pulled his pistol and told her that "she was his property, and that she must go home with him," whereupon she was "made to sleep upstairs." The issue was not whether the woman had been compelled to do anything, Overton made clear, but rather who had made her do it. It was "of the first moment," he wrote, that "this species of property should be inviolably guarded from the control of others than their master." Instead of locating the master's sovereignty within his household or confining it to well-governed territory, Tennessee's laws should deploy it wherever his chattels might go.[44]

True to their roots, both Overton and Jackson wanted a strong judiciary to turn the different states into a single jurisdiction for property seekers like them. Overton made sure of it while enforcing out-of-state wills and contracts. Jackson demanded it while alerting everyone "through the states of Kentucky and Ohio, or the upper part of Louisiana" of his runaway slave. The toasts he drafted for an Independence Day celebration in Nashville in 1805 suggest how he began to fit such convictions into the national consensus forming around Jefferson and the Constitution. Of course he described the "blood" sacrifice of the Revolution, the divine favor of the American people, and the duty of every "true american" to despise aristocrats and Federalists. More pointedly, he raised a glass to the state and federal governments, "confined within their constitutional sphere," while hoping that Liberty herself would "range unconfined over the earthly globe."[45]

Government in America had to be carefully "confined," Jackson believed, so that Americans could "range unconfined" over everything that had been won in 1783. He hereby made a claim for expansion far more aggressive than that of any squatter. Now that people like him had brought modern property rights to the territories, he was, or should be, totally free to bring cotton and the slaves who grew it from the point of production to the point of sale. He was, or should be, totally free to chase unpaid debts and runaway labor across an unbroken terrain of commercial order. In this sense the Constitution was less a framework for governing North America than a grant of power to its more enterprising citizens, a promise that they could pursue property and justice without further interference from the laws that defined property and justice. Anything less would dampen a patriotic spirit that had always been a matter of choice for ambitious elites along extreme frontiers.[46]

Here again, Jackson and Overton were partners in effect if not in name, the one emotional and ideological, the other cool and pragmatic. Faithful to the story of his own innocence, Jackson recoiled from every ambiguity, holding ever tighter to "sacred" principles and righteous anger. Federal protection for those who had shed Christian blood was an outrage, a crime, a betrayal. More relaxed and cynical, Overton made similar arguments in decisions like *Glasgow's Lessee v. Smith* (1805), which recognized pre-emption rights to Indian country. He later called for "latitude in surveying" rather than close scrutiny of treaty lines and title histories, since many surveys had been made when Tennessee was "infested by an Indian enemy." The people had faced their "very extermination" in the 1790s, and so retained more of their sovereignty than officials back east could understand. Government should thus enable what Overton called "a contest for the first choice or pre-emption," not pretend that Indians had any real claim to North America or that the state knew better than individuals how to divvy up its riches.[47]

MURDER, TREASON, AND SUICIDE

Although he resigned his judgeship in 1804 to better focus on his faltering business, Jackson remained major general of the West Tennessee militia. This post fit his talents and temper better than law or commerce. It channeled his energy into discrete tasks and clear roles, giving him a greater sense of control and his men a larger sense of purpose. At least once he studied a US Army detachment along the Natchez trace. He later devised a plan to give younger militiamen more intensive training in the "knowledge and art of war." Always he made clear that he was in charge. When in 1802 he learned that a frontier militia leader was planning to "break up" Indian "camps" over the Tennessee border so as to pre-empt native retaliation for the murder of a Cherokee, Jackson denounced the "illegal enterprise" and ordered the man arrested. The initial murder was an affront to "civil authority," he noted, while the violence that might follow would fall upon both the innocent and the guilty. Such mayhem violated "the peace of our country" and "the law of the land."[48]

Both Governor Sevier and President Jefferson could tell Jackson what that law was, but of course Jackson preferred to answer to Jefferson. After news of the Louisiana Purchase reached Tennessee in the summer of 1803, he offered the president "the unanimous congratulations of the citizens of Mero," who felt more American than ever. Jefferson replied that the purchase was of "immense importance to our future tranquility," in that it deprived Indians of potential European allies. Expanding the range over which households could settle or trade, the president was sure, would bind them to the Union by their own self-interest. In late 1805 and 1806, the administration further secured Tennessee's loyalty by purchasing large swaths of Indian country south and east of the old Mero District, using the unpaid debts of Chickasaws and Cherokees as leverage. While thus shifting some of the onus of commercial order onto non-Americans, these treaties united middle and eastern Tennessee and encouraged a new wave of emigration from the older states. Jackson rushed to secure his pre-emptions south of Nashville and to alert other speculators to re-mark their lands before the treaties became official.[49]

While Jefferson tried to expand the United States with all constitutional speed, his first vice president, Aaron Burr, sought to leap beyond the political schedules of lesser men. Burr was the dark wonder of the age. Something about his icy wit and macho gentility was "inconceivably fascinating," even before he killed Alexander Hamilton in July 1804. Indicted in both New York and New Jersey, Burr cooled his heels in Philadelphia before moving some senators to tears with a farewell address in the capitol in March 1805. Then he ventured west, assuring his daughter that his trip had "other objects than mere curiosity." After descending the Ohio River and proceeding overland through Kentucky and into Tennessee, Burr arrived in Nashville in late May 1805. For the following week and again later that summer, the Jacksons hosted him at the Hermitage.[50]

Historians David and Jeanne Heidler have commented on the contrast in personalities at hand: Burr, the rakish New Yorker whose progressive comments about women did not check his womanizing, and Jackson, the reformed sinner who raged at the slightest "pollution" on Rachel's honor; Burr, the smug descendant of New England theologians and living testament to the futility of Puritan self-denial in the new republic, and Jackson, orphaned son of Ulster and Carolina border people who scandalized pious opinion in other ways. They hit it off all the same. Burr called Jackson "one of those prompt, frank, honest souls whom I love to meet," and Jackson fell for Burr's audacity. Both reveled in their desire to risk life and limb for fortune and glory, and both were frustrated by the political maps stabilizing around them.[51]

No direct evidence of their meetings survives, but they clearly understood each other on a few points. First, war with the Spanish in the Floridas or Texas was both imminent and necessary. The Catholic sovereign to whom Jackson had sworn a borderlands kind of loyalty sixteen years before was on the wane, and thus unable to control its native populations. American forces would have to fill the void. Second, something had to be done about the Orleans Territory. Its population was ripe for revolt against American authority, for its people clung to the Old World ways that vexed Jackson the merchant. Deprived of their informal land claims and protected markets, they condemned the "hard Conditions" of Anglo-American common law and pined for "Spanish generosity." A rapid influx of Caribbean slaves to man the region's new sugar mills made it even more unstable. In the event of war, Jackson and Burr likely agreed, armed vessels would have to descend the Mississippi and secure New Orleans.[52]

Jackson had been building gunboats for the Jefferson administration since late 1803, and he arranged river transport for Burr as the "little Emperor" continued his mysterious voyage in the late summer of 1805. Bored and restless, Jackson then fell into another cycle of daring and fighting. This one started with a horse race rather than an election. Shortly after Burr's departure in 1805, Jackson and an east Tennessee rival, Joseph Erwin, had arranged a match race between their favorite steeds, which the latter called off. Disagreement arose over how and when the $800 in forfeit money would be paid. At some point another young lawyer, Thomas Swann, took the side of Erwin and of Erwin's son-in-law, Charles Dickinson, causing Jackson to question Swann's truthfulness. Swann demanded satisfaction, whereupon Jackson told Swann to mind his manners or risk a caning. When the two happened upon each other in a Nashville tavern in January 1806, Jackson made good on his threat, beating Swann as one would a servant or other subordinate.[53]

Jackson wanted to shoot Dickinson, not Swann. Apparently the young lawyer from Maryland had slandered Rachel Jackson, and his breezy arrogance provoked the general at the deepest, most visceral level. That Jackson pursued Dickinson despite warnings that the newcomer could put a bullet through his heart at fifty paces speaks to the intensity of Jackson's rage. He imagined the worst about his enemies and then let the excruciating images spin around his mind, tormenting him until either he or they had to die. He was more like Achilles than Jesus, and this is what bothered anti-dueling activists. Especially in the wake of Hamilton's death, the code of honor was widely condemned as illegal and impious. Critics drew from both enlightened and evangelical themes to insist upon a wider, deeper respect for public order and civil society. At the very least this forced duelists to avoid appearing to be as ready to kill someone as Jackson was in 1806.[54]

Even James Robertson tried to dissuade Jackson. The former leader of the Cumberland had once preferred to pay for Indian scalps rather than identify the guilty with greater care. In "former days," Robertson acknowledged, he might well have shot the man who insulted him. But age, reflection, and a clear change in public opinion now moved him to denounce dueling as a violation of God's law and "the laws of my contry." Nashville was improving and maturing along with the rest of the state and Union. The light of law and Christ had even reached some Cherokee children in eastern Tennessee, who now studied at a missionary school run by a Presbyterian veteran of past horrors. (John Sevier is said to have wept while watching these children sing hymns.) So Robertson cautioned Jackson not to take or risk life so rashly, to no avail.[55]

Early in the morning of May 30, 1806, Jackson and Dickinson met just over the border in Kentucky, where dueling was no less illegal but where Tennessee's 1801 statute did not apply. They took their places twenty-four feet apart, standing sideways to present a smaller target. Legend has it that Jackson wore a long, loose overcoat to conceal his thin frame. Still, Dickinson's shot caught him in the chest, breaking a rib and tearing some of the pleural lining from the lungs. Bleeding but still standing, Jackson tried to return fire. His gun "clicked" but did not discharge. On many occasions a single exchange was enough to restore honor even if one pistol did not fire correctly. But Jackson wanted blood along with honor, so he recocked his pistol and shot Dickinson through the midsection, perhaps piercing the ultra-sensitive lining of the liver. The general and his entourage hurried away while the younger man was taken to a nearby home. There Dickinson spent the day screaming in agony, expiring of blood loss or septic shock just before his young wife arrived.[56]

The "honest, unsuspecting part of society" had to beat back the "reptiles" in their midst, Judge Overton told General Jackson right after the duel. "God has so ordained it. You have been the instrument of doing so. Fear nothing." In other words, Jackson would face no charges in either Kentucky or Tennessee for having taken life in very cold blood. But the court of public opinion was not so kind. Having caned one man, killed another, been convicted of assault and battery on a third, and nearly arranged a duel with a fourth during the first half of 1806, Jackson was beginning to look more like a lunatic than an assassin, but no more like a Christian or gentleman. He seemed surly, vindictive, and cruel.[57]

While recovering at the Hermitage, he sent a menacing letter to a Nashville paper that was planning to frame its next edition in black. Anyone who wanted this "mourning border" would have to answer to him, Jackson warned. Several dozen Nashville citizens stood up to him that June, their names appearing in print along with his ugly threat. As his reputation plunged, Jackson scolded everyone for meddling in a "private dispute" while also denying that Dickinson's death had moved "the Publick feeling." The dead man had rendered no "esential service to the Publick," Jackson wrote. In fact, Dickinson was "engaged in the humane persuit of purchasing Negroes in Maryland and carrying them to Natchez and Louis[iana] and thus making a fortune of speculating on human flesh." Talk of the grieving widow and orphaned baby made Jackson angry, not sad.[58]

In September he received another letter from John Overton. It reads very much like an intervention. After hearing rumors of still another duel involving Jackson, Overton began, he had talked things over with "many judicious men of honor." By general consensus, Swann and friends were a "*dirty band*," a pack of "boys" whom Jackson ought to ignore. No one would doubt his bravery if he declined to fight, whereas if they did duel and Jackson killed them, "it would be said that you delighted in human blood." In any event, Jackson should remember his duties to his family and country, not to mention "the respect you owe to the opinion of your friends." Chastise your equals if you must, Overton concluded. "But *never, never* my dear sir, hurt the feelings of your friends, by putting yourself on a level with *boys, instruments, mere tools of others*." Jackson did not reply.[59]

It was at this low point that Aaron Burr returned to the Hermitage, inviting Jackson to make history. Burr had spent the previous year moving from the borderlands to Washington and back again, convincing some volunteers that Jefferson had to go and others that Jefferson wanted them to invade Mexico. All they needed was a bit of his daring—and a few good boats. On October 4, 1806, with Burr staying at his home, Jackson issued a new call to action to friends and subordinates. Since the president's most recent bid to buy the Floridas had failed, he enthused, war was at hand. Bold action "can conquer not only the Floridas, But all Spanish North america." Together they could "give freedom and commerce" to a vast new country and reveal their "laudable ambition of avenging our countries wrongs." "Should there be a war," Jackson saw fit to mention, "this will be a handsome theatre for our enterprising young men, and a certain source of acquiring fame." When peace dragged on for another month, he assured Jefferson that he was ready to strike "at one moments warning."[60]

Just days later, around November 10, another visitor brought some mortifying news. Burr's ultimate plan, it now appeared, was to set up a government hostile to the United States on the western side of the Mississippi. Far from trying to get rid of Spanish North America, Burr wanted to expand it. He was planning a continental coup d'état, an anti-Jefferson conspiracy instead of a Jeffersonian mission. Other reports had Burr riding into the capitol to kidnap or kill the president while his co-conspirators converged on New Orleans. Jackson had always known that he and Burr were taking liberties with their mandates, probably under the assumption that they were doing what national authorities desired but could not avow. In his experience such action could mean the difference between life and death, or in any case between honor and obscurity.[61]

"I love my Country and Government, I hate the Dons," he told the governor of Orleans Territory on November 12. "I would delight to see Mexico reduced, but I will die in the last ditch before I would yield a part to the Dons, or see the Union disunited." In the course of human events, he explained that same day to a US senator, patriotic citizens might well respond to the idea of "an attack on Mexico on the event of [diplomatic] failure . . . either under the auspices of government, or under circumstances that government would wink at." The goal of these unnamed patriots, Jackson continued, would have been to annex Mexico, or to make it friendlier, or in any case to promote "the growing greatness of am[erica]." Bold actions by heroic men not only advanced their nation's interests but also revealed its most admirable passions. Free to act in ways that their law-bound governments could not, they glorified their nations no less than themselves. In any case, Jackson had signed on for what Burr's followers called a "daring enterprise" rather than for what Jefferson now labeled a "criminal enterprise."[62]

In early December the president replied to Jackson's premature offer of service. As a "friend to peace," Jefferson had not despaired that the differences with Spain could be settled. Diplomacy was the best policy for a free and decent society that wanted to reform but still respect the law of nations. "The offer of service which your patriotism has now made to your country," the president intoned, "is a pledge that it will not be withheld in whatever form the National councils may authorize [its] use." In other words, Jackson would do as he was told. The day of the frontier avenger was over. Tennessee was now a member state of liberty's empire, bound to Washington as it had never been to Philadelphia. Underscoring the point, Nashville citizens burned Burr in effigy just before New Year's and damned his friends and co-conspirators for much longer. Once the advance guard of national law, Andrew Jackson had launched himself onto the wrong side of national loyalty.[63]

REDEMPTION AND RESENTMENT

Burr initially turned himself into local authorities in the Mississippi Territory, where a grand jury refused to indict him. After US soldiers captured him on his way to West Florida in early 1807, he stood trial for treason in the US Circuit Court in Richmond, Virginia. Called to testify to the grand jury that summer, Jackson made the long trip to defend his name. He and Burr had mostly talked about land speculation during their time at the Hermitage, he reported, and he had made clear that he would "only march by orders of gov[ernment]." Frantic for vindication, the general also made his views known on the street. One man overhead Jackson, a "great blackguard from Tennessee," defending Burr and cursing Jefferson to passersby. The Federalist judges were oddly sympathetic to Burr, who went free that fall and then set out for Europe, trying in vain to convince the British or French that he still mattered.[64]

Glory went instead to US sailors and marines on the shores of Tripoli. Jefferson's election had signaled a more militant approach to the Barbary states of North Africa, for unlike Vattel and most Federalists, the new president saw commerce as a natural right. He did not think that two nations had to sign a treaty before its citizens could exchange goods and credit. Jefferson was also looking for trading partners besides Great Britain, and the Mediterranean was full of potential buyers. In any case, the bashaw of Tripoli declared war early in 1801, whereupon Jefferson sent a squadron across the Atlantic. The entire crew of the U.S.S. *Philadelphia* was captured in 1803, adding to over one hundred Americans taken by Barbary ships during the 1780s and 1790s. The former US consul to Tripoli wondered if the crew should have blown the ship—and themselves—up. Such a "glorious death," he mused, would have done much for America's "national character." Instead, a daring raid led by Stephen Decatur burned the ship right under the bashaw's nose.[65]

Narratives of Barbary captivity shared much with stories of Indian atrocity: the graphic details, the tearful appeals, the constant focus on bodily violation. In both cases, white Americans pursuing happiness ran into dark, demonic foes whose cruelty marked out a new timeline of first injury and eventual justice. In both cases, radical evil called for some final and God-like vengeance, especially since the government could not or would not do anything less. The number of victims on the continental and oceanic frontiers was of course very small, but they had been targeted precisely because they were Americans, making their ordeal relevant and personal to their countrymen. To read about their suffering and to feel for the loved ones left behind gave ordinary Americans a taste of the frontier violence that had shaped and scarred people like Andrew and Rachel Jackson.

This link between the physical security of Americans abroad and the larger fate of the "American nation" was all the more pronounced in the face of its original foe. Even after the British wiped out the French and Spanish fleets at the Battle of Trafalgar in the fall of 1805, the Royal Navy needed thousands of new sailors each year for its blockade of Napoleon's Europe. Press gangs scoured London and other ports, but demand was overtaking supply. As Jay's Treaty expired and the British fleet clamped down on neutral carriers, then, the Crown stepped up the search for British (usually Irish) deserters on American ships, where wages were higher and discipline less brutal. These men remained British even if they lived in the United States and got drunk on the Fourth of July, imperial officials reasoned. Anyone who was born British would die British—whether in honorable service aboard a Royal Navy vessel or at the end of a hangman's noose.[66]

Throughout Jefferson's second term, a squadron of twenty British ships loomed just off the Atlantic coast, often stopping in American seaports to take on supplies. Meanwhile, the *National Intelligencer* reported in late 1807, thousands of Indian braves were massing at British forts near Detroit. "In case of war, it is expected that, under the auspices of the British, a general massacre will take place." The entire Michigan Territory was a "double frontier," its chief justice noted, as isolated from the nearest American settlements as the Mero District had been twenty years before. The British seemed to threaten all around the Union, or even inside it. Just before news of the Burr conspiracy broke, Republicans heard about a secessionist plot from Federalist New England, supported by the imperial strongholds across the Great Lakes. Above all, the ubiquity of British imports testified to the reach and power of the empire. English and Scottish merchants were "playing the same game over again of inundating this country with British goods," noted one Philadelphian. "[Their] influence here is beyond calculation."[67]

While in Virginia for part of the Burr trial in June 1807, Andrew Jackson learned that the H.M.S. *Leopard* had waylaid the U.S.S. *Chesapeake* just off the coast. The British captain was looking for four deserters who had enlisted in the American Navy. The commander of the *Chesapeake* refused to let the British board, since a naval vessel was understood to be the soil of its country. So the *Leopard* opened fire, crippling the smaller ship, wounding eighteen sailors, and killing three. Fearing further attacks

Figure 4.3 This Victorian-era engraving imagines how British officers might have impressed American (if British-born) sailors around 1810.
Courtesy of Library of Congress, Prints and Photographs Division, LC-USZ62-75535.

by a far superior fleet, the governor of Virginia ordered the militia to the port of Norfolk, where hatred of the Royal Navy ran deep. As the news traveled up and down the coast, angry crowds turned on the enemy in their midst while Jefferson ordered all British warships out of harbor. He also sent the U.S.S. *Revenge* to Britain with a list of demands to be delivered by the American envoy, James Monroe.[68]

One of the public meetings to denounce this "British Outrage" was held in Richmond on June 27. "All appeared zealously to vie who should be foremost in manifesting a patriotic indignation at the insult offered," one of Burr's prosecutors reported. Jackson was probably there, and he certainly fit the description. "The degradation offerred to our government by the British . . . has roused every feeling of the American heart," he wrote that day, "and war with that nation is inevitable." The attack was a "humiliating blow against our independence and sovereignty." When would the government avenge the nation it was supposed to represent? Back in Nashville one month later, Jackson made his presence well known at another public meeting on the incident. So did John Overton, who broke with his usual moderation and called for war. We, the citizens of West Tennessee, Jackson and other firebrands wanted to declare, have too long watched "the friendly and forebearing disposition of the nation ascribed to cowardice and fear."

This was too strong for James Robertson and other loyal Jeffersonians at the meeting, and they added assurances of that loyalty to the declaration.[69]

Jefferson was counting on such cooler heads. That summer and fall he ordered war preparations while waiting for the British explanation for the *Chesapeake*. It came at the end of November, "unfriendly, proud, and harsh." On December 17, reports surfaced of a new Order-in-Council, whereby any ship wishing to trade with Napoleonic Europe would first have to land at a British port and obtain a special license. The next day, Jefferson asked Congress for a total suspension of foreign trade by US vessels. Instead of going to war, the republic would refrain from foreign commerce until the great powers recognized its neutral—and natural—rights. A separate non-Intercourse Act blocked specified British goods from coming ashore. "Till [England and France] return to some sense of moral duty," Jefferson wrote, "we keep within ourselves." It was "much to be regretted," one of his New York supporters declared, that the European superpowers had forsaken "that ancient and venerable fabric called the Laws of Nations." Behind the "philosophic calmness" of Jefferson, the republic would now carry civilization's torch, proving its national character by preserving international society.[70]

The embargo drew predictable outrage in New England, where it brought high unemployment and low wages to seaports reliant on British trade. Jefferson damned Yankee merchants for exporting American iron to England and then importing the axes and nails, thereby profiting twice over at their country's expense. Popular support for the president was stronger in New York and Philadelphia, where Anglophobia was intense and where the recent boom offered a cushion. The embargo was both painful and popular in Virginia. Unable to export their tobacco, its planters watched staple prices fall and their debts climb. By the time Jefferson gave up in early 1809, the storyline of the Old Dominion's heroic sacrifice for the more commercial states had taken hold, one of several regional patriotisms of the early republican period.[71]

By denying planters and merchants their foreign markets, the embargo also underlined the need for manufacturing: everything from iron forging and cotton weaving to glass and paper making. These skilled, small-scale enterprises had been clamoring for protective tariffs since the 1780s. For all his faith in free trade and his dislike of shops and cities, Jefferson came around to the idea as global war and British hostility changed his sense of the possible. "I have lately inculcated the encouragement of manufacturers," he confided in 1809. A few years later he celebrated the spread of spindles across the west and south. Especially in New York and Pennsylvania, where manufacturers made up a fifth or more of households, the Republicans embraced them as the nation's forgotten producers. By selling their wares to the farmers who fed them, they would free the republic from the invisible fist of European credit. They would give the Union "internal sufficiency."[72]

This kind of economic nationalism took shape in conscious opposition to the Federalists and to the more general dominance of agriculture and commerce in American economic thought. It flourished in towns and cities just north of slavery. In the new states south of the Ohio River, where there were fewer manufacturers and fewer Federalists, such ideas had less traction. Its leading men lined up more against Britain than for the embargo, inviting the public at large to show the kind of anger and "resentment" otherwise reserved for people like them. Indeed, the sheer emotionalism of anti-British politics during the embargo made genteel self-control suspect, compelling elite men to unbosom themselves and share in what one scholar calls "the passions of patriotism."[73]

Andrew Jackson was uniquely suited for such a role at such a moment. His Jeffersonian Anglophobia was especially furious, in part because of the questions around his own patriotism and in part because the embargo killed his mercantile business once and for all. (In early 1808, he learned that his merchant contacts would not accept cotton "at any given price.") First he berated the government for its forbearance. Then he aligned with the small faction of dissident Republicans who wanted James Monroe rather than James Madison as the next president and who began to complain of the congressional caucus that had already decided things. Why they favored Monroe is not clear. The former governor of Virginia was not known for his talents ("dull and stupid," Aaron Burr concluded) and his diplomatic record since the Louisiana Purchase had embarrassed Jefferson and satisfied Britain. On the other hand, he was a firm and simple Republican who deplored federal corruption, resented European insults, and wanted West Florida. Tired of an administration that was too meek and lawful, Jackson tried to drum up support for Monroe during the spring of 1808.[74]

Just two years removed from his brush with treason, Jackson knew to keep one foot firmly planted in law and order even as the other reached for vengeance and glory. When word came to Nashville in April 1808 that the Creeks had broken fourteen years of peace and slaughtered three families southwest of Nashville, Jackson resumed his correspondence with Jefferson. "The blood of our innocent citizens must not flow, with impunity—Justice forbids it." In a lawless world, God's will had to be inflicted by virtuous men, not administered by any state. Should the hellish alliance between Europeans and Indians ever reform, Jackson swore, "I pledge myself to my government, that I will destroy [it]." That said, his troops would only cross the Tennessee River in cases of "imperious necessity." He linked this alleged violence to the war for independence. As Jefferson himself had once declared, dark forces had "raised the scalping knife and Tomahawk, against our defenceless weomen and children." Now that awful past was about to repeat itself farther west.[75]

Such themes were central to early Tennessee patriotism, and they helped to reconcile frontier elites not only with the United States but also with each other. In early January 1809, for example, John Sevier wrote to Andrew Jackson for the first time since they had nearly killed each other back in 1803. Now that the embargo had failed, the governor, in his sixth and final term, reached out to his old foe in the name of national dignity and public safety. Their government had shown nothing but "friendship, honest neutrality, [and] accommodating measures" toward European tyrants, Sevier noted. Its lawful tendencies were now the source of his rage, not its target. Indeed, the governor continued, we Americans "have not trespassed upon, or violated the rights of any neighboring, or foreign Nation." The United States had behaved lawfully "in all cases." So Jackson was to ready his men for a just and inevitable war. The younger man acknowledged receipt but did not reply, for he had already called a meeting of his officers in Nashville.[76]

Jackson served as president of this January 16, 1809, conference while Thomas Swann, the lawyer he had caned three years earlier, sat beside him as secretary. Again, though, this was no time for awkward silences. The "critical situation" of the United States obliged the officers to stand in readiness with whatever "Volunteer Corps" they could muster. The British and French, the officers resolved, had "by the most unprecidented Edicts and orders of Council violated the laws of Nations and committed infractions upon the commerce of the Nutrals." The United States had scrupulously obeyed the rules of European civilization, answering every insult and injury with patience and forbearance. Just like Jackson, the Union had suffered for its lawfulness.[77]

Jackson actually attended two meetings that day, one with his officers and the other with a larger but more obscure group of citizens. They had also been organizing, signing letters and petitions that did not always make it into the papers. One such petition from settlers south of the French Broad made clear that they were angry with Britain and worried about their fellow Americans on distant shores. But they had a more immediate problem. Although the legislature had given them relatively easy terms of payment three years earlier, they had spent most of their money on down payments for the lands they had originally improved. Many had taken loans from merchants to buy labor, seeds, and animals, apparently using their cotton as collateral. Yet cotton prices kept tumbling. After two bad seasons in a row, their creditors had changed their obligations into "money debts," requiring payment in either specie or bank notes. The Bank of Nashville, of which Jackson was an early stockholder, had just opened, but it had no reason to extend loans to hardscrabble settlers.[78]

A "very large majority" of them could not make their next payments, due in March 1809. If the law was "Strictly attended to" they would be "turned out their possessions, destitute of homes." Local sheriffs and constables would seize their properties and sell them to "money holders and Speculators." That was what always happened when the legal privileges of "money holders" trumped the natural rights of laboring households. They therefore asked Governor Sevier to pass an emergency stay law until the crisis passed. The petitioners did not expect any sympathy from federal magistrates. But if state judges acted in unison with Tennessee's executive and legislature, "the process of the federal courts" would break down. The auctions would never happen. Local sovereignty and republican solidarity would overrule the cold logic of the law.[79]

In Kentucky, too, the young legislator Henry Clay studied a petition for an act "relaxing the usual summary course of the law for the recovery of debts," which he found "reasonable." Indeed, emergency measures to prevent what the *National Intelligencer* called "a general sacrifice of property, to monied capital, and nefarious speculation" held wide and deep appeal throughout the debt-ridden South. In May 1808, the Georgia legislature halted all executions on any debtor who could show that he might pay later. Virginia, North Carolina, and Maryland passed similar protections. A Tennessee newspaper praised these "public acts of benevolence and humanity" and wondered if its state would be left behind, a "strong hold of avarice and barbarous cupidity" during Jefferson's brave stand against Britain.[80]

In Tennessee, much of this new agitation for stay and replevin laws came from militia officers, who generally saw Jackson as their zealous supporter. As recently as May 1808 he had called for better pay and supplies for them, noting also that "the poor always make the best Soldiers." Perhaps this is why Jackson was the chairman of the January 16, 1809, meeting in Nashville. But if the captains hoped he would endorse relief laws, or indeed any economic policy, they were disappointed. Jackson simply said that the people were "burning with indignation and resentment" against both European superpowers. "Attempts have been made to divide the union, such attempts may be made again." During such a crisis, he was sure, the people would reaffirm their attachment to "the federal compact" and declare to the whole world, "United we stand—divided we perish."[81]

The "friends of the people" thus pressed on without Jackson, and the legislature obliged later that year with a stay law for cases involving smaller debts. One lawmaker said that "a large majority" of his constituents wanted such protection from "the fangs of the rude and unmerciful creditor." If the people could feel rage against foreign threats, why should they not show compassion for each other? A Virginia Federalist who had risen from a shoemaker's shop to the state assembly answered these sentiments most directly. He could not "suffer the feelings which [hardship] inspired to govern me," he explained. His duty was instead to "the great and leading principles of justice" whereby contracts were honored and debts were repaid, come what may. For his part, Jackson quietly pressed his many debtors to pay up that year, often with the help of the younger lawyers he now patronized. One of these later spoke of "General Jackson's collecting business." Another reported that too many Kentucky debtors were "secure from the grasp of Justice." Eluding the law in a way that Jackson could never abide, such men were no part of the innocent nation he wanted to avenge.[82]

CHAPTER 5

The Hour of National Vengeance

In November 1811, Andrew Jackson left Nashville to take care of "imperious business" in Natchez. More than twenty years after making his first contacts in that downriver trading center, he learned that one of his newest partners had failed to sell two dozen slaves, leaving them there. So Jackson bought out this partner's share and went to take charge of the chattel workers. Despite his disdain for the "humane persuit" of slave trading, Jackson told Rachel that he would "sell some of them on the way at good prices," whether to whites around Natchez or to those natives who had converted to cotton planting. Unsold slaves would return to the Hermitage, where, Jackson trusted, his wife and overseer would make accommodations. The trip took Jackson through Choctaw land, and thus past the customs house of the US agent to that nation, Silas Dinsmoor.[1]

According to the 1796 Act to Regulate Trade and Intercourse with the Indian Tribes, US citizens south of the Ohio had to obtain a passport before entering treaty-certified native land. They were also supposed to account for any dependents traveling with them. The Jeffersonians had relaxed these rules, not least because subsequent treaties could be read to authorize more travel rights for US citizens. While handing out passports they also pressed native leaders for new road concessions. After 1808, as the effects of the embargo and the ban on the Atlantic slave trade took root, large numbers of Georgia and Carolina slave owners took their chattels along these roads. The inhabitants could plainly see that these planters were coming to stay, and they relayed their concerns to federal Indian agents like Dinsmoor. A high-strung New Englander, he resolved to heed the letter of national law and crack down on all the smugglers and fugitives of the borderlands. In 1811, Dinsmoor detained 25 of the 212 blacks who approached his custom house. On December 10, his deputy refused to let Jackson move on without a passport.[2]

Of course, Jackson objected. He did not need permission to traverse the Choctaw nation, the general told the deputy. The "good Citizens" did not owe anything to the national government; rather, the federal state owed *them* for having imposed a multiracial civil society over their individual commercial rights. The only passport he or any other US citizen required was "an honest face and a good reputation." According to a later version of this encounter, Jackson had pulled back his coat to reveal his pistols, announcing, "*these are General Jackson's passports*!!!" The deputy backed down and the general went on to collect the slaves. Hearing that Dinsmoor was preparing a force of white and Choctaw gunmen to stop him on his return trip, Jackson armed himself and some of the slaves and again stormed past the custom house. Back home at the Hermitage, he could not forget what had happened, raging against Indian agents and swearing revenge on the larger version of law they represented.[3]

"That citizens are to be threatened with chains and confinement for peaceably travelling a road ceded by solemn Treaty" was bad enough, Jackson told the new governor, Willie Blount (William's half-brother). "That the savages and Indian country-men should be assembled to carry these threats into execution is too intolerable to bear." For those citizens, Jackson imagined, handing over a pass triggered uncomfortable comparisons with the slaves that they were transporting, while signaling to those slaves that their owners were not the sovereigns after all. After Dinsmoor stopped a white woman traveling with undocumented blacks the next year, Jackson could bear no more. "[And] *my god*," he wrote to US Senator George Campbell of Tennessee, "is it come to this—are we *free men or are we slaves is this real or is it* a *dream*?" Any regulation on trade or travel was another betrayal of the fundamental rights that "our Citizens" carried because of *who* they were, not *where* they were. "The wrath and indignation of our citizens will sweepe from the earth the invader of their legal rights," he warned, "and involve Silas Dinsmore in the flames of his agency house."[4]

There is little evidence that the people were as outraged about the passport rule as Jackson was. He remained controversial in mid-Tennessee and obscure everywhere else, a tarnished westerner whose extreme views did not align very well with any popular movement or national party. In 1812 as in 1776, however, total war made new heroes and enemies, new timelines and loyalties. In his letter to Campbell, Jackson compared Dinsmoor's detention of the white woman and her slaves to the spring 1812 kidnapping of Tennessee midwife Martha Crawley by Creek militants. He also likened federal "invasions" of Tennessee sovereignty to British outrages on "our rights as an independent people and a nation." At last, Jackson said, the people were ready "to burst forth in Vengeance," becoming the kind of nation to which he could finally commit himself.[5]

INTERESTS, PASSIONS, AND NATIONS

For Jackson, the official declaration of war against Great Britain in June 1812 was unforgivably late. The fighting had started the previous November, just before he set out for Natchez, when a mixed force of militia and US soldiers under Governor William H. Harrison of the Indiana Territory marched on the Shawnee revolutionaries, Tecumseh and Tensketawa. The eastern nations had "vanished before the avarice and oppression of the White Man, as snow before a summer sun," Tecumseh told his distant Creek relations, many of whom were on the brink of famine. Unless the survivors united to expel the invaders, the world would fall. A series of tremendous earthquakes that began along the Mississippi on December 16, 1811, convinced many men that the time had come. Rumors of native hostility moved white families from Georgia to Indiana to "fort up" or flee during the spring and summer of 1812. Most everyone thought that the British were inciting the attacks, which along with their Orders-in-Council and their impressments called for war.[6]

And yet every Federalist in the US House and Senate voted nay, while the governors of three New England states refused to make their militias available for action against Upper or Lower Canada. A Boston paper declared that the region had been dragged into war "without a sense of enmity" against the so-called enemy. True, the British had seized nearly a thousand ships over the previous five years. And yet the ships in question were not lost to their Yankee owners, but taken to Halifax, where admiralty courts decided what goods and sailors could proceed. Once back on the ocean, the ships' captains could continue to Britain, by far the most important market. British governors also granted temporary licenses to bring cargoes to Caribbean or Canadian buyers. So long as New England's ships could leave port—so long as the "Damn-bargo" did not return—they could find profitable holes in the superpowers' blockades. For example, Napoleon relaxed his ban on ships coming from British ports in early 1809, briefly enabling merchants to unload their wares in occupied Amsterdam.[7]

"[The] protection of Commerce," noted the townsfolk of two Federalist strongholds in western Massachusetts, "was a leading object of the National Union." By this they did not mean that the government should wage war to open new markets. Rather, the federal compact obliged the national state to make treaties and build ships, regulating the business that its people did overseas and then protecting the legitimate claims that resulted. From this perspective, the British government was a model to emulate. Even its impressments were justified. New England seaports were filled with native-born sailors, who had nothing to fear from the Royal Navy. So why should Americans wage war "for the protection of English and Irish runaway sailors"? No longer the face of the United States as they had been during the anti-French *rage militaire* of 1798, New England Federalists now described the nation more in terms of how it should function than in how it might feel. They denounced their rivals' "youthful rage" along with the twisted notion of national honor that "thirsts after vengeance, and is appeased only by blood."[8]

Federalists in New York and Pennsylvania were no less unanimous in opposing war in June 1812, but they were quicker to moderate their views once the die was cast. Their more diverse seaports were full of Irish and French immigrants who hated the British ships just offshore and loved the personal freedoms of republican government, the glorious absence of a powerful state. Rising merchants in these ports sought new access to French markets and thus shared the popular anger against the Royal Navy. Mid-Atlantic manufacturers were also politically active. The embargo and nonimportation acts had briefly sheltered their wares from British competition, as did the new ban on British imports enacted by Congress with the declaration of war. They naturally saw this war as a second struggle for independence, a desperate fight to break free of the empire's long shadow.[9]

"New York is indeed a *middle*, but she is also emphatically a *frontier state*," noted a group of dissident Republicans as war broke out. The imperial foe threatened not only from the east, in Manhattan and Long Island, but also from the north and west, along the porous border with Upper Canada. Although vastly outnumbered by their southern neighbors, the Loyalists and Britons of that province had terrifying friends: the Shawnees, Miamis, Sauks, and Ottawas whom American settlers had been displacing for twenty years. Who could imagine that the Crown would stop those warriors from taking revenge on white households? Of course, Federalists in New York and Ohio argued that this awful danger was a good reason *not* to go to war, and the imprint that the national state had left on the region made them credible. Within a context of relative law and order, the Federalist ideal of a protective state within a wider society of nations remained viable.[10]

That ideal faded farther west, where William H. Harrison had been forcing land cessions from Shawnees and Miamis. It collapsed entirely after the Pigeon Roost massacre of September 3, 1812, when a dozen warriors attacked a group of Kentucky families who had crossed the Ohio River a few years earlier. More than twenty whites were killed, including fifteen children. A Lexington paper reported this attack under the heading "Anglo-Savage Affairs." It called Indians "a parcel of vagrants and scoundrels, who ought long since to have been driven entirely from our territories." One militia colonel told the president that the goal should be "to drive the Savages from our limits and destroy all we can find." *Our territories* and *our limits* referred here to wherever Kentucky families had settled, not to the more modest borders of the state. Instead of restraining speculation or offering protection from the enemies it created, Kentucky leaders promised to avenge their people all over the isolated settlements of the Indiana and Illinois Countries.[11]

Tennessee and Georgia were especially militant, for both had large areas of "unextinguished" Indian lands and large numbers of men with pre-emption claims to those lands. The "frontier" was all around: one-third of their counties bordered Indian jurisdictions or sparsely settled territories. In Tennessee these insecure geographies stretched along its southeastern corner and west to the corridor between the Tennessee and Mississippi Rivers, through which Tecumseh had passed to rally the Creeks. Removing all "hunting Indians" and granting the states "uncontrouled jurisdiction" was the only way to avoid the horrors of the 1790s, the new Governor Blount told one Indian agent in 1811. The May 1812 abduction of Martha Crawley and gruesome killing of several settlers near the mouth of the Duck River, just seventy miles west of Nashville, thus unleashed a torrent of hateful memories. Ever since federal treaties had begun protecting your bloodthirsty foes, one Nashville paper told its readers, Indian men had scalped as they pleased, knowing that the law-abiding whites bowed to "the softer emotions of humanity."[12]

Economic crisis worsened tensions throughout the region. Deerskin prices had long been falling along with whitetail populations, leaving Creek hunters to a grim, sedentary fate even before crop failures left them starving. Shut out of the carrying trade that kept New England merchants busy, the white planters of the region struggled to sell what their slaves were harvesting. As the Royal Navy kept a lid on potential markets, cotton prices collapsed below $0.10 per pound in 1811. For those who had spent big on enslaved labor, time was running out. Soon they would have to sell some of their lands and slaves, as Andrew Jackson had in 1804. The cotton bales piling up in New Orleans thus gave militant congressmen from the western states a keen sense of urgency. Led by Henry Clay, the Kentucky champion of domestic manufacturing, these "war-hawks" pushed the president to ask Congress to declare war.[13]

James Madison did so as both a Virginian and an American, and it was ultimately the Old Dominion and the South Atlantic states that gave the key votes and arguments for war. Virginia leaders had supported the embargo after the *Chesapeake* incident just off its shores. They had thought twice when hotheads from New York and Nashville called for vengeance. Experienced in national politics, they knew that war would swell both the federal state and the influence of the northern financiers who held its debt. Conquering Canada would also disrupt the emerging equipoise between slave and free states. But neither the embargo nor subsequent boycotts had worked. Neither the Federalist commitment to the law of nations nor the Jeffersonian goal of peaceful commerce had made the British or French any more respectful. "Let us consider what our government has done—how long it has borne with the repeated injuries," wrote one Virginian in April 1812. "Never before has there been an instance of a nation's bearing so much as we have borne," Jefferson judged that same month. Those who felt pride and indignation at this fact made up "the nation" as he now saw it.[14]

"If a long forbearance under injuries ought ever to be considered a virtue in any Nation," John C. Calhoun wrote on behalf of the House Committee on Foreign Relations, "it is one which peculiarly becomes the United States." His history of forbearance started in 1805, with the tightening of British controls over neutral trade. Georgians counted from 1802, when the federal government had promised to extinguish Indian claims. Ever since they had shown "a forbearance to which there is scarcely a parallel," their governor proclaimed. "Tears of the widows, and orphans of murdered Americans, have flowed in vain," the General Assembly of Ohio reported more vaguely. "[Forbearance] has stepped on the heels of forbearance, till the mind revolts at the thought of a prolonged endurance." The citizens of Lexington spoke of "a patience of Injury unparalleled in history," while those of Charleston described "the patient forbearance of our Government." During the course of "one continued series of insults—one long succession of oppressions," a group of New Yorkers declared, the republic had stayed true to "the established usage of nations." Any "longer forbearance" would reveal the republic as pitiful rather than lawful.[15]

The American forbearance story that came together in 1812 thus gave Republicans a shared and flexible way to imagine the United States. It also put their material motives in a new light. "Our population has been hitherto greatly retarded," Tennessee's delegates had complained to Madison in 1810. The state was not as rich as it could be because Indian and Spanish territories still blocked access to Gulf markets. Commercial access was now a matter of "the first laws of nature—self-preservation." Governor Blount told Jackson that citizens should be able to move through Creek lands "without passports, just as we do thro' our own settlements," a point that the general had already made to Silas Dinsmoor. While mobilizing volunteers in late 1812, Jackson employed a vengeance tale that began in 1794, when Tennesseans had lost their sovereign right to punish their native foes along with their constitutional right to pursue property across native lands. Now they were named by "nature herself" to enjoy free access to "the markets of foreign Nations or the atlantic States." The world according to Jackson was indeed a commercial state of nature, a place where virtuous people had to fight for what they desired.[16]

VOLUNTEERS AND MUTINEERS

"Your government has at last yielded to the impulse of the nation," Jackson had announced to the West Tennessee forces in March 1812. "Your impatience is no longer restrained. The hour of national vengeance is at hand." But peace dragged on, and in May he again had to leave Tennessee on urgent business. Ten years after he had bought eighty-five thousand acres south of Nashville for himself and other creditors of David Allison, Jackson learned that the US district court behind the auction had never had proper jurisdiction over the case. This left Jackson on the hook for all the warranted grants he had sold from those lands along the Duck River, the value of which had grown enormously since 1802. The shrewd lawyer rushed to Georgia and convinced Allison's brothers to transfer full title to him for the mere sum of $500 and a cancellation of outstanding debts. By the time Jackson returned in early June, word of Martha Crawley's abduction along that same river brought a new call to arms.[17]

"This cruel outrage must not go unrevenged," Jackson told the governor. "The assassins of Women and Children must be punishd." He was ready to march southeast to the nearest Creek towns, demand the guilty parties, and then, if refused, "lay their Towns in ashes." The attack hit close to home, and Jackson brought it even closer to those under his command. "He that can see the infant babe of nine days old torn from the arms of its mother and beat to pieces upon the walls of the house," he told them in July, "[he] that can view in the midst of this scene a distracted mother crying in vain for pity, and receiving from the hands of savage monsters stab after stab... He that beholds all this, and yet say no vengeance ought to be taken ... deserves not the name of a *man*." Indeed, "the mother who bore him should point with the finger of scorn, and say, '*He is not my son.*'" Jackson wanted his men to shut their eyes and "behold" their own damnation, to listen to the scorn of mothers and history and God. The lower

Figure 5.1 Andrew Jackson as he wanted to present himself to his volunteers and other soldiers during the War of 1812: angry, dignified, and powerful.
Courtesy of Library of Congress, Prints and Photographs Division, LC-USZ62-59036.

house of the Tennessee assembly duly threatened the Creeks with prompt and utter destruction, but the more cautious Senate tabled the idea.[18]

Desperate for war, Jackson reminded Tennessee readers that "the celebrated expedition against Nick-a-Jack" had been "a secret movement on the part of the people" against federal policy. He sent different letters to newspapers out of state, where people were less likely to know about Nickajack or to see Martha Crawley as family. During a recent trip from Nashville to Natchez, he reported anonymously, he had come upon some Creeks boasting of recent murders. Everyone in their villages hailed the capture of Martha Crawley, except for some older men. Since Indians rarely grew old, Jackson quasi-reasoned, only about one in ten Creeks could possibly qualify as an old man. "It is fair then to conclude that nine-tenths of the Creek Nation are heartily willing to cut our throats if they could." Since the Creek Nation's leaders could not be trusted with the highest forms of sovereignty, US authorities would have to punish the guilty members of their blood. If the Creeks delayed or objected, "the sword must reach them and their nation cease to exist." Jackson also conveyed his more personal motivations: "If I am successful . . . I will be hailed with laurels; if unsuccessful I shall be damned." Victory was the only way to "political salvation."[19]

To take vengeance on the necessary scale, however, Jackson had to convince several thousand men to leave their own families, and this proved difficult in the War of 1812. The administration initially authorized the expansion of the US Army from fewer than seven thousand to some thirty-five thousand men, hoping to attract soldiers with a signing bounty and the promise of a 160-acre land grant for five years of service. But farm hands and day workers could command a higher wage and then buy more land on their own, and their Republican leaders were unable and unwilling to compel them to arms. Even in early 1814, after the government had eased the terms of service, the effective number of regulars on the Canadian frontier was only about eight thousand men. And the War Department's plea for conscription went nowhere in the very House that had charged across the Rubicon two years earlier.[20]

So the government turned to "volunteers": independent companies drawn from militia rolls and commanded by state-level Republicans. These initially served for twelve-month terms, but six-month and even three-month stints would follow. (British authorities thought that new infantrymen needed three *years* of training.) Volunteers received a modest cash bounty and a handsome commission from the United States, but no land. Knowing that it could not pay for more, the War Department asked Tennessee to raise fifteen hundred men. Knowing that he would need more, Jackson aimed for twice that number. A modest number of hyperambitious men had already signed on to "drag [themselves] from obscurity," as the young lawyer Thomas Hart Benton put it. Benton also told Jackson that he could publish a journal of their mission in Tennessee papers. For the most part, though, the general relied on the captains whose demands for debt relief he had recently ignored to enroll some of Tennessee's twenty-nine thousand military-age men for actual service.[21]

The most eager captains rode door to door through their districts, no doubt using their general's frenzied arguments on reluctant husbands and fathers. One captain of the "brave citizen Soldiers" of Maury County, close to the sight of the Duck River attacks, reported that they were ready to "march to the heart of the Creek Nation" and "Teach" the natives "to respect and revere west Tennessee as a fractional part of the United States and revenge their barbarous acts practiced on our fellow mortals." Of the 498 privates in his company, 119 had volunteered. John Coffee, one of Jackson's business partners and most trusted men, mobilized 66 of 300 men on another militia roll into a cavalry troop. Jackson called these mounted men "the choice citizens of our country," a mix of substantial planters, their younger sons, and poorer, unattached men. He rejoiced when the governor and secretary of war ordered him to take these forces south to New Orleans.[22]

"Let it be remembered that the duty of a parent is to chastise and bring to obedience an undutiful child," Jackson told the 2,070 men who at last mustered in Nashville in December 1812. "The Major General has pledged himself to act towards you as a father, and now exhorts you to obedience." Their mission was to secure "the rights and liberties of a great and rising Republic" and redeem "the blood of so many thousand heroes" at the Crescent City, the very center of the American future. And yet he was already hearing complaints. Many men had signed up in response to the Duck River killings, which argued for an overland expedition to the Creek towns, not a longer trip down the Mississippi. Because the Gulf Coast was notoriously sickly, other volunteers wanted to go north, toward "upper Canedy." They were also upset about late pay. Straining at the leash, Jackson convinced the Bank of Nashville to release more funds and urged his men to accept its notes.[23]

They set out on foot and in boats in early January 1813. Frigid winds dimmed the initial "joy" that Benton managed to see on every face. Arriving on the outskirts of Natchez five weeks later, Jackson paused. "I am here without advice orders or directions," he realized. He found "no enemy to face—or anything to do." He did not know if he should proceed to New Orleans, or who would repay him for the supplies he was buying. Meanwhile the administration began to rethink the mission. Unable to move on Montreal because of New England's anti-war stance, Republican leaders had opted to attack Upper Canada at several points. This made more political than military sense, and the first campaigns of 1812 were fiascos. All energies now had to be focused on the northern front, and all pains taken to avoid a southern one. The secretary of war thus ordered Jackson to disband his volunteers and turn over their arms and supplies to General James Wilkinson, a career scoundrel. Jackson surmised that the secretary "must have been drunk" while writing the order and refused to leave his men in such unfaithful hands.[24]

True to his word, Jackson stayed with his men, even walking so that the sick and injured could ride. Veterans of Nickajack may have recalled this grim courage. Besides the name "Old Hickory," though, Jackson had little to show for his hardships. Most of his men wandered back to their farms. Thomas Hart Benton went to Washington in search of cheated glory, inevitably clashing with Jackson over the misbegotten campaign and other "affairs of honor." On September 4, 1813, Jackson and Benton and their well-armed friends came to blows at a Nashville hotel. Benton later swore that Jackson's posse had burst in with weapons drawn, obliging him and his brother to open fire. In the melee, a slug blew Jackson's left shoulder apart. He bled profusely and almost lost the arm. Never one for understatement, Benton called it "the most outrageous affray ever witnessed in a civilized country," not least because a judge was staying at the hotel at the time. "So little are the laws and its ministers respected!" This time, John Overton offered no counsel to his impetuous friend.[25]

As Tennessee's strongmen bickered, the Creek civil war intensified. Tecumseh's call to revolution had mostly resonated among younger men in the Upper Towns just south of Tennessee, where conditions were most dire. They painted their clubs red and renounced anything or anyone corrupted by whites, including the women who took part in the government's "civilization" program. Even worse were the pro-American and mixed-race Creek planters who profited from road cessions and took the lion's share of annual payments from the United States. To secure their standing with white authorities, this emergent elite also had several Red Sticks executed in the name of the "Nation." Red Sticks retaliated on property and on persons, leaving smashed spinning wheels and rotting cattle in their wake.[26]

Nativists rather than Jacobins, the Red Sticks still attracted small numbers of fugitive slaves from Spanish, French, and Anglo-American owners. Such runaways were dreadful reminders of recent upheavals in the Caribbean and of an 1811 rebellion just north of New Orleans. That uprising had ended with the execution of dozens of slaves, whose heads were posted along the roads leading to the city. It had also convinced Francophone sugar planters to join hands once and for all with the United States. Now, the possibility that Creek revivalists and ex-slaves might make common cause with the British gave warfare along the Gulf Coast both a class dimension and a nihilistic ferocity. It briefly united European Americans and their native allies against black and Indian men who had nothing to lose. From Louisiana to Georgia, masters once more saw murderers "in their bosoms," lurking inside their tyrannical homes.[27]

Such fears spiraled out of control after August 30, 1813. On that day, fugitive blacks helped to lead some one thousand Red Sticks to Fort Mims, just north of the border between American Mississippi and Spanish Florida. Built around the home of a Creek cotton planter, it harbored white and Creek families, slaves, and about 120 Mississippi soldiers. All of the defending soldiers died in the attack, along with between 75 and 120 women and children and 100 Red Sticks. Perhaps 100 slaves and Creeks left with the attackers. Then they disappeared from white view, perhaps to re-emerge in search of dozens or hundreds of Martha Crawleys. "The martial sons of Tennessee do well recollect the time when they and their fathers were isolated from the rest of the American family," Rev. Craighead declared in panic-stricken Nashville. "You can remember how many of your individual families have fallen in defense of their altars and firesides." The constant refrain of home invasions and "extensive inland borders" collapsed any sense of distance between the besieged nation and its vulnerable families. During the "fever" that Fort Mims had unleashed, one judge recalled, Tennessee women clamored as loudly as men for bloody deliverance.[28]

The only answer was what Jackson called a "war of destruction." Rather than burn through enemy country and then return home, as Griffith Rutherford and John Sevier had done from the 1770s to the 1790s, he would "drive the Indians and their Allies into the Ocean." He would cross the Tennessee River that had so long halted white avengers and attack the villages and cornfields along the Coosa and Tallapoosa Rivers. If the Spaniards gave the Red Sticks shelter in Pensacola or anywhere else, he would attack those places too. Fort Mims made these radical solutions possible: only then, with terrified refugees pouring over Tennessee's southern borders, did the state declare its own war on the Creeks. "Already do they advance towards your frontier with their scalping knifes unsheathed," Jackson warned in a new call to idled volunteers and fresh recruits. Either the Tennesseans or the Creeks were about to suffer beyond words. Time was also short because other US forces and Georgia militias were also moving in for the kill and the glory.[29]

His left shoulder in a sling, Jackson led his mixed force of white volunteers and militia and Choctaw and Cherokee warriors southeast from Tennessee in the fall of 1813. Actually, Cherokee and Creek guides led the way. The general knew these men as temporary but essential allies in a war for slavery and property, among other things. When some East Tennessee cavalry seized a Cherokee ally's horses and slaves, the general condemned this insult to "the laws of nations and of civil Society." Returning the man's property was a matter of "Justice" as enforced by "the laws of the united States." After destroying the village of the Creek insurgent Bob Cotalla, Jackson learned that one of the refugees and her three children had once belonged to a Choctaw, only to be captured, bought by Cotalla, and then given "for a wife" to Cotalla's "negro fellow." Impressed and worried by Choctaw power, Jackson took care to hold these captives until their original owner could be found. For now, he would do justice to lawful individuals (white or native) while bringing justice to lawless nations (white or native).[30]

As they moved into Creek territory, Jackson's cavalry seized whatever corn they could find and set fire to every field and village. Starving women and children filed into his camp. Many were widows, their hair and faces unadorned as required by Creek mourning rituals. Jackson's new favorite, John Coffee, reported little resistance besides the constant shortage of rations and directions. At times he had "no pilot or even any one that ever had been in the country." In early November, Coffee's men destroyed the town of Tallushatchee and all its defenders. "The enemy fought with savage fury," he reported. "[Not] one asked to be spared." Witnesses found family members burned into indistinguishable piles and surviving infants trying to nurse on their dead mothers' breasts. A week later Jackson's army attacked a Red Stick force near Talladega, killing more than three hundred and losing fewer than twenty. The lopsided casualties suggest that the Red Sticks' supply problem was far worse than invaders'.[31]

By mid-November, the rebel elements of the Creek Nation were crumbling at Jackson's feet. Redemptive glory was in his grasp, a simple matter of marching. Then his men said that they were leaving. They, too, were hungry, and some wondered if their commander had been so eager to attack that he had neglected his supply lines. The volunteers had enlisted on December 10, 1812, and to their minds the twelve-month clock had not stopped during their months of inactivity. So they would leave on December 10, 1813. One surgeon's mate reported that he was "previously engaged in business" and could not stay with the army. Another shrugged that "some occurrences" had "taken place," requiring him to go. As Jackson himself had declared, they were "free born sons of America" who fought as they desired, not passionless conscripts from Europe.[32]

One group of volunteers explained that they had signed on for "an expedition against the Villains who had murdered our fellow citizens at the mouth of Duck River." They wanted to kill Martha Crawley's attackers, not chase national glory to the Gulf Coast or Canada. At "great personal sacrifice," two dozen other troops told Jackson, they had mustered "to chastise our enemies, and avenge the blood of those who had already fallen victim to their cruelty." They had volunteered to punish recent atrocities, not to preemptively seize territory. Having killed and burned enough, they wanted to go home, all the more so because they were "extremely bare of clothing." "They do not like to Volunteer for they know [not] what," one officer discerned. Such were the "local principles" that stood in the way of national victories. Such were the "little spirits," as John Overton later told Jackson, who did not appreciate "the pursuit of fame, wealth, [and] honor."[33]

On December 9, Jackson ordered Coffee to return all deserters "in strings" and to open fire on those who resisted. The general called upon all his powers of intimidation to keep his army together, to convince his men that he would kill them as he had so many others. He used his glare, his uniform, his posture in the saddle. For a day or two he was able to turn the drafted militia against the much-vaunted volunteers, after which fresh volunteers arrived from East Tennessee. But they, too, took a strict reading of their military contracts, and his army melted away. "[We] have now a prospect of ample supplies of provision, and no troops to eat it," Jackson wrote to Rachel on December 14. "I fear the boasted patriotism of the State was a mere buble, that expires, on the approach of an enemy." She sympathized, although she also wondered how her husband could feel so intensely for other families while so often leaving his own.[34]

FIENDS OF THE TALLAPOOSA

Having little faith in the uncoordinated people, the Federalists saw the disasters of 1812 and 1813 as fitting if not deserved. "Where was the protection of the government, when your villages were in flames?" asked New York conservatives. Others decried the wickedness no less than the stupidity of Mr. Madison's war. "If your enemies have acted like savages," one pastor admonished, "take heed that ye do not as they had done." For their part, the Republicans intensified their call for sustained patriotic rage. Along with Fort Mims, the massacre of thirty or more prisoners along the Raisin River near Detroit in January 1813 became the focal point for such feelings. "Remember the Raisin!" was the battle cry of Kentucky volunteers at the Battle of the Thames that October, during which Tecumseh was killed and apparently skinned. Other units preferred "Remember Buffalo!" and "Remember Black Rock!" after those New York towns went up in flames in retaliation for the American burning of York (now Toronto). This was the ultimate speech act of the retaliatory spirit, a positive command to remember nothing but a deed so foul that it had to be punished somewhere, sometime, on someone.[35]

Vengeance became something like a national slogan and policy. After twenty-three British-born American POWs taken along the Niagara frontier were sent to Britain to stand trial for treason, President Madison ordered twenty-three British prisoners held as hostages. Congress authorized as much in the Retaliatory Act of March 1813, prepared in part by the Tennessee senator to whom Jackson had written about annihilating Indian agents along with Indian towns. In May, it ordered an investigation into a British raid on Hampton, Virginia. A newspaper account of the incident targeted those who might not believe that the soldiers of a civilized nation could be guilty of mass looting and gang rape. "Virginian! American!" the article cried. Anyone who was "feelingly alive to their country's wrongs" would commend their very bodies to "a thirst for revenge,"

Figure 5.2 *A Scene on the Frontiers as practised by the "humane" British and their "worthy" allies.* This grotesque image, completed in Philadelphia in 1812, speaks to the hatred and fury that pro-war Republicans felt and promoted.
Courtesy of Library of Congress, Prints and Photographs Division, LC-DIG-ppmsca-31111.

an "irrepressible desire of revenge." *The Barbarities of the Enemy,* a congressional report published in 1814, asked readers to hear "the shrieks of innocent victims of infernal lust at Hampton" and to recall that the rapists—"infatuated blacks" and invading Britons—were still at large with their carnal memories.[36]

As much as he wanted revenge, Andrew Jackson now knew that it was unreliable for long-term and long-distance campaigns. To win his "war of destruction," he needed a more professional army on the British or Canadian mold, not to say the Federalist one. In the early weeks of 1814, he fought two more battles before returning to his forward base to load up on food, clothes, and ammunition. For the first time he welcomed a large body of US regular soldiers: the six hundred men of the Thirty-Ninth Infantry Regiment. Jackson tried to remake his forces in their image and to establish himself as the only Tennessean whose military authority reached beyond Tennessee. He moved to court-martial the commander of the East Tennessee militia for refusing to bring more forces to the front. As new, sixty-day volunteers briefly swelled his total force to over four thousand men, he also tried at least eight others for disorderly conduct and told his commanders to "religiously" punish any insolence.[37]

The adverb is revealing, not only of Jackson's authoritarian impulses but also of the kind of authority to which he increasingly turned in 1813 and 1814. Total war and divine will played dangerously in his mind. With God's help, he told Rachel, he would drive into the heart of the Creek Nation and "slaughter the whole of them." Her pastor in Nashville had just led the call for all-out war; another Presbyterian minister read Coffee's report of Tallushatchee during a special service in Knoxville, blessing the carnage. Jackson leaned on still another Presbyterian pastor to enroll more recruits and on Jesse Denson, a holy man of more mysterious background, to rally his troops in the field. In a sermon given on December 9, 1813, Denson (unsuccessfully) called the volunteers to battle against a "Savage Satanic foe." Their mission was to honor the God of Israel by driving "Joshua like" through the darkness, "to trample down their false prophets . . . and send their superstitious heathenism to the bottomless pit from whence it came." They were called to "Slay them high and thick like Sampson Slew the Philistines," channeling God's will into bursts of violence. Only then would the "serpentine" foe learn "the awful consequences of Shedding the innocent blood of a peaceful Christian."[38]

Denson published a short, inelegant book called *The Chronicles of Andrew* just after the war, and it is fair to suppose that he had tried out some of the passages during the 1813–14 campaign. Jackson was a "mighty man of war" who "sweareth by the eternal God to executive vengeance" on barbarians and "Ethiopians." The fertile plains south of the Tennessee had been promised to his people, much as the fair lands west of the Jordan had been given to the Israelites three thousand years before. And like the Canaanites and Philistines who had stood against God's first nation, the "transgressing heathens" of the Coosa and Tallapoosa were marked for death, down to the last man, woman, and child. Denson noted that "all sexes and sizes" perished during Jackson's assaults. Elsewhere he insisted that the general had taken pity: "[We] consumeth their village with fire, and spareth the women and children." Narrated through the historic books of the Old Testament rather than the modern corpus of Euro-American law, Jackson's war became an epic drama between his genocidal mandates and his merciful gestures.[39]

By late January 1814, Jackson knew about a Red Stick stronghold at the so-called Horseshoe Bend in the Tallapoosa River, some sixty miles from his forward base. This was the new village of Tohopeka, or "wooden fence," just built by insurgent Creeks and now a refuge for nearby towns. This was the target. "[When] I move again I shall soon put an end to the creek war," he told Rachel, "carry into effect the ulterior objects of my government and then return to your arms to live and love together thro life." This time his army would move more deliberately. The awful tension between Jackson's thirst for glory and his need for prudence comes through in his letters home: "all things cautiously prepared . . . my march was slow but cautious." His successes were "providential." As they moved beyond the reach of letters early that spring, Rachel could only pray that "the same God that Led Moses through the wilderness has been and now is Conducting you."[40]

To his men, the general was indeed a "mighty man of war" who inspired more fear than love. Each night he had them form a hollow square of fallen trees around their camp, piled into chest-high "breastworks." At the first sight or sound of warriors he ordered infantry to form firing lines, gunners to load the cannon, and Coffee's white and Indian cavalry to cut off escape routes. He drove his thin body to the limit, getting by on tobacco and coffee and the tantalizing proximity of his ultimate goals. Not even the death of one of his nephews fazed him. "[He] *died* like a *hero* he fell roman like," he told a distraught Rachel. Death was nothing next to the "disgrace," not to mention another year wondering if a war party might burst through the door. So he asked his wife to recover her "usual firmness" and required the same of his troops. On March 14, the general approved the execution of an eighteen-year-old militiaman of "rebelious and obstinate temper of mind." A squad of US soldiers did the job, shooting the young man in front of the startled Tennesseans.[41]

After a grueling march during which their commander did not allow campfires, the bulk of Jackson's men approached Tohopeka on the morning of March 27, 1814. The new town already had a square and several rows of houses. The inhabitants had also built tall breastworks, although they were hoping that the whites would never find this remote place. Archeological evidence suggests that most of the warriors had no rifles, and their ammunition was always scarce. The general had already sent Coffee's men across the Tallapoosa, trapping the thousand or so people on the one-hundred-acre peninsula. Observing the small, elevated spot from a distance of a few hundred yards, Jackson sketched a map and placed his cannon. To his men, Tohopeka probably called to mind Fort Mims, although their commander later described it more like Sodom and Gomorrah.[42]

For two hours, Jackson's cannons and rifles fired at the breastworks. From the other side of the river, Coffee saw many warriors and "all the squaws and Children" running in terror. They had nowhere to go. The Cherokees and Creeks fighting with Jackson crossed the river and set fire to some buildings, intensifying the panic. Around noon, the sound of this fighting moved Jackson to order a charge. "[The] history of warfare furnishes few instances of a more brilliant attack," he reported. Supported by "a most tremendous fire" from his cannons and snipers, his men—led once more by the US regulars—charged into the breastworks. After a short, brutal fight at close range, Jackson's troops methodically shot, stabbed, and beat the defenders to death. The killing went on all afternoon. Many people tried to swim away, but Coffee's men were waiting for them, pouring round after round into the bloody water. One soldier fired no fewer than fifty times, Coffee reported, "and no doubt [did] much execution."[43]

"The *carnage*," Jackson told Rachel, "was *dreadfull*." The peninsula was wrapped in smoke and clogged with bodies, and the river turned red. In both letters and reports, he used a kind of battlefield sublime common to this war. Columns of smoke and puddles of gore were both beautiful and terrifying, "brilliant" signs of destiny and providence working through human events. The general also gave a careful body count: 557 Indian men lay dead in the village, while another 300 people of undetermined age and sex were "sunk and could not be counted." Jackson's men cut off noses as they counted, and some skinned the legs of their victims to form stirrups. The US regulars accounted for 17 of the 32 whites killed and more than half of the 99 injured. Jackson's Cherokee and Creek allies together lost 23 killed and had about 50 injured. Here as throughout the campaign, his men committed their dead to the rivers, fearing that Red Sticks would desecrate any other bodies.[44]

Jackson reported that all but three of their 350 prisoners were women and children. This was of special interest to his childless wife. "Aunt Rachel," as her Nashville neighbors now called her, had never given birth. She and her husband had legal custody of more than a dozen relatives and friends, and in 1809 they had adopted an infant boy, Andrew Jr. In November 1813, Jackson's men had come upon Lyncoya, a Creek infant found near his mother's corpse. (Evidently she had not been spared.) "He is a Savage [but one] that fortune has thrown in my hands," Jackson explained to Rachel. "[As] to his relations [he] is so much like myself [that] I feel an unusual sympathy for him." So he sent the child to the Hermitage, asking Rachel to "treat him like an orphan" and to offer him as a plaything to their white son. "[Tell Andrew Jr.] his sweet papa will be home shortly," he wrote while preparing for holy genocide, "and that he sends him three sweet kisses." He never asked Rachel if she wanted to take a native child into her home.[45]

No such adoptions took place after American battles with British and Canadian forces. No matter how bitter the fighting between the states and the provinces became, neither side thought to eradicate the enemy population. By contrast, the Creek women and children in Jackson's camp were the remnants of a heathen foe he meant to wipe off the earth.

Given the centrality of white women and children in vengeance stories and Cumberland memories, the bodies of these captives were certainly marked. On the other hand, no one imagined that they had taken part in attacks against white households, and most assumed that they could not "contend" for life in battle. To spare them became the last frontier between what Jacksonian avengers said they were and what they said their enemies were. To adopt one was to bring an end to the bloody saga, to consign all the grief and hatred to the master's home.[46]

Also in contrast to the northern theaters, where witnesses and participants quarreled endlessly over who had done what, Jackson was free to narrate the history he had just made. "The fiends of the Tallapoosa will no longer murder our women and children," he told his men one month after Horseshoe Bend. Just weeks ago, these "fiends" had danced around fires, their "infernal orgies" lighting up the dark woods. They had boasted of their invisibility, mocking God's all-seeing justice. And then, after enduring "*twenty years*" of insolence and abuse, the avengers brought fire. "The retaliatory vengeance with which we threatened them, has been inflicted," earth and water now "lighted up" by their burning villages. "[We have] seen them flying from the flames of their own dwellings," he recounted. "We have seen the ravens and the vultures preying upon the carcases of the unburied slain." Now, the Creeks "must be made to atone . . . by still farther suffering," so that their evil hopes could be "driven from their last refuge." It was a pity that the way to peace was strewn with smouldering towns and starving families. But it was not for them to decide, for "it is in the dispensations of that providence which inflicts partial evil, to produce general good."[47]

Jackson's victory at Horseshoe Bend made him a household name in all those states, regions, and territories where Indian attack felt like an imminent threat. His name was now tied to their most vivid nightmares and shocking desires. "The BLOOD of our citizens cry loud for VENGEANCE," a St. Louis paper bayed in May, after reporting that a white man's body had been found floating down the Missouri. "The general cry is let the north as well as the south be JACKSONISED!!!" When a vacancy in the officer corps opened in the early summer of 1814, the secretary of war also named Jackson a major general in the US Army: one of eight generalships issued in 1814, only two of which went to men coming from outside the regular army. All at once, the Cumberland strongman and Tennessee "blackguard" was an American general, a servant once again of the United States rather than of any mere state. Jackson took this as further evidence that he could act on the "ulterior" motives of the government, speaking for his nation while destroying those in its way.[48]

First he had to muscle out his senior officer, General Thomas Pinckney, and the meddlesome US Indian agent to the Creeks, Benjamin Hawkins. Pinckney was in Charleston, so easy to ignore; Hawkins had many native and federal supporters, but no army. Thus, it was Jackson who summoned the mostly pro-American Creek leaders to his new command center in early August 1814 to listen to a treaty that has no parallel in early US diplomacy. In lieu of the conventional platitudes, this Treaty of Fort Jackson began with a vengeance story: "Whereas an unprovoked, inhuman, and sanguinary war" had been waged by hostile Creeks against American homes, the United States would now issue its demands. It named "more than two-thirds" of Creek warriors and chiefs guilty, announced the cession of more than half their nation, and established an unlimited right to build roads, forts, and trading houses in what remained. The terms were so harsh that the Senate left it on the table throughout the year, while Hawkins resigned in protest.[49]

The goal behind such measures, Jackson now explained to national officials, was to turn southeastern North America into a vast domain of "wealthy inhabitants unmixed by Indians," a US frontier rather than a multinational borderland. He had wanted this for twenty years, and the long, bitter wait gave his actions an internal coherence that startled everyone else. Suddenly he turned on the long-friendly Chickasaws and Choctaws, noting that they had failed to keep America's enemies from passing through and thus forfeited any right to hold any land within the United States. For the moment he wanted the Chickasaw land between the Tennessee and Mississippi Rivers, as well as the Cherokee territory separating Tennessee from Georgia. He felt merciful for not taking further vengeance and angrily dismissed the stunned protests of his Creek allies. Betrayed and dejected, one refused to take part in running the new boundary lines: "I will sit still and hold down my head."[50]

The Treaty of Fort Jackson promised that the United States would feed the famine-stricken Creeks, and Jackson directed that the women and children in his camp receive food and clothing. Most of the native captives were turned over to Cherokee and Creek allies. A few probably ended up in white slave markets, sold away as exotic-looking "mulattoes." Jackson also saw to it that fugitive blacks were returned to their owners. "I intend putting the women in the citchen, the husband in the field," he told Rachel of other slaves who had fallen into his hands. And when he could not bring slaves to their master, Jackson auctioned them, with the proceeds marked for the widows and children of his fallen troops. As the Creek Nation was burned and liquidated, white households would be

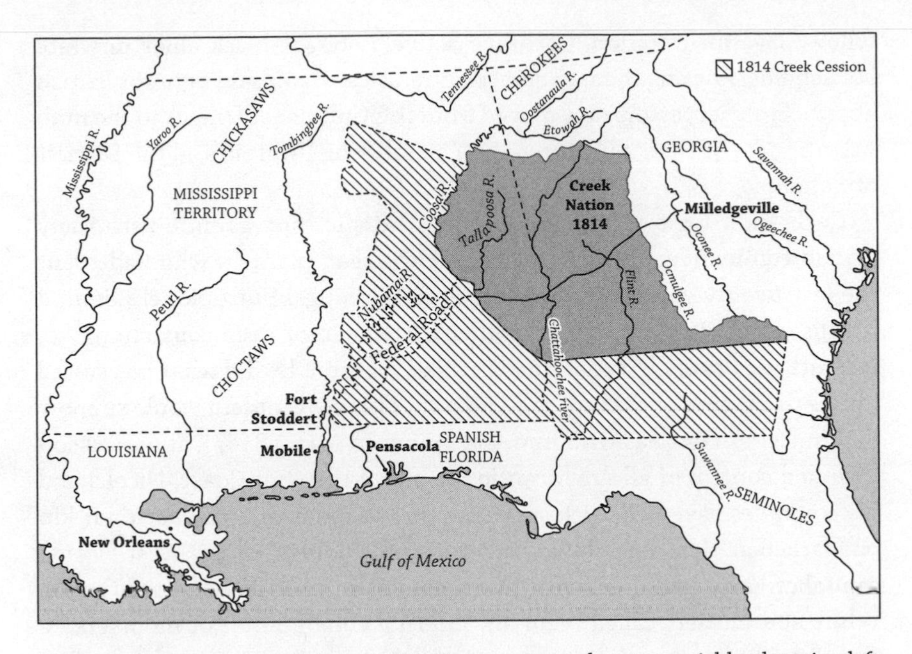

Figure 5.3 Treaty of Fort Jackson, 1814. This massive and controversial land cession left the Creeks surrounded by hostile American states and opened the rich cotton lands of Alabama and southern Georgia to white settlers and speculators.
From Kathryn Braund, "Summer 1814: The Treaty of Ft. Jackson Ends the Creek War," at https://www.nps.gov/articles/treaty-of-fort-jackson.htm.

protected and reconstituted, their nation free at last to spread over the bloody lands.[51]

NATURAL LAW AND PERFECT SAFETY

Just as Jackson emerged as the face of American vengeance, the United States faced a new degree of imperial retribution. Upper Canadian leaders had long cited their "forbearance" in the face of southern aggression, and after American troops burned towns on the Niagara Peninsula and the north shore of Lake Erie in late 1813 and early 1814, they called for "a full measure of retaliation" to recall the United States to "that system of warfare which ought to subsist between enlightened and civilized nations." The new commander of the Royal Navy in the North American theater, Sir Alexander Cochrane, was eager to oblige, not least because his brother had been killed at Yorktown. He ordered his commanders to "lay waste" to the mid-Atlantic coast for what had happened along the Great Lakes. And while his predecessors had worried about the "atrocities" that might follow slave insurrection, Cochrane actively sought black allies in white households, inviting them to quit the tyrannical states and fight for British liberty. Frontier terrors now moved from the Gulf Coast fringes to the mid-Atlantic core of the republican nation, paralyzing Virginia and the District of Columbia.[52]

Cochrane's logic was punitive and strategic, not abolitionist. Many British commanders were themselves Caribbean planters who had spent the last twenty years stamping out slave uprisings. But Colonel Edmund Nicolls of the Royal Marines, another Ulsterman of deep conviction, was violently dedicated to racial equality. Like Jackson, he did what he wanted on the far reaches of the war, convinced that his government would support him and that God was with him. Beginning in May 1814, just as Jackson assumed control of all American forces along the Gulf Coast, Nicolls and his comrades gave Red Stick survivors the weapons and powder their kin had lacked at Horseshoe Bend. They also took control of the West Florida capital of Pensacola, calling for race revolution in the name of the Crown. White southerners called them an "infernal combination of monsters," a "horde of Indian and Negro assassins," a "renegado and motley crew" of races and nations.[53]

"Does the law of nations, or the policy of the republic, forbid us to go there and bayonet these villains?" asked Thomas Hart Benton about the Indian rebels in West Florida. On this, at least, he and Jackson heartily agreed. For years the general had warned about the weak masters and impertinent slaves of the Gulf Coast, and Nicolls's proclamation of July 1814 convinced him that the empire's ultimate goal was "exciting the black population to insurrection and massacre." For the next three months he focused on the strip of coast between Mobile and Pensacola. When Nicolls was badly injured in one engagement, Jackson chortled that Americans would hear no more emancipation proclamations from "the Colonel." He also threatened the governor of West Florida, Mateo Gonzáles Manrique, with a "day of retribution" if Spanish authorities did not deliver up the "Matricidal band" in their midst. Incensed by Spanish claims to piety, Jackson countered that "*Our* Christianity" did not counsel forgiveness for a "murderous rebellious barbarous Banditti." The United States followed another coda: "An Eye for an Eye, Toothe for Toothe, and Scalp for Scalp." A subsequent letter also cited the law of nations.[54]

In early November Jackson brushed aside concerns about another war with another European power and seized Pensacola. Red Stick and black fighters fled east, while resident slave owners greeted him as a liberator. Just as Jackson restored his kind of law and order to this Spanish port, though, the administration received word of a British invasion force massing in Jamaica. The new secretary of war, James Monroe, shared Jackson's fear of revolutionary abolitionism, not least because he had served as governor of Virginia during an 1800 rising. But like every American leader, he saw New Orleans as the key to everything. Monroe thus ordered the general to leave Pensacola and protect the Crescent City. Jackson arrived there at the beginning of December, determined to stop the British and to punish the spies, traitors, and "hellish banditti" he saw all around.[55]

Unfamiliar with the terrain, the British moved slowly across the swamps and lakes between their landing point and their target. This gave Jackson time to study possible approaches, drawing in part on the expertise of the region's many pirates. He prepared a defensive line south of New Orleans, between the river and a swamp. On December 16, he declared martial law in the jittery metropolis, ruling its diverse population as he would an army camp. Four days later, dozens of flatboats cruised in from the north, bringing some 1,500 Tennessee militiamen under the able command of William Carroll. About 2,500 Kentuckians turned up on January 3, although many had no weapons. Louisiana's militiamen, for their part, had become a potent force since the 1811 slave rebellion, and as of January 8, 1815—the four-year anniversary of the insurrection—they made up another 1,000 of Jackson's total force of 5,200 militia, regulars, dragoons, free blacks, and newly patriotic pirates.[56]

One British officer felt an "evil foreboding" when the artillery opened fire just before dawn. Some of his comrades made a flanking maneuver over the Mississippi, routing the Kentuckians and exposing Jackson's flank. But the British commander, Edward Pakenham, sent the bulk of his troops over the wet, open ground in front of the "Jackson Line," at the center of which a single American flag was flying. First the cannons opened fire, followed by the rifles, and finally by the muskets. Carroll's Tennesseans stood four deep behind the solid wall of mud and wood, one man shooting and the rest reloading. A Kentuckian recalled his officer yelling, "Remember the Raisin!" as his unit blasted away, taking revenge two years and a thousand miles from the scene of that crime. Proud and disciplined, the redcoats trudged into the withering fire, and when the smoke and fog cleared, their bodies were spread over the fields of Chalmette. Among them was Pakenham, who had ridden into the abattoir to salvage one more victory. Around noon Jackson agreed to a ceasefire so that the British could dump their dead into a mass grave.[57]

The Battle of New Orleans gave Jackson all the glory he had ever wanted. The incredible body counts—some nine hundred British killed or mortally wounded, against just thirteen dead Americans—convinced a broad mass of people that God had directly intervened to save his most favored nation. The widespread belief that the British had planned to rape the women of the city fortified the dramatic link between Jackson's killing power and their physical safety. In any case, the general had given Americans the clean victory they so desperately wanted in the waning months of this harrowing conflict. Having at last defeated Napoleon, British leaders were content to fix a northern limit on the dangerous republic, forsaking their black and native allies and calling the war a draw. The debacle at New Orleans convinced them to honor the Treaty of Ghent much more quickly than they had the Treaty of Paris. All at once, Americans were safe from their nightmares, and they thanked Jackson for it.[58]

And yet the return of peace also meant a reassertion of laws he could not make. Jackson did not lift martial law until March 13, on guard as he always was against the "lurking traitor." He was floored when a US district judge whom he had detained promptly charged him for contempt of court and heartened when adoring locals offered to pay some of his $1,000 fine. Give it to war orphans and children, Jackson advised. Later that year he stormed to Washington and shut down any talk of further charges, but national leaders continued to act as though Indian nations were sovereign entities. In March 1816, the government all but apologized to the Cherokee for Jackson's "treaty" of 1814, assuring them that their southeastern borders were secure from American reprisals on the Creeks. The perennial cabinet member William H. Crawford then scolded Jackson for rushing surveys of the conquered land. Tennesseans had served well during the war, Crawford noted, so he hoped that they would not "forfeit their claim to the respect of the government by a different course of conduct in time of peace." Its *claim* to *respect*? Jackson pressed on for new land cessions in 1816 and 1818, clearing central and western Tennessee of Chickasaw claims. Still, a wide band of Indian country remained between the older settlements of Georgia and Tennessee and the new Gulf Coast lands.[59]

Worse, Florida was still Spanish, and no demographic force or political consensus was ready to change that fact. Southern migrants were headed west, not south. The few and poor settlers on the Georgia–Florida frontier complained about Indian cattle thieves, but they had little influence with state or national officials. Taking Florida would displease northern congressmen, the administration knew, especially since their hopes for adding the Canadas as nonslave states were now gone. Any invasion was sure to provoke the restored monarchies of Europe, and the United States was in no shape for another war. As for the Chickasaw lands that still separated central Tennessee from central Mississippi, Crawford deemed them "no great inconvenience." Seizing them would be an "act of injustice," as well as an unwise provocation. "In an enlightened nation," Crawford lectured Jackson in June 1816, "submission to the laws is the fundamental principle upon which the social compact must rest."[60]

Convinced that Crawford's idea of the rule of law would jeopardize the nation that now loved him, Jackson also waged his own war against the "*Land Pirates*" of Florida. To do so he relied on two key figures in the US military and government. In the army, that was Edmund P. Gaines, a young Virginian who had arrested Aaron Burr back in 1807. He was promoted to brigadier general after the 1814 siege of Fort Erie, during which large numbers of British troops blew up along with a powder magazine (a "*majestically* splendid and terrible" explosion, Gaines wrote). He seems to have quarreled with every superior except Jackson. The two men agreed that their primary target was the so-called Negro Fort that Nicolls and the British marines had built. Sitting on a tall bluff over the Apalachicola River, this fort was now manned by well-trained black regulars. They guarded a huge cache of weapons and several hundred people who farmed nearby. Jackson ordered Gaines to "destroy it and restore the stolen negroes and property to their rightful owners." To his mind, black fighters could never be lawful soldiers, and it was safer to suppose them "stolen" than to admit that they fought for freedom or vengeance.[61]

The first step was to build a fort just over the Spanish border, directly north of the target. Such a facility could only be supplied by gunboats ascending the Apalachicola, and the black soldiers would surely fire on any American vessel. In July 1816, Gaines led a force of US regulars and Creek allies south by land, while gunboats approached from the Gulf. Early in the morning of July 25, with Gaines's troops already besieging the fort, these boats took and returned fire. Moments later the powder magazine went up in a blast that spread burning flesh over distant trees. An official report would conclude that a heated shell from one of the boats had landed inside the magazine, an incredible shot. Perhaps the shell ricocheted off nearby trees and ignited some cartridges, which in turn detonated the magazine. Or perhaps Gaines had found another way to destroy another fort. In any case, Jackson's black enemies fell victim to their surplus of ammunition in 1816, while his native opponents had been doomed by their want of it in 1814.[62]

Survivors again fled east, joining Red Stick refugees among the Seminole villages near the Flint and Suwanee Rivers. Jackson and his lieutenants would not let them go. "You harbor a great many of my black people" at Suwanee, Gaines told the resident headman, King Hatchy. Let me pass through to capture them and all the murderers among your people, Gaines declared, "and I will shew them my law." No, Hatchy replied. When another chief told Gaines to keep his men on the west side of the Flint after soldiers crossed to gather wood, Gaines sent a force of mounted men to arrest him. The troops burned some of the town and shot several people trying to escape; one of them, Gaines told Jackson with "deep regret," was a woman. A large war party then attacked an American ship near the remains of Negro Fort in late November 1817, killing or capturing forty soldiers and six women. This latest attack, Gaines told Jackson, "place[s] our troops strictly within the pale of natural law," liberating them from any other command. In late December the War Department summoned Jackson to take over for Gaines along the Florida frontier, wrongly assuming that the major general would heed national, as well as natural, law.[63]

Now Jackson turned to his other ally at the national level, James Monroe. This Republican stalwart had begun the War of 1812 hoping to "open our ports *and trade and fight, and fight and trade*." He ended it by proposing huge citizen-armies to overrun Lower Canada, the New Englanders be damned. The two men had always understood each other. "Permit me to remark," Jackson wrote to Monroe in early January 1818, "that the arms of the United States must be carried to any point within the limits of East Florida, where an Enemy is permitted or protected." That included the interiors of the four Spanish forts, heretofore off-limits, along with the mouths of every river that reached back into the Union. Jackson offered to do the job "without implicating the Government." Historians long wondered whether Monroe ever replied; the scholar Daniel Feller has recently shown that Jackson did receive a high-value letter on the matter, which the general asked Rachel to "preserve with care" in anticipation of future controversy.[64]

Jackson quickly amassed a force of some five hundred US regulars, one thousand militia or volunteers, and eighteen hundred allied Creeks. They streamed into Fort Scott in February and March 1818, their ears ringing with new details of murdered families and captive women. First they moved south, past the remains of Negro Fort, then east through the towns that had been blocking US soldiers and slave hunters. Burning as they went, they continued east to St. Marks, and then 100 miles farther to the black and Seminole villages along the Suwanee. A Georgia volunteer recalled the campaign as a cold, hungry trudge through eerie woods and wetlands. All was quiet, deserted, destroyed. On the few occasions when native or black fighters were sighted, the "Tennessee horse men" rode them down. In mid-April, their commander ordered them to turn around and march back west, for this was a man-hunt no less than an invasion.[65]

Jackson's ultimate targets were the Red Stick "prophets" and British incendiaries who had succeeded Colonel Nicolls. "As long as *they* live," the general had told the Creeks, "they will try again to bring you into war, and destroy the remnant of your people." Chief among these were Alexander Arbuthnot, a sixty-eight-year-old Scot and Bahamian merchant who sold goods out of St. Marks. He had foolishly written to Gaines in early 1817, pleading the cause of the "infortunate Indian" against the relentless Americans. The other was Robert C. Ambrister, the twenty-one-year-old son of a Loyalist refugee. He had served in the Royal Navy before joining Colonel Nicolls in Florida. Thereafter he visited the Negro Fort refugees and their Seminole hosts, telling Arbuthnot's son that he would see justice done and "the negroes righted." This was a dangerous way to get back at the rebel slave holders who had betrayed their king and his father.[66]

Jackson had Hillis Hadjo and another Red Stick leader executed right away. At the end of April, he tried Arbuthnot and Ambrister in what surely qualifies as one of the strangest trials in American history, no small feat. Since they posed no threat to the angry troops all around them, the two prisoners could not very well be killed in the "heat" of battle or the midst of flight. But they also stood alone in a Florida wilderness that no European nation had effectively claimed, in the half-light of a war that no European nation had officially declared. At the general's headquarters in a pine forest outside of St. Marks, Jackson's sense of justice *was* the rule of law, although he still tried to make the distinction. He directed Gaines to organize a "special court" for the two Britons, made up of Gaines and a panel of officers. Arbuthnot denied the charges and asked for counsel, presumably with a straight face. He was sentenced to death.[67]

Ambrister pled guilty to leading Indian warriors against Jackson's army but not to exciting "the negroes and Indians" more generally. He then threw himself at the mercy of the special court. After first sentencing him to death, the officers settled on fifty lashes and a year's hard labor. Only then did Jackson intervene. "It is in an established principle of the laws of nations," the general intoned, "that any individual of a nation making war against the citizens of any other nation, they being at peace, forfeits his allegiance, and becomes an outlaw and pirate." The enormity of the crime was the only issue: Ambrister had waged war on American households. He could not be allowed to go on living or to return to British soil with his own version of events. At Jackson's orders, then, Arbuthnot was hanged (with genteel stoicism, it is said), while Ambrister was shot (dying "more like a woman than a man"). A few days later, Jackson wrote that this would serve as an "awful example" that "certain, if slow retribution" awaited the "unchristian wretches" who spilled American blood. He told Rachel that he had taken the "Just Vengeance of heaven" and destroyed "the babylon of the South."[68]

Seven years of war had made the fifty-one-year-old Jackson an old man. His tall frame was now skeletal, his weeping wounds sapped his energy, and he was coughing blood. Now the killing was finished, or so he thought. But in May he learned that some Georgia militiamen, seeking revenge for a frontier murder, had fallen upon a Chehaw village whose warriors were then guiding Jackson's army. The young men returned to find older men and women dead, houses burned, and livestock gone. Once more Jackson lashed out at such dark reflections of himself, calling the militia captain "a cowardly monster in human shape." Where was this *brave* band of murderers, he demanded of Georgia's governor, when Chehaw men had marched against those who held "the *bleeding scalps* of *your citizens*?" No governor of any state had the right to wage war "whilst I am in the field." Swearing as always to punish the guilty, Jackson told the Chehaws not to "attempt to take any satisfaction themselves," bearing patiently until "their father, the president of the U. States," did them justice.[69]

A GREAT NATIONAL QUESTION

President Monroe's cabinet members now saw Jackson as a threat. The secretary of war, John C. Calhoun, was trying to strengthen the US armed forces and had little patience for loose cannons who defied the chain of command. The secretary of the treasury, William H. Crawford, had already tired of Jackson's insubordination and probably resented the general's harsh words for his home state of Georgia, not to mention Jackson's preference for Monroe as president in 1816. Crawford had almost secured the caucus nomination that year and was determined to have the highest office one way or another. Wily and domineering, Crawford saw a dangerous new rival emerging from the deep southern frontiers. As for the secretary of state, John Quincy Adams, he had already heard outraged protests from his British, Spanish, and French counterparts before the cabinet met to discuss the invasion on July 15, 1818. Another generation removed than his father from Puritan doctrines of original sin, the younger Adams understood history as both collective progress through secular time and individual reconciliation with a benevolent God. He saw slavery as a violation of the natural rights that civil society was supposed to advance. He deplored the cruelties of war and called the violence in Florida "unexpected" if not unauthorized.[70]

Like his father, though, Adams had always resented Great Britain in ways that other New England Federalists did not. He had renounced the party after the *Chesapeake* incident revealed its degrading tolerance for the "British piratical Law of Nations." He thus admired Jackson's service to the emotional "nation" that had taken form during the long struggle with the empire. Adams also knew that anyone who crossed Jackson would "encounter the shock of his popularity," which the Florida invasion had intensified in many circles. *Niles' Weekly Register*, a major paper out of Baltimore, ran a summer 1818 series on "Indian War" that used Jackson's own reports to prove that the villages he burned were guilty, bleeding places. *The Tragical Death of Darius Barber*, published that year in Boston, immortalized a Georgia woman who had watched Indian men murder her sleeping family and then survived weeks in the Florida wilderness. She escaped after dispatching her captor with the same hatchet that had been stained by her children's blood. "It may be a gratification to the reader," the narrative commented, "to learn that the said tribe of SAVAGES have since been exterminated by the brave and intrepid GENERAL JACKSON."[71]

That November, then, Adams crafted a defense both of Jackson and of national vengeance. "The task is of the highest order," the dutiful New Englander confided. "[M]ay I not be found inferior to it!" First and foremost, he described Florida as what we now call a failed state. The Spanish did not control its native population as required by both the general or "necessary" law of nations and the explicit terms of the 1795 Treaty of San Lorenzo. As a result, the peninsula had drawn the very dregs of humanity. His anti-slavery hopes swept away by his patriotic fury, Adams condemned the Negro Fort as "a receptacle for fugitive slaves and malefactors." He echoed Jackson in calling it a "nuisance," a malignant spot that could be removed in the name of public safety. Even after the fort's immolation, though, Florida paid host to a "mingled horde of lawless Indians and negroes." Mixed and motley in one of Adams's sentences, this "horde" or "banditti" was single-minded and determined in the next, united in a "savage, servile, exterminating war against the United States."[72]

Adams hung vague but vivid generalities on neat and simple chronologies, inviting the reader to see dark, usually British intentions behind every atrocity. "No sooner" did Arbuthnot arrive in 1817 than "the peaceful inhabitants" of the Georgia frontier faced "all the horrors of savage war." He gave graphic details, taken from official reports yet eerily similar to Old

Testament narrations. When Seminoles found a few children on Lieutenant Scott's boat in late 1817, he reported, they dashed their brains out against the vessel. One sailor was covered in tar and burned alive. A three-year-old Georgian had his scalp taken along with his life; not even his two-month-old sibling was spared. Jackson had put an end to all the deviltry, acting from motives "written in every page of the law of nations, as well as in the first law of nature—self-defense." He had shown "the purest patriotism," a willingness to obey natural law and enforce natural rights against those who hungered for American blood, hair, and skin.[73]

Jackson's conduct in Florida came before Congress just after Adams wrote his vindication, when a House committee criticized the execution of the two Britons. "Whenever severity is not an absolute necessity," the report copied from Vattel, "mercy becomes a duty." The general had departed from "that clemency, of which the United States has heretofore so justly boasted." Richard M. Johnson, the Kentucky war-hawk who had supposedly killed Tecumseh, loudly objected to any such criticism of Andrew Jackson. Thomas W. Cobb, a young Georgian and Crawford supporter, countered by demanding a further exposé of the general's misdeeds. A Mississippian then jumped in, defending the man who had just created his state and warning Congress not to "forget the wrongs inflicted on us by foreign nations." The longest debate in congressional history up to that point ensued. Closely followed by audiences in the galleries and readers around the republic, this referendum on whether Jackson had served or disgraced his people became, as one participant put it, a "great national question" about America's place in the world, in history, and in the eyes of other nations and of God.[74]

Several dozen congressmen recoiled from the general's "desolating vengeance." Among them were the remnants of the Federalist Party, now discredited by their opposition to the war. Adams also identified "the high sticklers for State rights" as Jackson foes, including "all Virginia." In fact, four of the eight Virginians who spoke condemned Jackson, always in constitutional terms and once for his "degradation of State authorities." For "old Republican" purists he was federal power incarnate, a high-handed warmonger with no regard for old states and charter liberties. But most of the anti-Jackson arguments of 1819 were voiced by young delegates who saw themselves as the new nationalists of a postcolonial, postfrontier America. Retaliation was "an attribute of sovereignty" that the nation alone could invoke, they argued. It was something "placed upon the nation," authorized by its highest representatives during the most pressing emergencies. Hence the Retaliation Act of 1813. With war over—or at least not declared—such suspensions of the rule of law lost their cover, casting doubt on everything Jackson, Gaines, and even Monroe had done since 1815.[75]

Whereas Adams had focused on the killings on board Lieutenant Scott's boat in late 1817, these critics wanted to know why his vessel was there in the first place, fifty miles south of the border. Others asked about the Negro Fort. Why had American military personnel destroyed a target deep inside lands that were technically Spanish and effectively Seminole but certainly not American? And even if Jackson had been justified to seize the forts in 1818, how could he execute British nationals as "outlaws"? That term referred to those who had forsaken the protections and risked the vengeance of *their* sovereign. It was not for the republic, still less for one of its servants, to punish foreign nationals on foreign soil.[76]

Whereas Adams had described the natives of Florida as "prowling" and "stalking," the Seminoles and Creeks in these speeches were "wretched," "miserable," and "beggarly." They no longer threatened the republic and so had a right to live somewhere. A war-hawk in 1812, Henry Clay did not want to hear any more about how various prophets had deceived and incited the Indians. "They were *their* prophets—the Indians believed and venerated them, and it is not for us to dictate a religious belief to them." He was especially shocked by the execution of Hillis Hadjo. The only justification for capital punishment was to deter crimes among those who lived under the same laws, much like the only rationale for retaliation was to recall combatants to the rules of war. Because the natives were not subject to American jurisdiction, putting them to death was a matter of cold-blooded murder, of pure revenge. The brutal logic of *lex talionis* seemed all the more backward now that enlightened laws had renounced ancient notions of "corrupted" blood.[77]

The working assumption behind these arguments was that the world was properly divided into political territories, each of which regulated the natural liberties of the people living in and beyond their borders. "Indian country" was still a part of the maps they projected onto North America. Expansionist or not, they assumed that the nation's laws would have to precede or accompany its migratory citizens, organizing a civil society for any state or territory calling itself American. The union was a national society within a larger society of nations, and its respect for civilized norms was one reason it was special—or, perhaps, one reason it *had* been special. "In one day has the fair character of this nation been blasted!" yelled Cobb of Georgia. The watching world would now say, "boast no more—you are not less cruel than other nations." Less despairing, a young Federalist from Virginia argued that national glory was "more comprehensive" than military honor. It was best advanced "in refusing to wage war for revenge" and promoting "the wide diffusion of [the people's] happiness" under conditions of peace. Glory belonged to those nations that advanced their own well-being and the wider work of civilization, not to those that would "replunge the world in barbarism" to get back at those they hated.[78]

Although we live "beyond the control of the policy or force of Europe," Joseph Hopkinson of Pennsylvania admonished, "let us not forget that we belong to the family of enlightened nations" and to the march of progress that had fostered it. The son of an eccentric Federalist who once warned that the rule of law could turn men into cowards, Hopkinson had no illusions about social contracts. Europeans, he noted, entrusted some of their sovereignty to their governments because they were surrounded by other sovereigns, not because they were intrinsically moral. By contrast, Americans could do as they wanted with their weak neighbors. "This, sir, is a trying and a tempting situation!" Now that it had established self-government within its own borders, the republic was called to do the same in the international realm, honoring "those rules of conduct which the experience and wisdom of ages have established." It was America's duty and glory to show that law mattered more than force, even for an unbound Prometheus within a New World garden.[79]

Jackson took his support from the broad ranks of Republicans, and his defenders on the House floor came from Pennsylvania and New York, as well as Kentucky and Mississippi. They were just as likely as his critics to refer to the law of nations, with one citing Vattel more than twenty times. They echoed John Quincy Adams: Florida was derelict; the Indians and slaves were monsters; the British meddlers were "beyond the protection of civilized society." Hillis Hadjo was "a prophet, the crucifix of whose religion is the tomahawk and the scalping knife; the libations to whose worship is the blood of the white man." Others kept up the theme of "extraordinary forbearance," recounting how the government had meekly endured the worst abuses until "the nation rose in the majesty of its strength, and hurled destruction upon the foe!" Above all, they invoked the lawfulness of vengeance within a savage world. "Are we alone, of all the nations of the world, forbidden to deprive a cruel and perfidious enemy of the means of injuring us in the future?" demanded one Virginian.[80]

Look at the remains that Jackson had found in Seminole villages, the New York delegate James Tallmadge begged of the general's critics. Just a month before he provoked a sectional crisis over the admission of Missouri, Tallmadge went to full nationalist boil. "Sir, you are an American! Go, count the bleeding scalps of your murdered countrymen, of all ages and sexes . . . and then return, and tell to this House if this Seminole war was, on the part of your country, an offensive war!" The willingness to weep and rage at the awful fate of distant Americans was the fundamental duty of all Americans, the crucial quality that made them something more than a political union of self-interested persons and semiautonomous states. John Holmes of Maine dramatically spoke as a murdered woman from the southern frontiers: "the midnight yell was heard . . . the doors were forced," and her husband and children were "mangled and murdered" before she was burned alive. Now, from heaven, she watched representatives of her own nation make excuses for her killers. "Go tell the advocates of false humanity," the congressman concluded, "that there is an avenging God . . . that duty and policy demand that you should punish, with instant death, every instigator of Indian barbarity, wherever he may be, and whenever he may be found."[81]

For the Jacksonians of 1819, the American people were part of an epic drama, not a historical process. Because their households were in constant danger, they lived in emergency rather than ordinary time, and could transcend the law they meant to impose. The nation was more like a frontier home than a secure society, a "scene of slaughtered innocence" whose victims made up "a family group . . . almost a national group." Vengeance was a male duty, not a youthful sin. Especially on behalf of distant Americans rather than family or friends, it was indeed a civic duty, a bloody remaking of the "liberality" that the framers had once invoked. Instead of worrying about how civilized they appeared to polite and commercial nations, the general's followers argued, Americans should focus on instilling fear in savage ones. They had to convince their most depraved foes that anyone who harmed an American, anywhere, would suffer "instant death." They had to follow that "great and fundamental principle, that 'the safety of the people is the supreme law.'" That such thinking took hold *after* the young republic's years of greatest peril is further evidence that ideologies have their own logics.[82]

As grim as the world might sound in their speeches, however, these first Jacksonians did not despair. National vengeance was a glorious commandment to a people whose shared history was "written in characters of blood along your whole southern frontier," a tearful fellowship of love and hate. Justice would be done in this life rather than the next—not by law, or even by God, but by the United States. It was up to the republic to deliver his "dispensations," for only Americans retained the sovereign power to punish their foes along with a legacy of forbearance to authorize their wrath. As Romantic as it was Calvinist, this version of American nationhood imagined the people as the suffering Jesus while also empowering them to act like his grieving father. It pictured them as inherently innocent rather than conditionally lawful, entirely blameless "on all occasions, without a single exception to the contrary." And it named Jackson the man "appointed by Heaven to tread the wine press of Almighty wrath," to become justice rather than pray for it.[83]

The general returned to Washington in the middle of the debates in January 1819, more convinced than ever that the people understood him as no person ever had. He gathered rumors about what was happening inside Congress, trying as always to divide the world between friend and foe, good and evil. He also bought a young girl named Sally, a gift for Rachel. Three days after the House exonerated him in early February he left for a tour of the eastern seaports so long tormented by the Royal Navy. He sat for portraits and soaked in the people's joy. After the Senate issued a critical report on his conduct in late February, though, Jackson returned in a different mood to the capitol. Rumor spread that he was going to cut off the ears of its authors. To defend himself, one senator began carrying a concealed weapon—sad evidence, he lamented, that civil order had failed at the very center of the republic. Another senator recalled the general and his "ruffians" stalking around the city like a pack of dry drunks, waiting for someone to cross them, wanting someone to cross them.[84]

One Jacksonian all but dared Congress to censure "the people's great defender, their great avenger." It did not dare. More than 60% of representatives approved the executions of Ambrister and Arbuthnot; support for the seizures of the Spanish posts was almost as strong. The state legislatures of Louisiana, Mississippi, Alabama, and Pennsylvania added their official thanks to the general, who understood his support as all but universal. Pro-Jackson sentiment was certainly wider and louder in the American population than in Congress, although it was far stronger in some places and circles than others. Rooted in the extreme devotion of white households from enemy country and the proliferating institution of slavery, it reached into the raucous seaports of the East Coast, the camp meetings of frontier towns, and the officer corps of the US Army and Navy. It included women and men, children and parents. It was mostly Republican but vaguely Federalist, largely southern and western but also urban. It was, in a word, Jacksonian.[85]

As early as 1814, the general's oldest friend, John Overton, had told him that total war on the Creeks would bring national acclaim. In 1818, Overton offered a pre-emptive defense of the Florida campaign, and the Senate's criticism in early 1819 led the judge to publish a 150-page *Vindication* that fall. Again and again, Overton named the American people a "nation" and Jackson its most faithful servant. Again and again, he cited Vattel while insisting that no other nation cared about any law but force. If the British incendiaries or hostile towns had been spared, Overton insisted, "Indian wars would never cease, and innocent blood would forever flow!" In the end, he ruled, safety was "a *natural* right, anterior to the laws of nations, and it is a *perfect* right which can be asserted by force." Since most congressmen and the administration understood this, Overton named 1819 "a *golden age* in American politics" in which his famous friend could at last retire.[86]

CHAPTER 6

The People's Choice

Ever since he had emerged as a national hero, Jackson had moved to extinguish as much native territory as fast as possible. Two years after seizing much of the Creek Nation with the 1814 Treaty of Fort Jackson, he told the Chickasaws that they were trespassing on lands that had belonged to the Creeks, now retroceded to the United States. This "alarmed and seemed to iritate" some native delegates, the general noted, but he prevailed with "firm and decided stands" and well-placed bribes. He then urged John Coffee to tell the Choctaws that "no reservation to [their] nation can be granted." Although he had just taken similar positions against Indian nations in the northwest, the secretary of war, William H. Crawford, instead argued that the government should bring natives into "the pale of civilization" by giving them headright claims to tribal lands. The only other option, Crawford noted, was to turn white–native relations over to "individual enterprise," which would result in the Indians' "extermination or expulsion." Jackson fumed that the secretary simply wanted to stem emigration from Georgia "[and] wishes at the hazard of the safety of the union to cramp our growing greatness." Relations between the two men suffered accordingly.[1]

The general's second and related goal for the postwar years was "to bring into markett this land and have it populated." He suggested pre-emption rights for settlers, but his priority was to get the land sold quickly. Jackson was "so deeply impressed with the importance of this subject" that he wrote to Monroe twice over three weeks in 1816, having already told Coffee to start surveying. This no-holds approach to land sales troubled young nationalists who wanted to coordinate those sales with public improvements. It also dismayed poor settlers hoping to avoid auctions and land offices altogether. Tennessee settlers on "heathen lands" sent long petitions to the assembly, asking the state to secure "a more Equal distribution" of property by simply granting them plots as Spanish and British authorities once had. Otherwise, the speculators who had already done more harm "than all the wars that ever reached our continent" would take everything.[2]

Jackson got his way on both counts, and a postwar boom seemed to vindicate his vision of "growing greatness." Enterprising as always, the general made several "conditional contracts" for land along the Louisiana coastline and considered plans to export sugar as well as cotton. He offered to buy land for eastern investors, assuring them that the Gulf Coast regions he had conquered "present to the capitalist greater prospects of advantage—than any other." He owned shares in two land companies and also partnered with four other Tennesseans to buy land for some Philadelphia investors. These plans did not get very far, but no matter: cotton prices on the British market rose to what one group of Alabamians called "a most extravagant price," imparting an "unreal value" to cotton lands and enabling Jackson to expand the Hermitage into an eight-room mansion, complete with a central hall and French wallpaper. His earlier struggles long behind him, he identified more than ever with the just rewards of commercial striving within economic spheres as wide as Creation.[3]

After years of embargo and war, European manufactured goods once again poured into American seaports, despite the tariffs that Congress imposed in 1816. New land offices also opened, including the one where Jackson bought a piece of the long-coveted Muscle Shoals. The federal government encouraged such sales by issuing $4 million in "Mississippi stock," receivable as cash in the land offices of the new states of Mississippi and Alabama. State governments also fed the inflationary cycle by issuing new bank charters at the behest of entrepreneurs and boosters, not to mention rural communities that always wanted for currency. From just four banks at the start of the war, Pennsylvania had forty by the end of 1816, while Kentucky matched that number in 1818 alone. In Virginia and Tennessee, by contrast, the well-connected older banks held back the competition. Instead of issuing new charters, their legislatures increased the authorized capital of the established banks, including those controlled by Jackson's confidante, John Overton.[4]

As good weather and mass demobilization boosted crop production in Europe, however, demand for North American wheat, corn, and pork sagged. The British also found new sources of cotton in Brazil, which had two million slaves, and in India, where, one economist worried, the empire controlled "a coloured population, *full sixty times*" that of the United States. The price of US cotton dropped 30% in the early months of 1819, sending

American ships home with disappointing loads of coin and credit. The directors of the Bank of England began to call in North American debts, while British merchant houses turned off credit lines to East Coast wholesalers. The Second Bank of the United States (BUS), chartered in 1816, followed suit beginning in the summer of 1818, and its specie reserves grew steadily over the next few years even as the working total of "money" dried up. And since private indebtedness had risen so quickly since the war, this credit crunch turned into something much more serious than previous "panics."[5]

At least 85 of the 392 banks in the Union folded in 1819. Popular opinion now shifted against the "horse-leeches" who refused to pay the sums described on their notes while somehow escaping the usual course of the law. The newer and smaller banks instead blamed the legislators who had favored the older and richer ones, not to mention the currency traders who played havoc with the value of all bank notes. Matthew Carey, an Irish-born foe of British power and a well-known Pennsylvanian, pointed instead to the "radically wrong" policy of free trade. The problem was not so much the ubiquity of bank notes, he argued, as of imported goods from high-tech, low-wage Britain. For his part, the Tennessee war-hawk Felix Grundy faulted a wealthy few for buying too many foreign luxuries. He did not name any of these gentlemen-consumers, least of all his hero, Andrew Jackson.[6]

Although President Monroe saw the "extraordinary occurrences" of the European world as the root of all "pressures," these hard times could not be blamed on Britain in the same way as the economic crisis leading up to the War of 1812 had been. The problem clearly came from within, casting doubt on both the standard Republican faith in commercial agriculture and the more fundamental rules of commercial order. Hard times raised new questions about everything from trade policy and public spending to poor relief and building regulations, fomenting what John C. Calhoun famously called "a general mass of disaffection to the Government . . . looking out anywhere for a leader." It fostered new ways of thinking about national economic policy, starting with the idea that the nation itself *was* an economy, a common market whose citizens should enjoy certain privileges and protections. All of this prompted Andrew Jackson and his closest allies to re-enter national politics with their own kind of national solution.[7]

RELIEF AND PROTECTION

The depression left shuttered buildings all over the states. In Philadelphia and Pittsburgh, these were the "noble" workshops and factories that Matthew Carey and most Pennsylvanians wanted to protect with higher tariffs. To the west and south, the epicenters of crisis were the banks that folded to the injury more of note holders than stock owners. The lots and buildings they had owned were now deserted, often snapped up by the BUS. Everyone wanted to pay with the lesser bank bills that no one wanted to accept. "All things are changed, the rich have become poor," one Ohio banker summated. "[Tis] want, and fear and prosecution and suspicion and terror and dismay and bankruptcy and pauperism on all sides and on all hands." Then there were the federal land offices that had just been thronged with buyers claiming 160-acre plots for 5% down and 20% more in forty days. By the fall of 1819 they fell quiet, their clerks trying to make sense of how much was owed and to imagine how it could be paid.[8]

The grim arithmetic found its way to the Treasury Department, where Jackson's nemesis, William H. Crawford, had taken over three years before. Although better known for his intrigue than his intellect, this Republican stalwart had quickly discerned that too many people were "paying" for public lands with unreliable bills. Some of his predecessors at the Treasury and on the Senate Public Lands Committee had suggested abolishing the credit system altogether. Once the boom went bust, most congressmen embraced this view. Fresh off their resolution of the Missouri crisis, they transformed federal land policy in early 1820 by requiring all purchases of the public domain up front and in cash—BUS notes or specie—for 80-acre tracts (down from 160 acres) at a minimum of $1.25 per acre (down from $2). Crawford subsequently granted certain banks' notes purchase rights in certain offices, essentially declaring their bills to be cash too. Of course, these stabilizing measures did nothing to help the "public debtors" who had already bought on credit.[9]

As of 1820, such debtors owed the government some $22 million, at a time when Henry Clay, chief counsel for the BUS in Kentucky and Ohio, was collecting $2 million owed to that bank in those states. Pre-1820 purchasers were supposed to pay their balance in four yearly installments at 6% interest; if they were still behind after a fifth year, they forfeited their land, receiving only the difference between what the resold land brought in and the amount still due. In the doldrums of 1820, there was no resale market, especially after Congress abolished credit purchases that year. Nor was there any cash. Across the southwestern and northwestern states, then, many thousands of debtor-residents stood to lose their properties for a fraction of the precrash values, falling to those rules of commercial order that most offended popular ideas of fairness. Would the government act as "a rigid creditor"? Or would it forgive? Entire regions were waiting "in awful suspense," one senator noted. "The whole population trembled upon the brink of ruin," a westerner recalled.[10]

"The propriety of legislative interference to change the relation between debtor and creditor for the benefit of either may well be questioned," Crawford noted in his December 1820 report to the Senate. But the creditor here was the nation itself, at least in the institutional forms it took during peacetime. The government had already granted eleven extensions for public land purchases since 1809. It had tolerated a range of interventions by the states during the embargo, not to mention a variety of land laws in those states. (Crawford's Georgia was the most eccentric, relying on periodic lotteries to divvy up lands taken from Creeks.) So he recommended "relinquishment," whereby a public debtor could walk away from those portions of land for which he could not pay and use his previous payments to secure title to the acres he wanted to keep. Crawford also called for extra time for buyers who did not want to relinquish anything. The alternative, one congressman noted, was a land policy that once again fell short of the Spanish for charity. Even the laconic Monroe spoke of the need for "reasonable indulgence."[11]

With minor changes, Crawford's ideas became the Relief Act of early 1821. It passed the Senate thirty-six to five and the House ninety-seven to forty, another achievement of the Sixteenth Congress and, to some extent, of William H. Crawford. Because he and his followers were highly suspicious of federal power, however, they made only vague references to his "judicious" handling of the crisis. Otherwise, the act disappeared from national politics while its benefactors returned to the land offices to clear or extend their debts. "It is not easy to imagine a crisis more perilous" than that of 1820 and early 1821, one witness reflected. To judge by the consensus that had quietly formed around the Relief Act, "no one would have guessed the magnitude of the interests at stake." By September 1822, the total debt owed by western buyers had fallen 50%. Among the thousands of beneficiaries was Thomas Lincoln of Indiana, whose son, Abraham, wanted to be anything besides a frontier farmer.[12]

Andrew Jackson had little to say about the 1821 relief law, which was less relevant in Tennessee or Kentucky than in western states with federal land. Certainly he did not want to see the spoils of the Creek War wiped out by foreclosures, and he thought about "relinquishing" one of his own Alabama estates. Yet he said nothing in favor of this extremely popular measure, even when asked. He also grumbled when the relinquished land stayed off the market. Jackson also associated the relief law with William H. Crawford, who had long criticized the general's extreme hostility to Indian country. To Jackson, such ingratitude to those who had risked their scalps for the nation went hand in hand with the scheming and corruption he so despised. "[Crawford's] name and intrigue are intermixed where ever any election is on hand," he later told Coffee. If the man ever finagled his way to the White House, "it would be a great curse to the nation."[13]

Far more threatening than any federal reforms were the nearer, bolder calls for "Relief" that once again emerged outside of gentry-led politics as usual. In June 1819, a "numerous public meeting" in Frankfort, Kentucky, urged quick action to stop the auctions in the name of the "general welfare."

Figure 6.1 *General Andrew Jackson*, 1819 painting by Samuel Lovett Waldo. This likeness of the stern, frail warrior captures the inflexibility that Jackson would bring to the political turmoil of the early 1820s.
Metropolitan Museum of Art, New York.

In July, a similar rally took over the steps of the Tennessee state house, presenting a slate of new candidates for the assembly. This stunning challenge brought a 40% surge in voter turnout for state representatives in Davidson County. During the fall session, a fiery core of about a dozen delegates pushed to confiscate the property of the two biggest private banks and their stockholders. Their more cautious leader, Felix Grundy, instead passed a stay law in November that gave a debtor two years to pay, unless the creditor accepted current bank notes rather than specie. Grundy also sponsored a plan to "quiet" those who had never completed their grants. Seven years of "legal possession" should secure people from eviction, period. In the fall of 1819, speculators who displaced long-term residents were nearly as unpopular as bankers who refused to redeem their notes, and the measure passed almost unanimously. Among the few hold-outs was one of John Overton's closest allies, Pleasant M. Miller, an arch-conservative who was already trying to shift blame toward the BUS.[14]

During the summer of 1820, the Pennsylvania-born governor of Tennessee, Joseph McMinn, called an emergency session of the new legislature. He then argued for the further "care and protection of government" against the pitiless rules of modern commerce. Individuals would and should pursue "private gain," he said. "But public prosperity should not be sacrificed to the gratification of a few," as when productive wealth went for a song at sheriffs' auctions. Economic "emergency" called for an "indulgent policy" for the "debtor class," indeed for an "extraordinary effort" by and for the people. For the moment that meant a halt to land sales and debt prosecutions, so that the state could use what had been taken from the Indians to finance a new, more ambitious agenda. In Kentucky, a similar uprising had begun in late 1818 as an effort to tax the charter banks along with the BUS, which both the federal district courts and the Supreme Court disallowed. As the depression worsened, though, "Relief" became a more proactive project led by the governor and legislature against the courts.[15]

The basic idea of "indulgence" for debtors had been "put in force every day, and a thousand times a day perhaps" during Tennessee's 1809 stay law, one supporter noted. McMinn had sat in the state's upper house at that time, and he recalled "the happiest effects" for everyone. But while William H. Crawford used such precedents to excuse measures he would otherwise oppose, state-level relief often carried a deeper critique of the laissez-faire rule of law. Experience had shown the need for some "visitorial superintending authority" over private interests, some sovereignty that could secure "the safety of the community" against those who had no lasting ties to any community. Kentucky's governor spoke of a "fatal tendency in the progress of society" to make life harder on the poor and unfortunate, while the Frankfort public meeting called for "merciful forbearance" to head off "*general* calamity." A Virginia assemblyman used his state's revolutionary record against British creditors to argue for the people's ongoing authority over "*legal process* within her domain," that is, over the proper remedies to private obligations. "Creditors must take the law, as the Legislature choose to make it."[16]

In Kentucky and Tennessee, especially, this movement tried to challenge the private, state-*chartered* banks with public, state-*owned* banks. The Bank of the State of Tennessee opened in the fall of 1820 under Grundy's direction. Its mission, McMinn declared, was to help small settlers buy small tracts, creating a class of citizens "who, though possessed of moderate capital, should be furnished with motives of National attachment." It was to increase the sum of money that answered to the "public welfare," thereby shifting economic power away from the large planters, cotton gin owners, and interstate merchants who otherwise lent credit and recalled loans. This "New Bank" would be "a blessing to the people of this State," supporters in Nashville insisted. A grand jury in Jackson's home county warned the other bankers to respect it as such, also noting that the charter banks were "barely tolerated by the people." The notes of the Bank of the Commonwealth of Kentucky began to circulate in early 1821. This, too, was a "republican bank," the answer to both the monstrous BUS and the smaller institutions that the old legislature had foolishly chartered.[17]

These new state banks or "loan offices" partly relied on land sales and taxes to underwrite their notes. Instead of declaring those notes legal tender, which the courts would never allow, they attached themselves to the new stay laws: creditors who would not accept their bills were barred from suing their debtors for two years. Of course, out-of-state lenders and foreign merchandisers might still refuse or discount the notes. But so what? McMinn asked. The "economical planter who lives as he ought upon the products of his own farm" would find in its bills "a medium of exchange suited to the nature of all his wants." The goal of this bank was to secure the independence of state residents, not to facilitate business across state or national lines. It was to let Tennesseans "command the common destinies of the soil they tread," recycling the values they created for the mutual benefit of those who lived and labored there. McMinn also thought that the bank might fund various "schemes of national prosperity and wealth," such as canals and river improvements.[18]

Relief was strongest in prosperous farming counties where the depression was most shocking, but its support was wide and deep. Since debtors were also creditors and vice versa, and since some debtors were (for the moment) wealthy, it did not represent a class uprising in any conventional sense. Rather, it exposed the deep social divide in the early United States between the local and the cosmopolitan and the related controversy over what "the people" could do for themselves within a given place and time. Henry Clay's reaction is illustrative. "Our Legislature consists almost entirely of new members," the Kentuckian told the president of the BUS in late 1819. The next year he reported that his state had passed "unfavorable laws to creditors," by which he meant creditors from New York or London, as well as Lexington or Frankfort. No one was more concerned about the image that his state and nation made on the world stage than Clay. So the new efforts to secure local competence against Atlantic credit worried him. Yet he shared the general enthusiasm for an active public and tried to turn the nation at large into a more self-contained economy in which Americans would interact not only as free agents but also as fellow citizens.[19]

Having just seen the manufacturers of Lexington wiped out by an influx of Scottish and Russian cordage, Clay began to devise a vast project for American economic development. By holding on to its western lands and imposing higher tariffs, he argued, the national state could pay for new roads and canals. Farmers and tradesmen would then sell more to each other rather than to foreigners, enabling the United States and perhaps the entire Western Hemisphere to replace Britain as the global hegemon. Otherwise, the republic would remain a neocolonial economy, in thrall to British theories of free trade that the British themselves ignored as needed. Matthew Carey had been making this point for years. In the face of what he now called "a paralysis of all the active energies of our country," the duty of government was to intervene on their behalf. Delegates from nine states attended a Convention of Friends of Domestic Industry in New York in early 1820, making "Protection," as Carey called it, an electoral force that spanned from Kentucky to Pennsylvania and into the Northeast.[20]

More western and southern, relief was far less acceptable to national-level leaders—and, for that matter, to the manufacturers who wanted fast and solid payments. The growth of domestic markets since the 1780s underlined the demands of these and other *American* creditors, not just of British ones as during the founding. Besides Pleasant M. Miller, one of the staunchest opponents of Tennessee's stay law and state bank in the special assembly of 1820 was Sampson David, a wealthy distiller and tanner who later freed his slaves. He saw the public as a collection of equal and autonomous rivals, none of whom owed anything to each other besides what they had promised to pay. All efforts to clutter those obligations with stop laws and "paper institutions," he warned, were "demoralizing" for a "free and virtuous people." Matthew Carey denounced "*acts of legislature, suspending the collection of debts*" as one of the worst effects of the panic along with "the emigration of American citizens to a Spanish colony" (Texas, a debtors' haven). Disgusted with most politicians, he generally preferred Clay. On the other hand, Carey had long called for a warrior who could "fully avenge the injured honor of America" against its savage foes.[21]

REACTION AND ALIGNMENT

"The distressed state of the mercantile world," Andrew Jackson told his nephew in the fall of 1819, had brought "the great mass of mankind into distress." He was especially disturbed by the absence of "foreign notes," exchangeable for pounds sterling in London banks. Writing with a palsy, the aging general shrugged: "there is no escape but . . . industry and [eco] nomy." Ten years earlier he had held his tongue in the face of relief laws that upset his sense of law and justice, indeed his deeper and ultimately religious conviction that life was and should be a struggle. Now, he was a national hero and US general, and in no mood to compromise. In June 1820, he drafted an anti-relief proclamation with some Nashville notables. Wondering why "so much sympathy should be indulged for the *debtor*, and none for the *creditor*," it denied the legislature's right to interfere on behalf of either party, as if they otherwise arrived equal in court. Citing "judicious" rules of political economy, this essay also celebrated the "enterprising commercial adventurers" who risked their fortunes while seeking "markets abroad." Only by enabling such men to collect and sue could Tennesseans preserve "our respectability abroad as well as our confidence at home." As for the people at large, they should rediscover "our former habits of industry and simplicity," saving themselves rather than helping each other.[22]

Jackson traveled to Murfreesboro for the start of the special summer session of 1820. He had done the same thing the previous fall, apparently staying quiet as the rabble-rousing began. This time he waited outside. Possibly in military dress, he physically confronted the delegates as they filed in, warning them not to perjure themselves by voting for the state bank or other unconstitutional measures. He also helped to organize anti-relief resolutions in two other counties that summer. Like any westerner who did not want to commit political suicide, Jackson questioned the constitutionality of the charter banks. But his main targets were the state banks and fiat money that outraged the "principles of general Justice." They were "not voidable, but absolutely void," and he would oppose them "as long as I live." No state was "an independent government" when it came to the fundamental and global laws of commerce, Jackson made clear. State assemblies had no more right to depart from "the social compact of the union" than their citizens did to forsake the legal frameworks that made them innocent and sovereign.[23]

Yet the relief laws did pass, and the state banks did print money. From the fall of 1819 to the spring of 1821—the worst of the depression—the debtors and creditors of Tennessee thus faced off in a legal, political, and monetary context that Jackson found intolerable. Relief began a few months later in Kentucky, later still farther west, leading to much confusion as to when and where and how debts could be repaid. Measuring its effect is also difficult because the goal of relief was to *prevent* lawsuits. Still, the experience of Davidson County's circuit court is suggestive. It heard about fifty cases for debt prosecution and ejectment at its November 1818 term, a number that remained steady the following year—except for the fact that the Nashville Bank issued sixty-five depositions. Its directors knew that the legislature was about to change the rules of repayment and wanted to put its debtors on notice. In November 1820, after a year under the stay law, only about thirty cases for debt and ejectments were heard. A similar but less dramatic pattern played out in a poorer eastern county where neither the boom nor the bust had been so substantial. In such regions, support for Grundy's "legal resident" protections were stronger than enthusiasm for his new bank.[24]

"There are, no doubt, some hard cases of oppression and embarrassment, which require relief," conceded the September 1820 *Gazette* of Nashville, one of John Overton's mouthpieces. But the times were not so bad as to excuse such an "alarming violation of the Constitution of the United States" as a public bank. Such innovations would only make things worse while enabling improvident debtors to escape their obligations. A month later, with the people's bank up and running, the *Gazette* hardened its tone. Only "broken merchants, negro traders [and] land mongers and speculators" had suffered in the panic, they insisted. Only those who had spent beyond their means were in trouble. Why should others have to pay—or not be paid—for their mistakes? Why should the people bail each other out?[25]

Stay and replevin laws and other relief measures helped most during their first year, enabling debtors to complete a season without fear of prosecution and to keep some essentials safe from auction. After that the number of people they annoyed grew. Two modest-sized petitions declared in the summer of 1820 that the worst of the panic was "pretty well subsided" and that further interventions would only help "the Rich and speculating Class." And while poorer settlements balked at the reach and scale of a state bank, tradesmen in town centers often liked that bank more than the stay law. One group of petitioners made clear that they, too, wanted more money in circulation. But they had "allready Suffered a sacrifice of our property to pay our just Debts" and wanted their own debtors to do the same. Among them were tavern keepers and a cabinet maker, along with wealthier villagers.[26]

Popular fatigue with relief also reflected its fine print. Missouri's stay law, for example, enabled a citizen to reclaim foreclosed property within thirty months, at 6% interest. This brought little help to poor settlers and may have enabled speculators to cut overhead during the crisis and then reclaim the land after someone else had improved it. In Tennessee, the public bank was tied to the earlier stay or endorsement law, which had also encouraged creditors to accept the notes of the two major charter banks. Relief legislation thus buoyed the "money" of the very people most blamed for the panic along with that of the new, unproven "Bank of the people." John Overton's key ally in the legislature, Pleasant M. Miller, also pushed through some last-minute revisions to undermine its name. Its notes were not backed by the "faith of the state," he stipulated, but only by a limited number of land sales. Responding to a letter from the worried general, Miller assured Andrew Jackson that the people's bank was held in "universal detestation" by the right-thinking businessmen of Knoxville and that they were still working on "the proper course to be pursued." Evidently they decided to refuse the new bank's notes while Jackson denied its very existence. Miller was also closely involved in the lawsuit that challenged the emergency measures of 1819 and 1820.[27]

If public opinion about relief was complex and variable, judicial opinion was simple and shut. Federal courts had used the contracts clause against state laws since the 1790s, as did the highest court of North Carolina in 1814. These decisions and related parts of the state charter that Jackson had helped to write guided the Tennessee Supreme Court's ruling in May 1821. Both the endorsement law of 1819 and the public bank act of 1820 violated contracts and justice, the judges ruled. They threatened to return the Union to the dark days of the 1780s, when capital fled, credit withered, and debtors forsook "personal exertion." One judge added that it would be "unconscionable" of creditors to press too hard during this "extraordinary state of things," but that he could not force them to act otherwise. The key decisions in Kentucky and Missouri came the next year, spurring more confusion as to when debts should be paid and with what bills. "On the one hand a legislature enacting, on the other a judiciary repealing them," one paper bemoaned.[28]

Upon leaving office in September 1821, Governor McMinn nonetheless told Tennesseans that their experiment in public banking was working, at least for in-state transactions. Pro-relief leaders in Kentucky took more dramatic action. In January 1823, large bonfires were held in Frankfort, during which more than $770,000 in Bank of Commonwealth bills were sacrificed to enhance the value of what remained. That October, an appellate court reminded the legislature that its first obligation was to each and every property owner in Kentucky, not to the general welfare. The protection of property—debts or investments just like plows or livestock—was a duty of strict justice that traced to Kentucky's membership in the American Union and to "the principles of international law" as recognized by "all civilized states." As one ultra-conservative judge made clear, a creditor's right to the sums owed to him moved with him; this was the "international principle" at the heart of modern civilization. One "national principle" of the Constitution was thus "to impose an obligation upon all the states to give free course to the coercion of contracts." If that obligation failed, "social justice would cease, and man would again return to a state of nature."[29]

By then, the hard times had already passed, and the rush to narrate what had happened began. Felix Grundy credited his stay law and state bank along with the people's industry with reducing Tennessee's private debts by three-fifths from 1819 to 1821. He saw no need for further interventions, not least because he had larger political ambitions. Kentucky supporters also stood by their new form of popular rule. "The relief measures sprang from the great mass of the people," the *Argus of Western America* declared in 1823, "and are by them sustained." The legislature best reflected popular will, and by extension "the eternal principles of *justice* and *mercy*" for a flawed but decent population. Surely they could authorize emergency departures from legal principles born in England and nurtured by Federalists. What Republican would say otherwise? What American would refuse to help his fellow citizen? The *Argus* tried to name them:

> Is there an Englishman in the country? He is one of them. Is there a non-resident land speculator? He is one of them. Is there an advocate for the surrender of the power of the states to tax the United States Bank? He is one of them. Is there an advocate for the many and flagrant usurpations of the Supreme Court? He is one of them. . . . Is there a man who denies the power of State Legislatures to grant indulgence to debtors even in times of the greatest calamity? He is one of them.

Relief had saved thousands of fellow Kentuckians from ruin and revealed the happy fact that "Man is a social being and will feel for his fellow man." Those who sided instead with the law forsook the better angels of human nature, not to mention "the sovereignty of the state." Stunned by the judicial backlash, one relief leader asked how any law that would "*grind to death* the debtor" could be more constitutional than one that forgave people for some of their decisions and applied "the feelings of humanity" to social and economic relations.[30]

In reply, anti-relief leaders drew bright contrasts between the foolish experiments in Kentucky and the promised land of Ohio, even though the latter state had a replevin law in place from its earliest days. Ohio's legislature, one paper argued, had stood firm against the popular urge for more money. It had "put down a host of swindling banks, banished a spurious medium, and restored the good old currency." Presumably, the "good old currency" was coin, while the "spurious medium" referred to the bills printed by the public banks, or by the "swindling" banks, or both. Through such vehement generalities, opponents of relief appealed to everyone who disliked one part or another of the legal and political tangle it left behind. Americans, they said, were done with "spurious banks" and "ridiculous" stop laws. Retiring the depreciated bills of the now-defunct state banks proved a major headache for western states, further discrediting state interventions in general. For his part, Andrew Jackson kept denouncing relief leaders as "wild speculators" and "unsound politicians" who had nearly tarnished the American name.[31]

Beyond the quintessentially conservative theme of personal accountability to unchanging rules, anti-relief claims drew from a national legal framework that now reached from state and district courts all the way to John Marshall. Just as the panic set in, the US Supreme Court had affirmed the inviolability of contracts in *Sturges v. Crowinshield* and *Dartmouth College v. Woodward*, while also disallowing efforts to suppress the BUS in *McCulloch v. Maryland* and *Osborn v. BUS*. In 1823, with the panic gone and relief fading, it struck down the old Kentucky laws that had pushed nonresident claimants to yield their titles to western occupants or to pay them for improvements made. It was the power and the duty of the Supreme Court "as well as of every other court in the Union" to annul any law that impaired contracts in any way, the justices ruled in *Biddle v. Green*. This was something "too firmly established" by three decades of constitutional nationhood "to be now shaken."[32]

Because it put about one-third of all Kentucky land titles in jeopardy, *Biddle* was widely disregarded and also challenged by Henry Clay. Otherwise, the Kentuckian sought to replace relief with protection, which he renamed the "American System." Knowing that public banks and stay laws were asking too much of a traditionally weak public, he waited for the movement to stall and splinter. By 1824, he could exhale. Even the relief men knew that a political consensus had formed against their theory of peacetime sovereignty: a columnist who insisted that the people's "natural and inherent" power to make law "must yet remain with them" signed his articles, "Radical." Virginia's conservative legislature had held off a new round of stay and replevin laws, which its leading paper accused of "warring with the very elements of the social convention." Free-traders there and in South Carolina now disdained tariffs as an "experimental" departure from what had always worked for wealthy planters like them, mere "charity" for petty tradesmen who deserved no favors for being American. The northwestern states had been saved by federal relief in 1821 and showed only scattered enthusiasm for further measures. In the Deep South, a third cotton boom was about to begin, and with it new demands for more Indian lands and overseas markets. In the middle, in every sense, was Tennessee.[33]

The popular leader who emerged there was the man who had replaced Andrew Jackson at the head of Tennessee's militia, William Carroll. The two men had been comrades in the War of 1812, and Jackson had served as Carroll's second in an 1813 duel. Three years later, however, Carroll intimated that Jackson and Coffee had made fraudulent purchases in some of the lands they had conquered. Another ingrate, Jackson boiled. "I can scarcely believe it myself," Jackson told Coffee, "that I have huged such monsters to my boosom, called them friend, and risqued my life for [them]." At war's end, the Pennsylvania-born Carroll became a merchant, scrambling as Jackson once had to amass cash or credit and helping to form the Farmers' and Mechanics' Bank of Nashville in 1817. When the panic hit, it had $59,000 of notes in circulation, backed by $15,000 in silver. Both a borrower and a stockholder, Carroll owed this bank $300. A state committee proclaimed it "entirely safe" in October 1819.[34]

And yet the 1819 stay law and 1820 public bank law protected the new "people's bank" along with the old charter banks, but *not* the Farmers' and Mechanics'. A worse example of governmental partiality could hardly be imagined. A better spokesman for something new could scarcely be devised. Already known to militia captains, Carroll became the popular choice for governor in early 1821. Comfortable at country barbecues and impromptu rallies, he combined a loud, proud patriotism with targeted appeals to certain Tennesseans. He pleased creditors and merchants by denouncing the stay law. He attracted artisans and farmers by promising to force the charter banks to resume specie payments and by decrying Tennessee's dependence on export crops. The state should develop inside its own borders, Carroll said, funding new investments in roads, canals, schools, and prisons through more egalitarian taxes.[35]

In effect, the thirty-three-year-old Carroll offered a postpanic, postrelief vision of progress. His opponent, the much older Edward Ward, was a well-born Virginian, a large planter, and Andrew Jackson's friend and neighbor. Ward had signed Jackson's 1820 attack on the state bank, which was not necessarily a liability. But he was also a close associate of the older banks, which certainly was a liability. Like Jackson, he adapted to the general rage against bankers, but not very well. The charter banks were bad things, Ward conceded, but the public one was even worse. Ward praised "the government of a family" as a good model for the state and advised the people to choose wisdom and experience over name and popularity. Carroll supporters called him a closet Federalist and unfeeling aristocrat. Crawfordites suspected that Ward was simply the puppet of Andrew Jackson and John Overton, tapped to keep Tennessee out of Crawford's leger during the next presidential election.[36]

Of course, Jackson saw himself as a soldier rather than a politician. After the assembly spurned his anti-relief demands in the summer and fall of 1820, he had left home to serve yet again, this time bullying the Choctaws into a massive cession of Mississippi land. "You are advised to beware," he told them. The next spring Jackson had returned to Florida as the new territory's first governor. There he quarreled with Spanish officials and pressed for stronger courts. Now more than ever he saw the judiciary as "by far the most important branch" for any territory and wanted a safe choice like Edward Ward for his adopted state. Congressional cuts to the army meant that he had to resign as major general that summer, and he bitterly noted that many of his comrades were thus "thrown upon the world" by smarmy politicians. "I hope for the wellfare and happiness of Tennessee as well as for its respectability that [Ward] may be elected," Jackson wrote in July 1821. After two years of indulgence for debtors and austerity for soldiers, he still wanted to believe that most Tennesseans were "honest men." The election would "determine this point."[37]

But Carroll won 80% of the August vote, carrying forty-six of forty-eight counties. His inaugural address did little to assuage conservative fears. Instead of renouncing relief as immoral, the new governor said that "every feeling of [his] heart" wanted to help "the unfortunate debtor." However, the Constitution would not allow it, and the economy would suffer in the long run if the law was too lenient. For Carroll, then, the more sensible solutions were internal improvements, public education, and "*domestic or household manufactures*" rather than more imported goods. The answer was bold but constitutional policy to help the people compete with other states and nations. "Citizens of the same state—brothers of the same family," Tennesseans would "go speedily and energetically to work," with or without Judge Overton and General Jackson.[38]

Figure 6.2 William Carroll (1788–1844), Jackson's emergent rival in Tennessee politics. The Latin inscription suggests his more proactive idea of governance: "They can because they think they can, by virtue and toil."

THE MAKING OF A LEGEND

"Previously to the sitting of the Legislature in 1821," John Overton privately recalled three years later, "it forcibly struck me that [Jackson] ought to be the next President." This is plausible. The Tennessee legislature met in September, which would place Overton's revelation just after the disastrous vote for governor. The courts that Overton had organized had stopped relief in its tracks earlier that year, but now he and Jackson faced a young, popular governor who called "General Education" the main source of "a nation's happiness and glory" and who took inspiration from northern states and European nations. The answer, Overton realized, was to go national. Sometime in the winter of 1821–22, after Jackson resigned as governor of Florida, the judge and other confidantes convinced the general to run for president. Overton told "a leading member" of the new assembly, probably anti-relief man Pleasant M. Miller, of his plans, who in turn communicated them to formerly pro-relief Felix Grundy. At length the founder of the state bank "gave into" the idea. It was Grundy, after all, who in 1819 had proposed giving Jackson an honorific sword on behalf of the grateful people.[39]

Miller wrote the endorsement for the legislature and Carroll presented the sword at the 1822 Independence Day celebration in Nashville. In this context of orchestrated veneration, Jackson gave his first major address in Tennessee since accosting its pro-relief legislators two years earlier. Essentially he narrated "the whole British and Indian War" as the latest act of American independence. In 1818 as in 1815, he declared, he had simply been "the humble instrument in the hand of Divine Providence" to save the frontiers from "savage cruelty" and New Orleans from "ravages and pollution." Jackson then veered into a generalized critique of peacetime governance. The "*holy* zeal" that his soldiers had shown "ought to be fostered and cherished, not dampened, by the government." It was "this *zeal alone*," Jackson insisted, "that can defend and preserve the liberties of our country, and perpetuate the existence of our happy form of government." Later that month he reminded his nephew that relief was a threat to "Liberty" and that, once lost, the people would have to "bleed, fight, and conquer" to deserve it again.[40]

Overton had been supervising Jackson's image since 1793, when he advised Jackson to marry Rachel in Nashville, and again in 1806, when he implored his friend not to kill anyone else. In 1814, the judge had obtained a short and heroic biography of "General Jackson" and sent it to Jackson with instructions to entrust it to another officer. This officer, in turn, would give it to a Nashville editor, whereupon the story would spread on its own. As of 1822, Overton became something like Jackson's campaign manager, the center of a small group of close friends and allies sometimes referred to as the "Nashville Junto." They sent letters and handbills to editors and politicians around the Union, confidentially explaining why Jackson should be president. *The Life of Andrew Jackson*, first printed in 1817 by none other than Matthew Carey, reached a much wider audience. Written with the general's close cooperation by John Reid and John Eaton, both subordinates during the war, it gave Americans the picture he had always seen of himself.[41]

The full title gave fair warning of the content: *The Life of Andrew Jackson, Major-General in the Service of the United States: Comprising a History of the War in the South, from the Commencement of the Creek Campaign, to the Termination of Hostilities Before New Orleans*. As one reader noted, the book was "less a biography than a history." All but twenty of its more than four hundred pages were devoted to the campaigns of 1812–15, including long excerpts from Jackson's hand and documents showing British complicity in Indian atrocities. The book drew a narrative arc stretching from Jackson's first efforts to save Martha Crawley to his final defense of New Orleans' women. It described how Jackson organized his green troops during night marches, how he extracted food and provisions from greedy contractors, and how he alternately scared and inspired everyone around him. In these ways it was accurate.[42]

But it was the first chapter and final section—covering Jackson's first forty-six years and his overall "character," respectively—that were the most heavily sampled and reprinted around 1820. The opening chapter pictured Jackson as a poor, frail immigrant who might have fulfilled his mother's wishes had the British and Indian hordes not arrived. Then followed the stirring events of his Revolution: he and his brothers fought side by side; he refused to clean a British officer's boots; he still bore the scars of the ensuing blow. Once the shooting stopped, the chapter shifted gears, all but skipping over the key settings, problems, and choices of Jackson's life. His decisions were barely his to make. "The pulpit," as it happened, "was now abandoned for the bar." After a brief political career from 1797 to 1799, he retired to "an elegant farm" where he "enjoyed all the comforts of domestic and social intercourse" until dragged, yet again, into a war he never wanted. "Of the two great parties, which have distracted our country," the authors reported at book's end, "general Jackson is attached to the republican." Yet he was not "one of those blind infatuated partizans" who forgot the greater good, especially in times of great peril.[43]

Readers would have seen a close parallel with the nation's first Cincinnatus, George Washington. (Parson Weems's biography of the first president, the one with the cherry tree, was widely read by the 1810s.) The authors played with the comparison. Washington was the picture of neoclassical *gravitas*, a superb man around whom no one felt adequate. There was "nothing repulsive" about Jackson, either, Eaton and Reid assured everyone. But neither was he chilly or stately, and never did he keep people at arm's length. Instead, he was open and friendly, paying equal notice to "honest poverty" and "titled consequence." He had plenty of skeletons, real and figurative: the book mentioned his duels, his temper, his checkered past. The authors also relayed the rescue of Lyncoya, during which the general "is seen acting as a Christian, and sympathizing in others' woes." The picture that emerged was not so much complicated as colorful, a larger-than-life pastiche of love and hate, rage and mercy, honor and humility.[44]

Andrew Jackson wanted "a nation's gratitude" more than anything, Eaton and Reid concluded. He "possesses ambition, but it rests on virtue." Here, too, *The Life of Andrew Jackson* broke from the moral and cultural norms that had lifted George Washington to semidivine status. The first president's repeated efforts to retire were admirable because classical republican thought saw latter-day Caesars and large militaries as common threats to Western civilization. So long as other nations also respected this quality in Washington and the republic he embodied, the ethic of self-restraint was as prudent as it was virtuous. But "the general confusion of the world" had shown that "forbearance under injuries is construed into imbecility to redress them." Jackson had saved the country from its gentler delusions. He had avenged the frontiers "whilst the tomahawk and scalping knife were uplifted" and rescued the women of New Orleans just before the British raped them, inspired to great actions by his unbound passions. Alone in its lawfulness, the nation owed its survival to his raging ambition, his thirst for glory, gratitude, and even vengeance.[45]

As Jackson's legend spread and solidified, his closest friends began to soften and refine it. They knew that many important people saw him as a cruel, dangerous man who twisted the law into "a fierce vindictive power." The June 1822 endorsement from the Tennessee legislature thus described him as "calm in deliberation" and "cautious in decision," as well as "efficient in action." The following year, Overton and other handlers published another recommendation for those beyond Tennessee's borders. While every American understood Jackson as a great warrior, the piece declared, only his Nashville friends knew him as the caring neighbor who had no more axes to grind or laurels to win. They saw him "employed on his farm in our neighborhood, in the cultivation of which . . . no vestige of ambition can be traced." Jackson's age and accomplishments were further reasons not to worry about his passions. He had already avenged the nation and the people, and simply wanted to watch over his beloved country before he, too, passed on.[46]

Jackson thus had a unique appeal in the postwar, postpanic, and even postparty 1820s. The ideas were young, much like the nation itself, where only one white person in ten could remember the Battle of Yorktown. As the most controversial of the nation's veterans, Jackson epitomized its potential while tugging on its memory. He was older than most war-hawks and the only candidate for the White House who had fought in the Revolution. He was "the Old Hero." Descriptions of Jackson in the 1820s sometimes described him as God's right hand, from whom a wayward people could find direction and protection. The need to show gratitude to aging patriots also came out of cultural fears about commerce and backsliding, about the passing of great deeds and heroic times. "The gratitude of the American People is not to be questioned," a young officer (and business partner) of Jackson assured the general.[47]

Most people wanted to think that Jackson was on their side, which made it all the easier for his handlers to build a national coalition upon his few known positions. His extreme views on *salus populi* were obvious to all, and many Tennessee leaders had also encountered his equally extreme feelings about relief. In 1820, *Niles' Weekly Register* approvingly published his tirade against public banks and stay laws, while Jackson spelled out that opposition to the men who organized his campaigns. Chief among these was of course John Overton, who made clear that Jackson had always been a "firm and inflexible judge," as well as John Eaton, who in the revised *Life of Andrew Jackson* from 1824 added that the general was "scrupulously attentive" to financial obligations. In addition, the *National Intelligencer* had published Jackson's 1819 toast to "Domestic Manufactures" as essential to the "real independence" of the Union. The nation's most connected readers thus knew him as safely anti-relief and vaguely sympathetic to protection. Otherwise, Jackson turned the "general mass of disaffection" coming out of the hard times away from particular policies and toward his well-managed legend.[48]

That legend was most powerful in the same western and southern regions where relief had been most radical, burying that movement as no judicial reaction ever could. In 1824, for example, a relief supporter from Kentucky compared anti-relief conservatives to the New England Federalists who had almost committed treason during the war. These were the traitors, the writer noted, "whom General Jackson says he would have hanged if it had been the last act of his life." The article thus identified Jackson with the most passionate and extra-legal ways of dealing with Britons and Federalists, sweeping away the key differences over where, when, and against whom the American people were sovereign. As their movement broke down in 1826 and 1827, in fact, most relief men from Kentucky gravitated to the general, who at least had a history of defying politicians. Angry at the kinds of government that the law would allow, one argued that only a "Military chieftain" could break the rule of courts and lawyers, "and Jackson was the man."[49]

THE MAKING OF A CANDIDATE

The campaign to make Jackson the president hit two snags in 1823. The first was a dispute between the judge and the general. Ever the realist, John

Overton had supported some of Felix Grundy's resident protections during relief's 1819 heyday. Evicting such persons might satisfy the letter of the law more cleanly, but it would also sow uncertainly among other property owners. Ever the insider, Overton tried to convince the legislature to add a fourth, compliant justice to the state's supreme court, ensuring a favorable verdict on the matter. The general wanted nothing to do with this "verry corrupt combination" and favored a more narrow reading of the law, which would have empowered out-of-state claimants to dispossess long-time residents. He briefly began letters to Overton with a stiff "Dear sir," rather than the usual "My Dear friend," but the tension soon passed. In December, Jackson even asked his old friend if a new federal judgeship for Mississippi and Alabama might be of interest.[50]

The summer of 1823 also forced a strategic choice for the campaign. Governor Carroll was up for re-election, still promising to improve public schools and penitentiaries and to abolish debt imprisonment. At least one Junto member wanted Jackson to challenge Carroll and return Tennessee to more familiar ways of governing. Instead, Jackson opted to stand for the US Senate. In this way he could return to national office and defeat the incumbent senator, who was an ally of William H. Crawford, that "*great whore of babylon*." Once again, Jackson showed up in person on the steps of the Murfreesboro assembly, demanding entry as a last-minute candidate. He prevailed, thirty-five to twenty-five, and left that fall for the capital, describing himself as "astonished" at the rapid turn of events. Roadside crowds pressed to shake his hand, which he found "tiresome" but also "gratifying." To the melancholy Rachel, alone again at the Hermitage, Jackson swore that if God ever willed their reunion he would never leave again.[51]

Writing home that December on Jackson's behalf, John Eaton assured Rachel that her husband was getting along quite well. He was in good health, "constantly in motion to some Dinner party or other," and not involved in any disputes. "All his old quarrels have been settled," including the last of many lawsuits from the Allison affair. By early 1824, Jackson was "at peace with all the world," or at least with the elite men he met in Congress. Everyone either loved or feared him, and no one had much to gain in opposing him as they had during the Florida debate. Of course, Jackson despised Henry Clay, among others, for what the Kentuckian had said during that controversy. But Clay was in the House, exhorting everyone to protect American industry and develop American markets. Spared direct exposure to Clay's famous eloquence, Senator Jackson was cautiously open to new visions of economic independence, at least for the moment.[52]

By far his most important vote was his line-by-line support for a protective tariff schedule in 1824. Rich in potential benefits to what Jackson called "the great leading state" of Pennsylvania, the tariff had emerged as the most politically acceptable reply to the 1819–22 depression. It was widely popular in the free states and had just begun to alarm southern (and British) free traders. Jackson never spoke of tariffs as Clay or Carey did, but he acknowledged that manufacturing might enhance and complement agriculture and commerce. If "we the cotton growers" enjoyed governmental favors, Jackson mused, why should hemp growers be left to the wind? "I will be the President of the nation, [and] not of a party," he told his nephew. The general framed the tariff in terms of national security, pointing out that domestic production was essential during wartime. He also served as the chairman of the Committee on Military Affairs.[53]

The old man also budged somewhat during debates over "A Bill to Abolish Imprisonment for Debt," which, its supporters were quick to point out, was not a bill to abolish imprisonment for debt. Instead, it would replace prison with a series of oaths and bonds on the part of the defendant—but only for the interstate disputes heard in the federal district courts. Since most civil litigation was heard in county courts, Robert Y. Hayne of South Carolina took comfort in knowing that only a "very inconsiderable number" of debtors might benefit. He opposed it all the same. Another skeptic said that he had "seen enough in the Western Country of stop laws, occupying claimant laws, etc." to convince him that it was the creditor, not the debtor, who deserved help. Western delegates were more sympathetic to the bill. Creditors had every right to a debtor's property, conceded Richard M. Johnson of Kentucky. "But to allow the body of a citizen, under any circumstance, to be imprisoned at the discretion of his equal" was "a most flagrant violation of personal liberty."[54]

The whole point of enforcing contracts and collecting debts was not retribution but repayment. It was to turn a debtor's estate into a creditor's capital. Every senator agreed that "honest" debtors who had disclosed all their properties should be kept out of jail; the constitutions of North Carolina, Tennessee, Alabama, and Mississippi already prohibited such detention unless the court found "strong presumption of fraud." During his time on Tennessee's high court, Andrew Jackson had released some such debtors from custody. The greater issue was how to compel the more sophisticated investors whose wealth was hidden away in stocks and bonds to pay up. So the bill was nothing too dramatic. But what was the harm, supporters wanted to know, in "leading the people to the sweet belief, for a few weeks, at least?" At first it carried, twenty-four to nineteen, but when it returned from the House eight months later, the usual arguments for creditors' justice defeated the bill, twenty to twenty-three. In both cases Jackson voted yeah, his sole concession to what passed—in fact, did not pass—for relief in the Union's most prestigious club.[55]

If he was something like a moderate in economic policy, though, Senator Jackson once more stood for the most extreme solutions to frontier violence. North of cotton, the new boom on the western waters came in the form of beaver and bison. The fur trade had been reborn during the hard times, as St. Louis merchants casting about for new profits financed new expeditions up the Missouri and Yellowstone Rivers. This worried the Blackfeet, Arikara, Crows, and Mandans who preferred the devil they knew, the Hudson Bay Company. In the early summer of 1823, two Blackfeet attacks left at least eleven trappers dead and thousands of dollars in furs lost. "[If] we continue to forbear," one agent wrote, "this river will be discolored with our blood." Once again, some editors declared, the British Canadians were inciting scalp hunters to stop "the lucrative adventures of our enterprising citizens." Jackson's old comrade in Florida, General Edmund P. Gaines, readied to move troops from Florida to Missouri.[56]

Beyond the opposite end of the Union, along the Caribbean frontiers, American traders and investors now worried about pirates as well as slave insurrections, especially as "privateers" flying South American flags turned up in southern ports. They counted on Commodore David Porter, who had crippled Britain's whaling fleet during the war. As commander of the West Indies squadron in the early 1820s, Porter was just as aggressive, often burning Cuban fishing huts where pirates might take shelter. In the fall of 1824, one of his officers landed at Fajardo, Puerto Rico, in search of some goods stolen from a firm based in St. Thomas. After the locals roughed up this officer, Porter sent a force of 150 men to demand an apology along with the "American property" in question. He did not want to punish the innocent along with the guilty, but "[there] must and shall be an atonement." Recalled to Washington to explain this apparent invasion of Spanish soil, Porter cited the precedent set by Andrew Jackson in Florida, in which the general had acted on "the supposed will of the nation."[57]

In debating how to protect Americans along these northwestern and southeastern frontiers, most senators made clear that the hour of national vengeance was over. The United States was no longer under imperial siege; indeed, the British government had just proposed an Anglo-American alliance against the restored monarchies of Europe, from which Monroe adapted his famous doctrine in late 1823. This was "the most momentous" news for the United States since he had declared its independence a half-century before, Thomas Jefferson wrote. It signaled genuine recognition of the increasingly slaveholding republic by the increasingly abolitionist empire. So accusations of British–Indian collusion in the Upper Missouri attacks now seemed farcical, and not just because they were untrue. A New Jersey senator also noted that the mountain west was the Indians' last sanctuary, and that any incursions by trappers and hunters "will be, and ought to be" resisted by native men. If peaceful trade with the Blackfeet was not possible, "in the name of humanity let it be abandoned." Ultimately the Senate opted for an armed escort for American commissioners, while rejecting, thirty to twelve, a proposal to give the president a freer hand in sending troops to the Upper Missouri.[58]

As for the Caribbean, most senators were content to keep a naval squadron near Florida and accept that pirates would sometimes escape onto Spanish islands. They agreed with northern papers that condemned Porter's invasion of Fajardo as a "Shameful Aggression" against "all the recognized nations of the civilized world." By a count of thirty-seven to ten, they rejected a proposal to allow naval commanders to blockade suspected ports in consultation with the commander-in-chief. For Littleton Tazewell of Virginia, the very idea marked a troubling drift from the peaceful and lawful traditions of the republic. Tazewell described US history as a fifty-year struggle "to establish the reputation of being a just people," to respect the golden rule as instituted by the "high law" of "the whole civilized world." We Americans could not change those rules, he said, and must "come again within the pale of civil society." Quite apart from any high-minded motives, the senators did not want to transfer any of their war-making authority to the president.[59]

A militant minority had other concerns. Disdaining the "idolatrous reverence" for the law of nations, Philip Barbour of Virginia reprised his pro-Jackson arguments from the Florida debate. Pirates were "demons" who had to be annihilated, and in doing so it was impossible for the nation to go "*too* far." No longer trying to squeeze American militancy inside Vattel's clauses, he appealed to "the latitude of America" and "the right of self-preservation." Americans could go wherever their business took them, defending themselves by any means necessary. Their government should support those rights by using force on anyone—or any *place*—in the way. If pirates were suffered to live in Cuba, then the whole island was "contaminated by this deadly sin." Barbour called his colleagues to sacred violence: "You must cause vengeance to reach them—you must teach them there is justice still on the earth." Punishing them was the only way to protect and avenge "the blood of our people."[60]

While calling for action against the Blackfeet and Arikara, Senator Thomas Hart Benton described the southern states' forty-year ordeal at the hands of Indian savages and their European patrons. The people had only stopped bleeding with the conquest of Florida, he said, perhaps with a respectful nod to the Tennessee colleague with whom he had exchanged gunfire ten years earlier. A lawyer for a fur company, as well as a newspaper editor, Benton had helped to abolish government trading posts in 1822, arguing instead for "individual enterprize to take its course." The role of the government was to deploy military force on behalf of that enterprise, projecting "the will of the nation" over lesser peoples with other priorities. It was to focus the passions and interests of individual Americans in the "sovereign capacity" they retained against non-Americans.[61]

Jackson somehow stayed quiet during these debates, but he was one of just six senators to vote for both the anti-Blackfeet expeditions and the anti-piracy blockades. All of them were from slave-owning states, the eternal frontier. Indeed, South Carolina had trembled again in 1822, when a free black man named Denmark Vesey allegedly planned to burn Charleston and lead an exodus to Haiti. State militia and independent companies killed Vesey and three dozen others, after which all black sailors coming into Charleston had to spend their shore leave in jail. It did not matter if this Negro Seaman's Act violated international law, the state senate noted, because safety was "paramount to all *laws*, all *treaties*, all *constitutions*." Later that decade, petitioners just north of Charleston raged at an 1821 law that had stiffened penalties for murdering slaves. This naïve reform, they charged, might discourage a white man from shooting a black man who had "ravished his daughter." It would incite the bondsmen to "such acts of violence as call immediate vengeance down upon them." In a world of sovereigns and slaves, the only way to save the people from the brutal laws of nature was to let them keep the brutal rights of nature.[62]

JACKSONISM

Southern fears of federal power in the early 1820s grew out of two realizations. The first was that northern congressmen had less and less need for southern support and might impede the peculiar institution as they nearly had in Missouri. The second was that anti-slavery activists were targeting racial hotbeds like Baltimore. For a new generation of southern conservatives, in fact, the great peril no longer came from Britain and its native proxies but from the "insurrectionary doctrines" of northern abolitionists and the more subtle efforts by the federal state to promote "the *national welfare*." Among them was Roger B. Taney, a lawyer who began his career as a Federalist and critic of slavery. Shortly after moving to Baltimore in 1823, he lurched into anti-black fundamentalism, in which slave-holding polities reserved the right to protect white families from the "*moral contagion*" of abolition and the "walking pestilence" of free blacks. In 1824, Taney favored Andrew Jackson for president, noting that the general was "taken up spontaneously by the people." Besides, Taney confided, "I am sick of all Secretary candidates."[63]

The obvious "Secretary candidate" and choice of the congressional caucus was William H. Crawford, who had a stroke during the fall of 1823. This strengthened the hand of another southern secretary, John C. Calhoun, whose vigorous leadership of the War Department made him more than a sectional choice. The Kentucky slave owner Henry Clay also campaigned as a nationalist, and his protectionist ideas won over his home state, Missouri, and Ohio. Naturally, Jackson swept Tennessee, Alabama, and Mississippi; more impressively, he carried Maryland, North Carolina, Indiana, New Jersey, and, above all, Pennsylvania. John Quincy Adams dominated New England, ran well in the upper South, and had supporters everywhere. Adams finished with eighty-four electoral votes against Jackson's ninety-nine (and seventy-eight combined for Crawford and Clay). With no majority winner, the choice fell to Congress. There the various Republican blocs settled on Adams, who named Clay his secretary of state. Jackson retreated to Tennessee, cursing Clay as an "ambitious demagogue" while his supporters cried, "Corrupt Bargain." For the next four years they demanded Jackson's election in the name of popular sovereignty, even though recent research shows that Adams also had a strong claim to be the people's choice in 1824.[64]

Especially after Vice President Calhoun turned on Adams in early 1826, Jackson consolidated the support of all the slave states. There he did not need any authorized biography. The general had saved white Mississippians from "savage fury," one man had written after Horseshoe Bend, and could forever count on "the benedictions of a grateful people." "Every honest Louisianan is the personal friend of the old warrior," argued one southern paper. In frequent contact with the Junto, Jackson supporters all over the South made endorsements and organized celebrations on the eighth of January, the anniversary of the Battle of New Orleans, while appealing to "the sovereignty of the people as expressed in the last Presidential Election." The people worshipped Jackson "as a god on earth," one Mississippi resident noted while watching Jackson pass through, Overton at his side. They quite literally felt for him, because his name was so bound up with the security of their bodies.[65]

Gratitude to Jackson as a Tennessee soldier was coupled with suspicion for Adams as a Massachusetts politician. The administration's openness to a pan-American conference in Panama—the "national Congress in spanish america," in Jackson's disdainful words—looked like backdoor support for Haiti. One envoy told the recovering William H. Crawford that Cuba, as well, might become "a second black empire on our very threshold" on

Adams's watch. The president simply did not understand southern dangers. For the same reason he balked at an 1825 removal treaty forced upon Georgia's remaining Creeks, even considering the use of federal troops to protect Creek country until another treaty mooted the point. His White House hopes behind him, Crawford wrote that Adams's conduct "compelled every Georgian to oppose his re-election without regard to the character of his opponent." Almost every Georgian agreed: it was the most pro-Jackson state in the Union by 1828.[66]

The combined threat of Henry Clay and John Quincy Adams thus touched southern whites on points of what Brutus, the penname of an influential South Carolina author, called "exquisite sensitiveness." Clay marched on with plans for a deeper, more complex economy within the Union, as if its black population might someday have property or purchasing power. More of a free trader, Adams was no less committed to national progress. Under conditions of peace, the new president declared in December 1825, the goal of civil government was no longer mere protection, but rather "the improvement of the condition of those who are parties to the social compact." That meant roads, canals, schools, and even observatories for the common benefit of a national public. It meant policies designed for Americans as though they were "individuals of *one great* political society," Brutus lamented. He now saw federal roads as physical invasions of the "the State Sovereignties," just as tariffs were artificial impositions on planters' profits. He swore to protect the "*vital* sovereignty" of South Carolina and to vindicate the "*outraged sovereignty*" of Georgia.[67]

In the southern states, then, repeated demands to restore popular sovereignty after the scandal of 1824 combined with vivid fears of federal activism to foster an aggrieved enthusiasm that detractors called "Jacksonism." Brutus wanted every Carolinian to unite around the general: "As *Americans*, let us, without a noise, support him in 1828." Yet Brutus also worried that Jackson had voted for the 1824 tariffs, and that he would need strongholds north of slavery to topple Adams and Clay. Evidently that stronghold was Pennsylvania. Its Republican factions had united around Jackson in 1824, carrying the general to victory by a two-to-one margin after nominating him in a first-of-its-kind convention. They deplored the congressional caucus that had chosen Crawford. "My candidate requires no caucus," one state legislator declared. "*His* caucus was in the hearts of the people." But only 19% of Pennsylvania voters had participated in the election for president. By contrast, 64% had voted the previous year for a governor who promised a more active government as well as a more democratic one. Pennsylvania was thus a battleground not only between Jackson and the administration but also over what kinds of choices the mobilized people could make.[68]

The new governor, John Shulze, had taken power after both the depression and the judicial backlash. Like William Carroll in Tennessee, with whom he was in touch, Shulze could therefore make bold promises within a smaller range of choices. In 1823, he pledged "every measure" for "relieving the embarrassments of the community" and for "the promotion of the public welfare." His first priority was to make public schools "completely within the reach of all—the poor who could not pay for them as well as the rich who could." The legislature was more interested in canals, especially given the success of the Erie Canal for the rival Empire State. Pennsylvania's leaders now argued that its wealth had been "dissipated among strangers," requiring more direction by and for the public. Shulze worried about the price but approved a series of canal projects to the tune of $1 million per year, about the sum of all internal revenues normally collected in the state.[69]

In 1823, Shulze had won 58% of the more than 154,000 votes for governor. Four years later, after approving the canals and the state's first railroad, he ran virtually unopposed, taking 97% of 75,000 votes cast. He stood on the shoulders of a long line of Pennsylvania Republicans who argued for such spending on behalf of a "well-regulated society" whose leaders were "bound to promote by all possible means the welfare of their constituencies." The alternative was to let individuals pay their own way to market, which had always been best for those with the most capital and the least connection to local producers. Shulze told Pennsylvanians that he wanted to "completely protect American manufactures," citing the example of "the most enlightened and prosperous nations of Europe" in excluding whatever could be produced at home. Such was the political economy of independence as Pennsylvanians clearly wanted it—which is why Clay, in particular, hoped to carry the state over Jackson in 1828.[70]

"*We were all the supporters of Mr. Shulze's election,*" one group of Pennsylvania Jacksonians declared. They praised the new delegation system by which the governor had taken office as a "land mark of Democracy" and linked it to the nation-wide uprising against "King Caucus" that Jackson symbolized. More vaguely, the general's supporters endorsed a government that could "call forth the real resources of the country." To this end they pointed out that their man had voted for the 1824 tariff, and also that Rachel Jackson wore an American-made bonnet. A Pittsburgh businessman began this story in the spring of 1823 by sending Jackson the hat along with thanks for wartime sacrifices. Both the general and his wife replied in gracious and published letters, assuring readers that Rachel would don the "Jackson Flat" as "an emblem of the sphere in which [women] should move." For the most part this sustained the general's protectionist credentials even after Jacksonian congressmen from Pennsylvania voted against an 1827 bill to protect woolen manufacturers.[71]

More often, Jackson supporters focused not on what he might do in peace but on what he had already done in war. They identified him as "the only surviving soldier of the Revolution, whom . . . a grateful people can elevate to the Presidential chair." One preacher called him "a Saviour and a deliverour for his people" who was "justly entitled to the nation's gratitude." Pennsylvanians backed him in 1824 "chiefly from a sense of gratitude," one partisan told Jackson, and they would do so again because of the general's unique record of heroic violence. The hero from Tennessee "stands aloof from all the contemptible intrigue and management of the day," declared the *Letters of Wyoming*, a popular series that first appeared in a Philadelphia paper in 1823. Using the name of the Pennsylvania valley terrorized by Iroquois and Loyalists during the Revolution, Wyoming (actually John Eaton) called Jackson a soldier to whom "no parasite" was attached, an honest man who understood that the Constitution was "like the Holy Bible": simple and inflexible. No wonder he had been persecuted by two-faced politicians and secretive caucuses.[72]

If Jackson's Pennsylvania campaign had an economic theme, it was "retrenchment" or "integrity," a policy of purity that cast doubt on any public effort other than vigilance against non-Americans. The people did not trust plans for "governmental munificence" any more than they did the congressional caucus, the Jacksonians insisted. Americans did not want an American System. Nor were they fooled by the Woolens' Bill of 1827, which would mostly benefit President Adams's historically pro-British homeland. The bill was another example of "the diplomatic refinements of New England intrigue," another ruse by a man who had only "affected to become a republican" back in 1807. President Adams's political views "have been questioned," Wyoming intoned, "perhaps for the reason that he happens to be his *father's son*." He was "John the Second," the "*favorite* of the rulers and hangers-on of the *strong* governments of Europe." He had turned the White House into a "Palace" of courtiers, diplomats, and billiards tables, an un-republican replica of a union that had lost its way.[73]

Jackson men were convinced that the administration was Federalist at heart, much as Jackson was sure that Clay controlled a "secrete combination" in Washington. His creed came from "the old republican school," Jackson announced in a typical letter, "and is without change." Although light on details, such assertions bore special meaning in Pennsylvania, where the Federalists were a despised but significant minority. In addition to the hero of New Orleans against the party of treason, Jacksonians in the

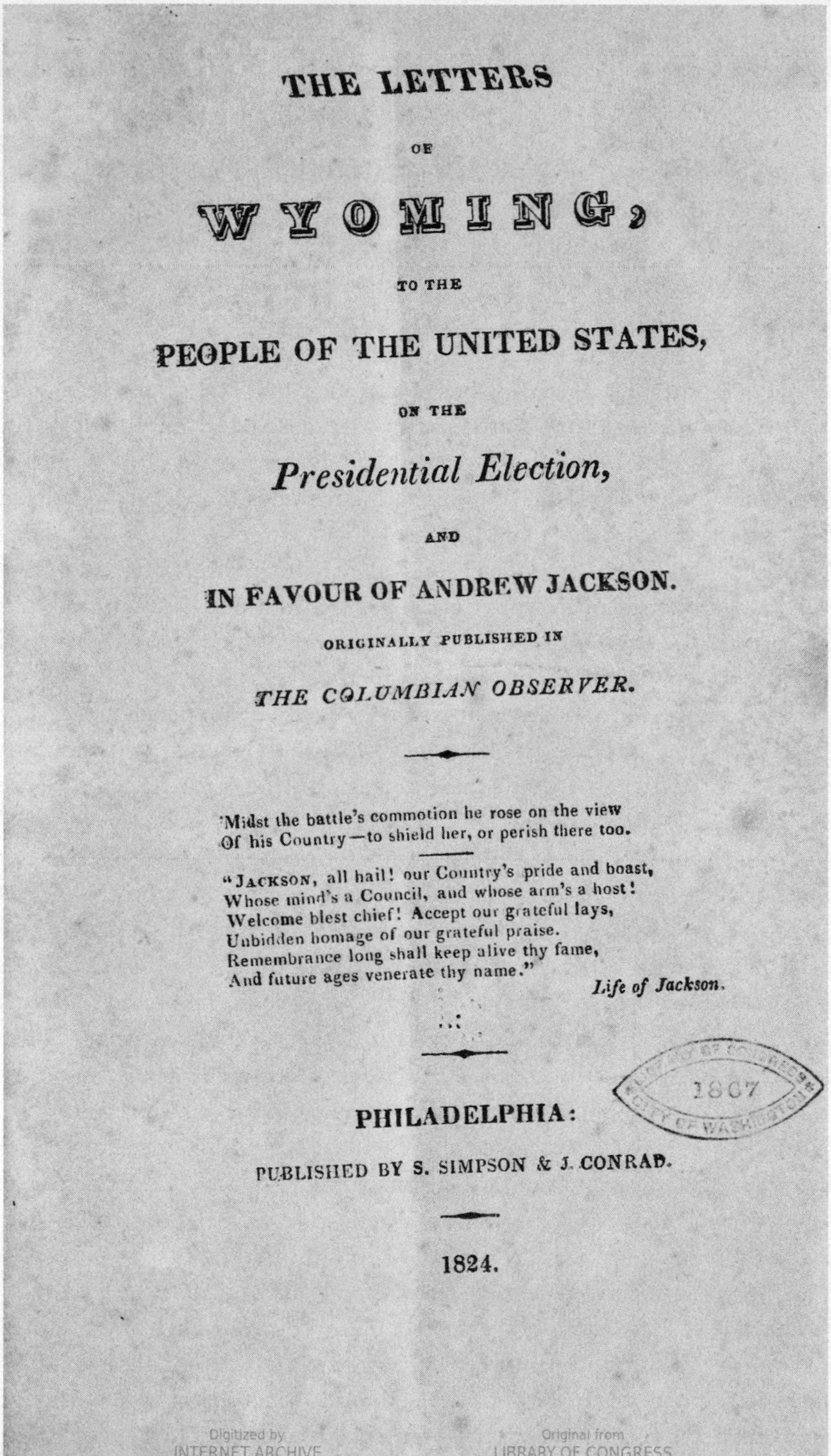

THE LETTERS

OF

WYOMING,

TO THE

PEOPLE OF THE UNITED STATES,

ON THE

Presidential Election,

AND

IN FAVOUR OF ANDREW JACKSON.

ORIGINALLY PUBLISHED IN

THE COLUMBIAN OBSERVER.

'Midst the battle's commotion he rose on the view
Of his Country—to shield her, or perish there too.

"JACKSON, all hail! our Country's pride and boast,
Whose mind's a Council, and whose arm's a host!
Welcome blest chief! Accept our grateful lays,
Unbidden homage of our grateful praise.
Remembrance long shall keep alive thy fame,
And future ages venerate thy name."

Life of Jackson.

PHILADELPHIA:

PUBLISHED BY S. SIMPSON & J. CONRAD.

1824.

Figure 6.3 *Letters of Wyoming.* Written by Jackson biographer and admirer John Eaton, this text presented the general as the one true nationalist amid a crowded field of corrupt politicians.

state declared, their man was a long-time Republican, and thus a trusted foe of "the whisky act, the alien law, the sedition law and all the measures of the reign of terror." Everyone in central and western Pennsylvania remembered when more than ten thousand nationalized militiamen had marched through to crush agrarian protest in 1794. Every German family in the eastern part of the state recalled a second crackdown in 1799. Federalist judges had taken up where Federalist troops left off, repeatedly frustrating popular measures to restrict land speculation, suspend debt collection, and raise taxes on the wealthy.[74]

Of course, Jackson was much like a Federalist judge on these issues. But few people knew about that, and even if so they could not vote against it, least of all at the national level. Their Andrew Jackson had rebelled against the other half of the Federalist project, the one that had tied the republic to a trans-Atlantic civil society of nations. Their disdain for European norms set them clearly apart. While figures from President Adams to Governors Carroll and Shulze praised European advances in education, science, and technology, the Jacksonians narrated the life of their hero and nation as a virtuous struggle against the powerful states and moral ambivalence of the Old World. Alone among his "race" of Irish settlers, they recounted, Jackson had survived to "avenge the wrongs of himself, his family, and his country" upon an empire "reeking with the blood of his ancestors." Now he would avenge the people against a government that ignored their love for him.[75]

Although these themes scared dead-end conservatives who openly disliked the unwashed masses, the basic idea of the American nation from which they drew was well established by the 1820s. Pennsylvania Jacksonians were both embracing and expanding that national concept, tying a history steeped in crying blood to a future of democratic reform. It was the National Republicans who offered the newer version of "Union," one that applied within rather than beyond the rule of law. It was Adams and Clay who appealed to patriotic duties in times of peace rather than war, for virtue in society rather than in nature. For good reason, Pennsylvanians were skeptical. For good reason, they recoiled from national plans to promote national commerce, even as so many of them supported such measures within their own state-nation. At the same time, Jackson appealed to those who did not share Governor Shulze's estimation of the people as "prosperous and happy beyond all former example," and who worried about their declining independence vis-à-vis their improvement-minded employers.[76]

As the November elections approached, Jacksonians rallied while their opponents sulked. The general's men marched through the streets, singing and chanting their way to another landslide in Pennsylvania and 56% of the overall popular vote, backed by a turnout that doubled the 1824 total. Fierce loyalty to the great avenger, confidence in their majority, and fear that they might be cheated again sometimes pushed them to more direct action. At a Fourth of July celebration in Pittsburgh, one speaker had declared that any congressman who again installed "an aristocratic president" would be "*tarred* and *feathered*." Jackson men in Philadelphia formed a committee to "take such measures" as would keep Henry Clay from setting foot there. Another crowd attacked the Philadelphia home and offices of an anti-Jackson printer. In the Juniata River Valley, where cabins that had served as forts during Indian scares still bore bullet holes, one township is said to have voted ninety-seven to three for the general. Supposedly, a crowd then beat up two of the suspected Adams voters, who after all seemed more like traitors than voters.[77]

If Jackson supporters outdid their foes in terms of physical intimidation, certain Adams men stooped lower when it came to character assassination. They went looking for dirt on the general and his family, and found plenty. They made much of his extended military rule over New Orleans and the execution of seven militiamen under his command in early 1815. One anti-Jackson editor from Ohio picked up where some high-society types in the Crescent City had left off that year, when they had called Rachel Jackson homely and fat. She was also a bigamist and a slut, the editor charged. For good measure he called the general's dead mother a whore. Rachel's niece, Emily Donelson, told her to ignore the slings and arrows, but Mrs. Jackson was in no shape for such disdain: "No, Emily, I'll never forget it."[78]

As for her husband, he let his Junto reply to the attacks, his restraint once more feeding his rage. "*You know me*," Jackson told Sam Houston. "I will curb my feelings until it becomes proper to act, when retributive *Justice will vissit* [Clay] *and his pander[ers] head*." He was slow to anger, then terrible in judgment. He never hurt women, children, or slaves, sheltering everyone in his power. Jackson mostly stayed at the Hermitage but released several dozen letters and statements during the campaign, making it all the more a referendum about him. He kept a dignified distance from the political maelstrom yet knew its every detail. The Nashville postmen often found the old man waiting for them at the end of his drive, eager for the latest.[79]

No wonder that news of victory left Rachel worried and depressed in the late fall of 1828. After spending so many years with Andrew gone, she would now have to leave her garden, her pastor, the slaves who waited on her, and the church she had helped to build on the Hermitage grounds. She would have to live in a city she despised, surrounded by uppity women and men who had heard all about her. Her checkered past would follow her east, she knew, tormenting her behind every fake smile. Instead she fell to severe chest pain on December 17, 1828, and died just before Christmas. Church bells tolled across Nashville to signal her passing. Stoic but distraught, Jackson walked with a cane at her service. The tombstone, added a few years later, covered her in the familiar arc of innocence, persecution, and vindication: "A being so gentle and so virtuous, slander might wound but could not dishonor." His enemies had pushed her to the grave, Jackson believed. Now, as the president of the people, he would make them sorry.[80]

Conclusion

Submit to Nothing

Andrew Jackson wore a mourning band as he made his way back to Washington in January 1829. Those who caught a glimpse of the legendary warrior saw a sad, tired old man whose body was giving out. He had taken a bad fall in 1825, possibly reopening the abscess that had developed on his breast plate after Charles Dickinson shot him in 1806. Thereafter he endured chronic swelling, which he morbidly treated by cutting his forearm. Years in the field without clean water returned in long bouts of diarrhea, and his left shoulder ached from his 1813 shootout with the Bentons. So he sat with his chest wedged against the back of a chair, bracing himself against the pain. In the White House he would lean on the care of Rachel's nephew, Andrew Donelson, and on Donelson's wife, Emily. She did her best to make "Uncle" feel at home, and he trusted her to run things. "You know best, my Dear," he would say. Others remember how this man of violence would gently pat children's heads as he sat with visitors, his long, bony fingers tightening whenever talk turned to politics.[1]

Historians have long wondered what his politics were on the day of his riotous inauguration. Jackson and his partisans had been deliberately vague on that score for seven years, and his early speeches followed suit. Besides his pointed praise for the British, they were measured and predictable, revealing him as little else than a practical Unionist who did not feel that the nation needed to improve as much as Adams had insisted.

Those who now see Jackson as an egalitarian reformer are left to assume that such improvement was unpopular, and to hang considerable weight on what the general had previously said about the "monied aristocracy" of eastern cities. In many cases the argument boils down to association: Jackson rode to power on a democratic wave that had already swept away suffrage restrictions and caucus selections, and then institutionalized those changes in the name of "the Democracy." Others infer that he had a change of heart on some key issues, embracing the more populist role that voters assigned him.[2]

There is no question that the presidency changed Andrew Jackson, perhaps more than it had his predecessors. He had less experience with national politics than "Secretary" executives like Adams, Monroe, and Madison, and his black-and-white view of things made life in Washington difficult. "It has pleased heaven to leave me alone in this world," the widower told his confidantes. "Not a drop of my blood runs in the veins of any American. I have no wife, no child. . . . Yet do I love my country." Often he felt both alone and surrounded, unable to see friend from foe and to control things as he could in military camps and slaveholding homes. The ambiguous hierarchies and incessant scheming of Washington made him angry and suspicious. Three members of his own cabinet betrayed and spied on him, he believed, and he could not even trust Andrew and Emily Donelson to respect his emotional support for Peggy Eaton, the wife of his first secretary of war. His grief over Rachel merged with his physical pain and general fatigue, and he asked about her tomb as if longing to rest his own bones.[3]

His only comfort, besides the large plantation that was waiting for him back home, was his fierce certainty that Americans were with him. "I was making a Cabinet for my self, as I told them," Jackson seethed as polite society shunned Mrs. Eaton. "I did not come here to make a Cabinet for the Ladies of this place, but for the nation." His goals and those of the nation were one and the same, and so his last mission was to give them what he had long demanded for himself: unlimited freedom to pursue whatever they wanted, wherever they wanted, bound only by constitutional rules of property and a "sacred" duty to avenge each other. It was to restore the lawful sovereignty of white Americans against their enemies, against their government, against society itself. As he liked to say, neither he nor they would submit to "anything that is wrong." These convictions guided President Jackson through Indian removal and the Bank War, among other struggles, forging a powerful link between his idea of the nation and its idea of democracy.[4]

SAVAGE STATES AND UNBOUND NATIONS

John Eaton is best remembered for his controversial wife, but as secretary of war he left his own mark. In early 1829, he received complaints from Cherokee leaders about recent efforts by the Georgia legislature to extend its laws over their five-million-acre homeland. The integrity of that national domain, the Cherokees noted, was secured not only by numerous treaties but also by their 1827 constitution. In addition to rules about contracts and "the African race" familiar to white Americans, that charter forbade individuals from selling their improvements to the United States and empowered the Cherokee state to "prevent the citizens from monopolizing improvements with the view of speculation." Eaton would have none of it. All "original Sovereignty" belonged to Georgia, he scolded. In light of all the times they had "waged war upon our frontier settlements," the Cherokees should be grateful for the "mildness and forbearance" that Georgia had shown. If they did not take the federal government's equally generous offer of western land, they would have to submit to the laws of the "Sovereign States" in which they lived.[5]

This was the general plan that Jackson worked out with his most trusted allies between 1828 and 1830. Along with the dismissal of many federal employees, the removal of all southern Indians was his top priority. Unlike his predecessors, he made his key appointments with this goal in mind and was ready to bear almost any cost—political, financial, or moral—to see it through. Never again, he resolved, would white households have to fear Indian country, or to get around it while rushing cash crops to foreign markets. As during the latter stages of war in the 1810s, Jackson never really had to defend these motives, enabling him to trot out various arguments about states' rights and humanitarian necessity without losing sight of what had to be done. Indeed, the deportation of the Choctaw, Chickasaw, Creek, Cherokee, and Seminole nations required every bit of force and guile against the strong opposition or simple foot-dragging of anti-removal chiefs, anti-Jackson congressmen, Choctaw women, Presbyterian missionaries, female-dominated churches, conservative judges, and unreliable militiamen. Rather than a linear process of "Indian Removal," then, we might describe three overlapping phases of this signature project of Jacksonian rule.[6]

The first phase was legislative activism. It began at the state level in Georgia in 1827 and continued over the next five years in Alabama, Mississippi, and Tennessee. Its keystone was "extension," the sudden application of state laws over the targeted nations. Speaking for their former commander in 1830, Eaton and Coffee told the Choctaws that Jackson, the "Great White Father," could not protect them from the Mississippi laws that would soon treat them like vagrants rather than citizens. In the case of Creeks and Cherokees within Georgia, extension also meant that individual improvements might be displaced by white claims, which only multiplied after the discovery of gold in the state's northern mountains. Like their allies in Washington, Georgia Jacksonians were especially harsh toward native elites. One law limited Cherokee owners to modest homesteads and forbade them from employing non-Indian slaves, tenants, or croppers. If any "aristocracy" had reason to fear Jacksonian democracy, it was the Cherokees.[7]

United in their desire to wipe out native jurisdictions, white Georgians were more divided when it came to the individual owners who wanted to stay. Governor George Gilmer, for one, thought that Cherokees should be able to bring suit in the courts that now governed them. This modest concession to the rule of law cost him in the 1831 election, when he faced Wilson Lumpkin. An "unwavering convert to the principles of free trade," Lumpkin wanted to connect Georgia to the Tennessee River by way of a canal—right through the Cherokee nation. The Cherokees refused, and Lumpkin made the disappearance of that nation the core mission of his public life. He narrowly defeated Gilmer by promising to open Cherokee lands for whites and to exclude Cherokee plaintiffs from courts. He swore fealty to "the unofficial, sovereign people" and worked hand in glove with the legislature to push the Cherokees out. He also counted on President Jackson, who duly told Cherokee leaders that "the arm of the Government" could not protect them from the restless states.[8]

And yet the bill for Indian removal that came to Congress in 1830 did not say anything about deporting anyone. It simply gave Jackson authority to negotiate "exchanges," whereby Indian nations would receive Oklahoma parcels and annual payments in return for their eastern homelands. The quiet linchpin of the bill was its $500,000 appropriation, which came with no strings attached. The more keen observers in Congress knew that this would give people like Coffee and Eaton a free hand to bribe, bully, and cheat native authorities. Most opponents were more appalled by the general idea. Relations with the southern tribes had been improving and stabilizing, they thought, especially since the arrival of dozens of respectable missionaries in their nations. How could the United States now turn on such men and the souls in their care? How could a peacetime government forsake "the great end for which human laws are made, that is, the protection of the weak against the strong"? Northern churches increasingly dominated by women flooded Congress with anti-removal petitions; one from Pittsburgh bore 670 names. Pennsylvania had always "plumed herself" for the fair way it had acquired Indian lands, one of the president's allies scoffed.[9]

"Yes, sir," Wilson Lumpkin argued during the congressional debate over removal, "amongst my earliest recollections are the walls of an old fort, which gave protection to the women and children from the tomahawk and scalping knife of the Indians." Georgia had forborne "for so many years," enduring all manner of "Indian perplexities" because bloodless politicians cowered from natural duties and pretended that Indians could become as Christian and innocent as white Americans already were. Lumpkin angrily affirmed the president's good faith. "No man living entertains kinder feelings to the Indians than Andrew Jackson." Having "chastise[d] them in times that are gone by," the Old Hero was now willing to show mercy. Another Georgian described his state's relation to the United States as one of creditor and debtor, reminding the representatives that the law required them "[to] be just before they can be generous." The bill barely passed the House, 102 to 97, with the slave states strongly in favor and everyone else divided or opposed.[10]

"I have exonerated the national character from all imputation," the president told one of his advisors a few months after the May 1830 vote. He had even traveled back to Tennessee to meet with native delegations and impress upon them the dangers gathering around them. "If now they shall refuse to accept the liberal terms offered," he told the US interpreter for the Choctaws, "they only must be liable for whatever evils and dificulties may arise." Despite the objections of a determined group of elder women, that nation was the first to encounter such evils. The removal treaty that Eaton and Coffee pushed through in September further divided these former Jackson allies, whose deportation began in late 1831—during an especially brutal winter for which they were entirely unprepared. Not until the summer of that year did the War Department seriously consider the logistics of moving some twenty thousand people in three waves over several hundred miles of deep forests, thick swamps, and icy rivers.[11]

The resulting misery of the Choctaw refugees led Eaton's successor as secretary of war, Lewis Cass, to draw up some regulations for the next removal, that of the Chickasaws. But the Creeks and Cherokees were not so easy to "get clear of," and in calling Jackson's bluff they initiated a second phase of the calamity, this one in the judicial domain. Famously, the Cherokee leadership brought suit to the 1831 session of the Supreme Court, which ruled that they could not do so as a "domestic dependent nation." The native plaintiffs may well have stopped to wonder just what white people wanted. In barely a generation, they had imposed a new rule of law over themselves. They had suppressed clan vengeance, converted to Christianity, and turned to staple crops and slave labor. Now, the state and federal governments condemned them for having formed a coherent nation while the highest court rebuffed them as something less than that. The *Cherokee Phoenix* could only conclude that the 1830 murder of one of their own was a ploy to provoke all-out war. "Forbear, forbear—revenge not," the paper urged of the citizens, "but leave vengeance to him 'to whom vengeance belongeth.' "[12]

The arrest of a white missionary in Cherokee lands prompted a more favorable ruling in 1832. John Marshall's decision in *Worcester v. Georgia* undermined the extension laws, and at least one justice from Georgia also registered his opposition to them. As Jackson himself had so often said, every civilized country had to give its property owners their day in court. But as the nation's president, Jackson would no longer abide any rival jurisdiction in its way. His national concept positively encouraged them to seek their fortunes in new lands and markets, where their interests were least likely to overlap and require regulation. So he dismissed Marshall's decision as "still born" while the Alabama Supreme Court used Vattel to annul all "pretension[s] to savage sovereignty" by the Creeks, whose 1832 treaty divided their nation into individual allotments without requiring them to move. Its three justices—two of whom were veterans of the 1813–14 holy war—paraphrased the long-dead Swiss theorist to establish that "the Indian" was incapable of progress or possession. Rather than the legitimate head of household that the treaty said he might become, the native man was more akin to "the beast of the same forest that he inhabits." For his part, Lumpkin vowed to hang the missionaries before bowing to "a few superannuated life estate judges."[13]

Jackson persuaded Lumpkin to release the missionaries and also insisted that the War Department use steamboats to rush the deportees out. Otherwise, the president kept his distance. Especially in what had been the Creek Nation of eastern Alabama, the sudden appearance of so much private property and its accompanying paperwork gave rise to what even Lumpkin admitted were "enormous frauds." Since native owners had no access to courts, white speculators defrauded them at will and took the lion's share of the allotments. Vermont native W. J. Beattie told friends back home that people were selling goods at 150% profits and that he was "emigrating Indians" for a private company. His correspondents were intrigued. "I should like to know what your speculation business really is," one wrote. Assuring Beattie that he was only interested in "*how to make fortunes*," this Vermonter offered to keep the details from Beattie's anti-slavery kin. The family wants to join you on the southern frontier,

Beattie's sister wrote in 1835. All except mother, who was afraid that the Indians would "rise and kill her."[14]

She had reason to worry, for a third and even more violent phase of the removals began that year. Unable to grow or buy food, the Alabama Creeks wasted away while government agents kept pressing them to move west. The War Department tried to step in and buy allotments directly from the Creeks, irritating the rival land companies that now held the titles. Small bands of desperate Creeks turned to violence in early 1836 and planned to burn the town of Columbus, Georgia, the site of one of the most hated companies. Some four hundred miles to the southeast, a larger rebellion began in northeast Florida. Outraged by burlesque treaties and subsequent demands of deportation, Seminole warriors and black rebels hid their families and attacked frontier plantations in late December 1835. Rushing to retaliate, Jackson's old comrade Edmund P. Gaines found the bodies of a hundred US troops in a pine forest south of St. Augustine. Some of them had apparently been axed to death by black fighters.[15]

Now an administration that had been pleading constitutional impotence on behalf of the sovereign states swept into action. Secretary of War Cass sent US troops into Alabama to stamp out Creek resistance. It was a pity that the president himself was not in command, one northerner mused, since the "very *name* of General Jackson would have terror struck them." The hungry insurgents quickly gave up, for the remains of their nation were already on the move. Private contractors and US troops eventually marched some eighteen thousand Creeks west to Memphis, where they boarded boats down the Mississippi and then up the Arkansas. In 1838, US troops and Georgia militia also forced some sixteen thousand people of the Cherokee Nation, now split into thirteen wretched camps, onto the long journey known as the Trail of Tears. Eager to hold down transport costs, the War Department's regulations prohibited the migrants from bringing horses or furniture. So while soldiers forced the Cherokees along, debt collectors took whatever they could find "for the payment of unjust and just Demands."[16]

With the help of Shawnee and Delaware scouts, American troops in Florida quickly captured Osceola, a Seminole leader and Horseshoe Bend survivor, while many black fighters gave up and fled to Oklahoma or Arkansas. Then the campaign stalled. Tracking a few hundred fighters through trackless woods and swamps, US officers complained of skittish civilians who saw "an Indian in every bush" and of faithless militiamen who wanted to go home. Frustration gave way to desperation. Federal officials heard plans for putting a $1,000 bounty on any Seminole, for sicking bloodhounds on blacks and natives, and for using hot-air balloons to scan the country by night. A series of scorched-earth missions in the summer of 1841 finally compelled all but a few die-hards to surrender. They, too, ended up in the middle of the continent, stateless and despised. "Anyone who has ever visited their beautiful villages," one officer remarked of the Seminoles, "would not be surprised at the reluctance of the Indians to exchange Florida for the cold country of Arkansas."[17]

This second Florida war cost some $30 million, sixty times the initial appropriation for the Removal Act. Choctaw removal alone cost another $5 million. Jackson saw no conflict between these high costs and his republican scruples, because his political ideas grew out of his military experiences no less than his legal precepts. To make the Indians disappear was a matter of physical safety, as well as commercial freedom. In some ways his closest ideological peers during the 1830s were the army and navy hardliners from the 1810s. Besides General Gaines, these included Secretary Cass, who as governor of the Michigan Territory had isolated the Kickapoos and Sauks from their British allies in the name of "the Sovereignty of the United States." President Jackson was doing the same for the South, and he bristled at moralistic carping from the Indian-free North. Jackson also oversaw a steep increase in the navy's budget. "Your Navy will not only protect your rich and flourishing commerce in distant seas," he maintained, "but will

Figure 7.1 Seminole villages, lithograph from 1837. Uprooting and deporting such communities to the far west took the US Army many years.
Courtesy of the State Archives of Florida.

enable you to reach and annoy the enemy." In a lawless world, "the enemy" might be anywhere, blurring the distinction between civilians and servicemen and inviting both to use violence in service to commerce.[18]

In 1831, for instance, Jackson learned that a merchant ship out of Salem, Massachusetts, had been waylaid by some Sumatran villagers. Three sailors had been killed, and large crowds had chanted, "Who great man now, Malay or American?" Jackson and his Navy secretary dispatched a frigate to find the guilty parties and stolen goods, or else. Arriving at the village of Kuala Batu in early 1832, the captain opened fire on the unsuspecting residents. Jackson was distressed by reports of many women among the 60 to 150 bodies left behind, but in his next speech to Congress he called the victims "a band of lawless pirates." Even with European nations, Jackson hinted that he would use military force to collect debts. When a new monarchy in France was slow to pay old damages as worked out in an 1831 treaty, he warned that the United States might "take redress into their own hands." If the French refused to pay, they would expose themselves to "the just censure of civilized nations and to the retributive judgments of Heaven," the wrath of a nation built equally on modern commerce and epic religion.[19]

FLUSH TIMES AND HARD MONEY

For a man whose name is forever tied to a "war" on the Second Bank of the United States (BUS), Jackson's prior views of that vast corporation are not clear. In 1817, he had heard complaints about the "money changers at Philadelphia" whose "*great* bank" presumed to regulate commerce in ways that he never liked. The BUS was widely resented by state-chartered banks of the kind that his inner circle in Nashville controlled. Nor did Jackson appreciate the efforts by Governor William Carroll to open a BUS branch in Nashville, which bore fruit in 1827. Then again, the general preferred "u states notes" to any other currency besides coin, for they did not lose value over state lines and helped Americans do business abroad. In that respect his anti-BUS crusade is all the more surprising: a national currency might have resolved his lifelong struggle against late payments and unreliable debtors.[20]

Popular opinion of the BUS had also improved since the 1819 crash, thanks in part to its new president, Nicholas Biddle. Privileged and precocious, Biddle was not yet forty when he took over in 1823. Not as tall or imposing as Jackson, Biddle did not need to boast or threaten; he knew that he knew best. Like his predecessor he was hard on lesser banks, discounting their bills while bolstering his own with the accounts of both private investors and the federal government. While marketing Treasury securities to wealthy men all over the Atlantic world, however, Biddle also authorized his branch offices to issue $5 or $10 "drafts" that passed as legal tender. Such bills were in great demand in an expanding economy and clearly superior to those of their competitors. Decrying the scarcity of money and resulting auctions of "poor mens cows," a Tennessee farmer and state-level politician appealed for a BUS branch in every state "and all other money put down." From this perspective, the fact that BUS notes accounted for one-fifth of the Union's total was not enough by four fifths.[21]

In late 1829, Biddle proposed paying down the remaining $49 million of national debt more quickly by assuming $13 million in old liabilities and retiring the $7 million that the government had paid for its BUS shares. In return Biddle wanted a new charter. Eliminating the debt was dear to Jackson's heart, but the general had also received word during the 1828 campaign that BUS operatives in Kentucky were paying down-and-outers to vote for Adams. Jackson was understandably appalled by the charge and characteristically sure that it was true. (Actually Biddle had voted for Jackson.) So he told Overton that the BUS had to be "*curbed*" and warned Biddle of his doubts about its constitutionality. If a republic should have any bank, he mused in 1830, it should be an "intirely national" one, issuing bills only when the people were at their most national—that is, during war. Then again, an anti-relief veteran from Kentucky told Jackson that a "great majority" of the people approved the BUS as a shield against "effigy Banks and their Bastard depreciated paper." Biddle's bank was popular not only with well-off farmers and manufacturers but also with most Pennsylvanians. Jackson's popularity in that pivotal state had taken a hit with Indian removal, one source confided. Securing its electors again would be "a *hard battle*."[22]

For most of his first term Jackson made vague threats in public while privately condemning "*that monster of corruption*" and considering a veto of its charter. He entertained ideas about a more constitutional BUS and even about a "National Bank" that could fund internal improvements. Support for the BUS, improvements, and tariffs tended to overlap in some of the president's nonslavery strongholds, but the West was wary of the BUS while the South was hostile to the tariff, leaving Jackson to temporize. The president "cannot satisfy both Pennsylvan[ia] and the South," one opponent noted, guessing also that Jackson leaned toward the free-trading planters rather than any "system of national policy." He signed bills to fund lighthouses and harbor improvements while showing less enthusiasm for roads and canals. He assured correspondents that he favored some projects but made clear that he would protect the nation's "individual owners," as one arch-conservative put it, from national expenses. As for the BUS, the president made no final decisions before January 1832.[23]

Then Biddle again pressed for a new charter, four years before its expiration. Although the first BUS had made a similar request, Jackson took this as another insult. When a House committee reported that spring that the BUS had bribed its way to good press, Jackson told a Presbyterian pastor that this "confirm[ed] what I had always thought, that it was, as at present constituted, one of the greatest Mamoths of corruption ever created." Once more his raging desire to humble his enemies overwhelmed his idle reveries of retirement. No matter that his own Treasury secretary, Louis McClane, approved the BUS or that the bill for recharter passed the House, 107 to 85, in early July 1832. Scrambling for allies, Jackson turned to Amos Kendall, a sickly New Englander who had once supported relief in Kentucky before taking a Treasury appointment. For several days Kendall, Jackson, and a few other advisors did nothing but write and rewrite the most famous veto in American history.[24]

Kendall's first draft warned that the "Generals, admirals, nobility and gentry of a hostile kingdom" might use their ownership of BUS stock to control their former colonies. In the final version as approved by Jackson, such anti-British tropes gave way to vaguer warnings about letting "subjects of a foreign power" inside the Union's fiscal house. But the veto was mostly about the American people and their Constitution. Inequality "will always exist under every just government," it concluded. People were "equally entitled" to the full protection of "the fruits of superior industry, economy, and virtue." The better governments "[left] individuals and States as much as possible to themselves," so that the rich and well born had no more favors (or duties) than "the humble members of society." The republic had no right to interpose on behalf of any citizen—and no more reason to under the democratic rule Jackson had restored, since all citizens were, a priori, equal. As the impartial guardian of commercial order, government was an "unqualified blessing." Otherwise, it was corruption waiting to happen.[25]

Biddle was so certain that the veto made Jackson look crazy that he paid for the printing of thirty thousand copies and helped to bankroll Henry Clay's run for the White House that fall. Jackson's attacks on the BUS, on Indians and missionaries, and on the balance of power cut into his Pennsylvania support, and Clay prevailed in his home state, Maryland and Delaware, and southern New England. The insurgent Anti-Masons, led by one of the Cherokee Nation's legal defenders, William Wirt, offered another alternative in the Northeast. But Jackson dominated slave country, especially the parts he had saved and opened. He took almost every vote in Tennessee, Alabama, Mississippi, Georgia, and Missouri and strengthened his grip on Virginia, North Carolina, and Louisiana. In the crucial battlegrounds of the mid-Atlantic and old Northwest, "Hickory Clubs" and Jackson parades gave the well-organized Democrats an intimidating edge, carrying the president to a decisive victory.[26]

At this point Jackson turned toward his southern base and away from the nationalist program that had seemed so strong ten years before. In March 1833, he vetoed Clay's comprehensive plan to use federal land sales to pay for improvements, education, and the colonization of free blacks. To his cabinet he now said that government should promote commerce and then "let all alone." He denounced the "misnamed American system" as a "British system of corrupt influence in Embryo," a tawdry "system of bargaining" and "system of favoritism" on behalf of "the monied classes." Always eager to prolong the emergency powers of war, Jackson took the opposite view of peacetime development, scaling back public works and national society as memories of the last Anglo-American conflict faded. At the same time he made clear that South Carolina's nullification of the revenue laws was treasonous, and that he would strike down their "Repleven laws" and enforce the compromise tariffs passed by Congress.[27]

Determined now to destroy the BUS rather than to reform it, Jackson relied on Roger B. Taney of the attorney general's office. In 1832, this former Federalist had supported South Carolina's quarantine of black sailors, arguing that black people could never be part of "the sovereignty of any state." The following year he fed Jackson new arguments against the BUS after a House committee found it to be perfectly solvent. Biddle's institution had wagered too much of the people's money while lending the people too many loans, Taney insisted. It was monopolistic rather than national, an unnatural force without constitutional or popular support. "My mind has for some time been made up," Taney told the president in August 1833, "that the continued existence of [this] powerful and corrupting monopoly will be fatal to the liberties of the people, and that no man but yourself is strong enough to meet and destroy it." Either Taney believed every word of this or he knew exactly how to rouse the old man to action.[28]

By the end of 1833, the president was convinced that the BUS had caused the hard times of 1819–22, that the people hated it, and that he had always been "opposed to the U. States Bank, nay all Banks." In lieu of a confused and overgrown money supply overseen by northern financiers, he imagined a simpler but radically decentralized cash economy. Over the opposition of his old and new Treasury secretaries, Jackson thus ordered the government's revenues to be redirected from the BUS to various "deposit banks," in effect dismantling what had passed for a national banking system. Biddle retaliated by calling in many of his bank's loans, a harsh and petulant move that caused a minor economic downturn. This only vindicated Taney's warnings and deepened Jackson's growing self-image as champion of the common man. The president called Taney a "sterling man" and appointed the Marylander first as interim secretary of the Treasury and then as Supreme Court justice.[29]

While Taney convinced Jackson that many deposit banks could handle the government's money, Thomas Hart Benton argued that gold and silver might displace bank notes altogether. The Missouri senator had first made this case while demanding full access to Chinese markets. Once they could sell their crops and pelts across the Pacific, Benton maintained, Americans would draw silver and silks from the Orient. For the president, this kind of hard-money fundamentalism was a reasonable outgrowth of lifelong views about contracts and commerce. For the American people it was a much more dramatic reversal of a century-long conflict, during which inflationary money had usually been the populist cause. As of 1833, the most popular man in the Union instead called hard money their best shot at a fair deal. This resonated especially with the new Workingmen's parties of New York and Philadelphia. If public banks were no longer possible and waged work was no longer avoidable, they at least wanted to be paid in something they could count on. Exploited by holier-than-thou employers, they rallied more than ever to the grim, principled man whose grim principles at least granted no more favors from above.[30]

If Jackson was ever happy during his presidency, it was while traveling back home in the summer of 1834. True, the emergent Whigs in Congress had censured him for removing the government's money from the one bank it could oversee. But the national debt was about to disappear, and Congress had approved a measure to encourage the importation and minting of gold coins. Traveling through friendly crowds, Jackson made a point of paying innkeepers with gold pieces, "which many had not for years seen." Soon the people would have all the gold they deserved, "as well dug from our soil as imported." The president saw "prosperity everywhere," and for good reason. Global specie flows had brought more Mexican silver to the Union, and British creditors were at last warming up to the lost colonies. As old concerns about the "law of debtor and creditor" in the revolutionary republic gave way to admiration of its resources and "national credit," and as the new South American states defaulted on their loans, British capital surged into the United States. Investors in London bought bonds floated by railroad and canal companies and by states where such improvements were more popular than ever, filling the role that some of Jackson's allies had once envisioned for a national bank.[31]

While Jackson celebrated the federal government's golden credit rating, then, state debts grew by 660% between 1830 and 1838. At least half of this growing sum was held by foreign creditors, and much of it went to the railroads and canals that paid long, slow dividends. In the states where native deportations were in full swing, however, over 85% of state debts were incurred to open or expand banks. More money was in high demand in Mississippi and Alabama because the white invaders of Choctaw and Creek lands had to get cotton to England as fast as possible, while prices were high. They could not wait for public investments or internal markets. The rapid rise in the number of deposit banks—from seven to twenty-two in late 1833 alone—and the removal of the BUS as a monetary clearinghouse further encouraged this new profusion of paper, which in turn accelerated the purchase of land.[32]

Jackson's campaigns against Indian country and the BUS thus began to feed off each other in unexpected ways. In 1833 and 1834, for example, two land offices in northern Mississippi sold nearly 5 million acres, mostly at the low minimum prices that the Jacksonians and the president himself preferred. With the Choctaws and Chickasaws physically gone or legally dead, the migrants kept coming. In 1835, the General Land Office in DC reported an unprecedented 12.5 million acres sold across the Union; 20 million acres followed in 1836, overwhelming this office much as Indian removal had the War Department. Judging by what they did with their money, however, British investors did not (yet) worry. Confident that they could recover their debts, the "American houses" of London kept lending credit, leading to a sharp rise in the US trade imbalance with Great Britain. And all under a president who symbolized anti-British patriotism.[33]

"This apparently preposterous state of things was at first a matter of exultation to the government," observed an English reporter. The unbound people were making the nation richer than ever, burying arguments for both relief and protection. And yet Jackson never forgot the 1819–22 depression that had spawned those movements and began to worry that something worse was on the way. Whenever "farmers" like us fall into debt, the president told his adopted son while waging war on the BUS, their estates "must go" to meet their obligations. Inflexible as ever about the stakes of business, he scrambled now to check its feverish expansion. Beginning in 1835, the administration required higher standards of payment for public lands and tried to drive smaller bills out of circulation. The following July, Jackson ordered the secretary of the Treasury to require gold or silver coin of anyone buying public land. The stated purpose of this Specie Circular was to discourage "the monopoly of the public lands in the

Figure 7.2 *High Water in the Mississippi*. Although decades removed from the boom times of the 1830s, this 1868 lithograph by English immigrant Frances F. Palmer captures the environmental and social chaos brought on by commercial agriculture, as well as the vast inequalities of the Cotton Kingdom.
Currier and Ives, 1868.

hands of speculators and capitalists," to cool off the blistering markets in lands and slaves.[34]

The Specie Circular along with supplemental transfers ordered by the Treasury drained gold from the deposit banks of New York City. As of September 1836 they held $7.2 million in specie reserves, some 10% of the nation's total. By March 1837, when Jackson left office and the first signs of trouble hit New Orleans, that sum had tumbled to $2.8 million. The rest languished in western vaults. Across the Atlantic, the directors of the Bank of England began to wonder if they should still accept notes from New York merchant houses. Cotton prices and interest rates wavered. Once again the economic fate of the republic turned on decisions made in the most exclusive corners of the empire. "The safety of the great body of the importing Merchants, and possibly of some of the Banks," Jackson's hand-picked successor, Martin Van Buren, reported in April 1837, "is supposed to depend upon the next arrivals from England." Bank runs hit the city a few weeks later, and by the end of the year about one-quarter of all banks had closed.[35]

Jackson blamed a concerted plan by Whigs and British creditors to "drain us of specie" and warned the banks to resume coin payments before the people regained "a proper sense of their own sovereign power." Even when he recognized Alabama and Mississippi as the epicenters of the crisis, though, he never made the link between the full-throttle expansion he required and the easy-money speculation he deplored. "But still it will produce good in the end," he told the new president. "[It] is like the [cholera], it sweeps off the dissapated and [those] of irregular habits." Van Buren was less clinical about the treatment but just as tied to hard-money solutions. "All communities are apt to look to government for too much," he declared. The business-friendly Whigs offered a more robust reply, for they saw the American people as a commercial society rather than just a commercial population. To do nothing but repress the money supply, Clay declared, was "narrow, selfish, [and] heartless." In the general's home state, the Whigs took over the legislature and launched new internal improvements.[36]

Rather than from the national parties, though, relief once more came out of governments willing to assert economic sovereignty within their boundaries. This included the Lone Star republic. Anglo-Americans had been settling the province of Coahuila y Tejas since the 1820s, and might well have stayed with the Republic of Mexico if it had authorized slavery and halted Comanche, Navajo, and Apache raids. Independent since 1836, Texas kept more of its Spanish past than it cared to admit, including debtor protections that dated to late medieval times. In early 1839, just before a second, more severe panic hit the United States, Texas introduced a "homestead exemption" law that kept fifty acres, household goods, and some livestock safe from seizure. Georgia, Mississippi, and Alabama followed suit. Six western states and Maryland put these exemptions into their constitutions between 1845 and 1860, and many others passed statutes to this effect. Supporters called them "sound" and "wholesome" laws that fostered a deeper tie between residents. Chief Justice Taney ruled against them, of course, citing the need to enforce contracts.[37]

SOVEREIGN CITIZENS

In his last addresses to Congress and the nation, Jackson warned about the speculating spirit that no government—least of all his kind—could contain. He also proposed sending a naval vessel to Mexico, authorized to take "immediate satisfaction" if its government did not pay outstanding claims due to American citizens. He had shown "great forbearance" on the matter, he noted. Upon his return to the Hermitage he found the church that he and Rachel had helped to build in the midst of a revival. Jackson had promised that he would officially join once his political career was over, and he kept his word after the standard evaluation. "General, there is one more question, it is my duty to ask you," the Presbyterian clergyman supposedly told the Presbyterian ex-president. "Can you forgive all your enemies?" Jackson is said to have paused and then replied that he could excuse his political foes, but not those "who abused me when I was serving my country in the field, and those who attacked me for serving my country." No exceptions, the pastor replied: God's children had to forgive their trespassers. The old man relented, although he never asked forgiveness of anyone.[38]

He spent his last years at the Hermitage, glad to be out of the game yet still drawn to it. The democracy spoke for the people against those who wanted to speak for them, he told visitors and correspondents. It gave them every chance in life against the rich and well born, and that was all they wanted or deserved. In 1842, he applauded the Dorr Rebels of Rhode Island, who rallied against an anachronistic constitution that denied urban workers the vote. If Van Buren was "weak" enough to send in troops to reinstall the old charter, Jackson declared, "the sovereign people" would fly to arms for their new constitution. He urged the government to annex Texas and his adopted son to set their slaves to cutting firewood, which was in great demand as fuel for steamboat engines. Often he was short of breath, unable to walk or talk, trapped in his own body.[39]

In April 1845, Jackson reluctantly agreed to add to his many portraits with a daguerreotype, an early form of photography just invented in France. The light bounced back a swollen mask of pain. "Humph!" he supposedly snapped. "Looks like a monkey!" Still he wanted to talk about politics and Texas and threats to the nation, preoccupied to the bitter end with what one Tennessee judge called "our great Slave and Indian border." On Sunday, June 8, 1845, Jackson could not attend church and realized that his time had come. He told his black and white caregivers to be good children and that he would see them all in heaven. The general died that evening, leaving most of his estate to his adopted son. Never good with money, Andrew Jackson Jr. later had to sell parts of the Hermitage to satisfy creditors.[40]

"This day the newspapers from Boston announce the death of Andrew Jackson," wrote John Quincy Adams, now a loose-cannon congressman who wanted no more expansion if it meant any more slavery. "Jackson was a hero, a murderer, an adulterer, and a profoundly pious Presbyterian." Another critic reflected: "Now that he is dead I find that I was very proud of him." Most people conveyed a simpler grief. Besides a living connection to the Revolution, Jackson had given them a solemn promise and an emotional bond. He had declared each of them worthy of the nation's passions, equals beyond the law, united not in the hum-drum management of society but by an extrahistorical mission to spread liberty and punish evil. Together with key investments in the navy, this blood bond gave the United States a unique capacity not only to project its power but also to see itself as innocent in doing so. It turned the military and moral liabilities of vengeance into a national resource.[41]

The panic-stricken Martin Van Buren could not carry Jackson's torch, but James K. Polk, barely elected in 1844, resolved to do so. "Young Hickory" was a Tennessee Jacksonian to the core. Humorless, childless, and pious, he had no doubts about his country and little curiosity about others. Seeing enemies everywhere, Polk rushed to expand US claims before the British or Russians set up hostile camps to the south or west. He blustered about war with Britain while carefully settling the Oregon question and pretended to negotiate with Mexico while preparing to invade it. Texas should have been included in the Louisiana Purchase, he argued in his March 1845 inaugural address. Now it was free to "merge her sovereignty" with the rest of the Union, whose expansion could only "extend the dominions of peace." Mexico had no say in settling the borders of its former province, or any reason to blame the United States for doing so. As long as it remained within its constitutional boundaries, Polk insisted, "our Government can not be otherwise than pacific." Nor would it restrain the "swarming millions" who were more or less loyal to it.[42]

The new president sent a navy squadron to Texas's Atlantic coast, ordered the US consul in Monterey to gin up anti-Mexican sentiment, and outfitted an overland mission to take Alta California. The Pacific squadron was to seize San Francisco when war began. After some stillborn negotiations, Polk ordered General Zachary Taylor into the disputed strip of land south of the Nueces River, down to the Rio Grande. In late April 1846, two weeks after Taylor blockaded that river, fighting broke out near the town of Matamoros. The news reached Polk just hours after he had begun a tepid war message that cited Mexican refusals to negotiate and repay debts. The revised product was much more Jacksonian. "The cup of forbearance" had already been exhausted, Polk declared. Now, after "repeated menaces," Mexico had "invaded our territory and shed American blood upon American soil." As in his inaugural address, he rhetorically repatriated the Anglo-Texans who had settled in Mexico decades earlier. One might say that he also posthumously repatriated the roughly two hundred Tennesseans, Virginians, Irishmen, Carolinians, and assorted adventurers killed at the Alamo mission in March 1836. Their blood made the ground it reddened American, no matter what the treaties said.[43]

As Congress fell into line, mixed forces of US sailors, settlers, and adventurers seized key parts of New Mexico and California. One group cried "New Orleans!" as they took Los Angeles on January 8, 1847, the thirty-second anniversary of Jackson's great victory. They neither required nor tolerated further direction from Washington. Precisely because the American government put few limits on their quest for vengeance and glory, they were loyal to the American nation. No one could stop what one paper called "the wild rapture of unchained passion" that Americans visited upon their foes, the "avalanche of American passion" that inspired every man to "sluice his veins" for his nation. In an 1836 speech that he reread to the Senate in 1845, Thomas Hart Benton equated Mexican demands that Anglo settlers turn in their arms at the village of Gonzales with the British incursion into Lexington, Massachusetts, back in 1775. "It was the same demand! and the same answer was given—resistance—battle—victory! for the American blood was at Gonzales as it had been at Lexington."[44]

Of course, this blood nationalism referred to the blood of white people. Benton even gushed about an "Anglo-Saxon character" and hoped that "old England" and young America would rejoice over its continental diffusion. Just as native deportation gained speed, in fact, free black men lost their right to vote in the new constitutions of Tennessee and North Carolina. Blacks were "outside the social compact," most delegates decided. The United States was "a nation of white people." Mississippi's 1832 constitution anticipated a "downright and absolute *democracy*," one delegate noted. It welcomed all white men into a racial order that made each of them a kind of sheriff against all nonwhites. After the 1831 Nat Turner uprising in neighboring Virginia, Pennsylvania banned the immigration of free blacks and required those who moved within the state to prove their right of residency. After reports that black voters bearing arms had tipped the balance in an 1837 election, Democrats called for direct action lest the "runaway" and "illegal" blacks "make the very streets run with white man's blood." The next year, a new constitution deprived Pennsylvania blacks of the franchise until after the Civil War.[45]

Besides free blacks, white abolitionists were the major targets of the riots that swept through the Union during the 1830s and of the lynchings that lasted much longer. Many anti-slavery activists were the sons and daughters of Federalists and veterans of the anti-removal campaign. They envisioned a deeper, wider rule of law infused with Christian love, a social contract of benevolent duty no less than constitutional liberty. As such they denounced violent men and passions, refused to defend themselves even when threatened, and opposed capital punishment. Especially after Nat Turner, public men in slave states agreed that these "fanatics" posed a clear and present danger to white households. Urban crowds no less than southern mobs thus targeted abolitionist meeting halls, black churches, and other mixed-race milieus as nuisances that aggrieved publics could forcibly—and, in a sense, legally—remove. So long as the cloying pretensions of civil society remained, how else could they convey their sovereignty than through summary justice? When else were they truly free and powerful, besides the exhilarating moment when the whip cracked and the rope fell?[46]

The promise of greater sovereignty for white Jacksonians was thus directly tied to the enhanced misery of black and native peoples in antebellum America. Rather than in the further regulation of any society, the citizens and their households took their new powers in a state of nature, at the expense of the traditional enemies in their midst. Their enhanced sovereignty required both the degradation of others and a certain kind of chaos in the nation at large: the daily freedoms for some to go armed, to seize lands, to vote, to take offense, and to threaten; the daily demands on others to retire, to hide, to bear quietly, and to forgive. Indeed, the foundational narrative that named white households as the original victims lent a violent edge to the roiling energies of the Jacksonian age, an enduring need to find sovereignty where the law did not reach and to go abroad in search of monsters to destroy.[47]

Even if we accept the dangerous formula that more democracy for some minus less democracy for others still makes a net gain, however, Jacksonian sovereignty cost the sovereigns too. For the citizens were only free within commercial order, never against it. Their liberty and power began with a lawfulness rooted in deeply conservative restrictions on what they could do for each other, a set of modern rules and artificial barriers that Jackson, more than anyone, renamed as permanent and natural—and democratic. What the people gained in individual sovereignty, they lost in their capacity to regulate the society they formed, to assert peacetime publics over the dizzying pace of modern economies. What the nation gained in avenging itself, it lost in its addiction to bloody pasts and its mistrust of human progress. Along with the healthy skepticism of state power and cultural snobbery that Jacksonian democracy has given us, then, we should also note how Jacksonian nationalism tends to push the people away from their futures and apart from each other, their love for their nation beat back ceaselessly by the terms of their nation.

ABBREVIATIONS

PUBLISHED MATERIALS: PRIMARY SOURCES

ASP — *American State Papers: Documents Legislative and Executive, of the Congress of the United States*. 38 vols. Washington, DC: Gales and Seaton, 1832–61.

AC — *The Debates and Proceedings in the Congress of the United States*, or *Annals of Congress*, 1789–1824, covering the First Congress through the first session of the Eighteenth Congress. For the sake of clarity I indicate whether the debates occurred in the House or Senate.

CAJ — *Correspondence of Andrew Jackson*. Edited by John Spencer Bassett. 7 vols. Washington, DC: Carnegie Institution of Washington, 1926–35.

CJP — *Correspondence of James K. Polk*. Edited by Herbert Weaver. 12 vols. Nashville: Vanderbilt University Press, 1969–.

CMP — *A Compilation of the Messages and Papers of the Presidents, 1789–1897*. Edited by James D. Richardson. 20 vols. New York: Bureau of National Literature, 1897.

CWT — *The Correspondence of William Tryon and Other Selected Papers*. Edited by William S. Powell. 2 vols. Raleigh: Division of Archives and History, Department of Cultural Resources, 1980, 1981.

DHAR — *Documentary History of the American Revolution*. Edited by R. W. Gibbes. 2 vols. New York, 1855, 1857.

DHRC	*The Documentary History of the Ratification of the Constitution*. Edited by John P. Kaminski et al. 27 vols. Madison: State Historical Society of Wisconsin, 1975–.
IT	*Indian Treaties, 1778–1883.* Edited by Charles J. Kappler. New York: Interland Publishing, 1973.
JGBP	*The John Gray Blount Papers*. Edited by Alice Barnwell Keith and William H. Masterson. 3 vols. Raleigh, NC: Division of Archives and History, Department of Cultural Resources, 1952–65.
KG	*Knoxville Gazette*, 1791–96, Knoxville, TN.
MJQA	*Memoirs of John Quincy Adams*. Edited by Charles Francis Adams. 12 vols. Philadelphia, 1874–77.
NWR	*Niles' Weekly Register*, 1811–49, Baltimore, MD.
PAJ	*The Papers of Andrew Jackson*. Edited by Daniel Feller et al. 10 vols. Knoxville: University of Tennessee Press, 1980–.
PGW	*The Papers of George Washington: Presidential Series*. Edited by Dorothy Twohig et al. 13 vols. Charlottesville: University of Virginia Press, 1987–.
PHC	*The Papers of Henry Clay.* Edited by James F. Hopkins. 10 vols. Lexington: University Press of Kentucky, 1959–92.
PJI	*The Papers of James Iredell.* Edited by Don Higginbotham. 2 vols. Raleigh, NC: Division of Archives and History, Department of Cultural Resources, 1976.
PJM	*The Papers of James Madison: Presidential Series*. Edited by Robert A. Rutland et al. 14 vols. Charlottesville: University of Virginia Press, 1984–.
PNG	*The Papers of General Nathanael Greene*. Edited by Richard K. Showman et al. 13 vols. Chapel Hill: University of North Carolina Press, for the Rhode Island Historical Society, 1976–2005.
RD	*Register of Debates* of U.S. Congress, 1824–37, covering second session of the Eighteenth Congress through the first session of the

	Twenty-Fifth Congress. For the sake of clarity I indicate whether the debates occurred in the House or Senate.
SL	*United States Statutes at Large*, vols. 1–18 (1789–1875).
TPUS	*The Territorial Papers of the United States*. Edited by Clarence E. Carter and John Porter Bloom. 28 vols. Washington, DC: Government Publishing Office, 1934–75.
TR	John Overton, *Tennessee Reports, or Cases Ruled and Adjudged in the Superior Courts of Law and Equity, Federal Courts, and Supreme Courts of Errors and Appeals for the State of Tennessee: Volume II*. Nashville, 1817. Original at Tennessee State Library and Archives.
WJQA	*The Writings of John Quincy Adams*. Edited by Worthington Chauncey Ford. 7 vols. New York: Greenwood Press, 1968.
WJW	*The Works of James Wilson*. Edited by Robert Green McCloskey. 2 vols. Cambridge, MA: Belknap Press of Harvard University Press, 1967.

PUBLISHED MATERIALS: SECONDARY SOURCES

AH	*Agricultural History*
AHR	*American Historical Review*
AHM	*American Historical Magazine*
AJLH	*American Journal of Legal History*
AP	*American Presbyterians*
APSR	*American Political Science Review*
AHRF	*Annales historiques de la Révolution française*
CH	*Church History*
DH	*Diplomatic History*
EAS	*Early American Studies*
ECHR	*Economic History Review*
ECI	*Eighteenth-Century Ireland*
EHR	*English Historical Review*
FHQ	*Florida Historical Quarterly*

GHQ	*Georgia Historical Quarterly*
IMH	*Indiana Magazine of History*
JAH	*Journal of American History*
JCHA	*Journal of the Canadian Historical Association*
JER	*Journal of the Early Republic*
JLR	*Journal of Law and Religion*
JNH	*Journal of Negro History*
JPE	*Journal of Political Economy*
JPH	*Journal of Presbyterian History*
JRSAI	*Journal of the Royal Society of Antiquaries of Ireland*
JSH	*Journal of Southern History*
JMH	*Journal of Mississippi History*
LH	*Louisiana History*
LHR	*Law and History Review*
MA	*Military Affairs*
MHR	*Missouri Historical Review*
MIH	*Modern Intellectual History*
MVHR	*Mississippi Valley Historical Review*
NCHR	*North Carolina Historical Review*
NEQ	*New England Quarterly*
NYH	*New York History*
PH	*Pennsylvania History*
PHR	*Pacific Historical Review*
PMHB	*Pennsylvania Magazine of History and Biography*
PNQ	*Pacific Northwest Quarterly*
RIS	*Review of International Studies*
RKHS	*Register of the Kentucky Historical Society*
RKSHS	*Register of the Kentucky State Historical Society*
SAPD	*Studies in American Political Development*
SCHGM	*South Carolina Historical and Genealogical Magazine*
SWHQ	*Southwestern Historical Quarterly*
THM	*Tennessee Historical Magazine*
THQ	*Tennessee Historical Quarterly*

TLR	*Texas Law Review*
UCLR	*University of Chicago Law Review*
UPLR	*University of Pennsylvania Law Review*
VLR	*Vanderbilt Law Review*
VH	*Vermont History*
VMHB	*Virginia Magazine of History and Biography*
WHQ	*Western Historical Quarterly*
WMQ	*William and Mary Quarterly*, Third Series
WMH	*Wisconsin Magazine of History*
WTHSP	*West Tennessee Historical Society Papers*

ARCHIVES AND COLLECTIONS

AJPLC	Andrew Jackson Papers, 1775–1874, Library of Congress, Washington, DC
BL	British Library, London
BNA	British National Archives, Kew
DL	David M. Rubenstein Rare Book and Manuscript Library, Duke University
HRB	Hargrett Rare Book and Manuscript Library, the University of Georgia Special Collections Library, Athens
HSP	Historical Society of Pennsylvania, Philadelphia
LCP	Library Company of Philadelphia
NA	National Archives, Washington, DC
NCC	North Carolina Collection, University of North Carolina at Chapel Hill
NCSA	North Carolina State Archives, Raleigh
TJM	Tennessee Judicial Museum, Nashville
TLP	Tennessee Legislative Petitions, 1799–1850, Tennessee State Library and Archives
TSLA	Tennessee State Library and Archives, Nashville

NOTES

INTRODUCTION

1 John Henry Eaton, *The Life of Andrew Jackson* (Philadelphia, 1824), 434, also quoted in Robert V. Remini, *Andrew Jackson and the Course of American Empire, 1767–1821* (New York: Harper and Row, 1977), 12. This quote appears in the 1824 edition of *The Life of Andrew Jackson*, but not in the original 1817 book by Eaton and John Reid. See also *The Life of Andrew Jackson, by John Reid and John Henry Eaton*, ed. Frank Lawrence Owsley Jr. (Tuscaloosa: University of Alabama Press, 1974), lxxix–lxxx. In addition to Remini's landmark books, recent biographies and studies of Jackson include Melissa J. Gismondi, "The Character of a Wife: Rachel Jackson and the Search for Zion, 1760s–1820s" (PhD dissertation, University of Virginia, forthcoming); Hendrik Booraem, *Young Hickory: The Making of Andrew Jackson* (Dallas: Taylor Trade, 2001); Andrew Burstein, *The Passions of Andrew Jackson* (New York: Alfred A. Knopf, 2003); Mark R. Cheathem, *Andrew Jackson, Southerner* (Baton Rouge: Louisiana State University Press, 2013); Matthew Warshauer, *Andrew Jackson and the Politics of Martial Law: Nationalism, Civil Liberties, and Partisanship* (Knoxville: University of Tennessee Press, 2006); and Tom Kanon, *Tennesseans at War, 1812–1815: Andrew Jackson, the Creek War, and the Battle of New Orleans* (Tuscaloosa: University of Alabama Press, 2014).

2 William B. Sprague, *Annals of the American Pulpit* (9 vols., New York, 1857–69), 3: 419 and 418–21; Booraem, *Young Hickory*, 19–21; Cheathem, *Andrew Jackson, Southerner*, 9–10.

3 Booraem, *Young Hickory,* 21 (Catechism quotes) and 170–71 (importance of Blackstone); William Blackstone, *Commentaries on the Laws of England*, 4 vols. (Dublin, 1771); Albert W. Alschuler, "Rediscovering Blackstone," *UPLR* 145 (November 1996): 1–55. In the United States, Blackstone's most prolific editor was St. George Tucker of Virginia. See Alschuler, "Rediscovering Blackstone," 3n and 5, and William S. Prince, "St. George Tucker: Bard on the Bench," *VMHB* 84 (July 1976): 266–82. There is a large and growing literature on the eighteenth-century law of nations. See Eliga H. Gould, *Among the Powers of the Earth: The American Revolution and Making of a New World Empire* (Cambridge, MA: Harvard University Press, 2012); Brian Richardson, "The Use of Vattel in the American Law of Nations," *AJIL* 106 (July 2012): 547–71; David Armitage, "The Declaration of Independence and International Law," *WMQ* 59 (January 2002): 39–64; David C. Hendrickson, *Peace Pact: The Lost World of the American Founding* (Lawrence: University of Kansas Press, 2003). English translations of Vattel appeared within a few years of its 1758 publication in French (*Le droit des*

gens; Ou Principes de la loi naturelle, appliqués à la conduit et aux affaires des nations et des souverains). By the end of the century, printings from Dublin and New York also circulated in the English-speaking world. Throughout this book I will use the quotations and page numbers from Emer de Vattel, *The Law of Nations*, ed. Béla Kapossy and Richard Whatmore (Indianapolis: Liberty Fund, 2008), which is based on a 1797 London edition that incorporated Vattel's own notes.

4 Stuart Banner, *The Death Penalty: An American History* (Cambridge, MA: Harvard University Press, 2002), 5–23 and 116–23. The Geneva Bible of 1599, which Protestants would have known best, translates Deuteronomy 32:35 as "Vengeance and recompense are mine, their foot shall slide in good time; for the day of their destruction is at hand" and Exodus 32:34 as "Go now therefore, bring the people unto the place which I commanded thee. Behold, my Angel shall go before thee; but yet in the day of my visitation I will visit their sin upon them." For the importance of the Geneva, see William Casey King, *Ambition, a History: From Vice to Virtue* (New Haven, CT: Yale University Press, 2013), 29–34.

5 Blackstone, *Commentaries*, Book II, chapter 1, p. 5 ("fairest"), p. 4 ("very *substance,*" emphasis in original), and p. 9 ("commercial traffic"); Book II, chapter 30, p. 442. See also Daniel Carey, "An Empire of Credit: English, Scottish, Irish, and American Contexts," in *Empire of Credit: The Financial Revolution in the British Atlantic World, 1688–1815,* ed. Carey and Christopher J. Finlay (Dublin: Irish Academic Press, 2011), 1–24. For the legend about Jackson's father, see Marquis James, *The Life of Andrew Jackson* (New York: Bobbs-Merrill Company, 1938), 9–10.

6 Blackstone, *Commentaries*, Book III, chapter 9, p. 145 ("secondary law") and Book II, chapter 30, pp. 464–70; Alschuler, "Rediscovering Blackstone," 28–36; Bruce H. Mann, *Republic of Debtors: Bankruptcy in the Age of American Independence* (Cambridge, MA: Harvard University Press, 2002), 6–33.

7 Blackstone, *Commentaries*, Book II, chapter 30, p. 466 ("now introduced") and p. 467 (statutes); Remarks by Robert Y. Hayne (SC), "Imprisonment for Debt," April 6, 1824, *AC: Senate*, 18th Congress, 1st Session, pp. 488, 489; Jane Kamensky, *The Exchange Artist: A Story of High-Flying Speculation and America's First Banking Collapse* (New York: Penguin Books, 2009), 14 and 14–70.

8 Blackstone, *Commentaries*, Book II, chapter 1, p. 15 ("grand ends") and Book II, chapter 30, p. 465 ("vast variety"); Vattel, *Law of Nations*, Book I, chapter 11, §110, p. 145 ("great end"), Preliminaries, §18, p. 75 ("dwarf as much a man," "naturally equal," and "nations composed of men"). Vattel self-consciously broke with Thomas Hobbes and other natural law theorists who stressed the overriding need for sovereigns to prevent violence. See Thomas Hobbes, *Leviathan: Or the Matter, Forme, and Power of a Common-Wealth Ecclesiastical and Civill*, ed. Ian Shapiro (1651; New Haven, CT: Yale University Press, 2010), 77, 78; Arash Abizadeh, "Hobbes on the Causes of War: A Disagreement Theory," *APSR* 105 (May 2011): 298–315; Abizadeh, "Publicity, Privacy, and Religious Toleration in Hobbes's *Leviathan*," *MIH* 10 (August 2013): 261–91, and email correspondence with Abizadeh, September 10, 2014; Richard Tuck, "Hobbes's Moral Philosophy," in *The Cambridge Companion to Hobbes*, ed. Tom Sorell (New York: Cambridge University Press, 1996), 175–207.

9 Vattel, *Law of Nations,* Book I, chapter 10, §109, p. 144; Comments by William R. Davie, North Carolina Ratification Convention Debates, July 28, 1788, at http://consource.org/document/north-carolina-ratification-convention-debates-1788-7-28/ (accessed September 24, 2015); Arthur K. Kuhn, "Local and Transitory Actions

in Private International Law," *UPLR* 66 (June 1918): 301–9. For Davie: Booraem, *Young Hickory*, 58, 132, and Peter N. Moore, "The Local Origins of Allegiance in Revolutionary South Carolina: The Waxhaws as a Case Study," *SCHM* 107 (January 2006): 31–32. For a forceful rejection of the universality of the law of nations, see Robert Ward, *The Foundation and History of the Law of Nations in Europe*, 2 vols. (London, 1795), I: xiii–xv.

10 Henry Home, Lord Kames, *Historical Law-Tracts*, 2nd ed. (Edinburgh, 1761), 19 ("darling privilege"), 35 ("greater importance"); Francis Hutcheson, *A Short Introduction to Moral Philosophy, in Three Books* (Glasgow, 1753), 226, 227; Blackstone, *Commentaries*, Book I, chapter 1, pp. 129–34. See also J. M. Opal, "Vengeance and Civility: A New Look at Early American Statecraft," *Journal of the Historical Society* 8 (March 2008): 61–88; David Boucher and Paul Kelly, "The Social Contract and Its Critics: An Overview," in *The Social Contract from Hobbes to Rawls*, ed. Boucher and Kelly (London: Routledge, 1994), 1–34; Susan Jacoby, *Wild Justice: The Evolution of Revenge* (New York: Harper and Row, 1983).

11 Vattel, *Law of Nations*, Book I, chapter 13, §176, pp. 194–97; Richard L. Bushman, *King and People in Provincial Massachusetts* (Chapel Hill: University of North Carolina Press, 1985); Guy Rowlands, *The Dynastic State and the Army Under Louis XIV: Royal Service and Private Interest, 1661–1701* (New York: Cambridge University Press, 2010); John A. Lynn, *Giant of the Grand Siècle: The French Army, 1610–1715* (New York: Cambridge University Press, 1997), 255–59. See also Luke Glanville, *Sovereignty and the Responsibility to Protect: A New History* (Chicago: University of Chicago Press, 2014), and Charles Tilly, *Coercion, Capital, and European States, AD 990–1992* (Cambridge, MA: Basil Blackwell, 1990).

12 Vattel, *Law of Nations*, Book I, chapter 2, §21, p. 88 ("labour at its own"); Book I, chapter viii, §94, p. 135 ("trade together"); Book I, chapter 8, §99, p. 139 (import duties); Book I, chapter 11, §111–13, pp. 145–47 (education); Book I, chapter 9, §101, p. 140 (roads and canals). See generally Book I, chapter 8, §89–92, pp. 133–35, and Book II, chapter 2, §21–34, pp. 273–80.

13 Vattel, *Law of Nations*, Book III, chapter 8, §152, p. 556 ("happily banished"); Book I, chapter 7, §81, p. 129; Book II, chapter 7, §97, p. 310; Book I, chapter 18, §209, pp. 216–17; Book III, chapter 9, §167, p. 570, and Book II, chapter 6, §78, p. 301; Gould, *Among the Powers of the Earth*, 48–78; Richard White, *The Middle Ground: Indians, Empires, and Republics in the Great Lakes Region, 1650–1815* (New York: Cambridge University Press, 1991), 50–51; Stuart Banner, *How the Indians Lost Their Land: Law and Power on the Frontier* (Cambridge, MA: Harvard University Press, 2005), esp. 150–90; Fred Anderson, *Crucible of War: The Seven Years' War and the Fate of Empire in British North America, 1754–1766* (New York: Knopf, 2000), 5–7, 12, 16, 46–47, 52–60.

14 Blackstone, *Commentaries*, introduction, section iv ("more distant"); James A. Henretta, "Magistrates, Common Law Lawyers, Legislators: The Three Legal Systems of British America," in *The Cambridge History of Law in America:* Vol. I, *Early America (1580–1815)*, ed. Michael Grossberg and Christopher Tomlins (New York: Cambridge University Press, 2008), 1: 581 (1720 quote), 558 (Penn quote), and 555–92; Claire Priest, "Law and Commerce, 1580–1815," in ibid., 1: 400–446, esp. 421–22; William M. Wiecek, "Somerset: Lord Mansfield and the Legitimacy of Slavery in the Anglo-American World," *UCLR* 42 (Autumn 1974): 109 and 86–146; David Brion Davis, *Inhuman Bondage: The Rise and Fall of Slavery in the New World* (New York: Oxford University Press, 2006), 231–49.

15 Blackstone, *Commentaries*, introduction, section iv; Vattel, *Law of Nations*, Book II, chapter 7, §97, p. 310 ("savages"); Book II, chapter 6, §78, p. 301 ("infested" and "haunts"); Book III, chapter 3, §34, p. 487 ("monsters"); Book III, chapter 8, §141, p. 544 ("When we are,"); Book III, chapter 15, §228, p. 613 ("suppose"); Alschuler, "Rediscovering Blackstone," 15 (Blackstone in Parliament). See also Jill Lepore, *The Name of War: King Philip's War and the Origins of American Identity* (New York: Alfred A. Knopf, 1998), 71–96; Simone Goyard-Fabre, "Guerre et paix chez les jurisconsultes du droit naturel et des gens," *Revue européenne des sciences sociales* 20 (1982): 89–120; Anthony Pagden, "Law, Colonization, Legitimation, and the European Background," in *Cambridge History of Law*, ed. Grossberg and Tomlins, 1: 5–14.

16 Quoted in Daniel J. Tortora, *Carolina in Crisis: Cherokees, Colonists, and Slaves in the American Southeast, 1756–1763* (Chapel Hill: University of North Carolina Press, 2015), 111. For the "Paxton Boys" (or "Hickory Boys") and their victims see Alden T. Vaughan, "Frontier Banditti and the Indians: The Paxton Boys' Legacy, 1763–1775," *PH* 51 (January 1984): 3–4 and 1–29; Peter Silver, *Our Savage Neighbors: How Indian War Transformed Early America* (New York: W. W. Norton and Company, 2008), 177–81; Daniel K. Richter, *Facing East from Indian Country: A Native History of Early America* (Cambridge, MA: Harvard University Press, 2001), 201–8; [Benjamin Franklin], *A Narrative of the Late Massacres, in Lancaster County, of a Number of Indians* (Philadelphia, 1764), 5, 8. The term "Paxton Boys" was widespread by 1764, and at least two other groups seem to have been directly inspired by it: the "Black Boys" of Cumberland County, Pennsylvania, and the "Augusta Boys" of Virginia. See Vaughan, "Frontier Banditti and the Indians," 6; Albert H. Tillson Jr., "The Militia and Popular Political Culture in the Upper Valley of Virginia, 1740–1775," *VMHB* 94 (July 1986): 292–93 and 293n; and James Mercer Garnett, "The Last Fifteen Years of the House of Burgesses of Virginia, 1761–1776," *VMHB* 18 (April 1910): 214; email correspondence with John Fea, October 2, 2014.

17 [Franklin], *Narrative of the Late Massacres*, 27. For native goodwill to Quakers and Moravians, see David Thomas, "Travels through the Western Country in the Summer of 1816," in *Indiana as Seen by Early Travelers*, ed. Harlow Lindley (Indianapolis: Indiana Historical Commission, 1916), 54, and James H. Merrell, *Into the American Woods: Negotiators on the Pennsylvania Frontier* (New York: W. W. Norton and Company, 1999), 84–90.

18 Alden T. Vaughan "'Expulsion of the Salvages': English Policy and the Virginia Massacre of 1622," *WMQ* 35 (January 1978): 77 ("Whereas we are"), and see also 57–84; Ronald Dale Karr, "'Why Should You Be So Furious?': The Violence of the Pequot War," *JAH* 85 (December 1998): 904 ("innocent blood" and "Lords revenge"), 876 (casualties), and 876–909; "Christopher Gale's Account of the Tuscarora War, 1711–1713," in *The North Carolina Experience: An Interpretive and Documentary History*, ed. Lindley S. Butler and Alan D. Watson (Chapel Hill: University of North Carolina Press, 1984), 17 ("What spectacle"); Richter, *Facing East from Indian Country*, 163–64.

19 Daniel K. Richter, "War and Culture: The Iroquois Experience," *WMQ* 40 (October 1983): 528–59, esp. 532–37; Tortora, *Carolina in Crisis*, 102–16; Alan Taylor, *The Divided Ground: Indians, Settlers, and the Northern Borderland of the American Revolution* (New York: Alfred A. Knopf, 2006); White, *The Middle Ground*, 75–82, 387–96; Cynthia Cumfer, *Separate Peoples, One Land: The Minds of Cherokees, Blacks, and Whites on the Tennessee Frontier* (Chapel Hill: University of North Carolina

Press, 2007), esp. 61–63 and 81–85; Merrell, *Into the American Woods*, 168, and see also 48–53; John Phillip Reid, *A Law of Blood: The Primitive Law of the Cherokee Nation* (New York: New York University Press, 1970); Kathleen DuVal, *The Native Ground: Indians and Colonists in the Heart of the Continent* (Philadelphia: University of Pennsylvania Press, 2006), 111–15.

20 British officers quoted in Tortora, *Carolina in Crisis*, 147, 141; White, *The Middle Ground*, 37; Tom Holm, "American Indian Warfare: The Cycles of Conflict and the Militarization of Native North America," in *A Companion to American Indian History*, ed. Philip J. Deloria and Neal Salisbury (Malden, MA: Blackwell Publishing, 2004), 154–74; Richter, "War and Culture," 537–39; Ned Blackhawk, *Violence over the Land: Indians and Empires in the Early American West* (Cambridge, MA: Harvard University Press, 2006).

21 Governor Fauquier quoted in Banner, *How the Indians Lost Their Land*, 98 and also 95–96; Gould, *Among the Powers of the Earth*, 14–15 (Acadians), 35–36 (Mosquito Coast), and 79–110. For examples of removing squatters, see Cameron B. Strang, "Michael Cresap and the Promulgation of Settler Land-Claiming Methods in the Backcountry, 1765–1774," *VMHB* 118 (2010): 106–35 and esp. 113–17, and Sherman Day, *Historical Collections of the State of Pennsylvania* (Port Washington, NY, 1843), 362–68, 382–83, 538–39. For disgust with colonial currency, see Adam Smith, *An Inquiry into the Nature and Causes of the Wealth of Nations*, ed. Edwin Cannan (New York: Modern Library, 1937), 310–11.

22 Thomas Reid, *An Essay on the Active Powers of the Human Mind*, ed. Baruch A. Brody (1788; Cambridge, MA: Harvard University Press, 1969), 152; William Robertson, *The History of America, Books IX and X, Containing the History of Virginia to the Year 1688; and of New England to the Year 1652* (Philadelphia, 1799), 183 and 95; Samuel Williams, *The Natural and Civil History of Vermont* (Walpole, NH, 1794), 144 ("possession of his soul"), 162 ("diabolical"), 160 ("fierce, brutal, horrid"), vi.

23 For recent treatments see Craig B. Yirush, "The Imperial Crisis," in *The Oxford Handbook of the American Revolution*, ed. Edward G. Gray and Jane Kamensky (New York: Oxford University Press, 2013), 85–102, and François Charbonneau, *Une Parte Égale de Liberté: Le patriotisme Anglais et la révolution américain* (Montreal: Liber, 2013).

24 Thomas Jefferson, "A Summary View of the Rights of British America [1774]," in *The Life and Selected Writings of Thomas Jefferson*, ed. Adrienne Koch and William Peden (1944; New York: Modern Library, 2004), 274 and 273–89; Peter S. Onuf, "'To Declare Them a Free and Independent People': Race, Slavery, and National Identity in Jefferson's Thought," *JER* 18 (Spring 1998): 1–46; Robert G. Parkinson, "From Indian Killer to Worthy Citizen: The Revolutionary Transformation of Michael Cresap," *WMQ* 63 (January 2006): 97–122; Joseph J. Ellis, *American Sphinx: The Character of Thomas Jefferson* (New York: Alfred A. Knopf, 1996), 29–36.

25 J. M. Opal, "Common Sense and Imperial Atrocity: How Tom Paine Saw South Asia in North America," *Common-place* 9 (July 2009); David Waldstreicher, *Slavery's Constitution: From Revolution to Ratification* (New York: Hill and Wang, 2009), 21–56; Pauline Maier, *American Scripture: Making the Declaration of Independence* (New York: Alfred A. Knopf, 1997); Silver, *Our Savage Neighbors*, 230–42; Hendrickson, *Peace Pact*. Franklin distributed the copies of the Amsterdam version of Vattel's work he had received from France to Congress, the Library Company of Philadelphia, and the library of Harvard College. See Armitage, "Declaration of Independence and International Law," 49, 49n, and 39–64.

26 Ellis, *American Sphinx*, 53 ("our common blood," deleted from Jefferson's original) and 46–59; Armitage, "Declaration of Independence and International Law"; Annette Gordon-Reed, *The Hemingses of Monticello: An American Family* (New York: W. W. Norton and Company, 2008), 91–110. In addition to Jefferson's indictment of the British king's role in introducing and perpetuating the Atlantic slave trade, Congress deleted a section about the need for Americans to renounce their affections for England. It was in this deleted section that Jefferson mentioned "common blood."

27 Preamble, Constitution of Vermont, July 8, 1777; Preamble, Constitution of Pennsylvania, September 28, 1776; Preamble, Constitution of South Carolina, March 26, 1776; Preamble, Constitution of New Jersey, July 2, 1776; The Constitution, or Form of Government, Constitution of North Carolina, December 18, 1776, all at http://avalon.law.yale.edu/subject_menus/18th.asp; Franklin quoted in Gould, *Among the Powers of the Earth*, 79. See also Nicole Eustace, *Passion Is the Gale: Emotion, Power, and the Coming of the American Revolution* (Chapel Hill: University of North Carolina Press, 2008), and Bushman, *King and People in Provincial Massachusetts*.

28 Caroline Cox, "The Continental Army," in *Oxford Handbook of the American Revolution*, ed. Gray and Kamensky, 162 and 161–76; David C. Hendrickson, *Union, Nation, or Empire: The American Debate over International Relations, 1789–1941* (Lawrence: University of Kansas Press, 2009).

CHAPTER 1

1. John Drayton, *A View of South-Carolina, as Respects Her Natural and Civil Concerns* (Charleston, 1802), 98, 92–99; James H. Merrell, *The Indians' New World: Catawbas and Their Neighbors from European Contact Through the Era of Removal* (Chapel Hill: University of North Carolina Press, 1989), 88, 103, 190, and 204; Robert L. Meriwether, *The Expansion of South Carolina, 1729–1765* (1940; Philadelphia: Porcupine Press, 1974), 136–45. For Richardson's death, see [Charles Woodmason], "The Rev. William Richardson," n.d., in *The Carolina Backcountry on the Eve of the Revolution: The Journal and Other Writings of Charles Woodmason, Anglican Itinerant*, ed. Richard J. Hooker (Chapel Hill: University of North Carolina Press, 1953), 132–35. Woodmason mistakenly dated the death in June 1772, not July 1771. For a meticulous history of Jackson's early life, see Hendrik Booraem, *Young Hickory: The Making of Andrew Jackson* (Dallas: Taylor Trade, 2001).
2. "Journal of C.W. Clerk, Itinerant Minister in South Carolina, 1766, 1767, 1768," in *Carolina Backcountry*, ed. Hooker, 6–7 ("mix'd Medley"), 12 ("Shocking," and "impenetrable"), 25 ("lowest vilest"), 15 ("State of Nature"); [Woodmason], "Copy of a Remonstrance Presented to the Commons House of Assembly of South Carolina," [November 1767], in ibid., 226 ("Bands of Society and Government") and 214 ("State of War"); [Woodmason], "A Report on Religion in the South," 1765, in ibid., 81 ("Civil Police," here referring to North Carolina); "Josiah Martin's View of the Regulation," [Martin to Lord Hillsborough, August 30, 1772], in *The North Carolina Experience: An Interpretive and Documentary History*, ed. Lindley S. Butler and Alan D. Watson (Chapel Hill: University of North Carolina Press, 1984), 119 ("broken").
3. Andrew R. L. Cayton and Fredrika J. Teute, "Introduction: On the Connection of Frontiers," in *Contact Points: American Frontiers from the Mohawk Valley to the Mississippi, 1750–1830*, ed. Cayton and Teute (Chapel Hill: University of

North Carolina Press, 1998), 1–15; Jeremy Adelman and Stephen Aron, "From Borderlands to Borders: Empires, Nation-States, and the Peoples in Between in North American History," *AHR* 104 (June 1999): 814–41; François Furstenberg, "The Significance of the Trans-Appalachian Frontier in Atlantic History," *AHR* 113 (June 2008): 647–77.

4. Scottish observer quoted in Bernard Bailyn, "Worlds in Motion," *Colonial American History*, ed. Kirsten Fischer and Eric Hinderaker (Malden, MA: Blackwell Publishers, 2002), 212; Booraem, *Young Hickory*, 2, 37–38, 45; Peter Linebaugh and Marcus Rediker, *The Many-Headed Hydra: Sailors, Slaves, Commoners, and the Hidden History of the Revolutionary Atlantic* (Boston: Beacon Press, 2000), 8–70.
5. Bernard Bailyn, *Voyagers to the West: A Passage in the Peopling of America on the Eve of the Revolution* (New York: Knopf, 1986), 26 (emigration figures) and 29–66 (British policy); Maldwyn A. Jones, "The Scotch-Irish in British America," in *Strangers Within the Realm: Cultural Margins of the First British Empire*, ed. Bernard Bailyn and Philip D. Morgan (Chapel Hill: University of North Carolina Press, 1991), 284–313; James G. Leyburn, *The Scotch-Irish: A Social History* (Chapel Hill: University of North Carolina Press, 1962), 83–98; R. D. W. Connor, *History of North Carolina: Volume I, The Colonial and Revolutionary Periods, 1584–1783* (New York: Lewis Publishing Company, 1919), 162–79; David Hackett Fischer, *Albion's Seed: Four British Folkways in America* (New York: Oxford University Press, 1989), 605–782; Graeme Kirkham, "Ulster Emigration to North America, 1680–1720," in *Ulster and North America: Transatlantic Perspectives on the Scotch-Irish*, ed. H. Tyler Blethen and Curtis W. Wood Jr. (Tuscaloosa: University of Alabama Press, 1997), 76–97.
6. "Report of Governor Arthur Dobbs to the Board of Trade," [1755], in *North Carolina Experience*, ed. Butler and Watson, 89; Marjoleine Kars, *Breaking Loose Together: The Regulator Rebellion in Pre-Revolutionary North Carolina* (Chapel Hill: University of North Carolina Press, 2002), 10–11 (Moravians and Granville). For typical complaints about North Carolinians, see [Janet Shaw], *Journal of a Lady of Quality; Being the Narrative of a Journey from Scotland to the West Indies, North Carolina, and Portugal, in the Years 1774 to 1776*, ed. Evangeline Walker Andrews (New Haven, CT: Yale University Press, 1921), 153 and 177.
7. Drayton, *A View of South-Carolina*, 163; South Carolina assembly quoted in Alan Taylor, *American Colonies* (New York: Viking, 2001), 240; Philip D. Morgan, *Slave Counterpoint: Black Culture in the Eighteenth-Century Chesapeake and Lowcountry* (Chapel Hill: University of North Carolina Press, 1998), esp. 151–54, 329–30.
8. J. Hector St. John de Crèvecoeur, *Letters from an American Farmer* (1782; New York, 1904), 245 ("self-preservation"), 232 ("perpetual revenge"), and 226–45; Entry for Feb. 2, 1750, *The Colonial Records of South Carolina: The Journal of the Commons House of Assembly*, ed. J. H. Easterry (Columbia, 1962), 8: 383; Entry for Jan. 31, 1750, ibid., 8: 370; "For the Better Ordering and Governing of Negroes and Other Slaves in this Province," March 7, 1755, in *Colonial Records of the State of Georgia*, ed. Allen D. Chandler (Atlanta, 1910), 18: 138. See also Christopher Tomlins, *Freedom Bound: Law, Labor, and Civic Identity in Colonizing English America, 1580–1865* (New York: Cambridge University Press, 2010), 431–52, and Sally E. Hadden, *Slave Patrols: Law and Violence in Virginia and the Carolinas* (Cambridge, MA: Harvard University Press, 2003).
9. Scotus Americanus, "Informations Concerning the Province of North Carolina," [1773], in *Colonial American History*, ed. Fischer and Hinderaker, 230, 231, 232; Belfast paper quoted in E. R. R. Green, "Queensborough Township: Scotch-Irish

Emigration and the Expansion of Georgia, 1763–1776," *WMQ* 17 (April 1960): 186, 187, and 183–99. See also Bailyn, "Worlds in Motion," 196–219, and Leyburn, *The Scotch-Irish*, 157–83.

10. Green, "Queensborough Township," 190 (thirty-three of thirty-nine grants); Booraem, *Young Hickory*, 7, 9, and 123; "Deed from Thomas and Sarah Ewing," December 17, 1770, in *PAJ* 1: 3–4; "Map of the Waxhaw District," in *PAJ* 1: 8. For a superb study of the Waxhaws, see Peter N. Moore, "The Local Origins of Allegiance in Revolutionary South Carolina: The Waxhaws as a Case Study," *SCHM* 107 (January 2006): 26-41. On the Catawba Nation, see Kars, *Breaking Loose Together*, 14 and 11–13, and Meriwether, *Expansion of South Carolina*, 136–45. For African languages in the low country, see Morgan, *Slave Counterpoint*, 560–66.
11. Pennsylvania settlers quoted in Jones, "The Scotch-Irish in America," 296; William Tryon to John Stuart, June 17, 1766, in *CWT* 1: 312 ("shut out"); Petition of Mecklenburg County Presbyterians to William Tryon and the Assembly, (?) 1769, in *CWT* 2: 282 ("Savage Enemy"); Thomas M. Hatley, *The Dividing Paths: Cherokees and South Carolinians Through the Era of Revolution* (New York: Oxford University Press, 1993); Daniel J. Tortora, *Carolina in Crisis: Cherokees, Colonists, and Slaves in the American Southeast, 1756–1763* (Chapel Hill: University of North Carolina Press, 2015), esp. 155–68.
12. Governor William Tryon to the Earl of Shelburne, July 15, 1767, in *CWT* 1: 549; "Committee Report on the Boundary Between South and North Carolina," [April 4, 1769], in *Maroon Communities in South Carolina: A Documentary Record*, ed. Timothy James Lockley (Columbia: University of South Carolina Press, 2009), 32 ("hunt the Negroes") and 32–33; Booraem, *Young Hickory*, 8 ("the Nation"). On Watauga: Connor, *History of North Carolina*, 287–301, esp. 292–94, and Daniel K. Richter, *Facing East from Indian Country: A Native History of Early America* (Cambridge, MA: Harvard University Press, 2000), 218. The term "middle ground" comes from Richard White, *The Middle Ground: Indians, Empires, and Republics in the Great Lakes Region, 1660–1815* (New York: Cambridge University Press, 1991). See also Peter Silver, *Our Savage Neighbors: How Indian War Transformed Early America* (New York: W. W. Norton and Company, 2008), esp. 211–13.
13. John Underhill quoted in Ann M. Little, *Abraham in Arms: War and Gender in Colonial New England* (Philadelphia: University of Pennsylvania Press, 2007), 47, and see also 44–53; John Temple, *The Irish Rebellion; Or, a History of the Beginnings, and First Progress of the General Rebellion Raised within the Kingdom of Ireland, in the Year 1641* (Dublin?, 1751), 17; Eoin Magennis, "Belturbet, Cahans and Two Presbyterian Revolutions in South Ulster, 1660–1770," *Seanchas Ardmhacha*, 21 and 22 (2007–2008): 131 (first Presbytery); Booraem, *Young Hickory*, 2. On the 1641 rebellion, see also Thomas Morley, "From *A Remonstrance* . . . (1643)," in *Strangers to That Land: British Perceptions of Ireland from the Reformation to the Famine*, ed. Andrew Hadfield and John McVeagh (Gerrards Cross: Colin Smythe, 1994), 116–17, and Patrick J. Corish, "The Rising of 1641 and the Catholic Confederacy, 1641–45," in *A New History of Ireland: Volume III, Early Modern Ireland, 1534–1691*, ed. T. W. Moody, F. X. Martin, and F. J. Byrne (Oxford, England: Clarendon Press, 1976), 3: 289–316.
14. T. C. Barnard, "The Uses of 23 October 1641 and Irish Protestant Celebrations," *EHR* 106 (October 1991): 903 ("must this day"), 898 ("enemy's country"), and 889–920; Temple, *Irish Rebellion*, 122 ("REVENGE!"). See also Allan Blackstock, "Armed Citizens and Christian Soldiers: Crisis Sermons and Ulster Presbyterians, 1715–1803," *ECI* 22 (2007): 81–105.

15. Temple, *Irish Rebellion*, 58 (emphasis in original); Ezekiel 25:15–17; Booraem, *Young Hickory*, 92–94; Little, *Abraham in Arms*, 53–54; Jill Lepore, *The Name of War: King Philip's War and the Origins of American Identity* (New York: Alfred A. Knopf, 1998), 107–13.
16. Silver, *Our Savage Neighbors*, 87 (quote from William Bartram); Nicole Eustace, *Passion Is the Gale: Emotion, Power, and the Coming of the American Revolution* (Chapel Hill: University of North Carolina Press, 2008), 151–99.
17. Richard Maxwell Brown, *The South Carolina Regulators* (Cambridge, MA: Belknap Press of Harvard University Press, 1963), 4–5 (Long Canes Massacre); Albert H. Tillson Jr., "The Militia and Popular Political Culture in the Upper Valley of Virginia, 1740–1775," *VMHB* 94 (July 1986): 292–93 and 293n; James Mercer Garnett, "The Last Fifteen Years of the House of Burgesses of Virginia, 1761–1775," *VMHB* 18 (April 1910): 214; Silver, *Our Savage Neighbors*, 5–6 and 23–27.
18. [Woodmason], "The Presbyterians Urged to be Tolerant," January 1767?, in *Carolina Backcountry*, ed. Hooker, 93, 94 (quotes from sermon he wanted to give, although the Presbyterian elders of the Waxhaws apparently refused) and "Introduction," xiii (slaves and headrights).
19. Meriwether, *Expansion of South Carolina*, 136–46, estimates that South Carolina grants covered thirty thousand acres in the Wateree-Catawba valley, of which one-fourth were located in the Waxhaws. Some four thousand acres were held under North Carolina grants. For variations to the process whereby a claim "ripened" from entry to warrant to survey to patent, see William Tryon to the Earl of Shelburne, July 16, 1767, "State of Manufactures, Mode of Granting Land, Fees of Officers, etc. in America," BL. For Crawford properties and AJ's birthplace, see Booraem, *Young Hickory*, 8–9, 11–12, 16, and 53–54, and Max F. Harris, "The Andrew Jackson Birthplace Problem," unpublished manuscript at NCSA. For fears of horse thieves and plans to clarify boundaries in 1762 and 1774: Governor William Tryon to the Earl of Shelburne, July 15, 1767, in *CWT* 1: 549, and Drayton, *View of South-Carolina*, 3.
20. Tortora, *Carolina in Crisis*, 189–90; Rachel N. Klein, *Unification of a Slave State: The Rise of the Planter Class in the South Carolina Backcountry, 1760–1808* (Chapel Hill: University of North Carolina Press, 1990), 178–80; Annette Gordon-Reed, *The Hemingses of Monticello: An American Family* (New York: W. W. Norton and Company, 2008), 52–53; Allan Kulikoff, *Tobacco and Slaves: The Development of Southern Cultures in the Chesapeake, 1680–1800* (Chapel Hill: University of North Carolina Press, 1986), 45–77. Profits from rice and indigo exports hit a new high in the early 1770s. See Drayton, *View of South-Carolina*, 164–65.
21. Lt. Gov. Bull to the Earl of Hillsborough, September 8, 1768, in "State of Manufactures," BL; Laurel Thatcher Ulrich, "Wheels, Looms, and the Gender Division of Labor in Eighteenth-Century New England," *WMQ* 55 (January 1998): 3–38. On likely home styles and furnishings: Booraem, *Young Hickory*, 6–8; Jack Larkin, *The Reshaping of Everyday Life, 1790–1840* (New York: Perennial Library, 1988), 106–8, 32–48.
22. Booraem, *Young Hickory*, 17, 35–36, 38–40; Andrew Burstein, *The Passions of Andrew Jackson* (New York: Alfred A. Knopf, 2003), 3–9.
23. Physician quoted in Tortora, *Carolina in Crisis*, 87 and 123; Booraem, *Young Hickory*, 40–41; Drayton, *View of South-Carolina*, 154–59; Lindley S. Butler, *North Carolina and the Coming of the Revolution, 1763–1776* (Raleigh: North Carolina Department of Cultural Resources, 1976), 29–45; Klein, *Unification of a Slave State*, 1–8, 10. For a brilliant analysis of eighteenth-century cities and their hinterlands, see

Mark A. Peterson, "The War in the Cities," in *The Oxford Handbook of the American Revolution*, ed. Edward G. Gray and Jane Kamensky (New York: Oxford University Press, 2013), 194–215.

24. Klein, *Unification of a Slave State*, 9, 19–20, and 74–75; Anton-Hermann Chroust, *The Rise of the Legal Profession in America* (2 vols., Norman: University of Oklahoma Press, 1965), 1: 303–4; Richard J. Hooker, "The South Carolina Regulator Movement: An Introduction to the Documents," in *Carolina Backcountry*, ed. Hooker, 167; Tortora, *Carolina in Crisis*, 87; Charles Warren, *A History of the American Bar* (Boston: Little, Brown, and Company, 1911), 211–39. I borrow the phrase "ruling race" from James Oakes, *The Ruling Race: A History of American Slaveholders* (New York: Knopf, 1982). For prerevolutionary legislation and private bills, see James A. Henretta, "Magistrates, Common Law Lawyers, Legislators: The Three Legal Systems of British America," in *The Cambridge History of Law in America: Volume I, Early America (1580–1815)*, ed. Michael Grossberg and Christopher Tomlins (New York: Cambridge University Press, 2008), 1: 584–88.
25. "Journal of C.W. Clerk," in *Carolina Backcountry*, ed. Hooker, 45 ("for I counted") and 15, 15n (marriages and 1760 Proclamation); [Woodmason], "The Need for Education," in ibid., 120 ("expos'd"); [Woodmason], "The Baptists and the Presbyterians," 1768?, in ibid., 99–100 (pregnancies).
26. "Will of Alexander Craighead," April 9, 1765, in Brent H. Holcomb, *Mecklenburg County, North Carolina: Abstract of Early Wills, 1763–1790* (privately printed, 1980), 17, NCSA; "Journal of C.W. Clerk," in *Carolina Backcountry*, ed. Hooker, 14; William B. Bynum, "The Genuine Presbyterian Whine": Presbyterian Worship in the Eighteenth Century," *AP* 74 (Fall 1996): 157–70; Meriwether, *Expansion of South Carolina*, 144.
27. Booraem, *Young Hickory*, 27–32; "Deed from Thomas and Sarah Ewing," in *PAJ* 1: 3–4. On grammar schools: "An Act to Establish Queen's College," January 15, 1771, in *CWT* 2: 564–67. On Witherspoon: Roger F. Fechner, "'The Sacredness of Public Credit': The American Revolution, Paper Currency, and John Witherspoon's *Essay on Money* (1786)," in *Empire of Credit: The Financial Revolution in the British Atlantic World, 1688–1815,* ed. Daniel Carey and Christopher J. Finlay (Dublin: Irish Academic Press, 2011), 141–67.
28. Brent H. Holcomb and Elmer O. Parker, *Mecklenburg County, North Carolina Deed Abstracts, 1763–1779* (Easley, SC: Southern Historical Press, 1979), 191 (1772 sale) and 9; Meriwether, *Expansion of South Carolina*, 137–39; Robert Claude Carpenter, "Griffith Rutherford: North Carolina Frontier Military and Political Leader" (MA thesis, Wake Forest University, 1974), 4–8; James M. MacDonald, "Politics of the Personal in the Old North State: Griffith Rutherford in Revolutionary North Carolina" (PhD dissertation, Louisiana State University, 2006), 5, 15, 19–23, 38.
29. William Tryon to Lords of Trade, January 30, 1767, "State of Manufactures," BL; Kars, *Breaking Loose Together*, 9–75; Carl Ubbelohde, *The American Colonies and the British Empire, 1607–1763* (New York: Crowell, 1968), 62–63; Cameron B. Strang, "Michael Cresap and the Promulgation of Settler Land-Claiming Methods in the Backcountry, 1765–1774," *VMHB* 118 (2010): 106–35.
30. William Tryon to the Earl of Shelburne, July 1767, "State of Manufactures," BL; McCulloch quoted in Don Higginbotham, "The Making of a Revolutionary," in *PJI* 1: xlviii; William K. Boyd, "Introduction" to Henry McCulloch, "Miscellaneous Representations Relative to Our Concerns in America," [1761], in *Some Eighteenth-Century Tracts Concerning North Carolina*, ed. Boyd (1927; Spartanburg, SC: Reprint Company, 1973), 143–46.

31. Henry E. McCulloch to Governor Tryon and the Council, April 25, 1765, in *CWT* 1: 69 ("indefeazible") and 66 ("decision or direction"); "The Memorial of Henry Eustace McCulloch," November 5, 1783, American Loyalist Claims, Series II, McCullok, AO13/117, BNA ("Extent and quantity" and "desirable objects"). McCulloch estimated that one-half of all the land claimed by his father was "barrens." For alligators and swamps: *Journal of a Lady of Quality*, 149–51, 151n, and 202–3.
32. Kars, *Breaking Loose Together*, 29–30.
33. "Memorial of Henry Eustace McColloch," American Loyalist Claims, BNA ("Wood, Water, and Soil" and "annually migrated"); McCulloch to Governor Tryon and the Council, April 25, 1765, in *CWT* 1: 72 ("reasonable") and 72–73. For McCulloch grants near Jackson, see Holcomb and Parker, *Mecklenburg County, North Carolina Deed Abstracts*. McCulloch noted that settlers in the early 1760s had sometimes paid as little as 1 to 3 shillings per acre on lands they had improved, whereas he sold ready-made farms ten years later for 5 to 17 shillings per acre. See also Kars, *Breaking Loose Together*, 48–52.
34. William Tryon to the Earl of Shelburne, July 16, 1767, in "State of Manufactures," BL; Tryon to Shelburne, July?, 1767, ibid.; "Deed from Thomas and Sarah Ewing," December 17, 1770, in *PAJ* 1: 3; Mark R. Cheathem, *Andrew Jackson, Southerner* (Baton Rouge: Louisiana State University Press, 2013), 7. For estimates of how much sheriffs were in arrears, see Butler, *North Carolina and the Coming of the Regulation*, 31–33, and Marvin L. Michael Kay, "The Payment of Provincial and Local Taxes in North Carolina, 1748–1771," *WMQ* 26 (April 1969): 218–40.
35. [George Sims], An Address to the People of Granville County, June 6, 1765, "Extortion and Public Officials," in *North Carolina Experience,* ed. Butler and Watson, 112 ("cursed hungry"); Henry E. McCulloch to Tryon and the Council, April 25, 1765, in *CWT* 1: 73, 76. See also "Governor Dobbs and Riots, 1759," in *North Carolina Experience*, 110–11, and Connor, *History of North Carolina*, 287–320.
36. "Gov. Martin to the Earl of Hillsborough, December 26, 1771," in Hugh Talmadge Lefler, *North Carolina History Told by Contemporaries* (Chapel Hill: University of North Carolina Press, 1934), 54; "Instructions to William Tryon, December 24, 1765," in *CWT* 1: 183; Petition of Merchants in London Who Trade to North Carolina, in Lefler, *North Carolina History*, 52–53. See also Bruce H. Mann, "The Transformation of Law and Economy in Early America," in *Cambridge History of Law in America*, ed. Grossberg and Tomlins, 1: 391–92.
37. [Herman Husband], "A Fan for Fanning, and a Touchstone for Tryon," [1771], in *Some Eighteenth-Century Tracts*, ed. Boyd, 351–56. For taxes: Robin Einhorn, *American Taxation, American Freedom* (Chicago: University of Chicago Press, 2006), 79–81; Kay, "The Payment of Provincial and Local Taxes in North Carolina."
38. James P. Whittenburg, "Planters, Merchants, and Lawyers: Social Change and the Origins of the North Carolina Regulation," *WMQ* 34 (April 1977): 226 (figures from Orange County) and 215–38; Kay, "The Payment of Provincial and Local Taxes," 240. See also Henretta, "Magistrates, Common Law Lawyers, Legislators," in *Cambridge History of Law in America,* ed. Grossberg and Tomlins, 1: 574–77.
39. Kars, *Breaking Loose Together*, 73 (quote) and 72–73 for auctions; [William Tryon], "A View of the Polity of the Province of North Carolina in the Year 1767," in *CWT* 1: 526 (number of lawyers); Chroust, *Rise of the Legal Profession*, 1: 310–24. For courtroom spaces, see Henretta, "Magistrates, Common Law Lawyers, Legislators," in *Cambridge History of Law in America*, ed. Grossberg and Tomlins, 1: 571.

40. [George Sims], An Address to the People of Granville County, June 6, 1765, "Extortion and Public Officials," in *North Carolina Experience,* ed. Butler and Watson, 111 ("not our mode"), 112 ("Are not your lands"); [Herman Husband], "A Fan for Fanning," in *Some Eighteenth-Century Tracts*, ed. Boyd, 343 ("Pettyfogging Lawyers"), 358 ("Bomb Sheriffs"); Connor, *History of North Carolina*, 302–20.
41. "Regulators to William Tryon and the Council: Advertisement No. 11, May 21, 1768," in *CWT* 2: 115 ("unequal Chances"); [Husband], "A Fan for Fanning," 358 ("to consult Lawyers"); Kars, *Breaking Loose Together*, 94 and 79–129; Wythe Holt, "The New Jerusalem: Herman Husband's Egalitarian Alternative to the United States Constitution," in *Revolutionary Founders: Rebels, Radicals, and Reformers in the Making of a Nation*, ed. Alfred F. Young, Gary B. Nash, and Ray Raphael (New York: Alfred A. Knopf, 2011), 253–72.
42. In 1768, some £60,106 in proclamation money and interest-bearing notes circulated in North Carolina, down from over £95,000 in 1761. See Kars, *Breaking Loose Together*, 66. For rural unrest in other colonies, consult Brendan McConville, *Those Daring Disturbers of the Public Peace: The Struggle for Property and Power in Early New Jersey* (Ithaca, NY: Cornell University Press, 1999), and Gary Nash, *The Unknown American Revolution: The Unruly Birth of Democracy and the Struggle to Create America* (New York: Viking, 2005), 1–43.
43. "Proclamation of Governor Tryon," July 16, 1767, in Colonial Governor's Papers: William Tryon, 1765–1771, 1783–1786, NCSA; "Western Boundary Agreement," June 13, 1767, in ibid.; Holt, "The New Jerusalem." Tryon's proclamation was issued in North Carolina the same day as a similar proclamation from George III, in which the king warned squatters and speculators to respect the natives' "just Rights and Possessions." See "Proclamation of George III," July 16, 1767, in Colonial Governor's Papers: William Tryon, 1765–1771, 1783–1786, NCSA. On Pennsylvania's loan office, popularly known as the "land bank," see Terry Bouton, *Taming Democracy: "The People," The Founders, and the Troubled Ending of the American Revolution* (New York: Oxford University Press, 2007), 36–41.
44. "The Hillsborough Riot," [*Virginia Gazette,* October 25, 1770], in *North Carolina Experience*, ed. Butler and Watson, 116 ("leaped"), 118 ("glutted"), 117 ("bloodthirsty"); Deposition of Waightstill Avery, March 8, 1771, in *CWT* 2: 623 ("Friend" and "all the Clerks"); Kars, *Breaking Loose Together*, 73–74.
45. Butler, *North Carolina and the Coming of the Revolution*, 32–33, 40–43; Connor, *History of North Carolina*, 314–20; "Council of War at Hillsborough, September 22–23, 1768," in *CWT* 2: 184–85; John Frohock and Alexander Martin to William Tryon, March 18, 1771, in ibid., 2: 638, 639n (Rutherford's role); Tryon to? Waddell, May 10, 1771, in *CWT* 2: 735; Tryon to the Earl of Hillsborough, April 24, 1769, in ibid., 2: 322; Tryon to Thomas Gage, March 19, 1771, in ibid., 2: 641; Kars, *Breaking Loose Together*, 197–203.
46. Rev. George Micklejohn, "A Sermon to Governor Tryon and his Troops" [1768], in *Some Eighteenth-Century Tracts*, ed. Boyd, 400 ("dreadful impiety"), 409 ("tenfold vengeance"); Kars, *Breaking Loose Together*, 204 (numbers who took oath); Holt, "The New Jerusalem," 257 (Tuscape Death). For more on the aftermath: "Josiah Martin's View of the Revolution," [Martin to Lord Hillsborough, August 30, 1772], in *North Carolina Experience*, ed. Butler and Watson, 119–20.
47. Micklejohn, "A Sermon to Governor Tryon and his Troops," 407 ("basest ingratitude," "foreign Enemies" and "domestic foe," "civil society"), 401 ("obey *Magistrates*" and "be no *brawlers*"), 403 ("*guardians* of the public," "God has been pleased," and "*powers that be*"); Presbyterian Ministers to William Tryon, August

23, 1768, in *CWT* 2: 178 ("Sacred Person"). See also "Appointment of Justices of Peace," April 29, 1768, in Colonial Governor's Papers: William Tryon, 1765–1771, 1783–1786, NCSA. On Mecklenburg's pro-government leanings, see also William Tryon to the Earl of Hillsborough, December 12, 1768, in *CWT* 2: 269–70.

48. Husband quoted in Kars, *Breaking Loose Together*, 25.
49. Einhorn, *American Taxation, American Slavery*, 81, 92–104; Meriwether, *Expansion of South Carolina*, 242–44, 259–61; Klein, *Unification of a Slave State*, 52. See also "Journal of C.W. Clerk," in *Carolina Backcountry*, ed. Hooker, 60.
50. [Woodmason], "Copy of a Remonstrance," in *Carolina Backcountry*, ed. Hooker, 229 ("Lawless and Idle"); "Journal of C.W. Clerk," in ibid., 27 ("Without Laws or Government"); [Woodmason], "The Justices of the Peace," 1771?, in ibid., 124 ("Widows Orphans"); Hooker, "The South Carolina Regulator Movement," in ibid., 167–68; Brown, *South Carolina Regulators*, 34–35 ("Ready Money" and Waxhaws incident).
51. [Woodmason], "Copy of a Remonstrance," in *Carolina Backcountry*, ed. Hooker, 214 ("shocking Outrages,"), 213 ("infernal Gang[s]"), and 229; Klein, *Unification of a Slave State*, 51 (Pee Dee Regulators) and 47–77 generally; Brown, *South Carolina Regulators*. For "rights in the woods," see Stephen Aron, "Pigs and Hunters: 'Rights in the Woods' on the Trans-Appalachian Frontier," in *Contact Points*, ed. Cayton and Teute, 181 and 175–204.
52. [Woodmason], "Copy of a Remonstrance," in *Carolina Backcountry*, ed. Hooker, 231 ("Coercive Laws"), 224 ("bid Defiance"), 229 ("raise Staple Articles").
53. John Frohock and Alexander Martin to William Tryon, March 18, 1771, in *CWT* 2: 638, 639n (Mecklenburg companies); "Petition of Mecklenburg County Presbyterians to William Tryon, and the Assembly,? 1769," in ibid., 2: 281–82; Booraem, *Young Hickory*, 27–44; Kars, *Breaking Loose Together*, 180; McDonald, "Politics of the Personal," 50–51; Moore, "Local Origins of Allegiance," 29–30.
54. "An Act to Establish Queen's College," January 15, 1771, in *CWT* 2: 564–67. In two samples (n = 100) of deeds from Mecklenburg County from the late 1760s and early 1770s, I found that 33% and 54%, respectively, mentioned payment in "proclamation money." See Holcomb and Parker, *Mecklenburg County, North Carolina Deed Abstracts*, 100–111 and 173–82. On the Privy Council's ban, see Bailyn, *Voyagers to the West*, 49–66.
55. "The Charlotte Town Resolves," May 31, 1775, at avalon.law.yale.edu/18th_century/charlott.asp (accessed October 13, 2016); Booraem, *Young Hickory*, 54–55 ("Lord Hook," probably the Loyalist Christian Huyck), 76 (Hessians); "A List of Such Persons in the County Who Have Not as Yet Taken the Oath of Allegiance to this State,"? 1779, in Doris Futch Briscoe, *Mecklenburg County Court Minutes, Book 3: 1774–1780* (Charlotte, NC, 1966), NCSA, listing just seventeen such persons. For more on the Mecklenburg Resolves and their link to the probably farcical "Mecklenburg Declaration of Independence" that came to light in 1819, see Pauline Maier, *American Scripture: Making the Declaration of Independence* (New York: Alfred A. Knopf, 1997), 172–74.
56. *Journal of a Lady of Quality*, 199; John Simpson to Richard Cogdell, July 15, 1775, in Richard Cogdell Papers, NCSA (Cogdell was the head of the Beaufort County Committee of Safety); Pitt Committee cited in Jeffrey J. Crow, "Slave Rebelliousness and Social Conflict in North Carolina, 1775 to 1802," *WMQ* 37 (January 1980): 85.
57. William Tennent to Council of Safety, September 1, 1775, in *DHAR* 1: 165 ("horrible conspiracy"); Affidavit of Jonathan Clark Concerning Cameron and Cherokee

Indians, August 21, 1775, in ibid., 1: 148; South Carolina—Ninety-Six District, September 12, 1775, in ibid., 1: 179–80; Joseph Hewes to James Iredell, July 8, 1775, in *PJI* 1: 313. See also Richter, *Facing East from Indian Country,* 217–18; Robert L. Ganyard, "Threat from the West: North Carolina and the Cherokee, 1776–1778," *NCHR* 45 (January 1968): 51 and 47–66; and Colin G. Calloway, "La Révolution Américaine en Territoire indien," *AHRF* 363 (janvier–mars 2011): 131–50.

58. Klein, *Unification of a Slave State*, 82–84; Kars, *Breaking Loose Together*, 212–14; Chroust, *Rise of the Legal Profession*, 2: 11 and 11n; "Introduction," in *Carolina Backcountry*, ed. Hooker, xxx (Woodmason's view).
59. [John Rutledge], "The President's Speech to Both Houses, April 11, 1776," in *DHAR* 1: 274–75; [James Iredell], "Causes of the American Revolution," [June 1776], in *PJI* 1: 409; Richard B. Sheridan, "The Jamaican Slave Insurrection Scare of 1776 and the American Revolution," *JNH* 61 (July 1976): 290–308. For reports of a "concerted scheme" between the British fleet, Loyalists, and Cherokees, see Rev. James Creswell to William H. Drayton, July 27, 1776, in *DHAR* 2: 30–31.
60. Entry for Feb. 8, Bethabara Diary, 1776, in *Records of the Moravians in North Carolina*, ed. Adelaide L. Fries (Raleigh, 1926), 3: 1092 ("evil reports"); Entry for October 14, Salem Diary, 1776, in ibid., 3: 1078 ("Northern Indians"); Entry for May 26, Bethabara Diary, 1776, in ibid., 3: 1097 ("wild men"); Entries for July 29 and 30, Bethabara Diary, 1776, in ibid., 3: 1107 (rumors of six thousand and six hundred); Extracts from Summary in the Wachovia Church Book, 1776, in ibid., 3: 1043 (New York); Entry for July 11, Salem Diary, 1776, in ibid., 3: 1069 (Rutherford). The British did consider hiring mercenaries from Russia. See David Hackett Fischer, *Washington's Crossing* (New York: Oxford University Press, 2004), 51–65. For the rumor, see "Proceedings of the Safety Committee for the Town of Wilmington, North Carolina" (Raleigh, 1844), 39–40, NCSA. For evidence of whites fighting with the Cherokee, see Rachel N. Klein, "Frontier Planters and the American Revolution: The South Carolina Backcountry, 1775–1782," in *An Uncivil War: The Southern Backcountry during the American Revolution*, ed. Ronald Hoffman, Thad W. Tate, and Peter J. Albert (Charlottesville: University of Virginia Press, 1985), 56–57, and Entry for July 15, Bethabara Diary, 1776, in *Records of the Moravians*, 3: 1099. For Rutherford and Moravians, see also MacDonald, "Politics of the Personal," 109.
61. Rutherford quoted in MacDonald, "Politics of the Personal," 66; Carpenter, "Griffith Rutherford," 10–14.
62. Francis Salvador to William H. Drayton, July 18, 1776, in *DHAR* 2: 25; MacDonald, "Politics of the Personal," 78–87; Moore, "Local Origins of Allegiance," 32 (Waxhaws volunteers); Llewellyn M. Toulmin, "Back Country Warrior: Brigadier General Andrew Williamson," *Journal of Backcountry Studies* 7 (Spring 2012): 6–7; Hatley, *The Dividing Paths*.
63. William H. Drayton to Francis Salvador, July 24, 1776, in *DHAR* 2: 29; William Hooper, Joseph Hewes, and John Penn to North Carolina Council of Safety, August 7, 1776, Continental Congress Delegates Collection, NHSA; MacDonald, "Politics of the Personal," 82 ("restrain the Soldiery," from September 11, 1776, letter); Reports of Colonels Christian and Lewis During the Cherokee Expedition, 1776, "Virginia Legislative Papers," *VMHB* 17 (January 1909): 62; Hatley, *Dividing Paths*, 191–203.
64. North Carolina horsemen quoted in Hatley, *Dividing Paths,* 196, and MacDonald, "Politics of the Personal," 91; William Lenoir, "Account of the Expedition Against

the Cherokee Indians in 1776," [June 1835], NCC; Will Graves, ed., "Arthur Fairies' Journal of Expedition Against the Cherokee Indians from July 8, 1776 to October 11, 1776," [1850], http://www.southerncampaign.org (accessed March 21, 2014); D. L. Swain, "Historical Sketch of the Indian War of 1776," *North Carolina University Magazine* 1 (May 1852): 132–56; Pension Application of James Cole, December 10, 1832, transcribed by Will Graves, http://www.southerncampaign .org (accessed March 21, 2014). See also "Speech of His Excellency, J. Rutledge, September 19, 1776," in *DHAR* 2: 34, and Elizabeth Fraas, "An Unusual Map of the Early West," *RKHS* 73 (January 1975): 62–69. See also Christina Snyder, "Native Nations in the Age of Revolution," in *The World of the Revolutionary American Republic: Land, Labor, and the Conflict for a Continent*, ed. Andrew Shankman (New York: Routledge, 2014), 77–96.

65. James Robertson to Felix Robertson,? 1806, in Paul Clements, *Chronicles of the Cumberland Settlements, 1779–1796* (self-published, 2012), 166–67 ("skinned over"); "The Clover Bottom Massacre," in ibid., 161 (dogs barking); Calloway, "La Révolution Américaine en Territoire indien," 140.
66. Jane T. Merritt, "Native Peoples in the Revolutionary War," in *Oxford Handbook of the American Revolution*, ed. Gray and Kamensky, 241–44; Silver, *Our Savage Enemy*, 239–40; Max M. Mintz, *Seeds of Empire: The American Revolutionary Conquest of the Iroquois* (New York: New York University Press, 1999); Joseph R. Fischer, *A Well-Executed Failure: The Sullivan Campaign Against the Iroquois, July–September 1779* (Columbia: University of South Carolina Press, 1997).
67. Motion by John Mathews, September 20, 1781, *Journals of the Continental Congress, 1774–1789*, 978, at http://memory.loc.gov/ammem/amlaw/lwjc.html (accessed August 31, 2015); Adams quoted in Fischer, *Washington's Crossing*, 376, and see 375–79; Thomas Paine, "The American Crisis, No. 6," October 20, 1778, in *Common Sense and Other Writings*, ed. J. M. Opal (New York: W. W. Norton and Company, 2012), 41 (threat to Bank of England and other buildings), and Opal, "Thomas Paine and the Revolutionary Enlightenment, 1770s–1790s," in ibid., xxiii–xxiv.
68. [George Rogers Clark], "Clark's Campaign in the Illinois," November 19, 1779, in *Col. George Rogers Clark's Sketch of his Campaign in the Illinois in 1778–9* (Cincinnati, 1869), 41 ("Devils"), 43 ("beneath the Character"), 45 ("blame no Person"), 36 ("great presents and promises"); MacDonald, "Politics of the Personal," 113–19.
69. Jefferson quoted in Merrill D. Peterson, *Thomas Jefferson and the New Nation: A Biography* (New York: Oxford University Press, 1970), 123, and see 123–24; Henry quoted in William Wirt, *Sketches of the Life and Character of Patrick Henry* (Philadelphia, 1817), 322 and 320–49; Richard B. Morris, *The Forging of the Union, 1781–1789* (New York: Harper and Row, 1987), 197 (sequestration figures); MacDonald, "Politics of the Personal," 107–8; Carole Watterson Troxler, "Refuge, Resistance, and Reward: The Southern Loyalists' Claim on East Florida," *JSH* 55 (November 1989): 563–96.
70. Benjamin Harrison to Governor Matthews, October 15, 1782, in "George Rogers Clark Papers, 1781–1784," in *Collections of the Illinois State Historical Library*, ed. James Alton James (Springfield: Illinois State Historical Library, 1926), 19: 130; Michael A. McDonnell, "Class War? Class Struggles during the American Revolution in Virginia," *WMQ* 63 (April 2006): 305–44; L. Scott Philyaw, "A Slave for Every Soldier: The Strange History of Virginia's Forgotten Recruitment Act of 1 January 1781," *VMHB* 109 (2001): 367–86.

71. "Jackson's Description of His Experiences During and Immediately Following the Revolutionary War," in *PAJ* 1: 5 ("shot him"); Booraem, *Young Hickory*, 45–61, esp. 50. See also John Shy, "British Strategy for Pacifying the Southern Colonies, 1778–1781," in *The Southern Experience in the American Revolution*, ed. Jeffrey J. Crow and Larry E. Tise (Chapel Hill: University of North Carolina Press, 1978), 155–73; John W. Gordon, *South Carolina and the American Revolution: A Battlefield History* (Columbia: University of South Carolina Press, 2003); and Allan Kulikoff, "The War in the Countryside," in *Oxford Handbook of the American Revolution*, ed. Gray and Kamensky, 216–33.
72. Booraem, *Young Hickory*, 53–84, 85–88, 91–95, 96–98; AJ to Amos Kendall, January 9, 1844, in *PAJ* 1: 9n. For "lying out," see "Colonel Robert Gray's Observations on the War in Carolina," *SCHGM* 11 (July 1910): 154.
73. Pension Application of John Clemmons, July 18, 1832, transcribed by Will Graves, http://www.southerncampaign.org; Pension Application of Jonathan Starkey, October 8, 1832, transcribed by Will Graves, http://www.southerncampaign.org; Pension Application of David Blalock,? 1833, transcribed by Will Graves, http://www.southerncampaign.org; Pension Application of William Bates, April 5, 1832, transcribed by Will Gates, http://www.southerncampaign.org; Pension Application of Jacob Schoolcraft, November 25, 1833, transcribed by Will Graves, http://www.southerncampaign.org (all accessed March 21, 2014); Joseph Johnson, *Traditions and Reminisces of the American Revolution in the South* (Charleston, 1851), 111 and 110–12.
74. Rutherford quoted in MacDonald, "Politics of the Personal," 165 ("imps") and 117 ("sons"), and see 131–32 and 136–38; Griffith Rutherford to Nathanael Greene, April 15, 1782, in *PNG* 11: 70 ("Wolves"), and Nathanael Greene to Griffith Rutherford, April 12, 1782, in *PNG* 11: 42 ("cause of America"); "Colonel Robert Gray's Observations," 156 ("perfect savage").
75. MacDonald, "Politics of the Personal," 144 (Greene quote) and 143–48; "Colonel Robert Gray's Observations," 158, 159 ("most calamitous" and "Common Cause") and 149 ("small murdering"). See also Caroline Cox, "The Continental Army," in *Oxford Handbook of the American Revolution*, ed. Gray and Kamensky, 161–76.
76. MacDonald, "Politics of the Personal," 156.
77. "Jackson's Description of His Experiences During and Immediately Following the Revolutionary War," in *PAJ* 1: 5; Booraem, *Young Hickory*, 106–8; Elizabeth A. Fenn, *Pox Americana: The Great Smallpox Epidemic of 1775–82* (New York: Hill and Wang, 2001).
78. "Advice to Andrew Jackson by His Mother," undated, Andrew Jackson Papers, 1788–1836, NCSA. According to this printed but undated document, Jackson relayed his mother's parting wisdom to close friends including John Eaton and William B. Lewis. The exact words supposedly passed down from mother to son inevitably vary by source. See also Booraem, *Young Hickory*, 108–9 and 253n, and "Jackson's Mother's Adieu," in box 18, folder 2, Provine Papers, TSLA. "Jackson's Mother's Grave," [1918 story], in William Alexander Provine Papers, 1552–1935, box 18, folder 2, TSLA, and "Mother of Andrew Jackson," in box 18, folder 2, ibid.
79. Booraem, *Young Hickory*, 111.

CHAPTER 2

1 [Andrew Jackson], "Jackson's Description of His Experiences During and Immediately Following the Revolutionary War," *PAJ* 1: 7; Hendrik Booraem, *Young Hickory: The Making of Andrew Jackson* (Dallas: Taylor Trade, 2001), 112–14.

2 Booraem, *Young Hickory*, 116 (quote) and 115–16; J. M. Opal, *Beyond the Farm: National Ambitions in Rural New England* (Philadelphia: University of Pennsylvania Press, 2008), 69–95. For "hewers of wood," see Joshua 9:23 and Peter Linebaugh and Marcus Rediker, *The Many-Headed Hydra: Sailors, Slaves, Commoners, and the Hidden History of the Revolutionary Atlantic* (Boston: Beacon Press, 2000), 36–70.

3 Booraem, *Young Hickory*, 118–29; [Andrew Jackson], "Jackson's Description of His Experiences During and Immediately Following the Revolutionary War," *PAJ* 1: 7; Allan Kulikoff, "'Such Things Ought Not to Be': The American Revolution and the First National Depression," in *The World of the Revolutionary American Republic: Land, Labor, and the Conflict for a Continent*, ed. Andrew Shankman (New York: Routledge, 2014), 134–64.

4 "Colonel Robert Gray's Observations on the War in Carolina," *SCHGM* 11 (July 1910): 149 ("small murdering"); *South Carolina Weekly Gazette* (Charleston), December 18–22 and December 22–25, 1784; Allan Kulikoff, "The War in the Countryside," in *The Oxford Handbook of the American Revolution*, ed. Edward G. Gray and Jane Kamensky (New York: Oxford University Press, 2013), 216–33; Richard B. Morris, *The Forging of the Union, 1781–1789* (New York: Harper and Row, 1987), 136–37 and 143–44. For Charleston's bar: Anton-Hermann Chroust, *The Rise of the Legal Profession in America: Volume II, The Revolution and the Post-Revolutionary Era* (2 vols., Norman: University of Oklahoma Press, 1965), 2: 11 and 11n.

5 Booraem, *Young Hickory*, 156 (quire), 139–40 (indent sale), 118–29, 130–38; Charles Sellers, *The Market Revolution: Jacksonian America, 1815–1846* (New York: Oxford University Press, 1991), 174–80; "Appraisal of Bay Horse," December 12, 1783, in *PAJ* 1: 9, and "Appointment as Agent to Receive Payment," October 24, 1785, in *PAJ* 1: 9–10.

6 Colin G. Calloway, "La Révolution Américaine en Territoire indien," *AHRF* 363 (janvier–mars 2011): 142–43; Paul Kelton, *Cherokee Medicine, Colonial Germs: An Indigenous Nation's Fight Against Smallpox, 1518–1824* (Norman: University of Oklahoma Press, 2015), 246n; Thomas B. Allen, *Tories: Fighting for the King in America's First Civil War* (New York: Harper Collins, 2010), 287–90; William Dykeman, *Tennessee: A History* (New York: W. W. Norton and Company, 1975), 64–65.

7 "An Act for Suppressing the Violences of the Indians," [October 31, 1787], in *A Digest of the Laws of the State of Georgia from Its First Establishment as a British Province down to the Year 1798*, ed. Robert Watkins and George Watkins (Philadelphia, 1800), 365–66; John Dickinson quoted in Daniel K. Richter, *Facing East from Indian Country: A Native History of Early America* (Cambridge, MA: Harvard University Press, 2000), 224. See also Stuart Banner, *How the Indians Lost Their Land: Law and Power on the Frontier* (Cambridge, MA: Harvard University Press 2005), 112–49, and Peter Silver, *Our Savage Neighbors: How Indian War Transformed Early America* (New York: W. W. Norton and Company, 2008), 265–76.

8 Carleton quoted in Lorenzo Sabine, *Biographical Sketches of Loyalists of the American Revolution, with an Historical Essay* (2 vols., 1864; Port Washington, NY, 1966), 1: 90; Maya Jasanoff, *Liberty's Exiles: American Loyalists in the Revolutionary World* (New York: Vintage Books, 2011), 92 ("Flee then") and 85–95. For Loyalist refugees, see Mary Beth Norton, *The British-Americans: The Loyalist Exiles in England, 1774-1789* (Boston: 1972), 8–9 and 35–38; "The Loyalist British

Atlantic, ca. 1775–1795," in *The Loyal Atlantic: Remaking the British Atlantic in the Revolutionary Era*, ed. Jerry Bannister and Liam Riordan (Toronto: University of Toronto Press, 2012), xxii–xxiii, and Mark A. Peterson, "The War in the Cities," in *Oxford Handbook of the American Revolution,* ed. Gray and Kamensky, 208–10. In 1784, Spruce McCoy (or Macay) purchased three plots of land in Rowan County seized from Henry E. McCulloch. One was 126 acres (£301), another 159 acres (£168), and a third just 2 acres (£301). It seems likely that his law office was located on this small plot, probably in Salisbury. See Robert O. DeMond, *The Loyalists in North Carolina During the Revolution* (1940; Hamden, CT: Archon Books, 1964), 249, and, for all confiscated sales between 1784 and 1787, Appendix B, 240–50, and Booraem, *Young Hickory*, 168–70, 156, 157.

9 Rutherford quoted in DeMond, *The Loyalists in North Carolina,* 177, and see also 170–80 and 256; McCulloch quote from Memorial of Henry Eustace McCulloch, November 5, 1783, in American Loyalist Claims, Series II: McCullok, AO13/117, BNA. Rutherford used this same line with other Loyalist claimants. See James M. MacDonald, "Politics of the Personal in the Old North State: Griffith Rutherford in Revolutionary North Carolina" (PhD dissertation, Louisiana State University, 2006), 163. In Orange County, McCulloch had owned sixty-nine separate properties, most ranging from two hundred to four hundred acres; one man, James Williams, purchased twenty-three of these tracts, but the others mainly went to single-plot purchases, so that the sixty-nine properties once owned by one man passed to thirty-six owners. In Rowan County, McCulloch had owned fifty-one of the fifty-four properties sold; after the confiscation sales, there were thirty-seven owners rather than three. See Demond, *Loyalists in North Carolina*, 240–50.

10 [Iredell], "Instructions to Chowan County Representatives," [Sept. 1783], in *PJI* 2: 449 ("narrow and contracted"); [Iredell], "Causes of the American Revolution," [June 1776], in *PJI* 1: 410 ("*Revenge*," emphasis in original) and 409 ("more than diabolical"). For newspaper clippings to McCulloch, see *Virginia Gazette*, December 27, 1787, included with notation "transmitted by Jas. Iredell Esq. from Edenton N. Carolina 22nd June 1788," in Memorial of Henry Eustace McCulloch, April 2, 1788, American Loyalist Claims, Series II: McCullok, AO13/117, BNA. For Iredell see also Don Higginbotham, "James Iredell's Efforts to Preserve the First British Empire," *NCHR*, 49 (April 1972), 127–45, esp. 127–30; Gordon S. Wood, *The Creation of the American Republic* (1967, Chapel Hill: University of North Carolina Press, 1998), 406–7; and Allan Nevins, *The American States During and After the Revolution, 1775–1789* (1924; New York: A. M. Kelley, 1969), 363.

11 [Iredell], "Resolutions of the Citizens of Edenton," August 1, 1783, in *PJI* 2: 431 ("not of Revenge"); Burke quoted in John C. Meleney, *The Public Life of Aedanus Burke: Revolutionary Republican in Post-Revolutionary South Carolina* (Columbia: University of South Carolina Press, 1989), 73.

12 Robert R. Livingston quoted in *The Law Practice of Alexander Hamilton: Documents and Commentary*, ed. Julius Goebel (2 vols., New York: New York University Press, 1964), 2: 216; [Alexander Hamilton], "A Letter from Phocion to the Considerate Citizens of New York," [January 1784], in *The Papers of Alexander Hamilton: Volume III: 1782–1786,* ed. Harold C. Syrett (New York, 1962), 3: 484 ("legal liberty"), and 492 ("little vindictive"), 486 ("scorn of nations"); [Hamilton], "Second Letter from Phocion," [April 1784], in ibid., 3: 556 ("*enact*," emphasis in original); Burke quoted in Meleney, *Public Life of Aedanus Burke*, 68 ("numerous democratic") and 80 ("fix disgrace"); Iredell quoted in William Boyd, *History of North Carolina: Volume II, The Federal Period, 1783–1860* (New York: Lewis Publishing Company, 1919), 11.

13 *An Address from the Committee Appointed at Mrs. Vanderwater's, on the 13th Day of September, 1784* (New York, 1784), 6 ("custom of nations"); Wood, *Creation of the American Republic*, 453–63; Robert M. Weir, "'The Violent Spirit,' the Re-establishment of Order, and the Continuity of Leadership in Post-Revolutionary South Carolina," in *An Uncivil War: The Southern Backcountry in the American Revolution*, ed. Ronald Hoffman, Thad W. Tate, and Peter J. Albert (Charlottesville: University of Virginia Press, 1985), 70–98; Ron Chernow, *Alexander Hamilton* (New York: Penguin Books, 2004), 194–99, and, for near duel with Hamilton, 284–85 and 308–9.

14 J. Hector St. John de Crèvecoeur, *Letters from an American Farmer, and Sketches of Eighteenth-Century America* (1782, New York: Fox, Duffield, 1904), 196 ("surprising!") and 197–99 and 224–5; Terry Bouton, "A Road Closed: Rural Insurgency in Post-Independence Pennsylvania," *JAH* 87 (December 2000), 859–60 (foreclosure figures). See also Bouton, *Taming Democracy: "The People," the Founders, and the Troubled Ending of the American Revolution* (New York: Oxford University Press, 2009); Stephen Mihm, "Funding the Revolution: Monetary and Fiscal Policy in Eighteenth-Century America," in *Oxford Handbook of the American Revolution*, ed. Gray and Kamensky, 327–54; Louis Maganzin, "Economic Depression in Maryland and Virginia, 1783–1787" (PhD dissertation, Georgetown University, 1967); John H. Flannaghan Jr., "Trying Times: Economic Depression in New Hampshire, 1781–1789" (PhD dissertation, Georgetown University, 1972); Paul Douglas Newman, *Fries's Rebellion: The Enduring Struggle for the American Revolution* (Philadelphia: University of Pennsylvania Press, 2004), esp. 29–36. For *scire facias*: William Blackstone, *Commentaries on the Laws of England* (4 vols., Dublin, 1771), Book III, chapter 26, pp. 416–17, and Henry Campbell Black, *Black's Law Dictionary* (rev. 4th ed., St. Paul, MN: West Publishing, 1968), 1513. Debt imprisonment seems to have followed from either *capias ad respondendum* or *capias ad satisfaciendum*. See Black, *Black's Law Dictionary*, 262.

15 Erwin C. Surrency, "The Pernicious Practice of Law—A Comment," *AJLH* 13 (July 1969): 249 ("safety and good order), 256 ("mere business"), and 287 ("men of enterprise" and "Justice"). This is a reprint of a series of essays first published in 1786, probably by Boston Anti-Federalist Benjamin Austin. For speculation in public securities, see Stanley Elkins and Eric McKitrick, *The Age of Federalism: The Early American Republic, 1788–1800* (New York, 1993), 136–45, and, for the Massachusetts Regulation: Leonard L. Richards, *Shays's Rebellion: The American Revolution's Final Battle* (Philadelphia: University of Pennsylvania Press, 2002); John L. Brooke, "To the Quiet of the People: Revolutionary Settlements and Civil Unrest in Western Massachusetts, 1774–1789," *WMQ* 46 (July 1989): 425–62.

16 Chroust, *Rise of the Legal Profession*, 2: 28, 29 (Massachusetts quotes), 62–63 (six state constitutions, plus Rhode Island's in 1842); "Introduction," in *DHRC: Virginia* 8: xxvii–xxviii; Gordon S. Wood, *Empire of Liberty: A History of the Early Republic, 1789–1815* (New York: Oxford University Press, 2009), 400–432; John Philip Reid, *Legislating the Courts: Judicial Dependence in Early National New Hampshire* (Dekalb, IL: Northern Illinois University Press, 2009), 123–31. In addition to the proposed constitution for Frankland in 1784–85, discussed later, the 1798 Georgia Constitutional Convention considered an amendment to ban lawyers along with clergy from the legislature. See Albert B. Saye, ed., "Journal of the Georgia Constitutional Convention of 1798," *GHQ* 36 (December 1952): 369.

17 Adams quoted in Warren, *History of the American Bar*, 220; Burke quoted in a 1782 letter in Meleney, *Public Life of Aedanus Burke*, 69; Wilson Lumpkin, *The Removal*

of the Cherokee Indians from Georgia (2 vols., New York: Dodd, Mead and Company, 1907), 1: 15; Jefferson in 1807 letter quoted in Wood, *Empire of Liberty*, 440, and see also 402, 418, 422, and 449. On Abigail Adams and speculation: Woody Holton, "Abigail Adams, Bond Speculator," *WMQ* 64 (October 2007): 821–38. Numbers of lawyers in Massachusetts from Gerard W. Gawalt, "Sources of Anti-Lawyer Sentiment in Massachusetts, 1740–1840," *AJLH* 14 (October 1970): 285, and see 283–307.

18 Booraem, *Young Hickory*, 116–17.

19 Booraem, *Young Hickory*, 158–59 and 165–66; James C. Curtis, *Andrew Jackson and the Search for Vindication*, ed. Oscar Handlin (Boston: Little, Brown and Company, 1976), 10–15.

20 Booraem, *Young Hickory*, 175–78; Stephen C. Bullock, *Revolutionary Brotherhood: Freemasonry and the Transformation of the American Social Order, 1730–1840* (Chapel Hill: University of North Carolina Press, 1998). It is certain that Jackson was a devoted Mason in Tennessee as of 1800, but Booraem suggests that he was also a member of the Old Cone Lodge in Salisbury around 1787 or a member of Nashville's Harmony Lodge from its founding in 1789.

21 Booraem, *Young Hickory*, 192–93; Alex M. Hitz, "Georgia Bounty Land Grants," *GHQ* 38 (December 1954): 341 ("steadfastly"), 337 (population and warrant numbers), 339–41 (schedule of bounties); Robin L. Einhorn, *American Taxation, American Slavery* (Chicago: University of Chicago Press, 2006), 92–93. See also Roger H. Brown, *Redeeming the Republic: Federalists, Taxation, and the Origins of the Constitution* (Baltimore: Johns Hopkins University Press, 1993), and David A. Nichols, "Land, Republicanism, and Indians: Power and Policy in Early National Georgia, 1780–1825," *GHQ* 85 (Summer 2001): 199–226.

22 Remarks of Judge Haywood, "Sevier and Anderson's Lessee vs. Hill," [Dec. 1808], in *TR* 2: 31–32 ("discourage large grants" and "lordly owners"); "Hampton's Lessee vs. M'Ginnis," [Sept. 1805], in ibid., 2: 10 (records from 1777 office lost or non-existent); Einhorn, *American Taxation, American Slavery*, 92–93 and 80–81. Land entries from State Agency Records: Secretary of State, Original Land Entries, Western Lands, 1783–1784, NCSA. Melissa Gismondi and Jonathon Booth were indispensable in making sense of this enormous set of records. The claims on the east bank of the Mississippi River made at Armstrong's office were overwhelmingly large; after throwing out a handful of claims whose descriptions were too ambiguous, I found that 78% (39 of 50) were for 5,000 acres, and no claim was for less than 1,000 acres. The median claim was 4,059, ten times that near the French Broad. A land office selling so-called county grants was opened in North Carolina in 1777, and Rutherford County was formed in 1779.

23 "Avery vs. Holland," [September 1806], *TR* 2: 73; Entry of Andrew Evans, January 4, 1784, Original Land Entries, Western Lands, 1783–1784; Entries of Griffith Rutherford, October 27, 1783, and May 7, 1784. For another reference to Christian's expedition, suggesting a large number of Virginia claimants, see Entry of David Campbell, October 21, 1783. Henry and John Rutherford made entries on October 28, 1783, and these and the October 27 purchase included a notation about Griffith Rutherford paying. On May 7, 1784, a Margaret Rutherford also made an entry. For Armstrong, see Demond, *Loyalists in North Carolina*, 250 (purchases two plots from McCulloch's estate), and Booraem, *Young Hickory*, 192–93 (meet AJ and Mason). In a large sample that I prepared with Gismondi (N = 875), 211 entries, or 24.1%, specifically mentioned tree markings. See also Angela Pulley Hudson, *Creek Paths and Federal Roads: Indians, Settlers, and Slaves and the*

Making of the American South (Chapel Hill: University of North Carolina Press, 2010), 37–38.

24 William Blount to John Donelson, May 17, 1783, in *JGBP* 1: 58 ("very punctually"); William Blount to John Donelson, Joseph Martin, and John Sevier, May 31, 1784, in ibid., 1: 168 ("make use of" and "transfer their Rights"); John Armstrong to William Blount, October 6, 1789, in ibid., 1: 507–8; Thomas Williams to John Gray Blount, August 12, 1784, in ibid., 1: 173–74; William Blount to John Gray Blount, September 22, 1795, in ibid., 2: 596; William Blount to John Gray Blount, March 28, 1795, in ibid., 2: 520–23, and William Blount to John Gray Blount, June 26, 1790, in ibid., 2: 67–72. See also Dale Van Every, *Ark of Empire: The American Frontier, 1784–1803* (New York: William Morrow and Company, 1963), 89–90, and Andrew R. L. Cayton, "When Shall We Cease to Have Judases?: The Blount Conspiracy and the Limits of the 'Extended Republic,'" in *Launching the "Extended Republic": The Federalist Era*, ed. Ronald Hoffman and Peter J. Albert (Charlottesville: University of Virginia Press, 1996), 156–89; "Jacob Blount's Family," in *JGBP*, 1: xiv–xv. A lawyer who specialized in scrutinizing land titles was a *conveyanier*. See Bettina Manzo, "A Virginian in New York: The Diary of St. George Tucker, July–August, 1786," *NYH* 67 (April 1986): 187 and 187n.

25 Entry of William Blount, October 29, 1783, Original Land Entries; William Blount to Thomas Blount, July 30, 1787, in *JGBP* 1: 328 (postscript) and 327–28; Andrew R. L. Cayton, "'Separate Interests' and the Nation-State: The Washington Administration and the Origins of Regionalism in the Trans-Appalachian West," *JAH* 79 (June 1992): 56–58 (Blount holdings by 1796). Over thirty entries in Original Land Entries, Western Lands, 1783–1784, mention Blount as the paying party. For figures of 3.7 million acres of warrants given out at Armstrong's office and of more than 7.5 million acres in the whole of the Southwest Territory, exclusive of Cherokee and Chickasaw lands, see "Report of the Secretary of State to the President," November 8, 1791, in *TPUS* 4: 85–93.

26 William Blount to John Donelson, May 17, 1783, in *JGBP* 1: 58; John Donelson to William Blount, September 24, 1783, in ibid., 1: 111–12; Jane Kamensky, *The Exchange Artist: A Story of High-Flying Speculation and America's First Banking Collapse* (New York: Penguin Books, 2008), 14–70. For the Muscle Shoals, see Daniel Dupre, "Ambivalent Capitalists on the Cotton Frontier: Settlement and Development in the Tennessee Valley of Alabama," *JSH* 56 (May 1990): 215–40.

27 William Blount to Joseph Martin, March 9, 1784, in *JGBP*, 1: 157 ("keep up a Report") and 156–57; William Blount to Arnold Delius, April 10, 1784, in ibid., 1: 162–64. For Muscle Shoals members: "Petition of William Blount and Associates to the Assembly of Georgia for a Grant of Land," Feb. 7, 1784, in ibid., 1: 536–37; A. P. Whitaker, "The Muscle Shoals Speculation, 1783–1789," *MVHR* 13 (December 1926): 365–86; Rachel N. Klein, *Unification of a Slave State: The Rise of the Planter Class in the South Carolina Backcountry, 1760–1808* (Chapel Hill: University of North Carolina Press, 1990), 181.

28 John Strother to John Gray Blount, May 3, 1785, in *JGBP*, 1: 197; Kristofer Ray, "Land Speculation, Popular Democracy, and Political Transformation on the Tennessee Frontier, 1780–1800," *THQ* 61 (Fall 2002): 161–81; Peter Onuf, "Toward Federalism: Virginia, Congress, and the Western Lands," *WMQ* 34 (July 1977): 353–74, and Onuf, "Liberty, Development, and Union: Visions of the West in the 1780s," *WMQ* 43 (April 1986): 179–213.

29 "State of Frankland, August Session, 1785," *Columbian Herald* (South Carolina), January 30, 1786; Boyd, *History of North Carolina*, 2: 11 (rough population of

twenty-five thousand); "State of Franklin," http://www.northcarolinahistory.org/commentary/99/entry (accessed March 28, 2014); James William Hagy, "Democracy Defeated: The Frankland Constitution of 1785," *THQ* 40 (Fall 1981): 239–56; Kevin T. Barksdale, *The Lost State of Franklin: America's First Secession* (Lexington: University Press of Kentucky, 2009). For Vermont, see Michael A. Bellesiles, *Revolutionary Outlaws: Ethan Allen and the Struggle for Independence on the Early American Frontier* (Charlottesville: University of Virginia Press, 1993).

30 *Maryland Gazette* of October 11, 1785, quoted in George Henry Alden, "The State of Franklin," *AHR* 8 (January 1903): 280. I used the descriptions of the locations mentioned in Original Land Entries and then drew up samples based on discernible regions. I threw out those descriptions that were vague or ambivalent, but even so these samples must be treated as rough estimations. Still, clear patterns emerge. The sample of single-entry claims that used the French Broad as a locator (n = 46) averaged 424 acres, with a modal entry of 200 and no entries larger than 2,000. Those supposedly in Greene County and using the Holston or Nolichucky Rivers as references (n = 100) had a larger mean size of 670 acres and included four maximum (5,000-acre) claims. Jonathon Booth did his own calculations using the same sample but his own sense of the locations referred to in each entry, and his findings were very similar. In the 1700s, "Franks" could refer to European Crusaders; see [Benjamin Franklin], "A Narrative of the late Massacres, in Lancaster County," [1764], in *Benjamin Franklin: Writings* (New York: Library of America, 1987), 549–50. But some of the more eccentric thinkers of the 1780s also endorsed "frankpledge." Among these thinkers was the British abolitionist Granville Sharp, who shared the idea with none other than Benjamin Franklin and imposed it upon some of the early settlers of Sierra Leone. See Adam Hochschild, *Bury the Chains: Prophets and Rebels in the Fight to Free an Empire's Slaves* (Boston: Houghton Mifflin, 2005), 146, 150, and 175. On the names Frankland and Franklin, see also Hagy, "Democracy Defeated," 240n.

31 Francis A. Ramsey, "The Provisional Constitution of Frankland," *AHM* 1 (January 1896): 52 ("sense of a majority" and "secure the poor," in preface by Houston), 54 ("*Commonwealth*"), 59 (Registers), 63 (inheritance); Richard Price as quoted by Arthur Campbell in Virginia, cited in Hagy, "Democracy Defeated," 244 ("power of *Civil Society*," emphasis in original). The six purchasers of land in Armstrong's office were David Campbell, William Cox, David Craig, John Blair, John Gilliland, and Joseph Tipton.

32 "Extract of a Letter from Caswell County in the State of Frankland, Dated May 26, 1785," *State Gazette of South Carolina* (Charleston), October 27, 1785; "The Provisional Constitution of Frankland," 61. For Frankland's ties to Virginia, see Peter J. Kastor, "'Equitable Rights and Privileges': The Divided Loyalties in Washington County, Virginia, During the Franklin Separatist Crisis," *VMHB* 105 (Spring 1997): 193–226. For Dumplin Creek and complaints about North Carolina's treatment of Indians, see Robert E. Corlew, *Tennessee: A Short History* (1969; Knoxville: University of Tennessee Press, 1981), 74 and 77–78.

33 "Provisional Constitution of Frankland," 51 (preface by Houston); Sevier quoted in Ray, "Land Speculation, Popular Democracy, and Political Transformation," 163 ("Chickamoggy"), and Alden, "State of Franklin," 273 ("Dragged into"); Corlew, *Tennessee*, 77 (Benjamin Franklin not interested). For Stockley Donelson as speaker of the Franklin assembly, see "State of Franklin, August Session, 1785," *Columbian Herald*, January 30, 1786. On Franklin as a front for Muscle Shoals

speculators, see "Extract of a Letter from a Gentleman Living in the Western Territory . . . Dated December 20, 1784," *Freeman's Journal* (Philadelphia), February 2, 1785.

34 "From the Knoxville Gazette, of May 1," *Southern Sentinel* (Augusta, GA), August 10, 1797 (Sevier trip down the Tennessee in 1785 and "warrants of survey"); "Treaty with the Cherokee, 1785," in *IT*, 9 ("United States" and "particular situation") and 8–11; Whitaker, "The Muscle Shoals Speculation." The four commissioners were Joseph Martin (a Muscle Shoals member), Benjamin Hawkins, Andrew Pickens, and Lachlan McIntosh.

35 "Treaty with the Cherokee, 1785," in *IT*, 10; "Extract of a Letter from Caswell County . . . Dated May 26, 1785," *State Gazette of South Carolina* (Charleston), October 27, 1785 (I assume the writer's birthplace from the destination of his letter); Bennett Ballew to George Washington, August 22, 1789, in *PGW* 3: 518. On Ballew, see *PGW* 2: 328n–329n.

36 "Georgia," *New-Hampshire Mercury and the General Advertiser* (Portsmouth), September 20, 1787 ("internal and external," from Sevier letter of June 25); "Intelligence from Georgia," *Columbian Herald* (Charleston), September 25, 1787 ("think it extraordinary," from Sevier letter of August 30); George White, *Historical Collections of Georgia* (New York, 1855), 479–80. See also Kenneth Coleman, ed., *A History of Georgia* (2nd ed., Athens: University of Georgia Press, 1991), 92–94.

37 Jessica Choppin Roney, "Institutional Violence: State-Making and Indian-Killing in the Early West," Society for Historians of the Early American Republic Annual Meeting, Raleigh, NC, July 18, 2015; J. G. M. Ramsey, *The Annals of Tennessee to the End of the Eighteenth Century* (Charleston, 1853), 419–20. For Georgia–Franklin negotiations and offers, see "An Act for Suppressing the Violences of the Indians," in *A Digest of the Laws of the State of Georgia*, 368, and "American Intelligence," *State Gazette of South-Carolina*, January 3, 1788. On Chota: Daniel J. Tortora, *Carolina in Crisis: Cherokees, Colonists, and Slaves in the American Southeast, 1756–1763* (Chapel Hill: University of North Carolina Press, 2015), 22, 41, 147–48.

38 "A Treaty Held Between the Officers of the State of Franklin and the Cherokee Indian Chiefs, July 31st and August 3rd, 1786," in Ramsey, *Annals of Tennessee*, 344, 345 (Old Tassel's words, emphasis in original), and see also 406–10 and 418 for seizures and arrest of Sevier. For report of drunken dispute: "American Intelligence," *Pennsylvania Mercury and Universal Advertiser* (Philadelphia), December 9, 1788. Corlew, *Tennessee*, 72–84, offers a clear narrative.

39 North Carolina had offered Sevier the post of brigadier general of a new western district in late 1784. He assumed this post upon pledging allegiance to the parent state in early 1789. See Corlew, *Tennessee*, 82–83.

40 "North Carolina: Cession of Western Land Claims," December 22, 1789, in *TPUS* 4: 7, 8, and 3–8; Corlew, *Tennessee*, 77–78 and 82–83.

41 [Alexander Hamilton], "The Federalist, no. 6," in *The Federalist, with Letters of "Brutus,"* ed. Terence Ball (New York: Cambridge University Press, 2003), 24; Hugh Williamson to George Washington, May 21, 1789, in *PGW*, 2: 360; Washington quoted in Eliga H. Gould, *Among the Powers of the Earth: The American Revolution and the Making of a New World Empire* (Cambridge, MA: Harvard University Press, 2012), 127. The classic study of the cultural mood of the Federalists remains Wood, *Creation of the American Republic*, 391–467. More recent studies relevant here include Bouton, *Taming Democracy*, 171–96, and Woody Holton, "Did Democracy Cause the Recession That Led to the Constitution?," *JAH* 92 (September 2005): 442–69.

42 Klein, *Unification of a Slave State*, 132 (quote from Camden grand jury) and 127–35; John Kean to Susan Livingston Kean, April 14 and 18, 1788, in *DHRC: South Carolina* 27: 296 ("put you off"); Boyd, *History of North Carolina*, 7–8; Nevins, *American States During and After the Revolution*, 336–37, 571. For replevin in British common law, see Paul Goodman, "The Emergence of Homestead Exemption in the United States: Accommodation and Resistance to the Market Revolution," *JAH* 80 (September 1993): 475–76 and 470–98.

43 Petition from Ninety-Six District quoted in Klein, *Unification of a Slave State*, 132; Nevins, *American States During and After the Revolution*, 518–19, 523–24.

44 David W. Robson, "Anticipating the Brethren: The Reverend Charles Nisbet Critiques the French Revolution," *PMHB* 121 (October 1997): 315, 316, and 303–28; Fredrika Teute Schmidt and Barbara Ripel Wilhelm, "Early Proslavery Petitions in Virginia," *WMQ* 30 (January 1973): 141, 145, and 133–46; *The Political Club of Danville, Kentucky, 1786–1790* (Louisville, 1894), 143 ("hated") and 130; "The Cumberland Compact," [May 13, 1780], in Paul Clements, *Chronicles of the Cumberland Settlements, 1779–1796* (self-published, 2012), 149 and 149–59; James Duncanson to James Maury, March 11, 1788, in *DHRC: Virginia* 8: 478–80; David Ramsay, *The History of the American Revolution, in Two Volumes* (1789; Indianapolis: Liberty Fund, 1990), 2: 452–62.

45 Eric Foner, *Tom Paine and Revolutionary America* (New York: Oxford University Press, 1976), 133; "The Dissent of the Minority of the Convention," [December 18, 1787], in *DHRC: Pennsylvania* 2: 624–25; [James Jackson], *The Letters of Sicilus, to the Citizens of the State of Georgia* (1795), 7 ("avarice" and "natural liberty"), 13 ("as near an equality"); George R. Lamplugh, "'Oh the Colossus! The Colossus!': James Jackson and the Jeffersonian Republican Party in Georgia, 1796–1806," *JER* 9 (Autumn 1989): 315–34.

46 [Jackson], *Letters of Sicilius*, 30 ("peaceable"), 48 ("speculating"), 46 ("break in"), 32 ("wreak their vengeance"), 49 ("language of Vattel"); Vattel, *Law of Nations*, Book I, chapter 11, §123, p. 154; Don E. Fehrenbacher, *The Slaveholding Republic: An Account of the United States Government's Relations to Slavery*, ed. Ward M. McAfee (New York: Oxford University Press, 2001), 137–38.

47 [Jackson], *Letters of Sicilius*, 13; [Alexander Hamilton], "The Federalist, no. 6," in *The Federalist*, ed. Ball, 24. See also Onuf, "Towards Federalism."

48 Adam Smith, *An Inquiry into the Nature and Causes of the Wealth of Nations*, ed. Edwin Cannan (New York: Modern Library, 1937), 862 ("regularly employed") and 669–81; Robert Green McCloskey, "Introduction" in *WJW* 1: 1–48, esp. 7–17; Claire Priest, "Law and Commerce, 1580–1815," in *The Cambridge History of Law in America: Volume I, Early America (1580–1815)*, ed. Michael Grossberg and Christopher Tomlins (New York, 2008), 1: 400–46, esp. 412–14; Wood, *Empire of Liberty*, 411–12, 451–52.

49 Wilson, "Of the Natural Rights of Individuals," [1791], in *WJW* 2: 605 ("repugnant"); Remarks by Wilson in debates of December 4, 1787, in *DHRC: Pennsylvania* 2: 500 ("how insecure" and contracts clause); Debates of August 28, 1787, in *Notes of the Debates in the Federal Convention of 1787 Reported by James Madison*, ed. Adrienne Koch (Athens: Ohio University Press, 1966), 541–43; Pauline Maier, *Ratification: The People Debate the Constitution, 1787–1788* (New York: Simon and Schuster, 2010), 77–82, 101–15; Clinton Rossiter, *1787: The Grand Convention* (New York: Macmillan, 1966), 247–48; Holton, "Did Democracy Cause the Recession," 450–56; Bouton, *Taming Democracy*, 134–35.

50 James Wilson, "Of the Study of the Law in the United States," [1790], in *WJW* 1: 86 ("scaffolding," "domestick society"), 92 ("great commonwealth"); Wilson, "Oration Delivered on the Fourth of July, 1788," in ibid., 2: 775 ("mild and modest"). For his support of canals and other improvements: Debates of September 14, 1787, in *Notes of Debates*, ed. Koch, 638, and Debates of December 11, 1787, in *DHRC: Pennsylvania* 2: 582. For his speculations, see McCloskey, "Introduction," *WJW* 1: 18–19.

51 McCloskey, "Introduction," in *WJW* 1: 39 ("consent of those"), and see also 37–38 for the lecture series; Debates of September 14, 1787, in *Notes of Debates*, ed. Koch, 637 ("*define* the law of nations," emphasis in original).

52 James Wilson, "Of the Study of the Law in the United States," in *WJW* 1: 92 ("How far"); Wilson, "Of the Law of Nations" [1790] in ibid., 1: 151 ("universal"), 153 ("law of the people").

53 Wilson, "Of the Law of Nations," in *WJW* 1: 163 ("civilized and commercial"), 153 ("I mean"), 167 ("stability" and "globe of credit"); Remarks by Wilson in Debates of December 11, 1787, in *DHRC: Pennsylvania* 2: 581 ("a NATION"). See also Maier, *Ratification*, 114; Anne-Marie Burley, "The Alien Tort Statute and the Judiciary Act of 1789: A Badge of Honor," *AJIL* 83 (July 1989): 461–93; Thomas Bender, *A Nation Among Nations: America's Place in World History* (New York: Hill and Wang, 2006), 155–57; David C. Hendrickson, *Peace Pact: The Lost World of the American Founding* (Lawrence: University of Kansas Press, 2003).

54 Wilson, "Speech Delivered on 26th November 1787 in the Convention of Pennsylvania," in *WJW* 2: 767 ("minute attention" and "predominating regard"); J. M. Opal, "The Labors of Liberality: Christian Benevolence and National Prejudice in the American Founding," *JAH* 94 (March 2008): 1095 (quotes) and 1082–107; Philip Hamburger, "Liberality," *TLR* 78 (May 2000): 1216–85.

55 [James Madison], "The Federalist, no. 10," in *The Federalist*, ed. Ball, 42; Rosenberg, *This Violent Empire*, 114–33; Madison in 1790 debate quoted in Elkins and McKitrick, *Age of Federalism*, 143 ("liberal"), and see 136–45.

56 Debates of September 17, 1787, in *Notes of Debates*, ed. Koch, 657 ("without committing"); William Blount to Richard Caswell, July 19, 1787, in *JGBP* 1: 323 ("perfectly independent") and 322–23; Rossiter, *1787*, 168, 236–37, and 251.

57 Davie quoted in Maier, *Ratification*, 419, and see 401–34; Joseph McDowell quoted in North Carolina Ratification Convention Debates, July 28, 1788, at http://consource.org/document/north-carolina-ratification-convention-debates-1788-7-28/ (accessed March 28, 2014); Jones to [McCulloch?], The Memorial of Henry Eustace McCulloch, April 2, 1788, American Loyalist Claims, Series II: McCullok, AO13/117, BNA; *State Census of North Carolina, 1784–1787* (Salt Lake City, 1973), 64 (Jones's wealth) and 57–71 (rest of Halifax County); MacDonald, "Politics of the Personal in the Old North State," 167–69 (Rutherford's anti-Federalism). See also J. Edwin Hendricks, "Joining the Federal Union," in *The North Carolina Experience: An Interpretive and Documentary History*, ed. Lindley S. Butler and Alan D. Watson (Chapel Hill: University of North Carolina Press, 1984), 147–57; Saul Cornell, *The Other Founders: Anti-Federalism and the Dissenting Tradition in America, 1788–1828* (Chapel Hill: University of North Carolina Press, 1999), 19–80; Boyd, *History of North Carolina*, 30–34 and 38–39.

58 Edward Countryman, *The American Revolution* (New York: Hill and Wang, 1985), 215 and 214–17; Morris, *Forging of the Union*, 148–52; St. George Tucker, *Reflections on the Policy and Necessity of Encouraging the Commerce of the Citizens of the United States of America* (New York, 1785); Wood, *Empire of Liberty*, 170

and 95–139; Albrecht Koschnik, "Political Conflict and Public Contest: Rituals of National Celebration in Philadelphia, 1788–1815," *PMHB* 118 (July 1994): 214 and 209–48; James Wilson, "Oration Delivered on the Fourth of July, 1788," in *WJW* 2: 773–80.

59 Iredell quoted in *The Case of Messrs. Brailsford and Others Versus James Spalding, in the Circuit Court for the District of Georgia* (Savannah, 1792), 26; "Opinion of Justice Wilson," *Ware vs. Hylton*, 3 U.S. 199, 281 (1796); McCloskey, "Introduction," *WJW* 1: 32; Saul Cornell and Gerald Leonard, "The Consolidation of the Early Federal System, 1791–1812," in *Cambridge History of Law in America*, ed. Grossberg and Tomlins, 1: 541–42 (Rhode Island stay law). Wilson went on to say that even if Virginia had been right to obstruct the payment of debts during the war, as other justices argued, the Treaty of Paris clearly annulled such measures. This was the decision of the court. See also Fred L. Israel, "James Iredell," in *The Justices of the United States Supreme Court, 1789–1969*, ed. Leon Friedman and Fred L. Israel (2 vols., New York: R. R. Bowker Company, 1969), 1: 121–32, and Charles Warren, "The First Decade of the Supreme Court of the United States," *UCLR* 7 (June 1940): 631–54.

60 Alan Taylor, "The Late Loyalists: Northern Reflections of the Early American Republic," *JER* 27 (Spring 2007): 9 ("subordination") and 5–6 (land grants); Booraem, *Young Hickory*, 184; Reid, *Legislating the Courts*. For a brilliant look at federal efforts to govern the northern borders, see Bethel Saler, *The Settlers' Empire: Colonialism and State Formation in America's Old Northwest* (Philadelphia: University of Pennsylvania Press, 2014).

61 Cayton, "Separate Interests and the Nation-State," 39–67; Michael D. Green, "The Expansion of European Colonization to the Mississippi Valley, 1780–1880," in *The Cambridge History of the Native Peoples of the Americas: Volume I, North America, Part I*, ed. Bruce G. Trigger and Wilcomb E. Washburn (New York: Cambridge University Press, 1996), 1: 469–75; Wilson, "Speech Delivered on 26th November 1787," in *WJW* 2: 761; Richard H. Kohn, *Eagle and Sword: The Federalists and the Creation of the Military Establishment in America, 1783–1802* (New York: Free Press, 1975). On Knox, see Alan Taylor, *Liberty Men and Great Proprietors: The Revolutionary Settlement on the Maine Frontier, 1760–1820* (Chapel Hill: University of North Carolina Press, 1990), 37–47. See also Van Every, *Ark of Empire*, 174–201.

62 Henry Knox to George Washington, July 7, 1789, in *PGW* 3: 136, one of two letters Knox wrote to GW that day; Henry Knox to George Washington, July 6, 1789, in ibid., 3: 124 (on McGillivray). See also David Andrew Nichols, *Red Gentlemen and White Savages: Indians, Federalists, and the Search for Order on the American Frontier* (Charlottesville: University of Virginia Press, 2008).

63 Andrew Ellicott to Timothy Pickering, September 24, 1797, in *TPUS* 5: 4 ("sovereign power" and "less the better") and 7 ("genuine americans"); *The Journal of Andrew Ellicott* (Philadelphia, 1814), 2; Catharine Van Cortlandt Mathews, *Andrew Ellicott: His Life and Letters* (New York: Grafton Press, 1908), esp. 7–11 and 206–7.

64 "Proclamation by the President," August 26, 1790, in *TPUS* 4: 34; "Treaty with the Creeks, 1790," in *IT*, 25–29; R. S. Cotterill, "Federal Indian Management in the South, 1789–1825," *MVHR* 20 (December 1933): 333–52; "An Act to Regulate Trade and Intercourse with the Indian Tribes," July 22, 1790, 1 *SL* 137–38; "An Act to Regulate Trade and Intercourse with the Indian Tribes, and to Preserve Peace on the Frontiers," May 19, 1796, 1 *SL* 469–74. The passport rule is in section 3 of the 1796 Act.

65 "Treaty with the Creeks," in *IT*, 27; David J. Farmer, "Kill the King: Foucault and Public Administration Theory," *Administrative Theory and Praxis* 17 (1995): 78–83.

66 "Treaty with the Cherokee, 1791," in *IT*, 31 ("retaliation"), 30–31 (Article VIII about squatters and Article IX about hunters and passports), and 32 (Blount as representative); Knox to Washington, July 7, 1789, in *PGW* 3: 142 ("many unprovoked"); "North Carolina: Cession of Western Land Claims," December 22, 1789, in *TPUS* 4: 7. For Knox and Washington see also Joseph J. Ellis, *His Excellency: George Washington* (New York: Alfred A. Knopf, 2004), 211–14.

67 "The Blount Journal, 1790–1796: The Proceedings of Government over the Territory of the United States of America, South of the River Ohio," William Blount Papers, 1790–1796, TSLA, 14 (GW's letter); William Blount to John Gray Blount, June 26, 1790, in *JGBP* 2: 67 ("I rejoice"). See also Cynthia Cumfer, "Local Origins of National Indian Policy: Cherokee and Tennessean Ideas About Sovereignty and Nationhood, 1790–1811," *JER* 23 (Spring 2003): 30–31, 40–41. See also Hugh Williamson to George Washington, May 28, 1790, in *PGW* 5: 422–23, and "To the United States Senate," in ibid., 5: 490. On the importance of the Society of the Cincinnati for Washington, see Cayton, "Separate Interests and the Nation-State," 50–51.

68 "The Blount Journal," 15, 29, 40–42.

69 *An Interesting Appendix to Sir William Blackstone's Commentaries on the Laws of England* (Philadelphia, 1773), 79–81 ("nations"); James W. Ely Jr., "The Legal Practice of Andrew Jackson," *THQ* 38 (Winter 1979): 434 (appendix to Blackstone and readings) and 421–35; Booraem, *Young Hickory*, 170–72 and 271n; Curtis, *Andrew Jackson and the Search for Vindication*, 10–15; Jennifer Hunsicker, *Young Andrew Jackson in the Carolinas: A Revolutionary Boy* (Charleston, SC: History Press, 2014), 136–37. Jackson did acquire two volumes of the *Laws of the United States* from a Philadelphia supplier; see Ely, "Legal Practice," 434.

70 "Law License in North Carolina," September 26, 1787, *PAJ* 1: 10; Chroust, *Rise of the Legal Profession in America*, 2: 63.

71 Booraem, *Young Hickory*, 147–48 (clothes), 136–38, 197–98; Reda C. Goff, "A Physical Profile of Andrew Jackson," *THQ* 28 (Fall 1969): 297–309, esp. 301–3. On the importance of horses in slave country, see Walter Johnson, *River of Dark Dreams: Slavery and Empire in the Cotton Kingdom* (Cambridge, MA: Harvard University Press, 2013), 222–24. Jackson presented this license to the county courts in Rowan, Surry, Guilford, and Rockingham during November 1787 alone. See *PAJ* 1: 10n–11n and "Jackson's North Carolina License, 1787," box 18, William Provine Papers, TSLA.

72 Andrew Jackson to Waightstill Avery, August 12, 1788, in *PAJ* 1: 12 and 12n; Vattel, *The Law of Nations*, Book I, chapter 13, §175, p. 194; "Record of Slave Sale," November 17, 1788, in *PAJ* 1: 15; Booraem, *Young Hickory*, 188–90. For dueling, see C. A. Harwell Wells, "The End of the Affair? Anti-Dueling Laws and Social Norms in Antebellum America," *VLR* 54 (May 2001): 1805–47, and Joanne B. Freeman, *Affairs of Honor: National Politics in the New Republic* (New Haven, CT: Yale University Press, 2001), 159–98.

73 "An Act Amendatory of, and supplemental to an act passed at the present session . . . for the adjudication of North Carolina land claims," in *Acts of a Public or General Nature, Passed at the First Session of the Thirteenth General Assembly of the State of Tennessee* (Nashville, 1819), 85–86 (Rutherford claim displaced by Greene); Samuel C. Williams, "Generals Francis Nash and William Lee Davidson," *THQ* 1 (September 1942): 250–68; Ramsey, *Annals of Tennessee*, 496–97; Theodore

Brown Jr., "John Overton," *Tennessee Encyclopedia of History and Culture*, at https://tennesseeencyclopedia.net/index.php (accessed January 21, 2016).

74 "North Carolina: Cession of Western Land Claims," December 22, 1789, in *TPUS* 4: 3–8; "The Blount Journal," 43, 46; Ray, "Land Speculation, Popular Democracy, and Political Transformation," 166.

75 Blackstone, *Commentaries on the Laws of England*, II, chapter 30, p. 464; Ely, "Legal Practice," 429–31 (clients and court time) and 426 (*scire facias*). In total, Jackson represented the Mero District of the Southwest Territory some eighty-five times after his February 1791 appointment by Blount, while taking part in about four hundred cases for private clients. See also Andrew Burstein, *The Passions of Andrew Jackson* (New York: Alfred A. Knopf, 2003), 20, 26–27, and Cheathem, *Andrew Jackson, Southerner*, 24. From a sample (n = 19) of people and firms represented by Jackson, I found that eight definitely owned property in Nashville. The others tended to be grant or pre-emption holders who had arrived near the onset of significant settlement in the early 1780s. See *Transcripts of the County Archives of Tennessee: Minutes of the County Court of Davidson County: Book B, 1791–1797* (Nashville, 1941), TSLA. For his purchase of a horse and service as a surety, see *PAJ* 1: 432–33. For the lay attorney, see notes from April 5, 1785, regarding William Gubbins, in Carol Wells, *Davidson County, Tennessee County Court Minutes, 1783–1792* (Bowie, MD, 1990), 26, and Maude Weidner, *Nashville Then and Now* (Nashville, 1930), 13–22, both available TSLA. Gubbins had his 720-acre grant for Continental service surveyed in December 1785, seven months after the county recognized him as an attorney "in fact." See Helen C. Marsh and Timothy R. Marsh, *Land Deed Genealogy of Davidson County, Tennessee* (3 vols., Greenville, SC, 1992), 1: 29, 50. Possibly he was the pro-debtor lawyer behind this statement in Erik McKinley Erickson, "Andrew Jackson, the Man and Mason," *The Builder* (June 1925), 165, filed in box 17, William Provine Papers, TSLA: "The only lawyer of the vicinity had been retained by a group of debtors, so the creditors were glad to retain Jackson." Van Every, *Ark of Empire*, 178, claims that Jackson personally brought news of the ratification of the US Constitution, available as of July 12, 1788, in Kentucky, to the Cumberland. For "the New Government" and its initial installation: *Norfolk and Portsmouth Gazette* (Norfolk, VA), July 9, 1788, and September 17, 1788, and Maier, *Ratification*, 404.

76 William Blount to James Robertson, January 2, 1792, in *TPUS* 4: 108; Booraem, *Young Hickory*, 194 ("great ambition"); AJ to Intruders on the Cherokee Lands, May 29, 1820, ser. 1, reel 29, AJPLC.

CHAPTER 3

1 "Extract of a Letter from a Gentleman in the Western Country to His Friend in Philadelphia, Dec. 22," *National Gazette*, January 2, 1792; H. H. Brackenridge, "Further and Concluding Thoughts on the Indian War," *KG*, June 2, 1792; see also Hugh Henry Brackendridge, "Modern Chivalry" [1792], in *A Hugh Henry Brackenridge Reader, 1770–1815*, ed. Daniel Marder (Pittsburgh: University of Pittsburgh Press, 1970), 174. For the United Indian Nations, see Alyssa Mt. Pleasant, "Independence for Whom?: Expansion and Conflict in the Northeast and Northwest," in *The World of the Revolutionary American Republic: Land, Labor, and the Conflict for a Continent*, ed. Andrew Shankman (New York: Routledge, 2014), 118–19. For the St. Clair disaster, see Gordon S. Wood, *Empire of Liberty: A History of the Early Republic* (New York: Oxford University Press, 2009), 129.

2 Grand Council quoted in Michael D. Green, "The Expansion of European Colonization to the Mississippi Valley, 1780–1880," in *The Cambridge History of the Native Peoples of the Americas: Volume I, North America, Part I*, ed. Bruce G. Trigger and Wilcomb E. Washburn (New York: Cambridge University Press, 1996), 479–80; James P. Whittenburg, "'The Common Farmer (Number Two)': Herman Husband's Plan for Peace Between the United States and the Indians, 1792," *WMQ* 34 (October 1977): 650 and 647–50.

3 Richard H. Kohn, *Eagle and Sword: The Beginnings of the Military Establishment in America* (New York: Free Press, 1975), 124–27, 141–57, and 157–70; Terry Bouton, *Taming Democracy: "The People," the Founders, and the Troubled Ending of the American Revolution* (New York: Oxford University Press, 2007), 218, 228, 216–43; Stanley Elkins and Eric McKitrick, *The Age of Federalism: The Early American Republic, 1788–1800* (New York: Oxford University Press, 1993), 375–488; Patrick Griffin, *American Leviathan: Empire, Nation, and Revolutionary Frontier* (New York: Hill and Wang, 2007).

4 Proceedings with the Cherokee, Tellico Blockhouse, December–January 1794–95, box 2, James Robertson Papers, 1784–1814, TSLA ("all Citizens"); "Governor Blount to the Bloody Fellow, a Chief of the Cherokees," September 13, 1792, in *ASP: Indian Affairs*, 1: 281 ("as much the care"); William Blount to Rev. Joseph Dorris et al., October 11, 1795, box 1, Robertson Papers.

5 Daniel H. Usner Jr., *Indians, Settlers, and Slaves in a Frontier Exchange Economy: The Lower Mississippi Valley Before 1783* (Chapel Hill: University of North Carolina Press, 1992); Donald J. Weber, *The Spanish Frontier in North America* (New Haven, CT: Yale University Press, 1992). For payments in skins and crops, see advertisements for Nelson and Company, *KG*, January 14, 1792; advertisements for David Deaderick's store, *KG*, July 28, 1792. For river distances, see "A Short Description of the State of Tenasee, Lately Called the Territory of the United States South of the River Ohio," [March 9, 1796], in Gilbert Imlay, *A Topographical Description of the Western Territory of North America* (1797; New York: A. M. Kelley, 1969), 514–20.

6 Andrew Jackson to Daniel Smith, February 13, 1789, box 17, William Provine Papers, TSLA; John Buchanan, *Jackson's Way: Andrew Jackson and the People of the Western Waters* (New York: J. Wiley, 2001), 115–16; Henry O. Robertson, "Tories or Patriots?: The Mississippi River Planters During the American Revolution," *LH* 40 (Autumn 1999): 445–62. On Natchez, see Usner, *Indians, Settlers, and Slaves*, 65–76, 111–14; Ronald L. F. Davis, *The Black Experience in Natchez, 1720–1880* (Natchez: National Park Service, 1993), 9–10; *The Natchez Court Records, 1767–1805: Abstracts of Early Records*, comp. Mary Wilson McBee (1953; Baltimore: Genealogical Publishing Company, 1979); and Imlay, *Topographical Description*, 423–25.

7 Francisco Cruzat to Esteban Miró, August 23, 1784, in *Annual Report of the American Historical Association for the Year 1945: Spain in the Mississippi Valley, 1765–1794: Volume III (part 2): Post War Decade, 1782–1791*, ed. Lawrence Kinnaird (4 vols. Washington, DC, 1946), 3: 117 (Cruzat was relaying words of a large native delegation, who described Americans as a "plague of locusts"); Kathleen DuVal, "Independence for Whom?: Expansion and Conflict in the South and Southwest," in *World of the Revolutionary American Republic*, ed. Shankman, 97–115; David E. Narrett, "Geopolitics and Intrigue: James Wilkinson, the Spanish Borderlands, and Mexican Independence," *WMQ* 69 (January 2012): 101–46, esp. 107–12; J. H. Elliott, *Empires of the Atlantic World: Britain and Spain in America, 1492–1830* (New

Haven, CT: Yale University Press, 2006), esp. 292–324; Claudio Saunt, *West of the Revolution: An Uncommon History of 1776* (New York: W. W. Norton and Company, 2014), esp. 54–115; William S. Coker, "The Bruins and the Formulation of Spanish Immigration Policy in the Old Southwest, 1787–88," in *The Spanish in the Mississippi Valley, 1762–1804*, ed. John Francis McDermott (Urbana: University of Illinois Press, 1974), 61–71; Gilbert C. Din, "Spain's Immigration Policy in Louisiana and the American Penetration, 1792–1803," *SHQ* 76 (January 1973): 255–76.

8 Carlos de Grand-Pré to Esteban Miró, May 26, 1782, in *Spain in the Mississippi Valley*, ed. Kinnaird, 3: 17 ("Americans by birth but not sentiment," as translated in an interview with settlers); "Memorial of Inhabitants of the Territory to the Land Commissioners," [n.d.] 1810, in *TPUS* 14: 383 and 382–97, 397n–398n; "Memorial to Congress by the Territorial Legislature," December 14, 1804, in *TPUS* 5: 365; N [?] Hunter to William C. C. Claiborne, enclosure, February 4, 1800, in *TPUS* 5: 100; Robert V. Remini, "Andrew Jackson Takes an Oath of Allegiance to Spain," *THQ* 54 (Spring 1995): 2–15. On Jackson's "opportunistic" loyalties, see Eliga H. Gould, *Among the Powers of the Earth: The American Revolution and the Making of a New World Empire* (Cambridge, MA: Harvard University Press, 2012), 112. Spanish grants were limited to three hundred *fanegas*, a unit of land over which one unit of grain could be spread. One *fanega* generally converts to 1.588 acres. See Wilkinson's Second Memorial, September 17, 1789, "Papers Bearing on James Wilkinson's Relations with Spain, 1787–1816," *AHR* 9 (July 1904): 757 and 757n, 748–66. My thanks to Jonathon Booth for this citation.

9 Miró quoted in DuVal, "Independence for Whom?," 105; William C. C. Claiborne to James Madison, Nov. 5, 1802, in *Official Letter Books of W.C.C. Claiborne, 1801–1816*, ed. Dunbar Rowland (6 vols., Jackson: Mississippi Department of Archives and History, 1917), 1: 217 ("Spanish *Customs*"), 219 ("Equitable"), and 214–15; "Memorial to Congress by Citizens of the Territory," December 6, 1800, in *TPUS* 5: 111, 113, and 114–17; See also "Memorial to the President and Congress by the Territorial Legislature," December 21, 1807, in *TPUS* 5: 588. For pro-debtor protections, see Donald E. Worcester, "The Significance of the Spanish Borderlands to the United States," *WHQ* 7 (January 1976): 12–13, and Regina Grafe and Maria Alejandra Irigoin, "A Stakeholder Empire: The Political Economy of Spanish Imperial Rule," *ECHR* 65 (May 2012): 609–51; Lena London, "The Initial Homestead Exemption in Texas," *SWHQ* 57 (April 1954): 440n and 432–53.

10 [?] Clark to John Overton, October 18 1797, box 4, Murdock Collection: Overton Papers, TSLA. Both the 1790 charter of the Southwest Territory and the 1798 plan for the Mississippi Territory forbade the importation of slaves from outside US lands. For protests: "Presentments of the Grand Jury of Adams County," June 6, 1799, in *TPUS* 5: 63–66; "Petition to Congress by Committee of Inhabitants," October 2, 1799, in ibid., 5: 83–86; and "Presentments of the Grand Jury of Pickering County," June 17, 1799, in ibid., 5: 66–68. For the native alliances, see DuVal, "Independence for Whom?," 103–4.

11 J. G. M. Ramsey, *The Annals of Tennessee to the End of the Eighteenth Century* (Charleston, 1853), 501; William Blount to Henry Knox, January 14, 1793, in *TPUS* 4: 231 ("extreme frontier" and dimensions). I know of no precise census of American-born settlers in Spanish Louisiana. My estimate is based on Weber, *The Spanish Frontier in North America*, 281, which cites a jump in population in Louisiana of twenty-five thousand (twenty thousand to forty-five thousand) from 1782 to 1792. Most of this increase was surely from immigration, the bulk of which would have come from the American states. For example, officials in

Natchez reported that 143 of the 195 new arrivals there from 1793 to 1795 (73.3%) were Americans, counting those from Kentucky and Fort Pitt. In Nogales, a list of origins reported that 313 of 466 new arrivals (67.2%) were Americans. See Lawrence H. Feldman, *Anglo-Americans in Spanish Archives: Lists of Anglo-American Settlers in the Spanish Colonies of America: A Finding Aid* (Baltimore: Genealogical Publishing Company, 1991), 205–17 and 218–29, and Albert Tate Jr., "Spanish Census of the Baton Rouge District for 1786," *LH* 24 (Winter 1983): 70–84. For the Cumberland land grants, see "Pre-emption and Guard Rights," 1782–1787, box 4, Provine Papers, TSLA. For the Continental grants, I took three different samples from Helen C. Marsh and Timothy R. Marsh, *Land Deed Genealogy of Davidson County, Tennessee* (3 vols., Greenville, SC, 1992), 1: 1–15, 50–65, and 90–105. Of the total sample of transactions (n = 291), 124 or 42.8% involved Continental Army grants. Of these, 59 or 47.5% were direct grants to Continental Army veterans. On "quitting the country," see Eric R. Schlereth, "Privileges of Locomotion: Expatriation and the Politics of Southwestern Border Crossing," *JAH* 100 (March 2014): 995–1020. The 1776 Constitution of Pennsylvania and the 1777 Constitution of Vermont each cited a "natural and inherent" right to emigrate in their respective Bills of Rights.

12 "The Dunham Pioneers to Middle Tennessee," [n.d.], box 4, Provine Papers, TSLA; Unknown to Joseph Brown, February 7, 1854, Papers Relating to Claim of Joseph Brown to Bounty Lands, Joseph Brown Papers, Correspondence re: Negroes Recovered from Indians, 1814–16, TSLA; James Robertson to John Sevier, August 1, 1787, James Robertson Letter, TSLA. Bledsoe reported twenty-four dead "in this country" over the previous two months. See also Colin G. Calloway, "Declaring Independence and Rebuilding a Nation: Dragging Canoe and the Chickamauga Revolution," in *Revolutionary Founders: Rebels, Radicals, and Reformers in the Making of a Nation*, ed. Alfred F. Young, Gary B. Nash, and Ray Raphael (New York: Alfred A. Knopf, 2011), 185–98.

13 Anthony Bledsoe to John Sevier, August 5, 1787, in Ramsey, *Annals of Tennessee*, 395 ("revenge the blood") and 394–95; Robertson quoted in DuVal, "Independence for Whom," 105 and 108 for the settlement north of Mobile. I have used Ramsey rather than John Haywood, *The Civil and Political History of the State of Tennessee, from Its Earliest Settlement up to the Year 1796* (1823; Nashville, 1891) because Ramsey had access to many other materials and tried to correct Haywood. See Ramsey, *Annals of Tennessee*, v–vi. For similar tensions in the Ohio Valley, see Griffin, *American Leviathan*.

14 James Robertson to Esteban Miró, September 2, 1789, in *Spain in the Mississippi Valley, 1765–1794*, ed. Kinnaird, 3: 279; DuVal, "Independence for Whom?," 104; Ramsey, *Annals of Tennessee*, 494; Buchanan, *Jackson's Way*, 51–64. In a 1787 census of Davidson, there were only 105 blacks between the ages of twelve and sixty. See Richard Carlton Fulcher, *1770–1790 Census of the Cumberland Settlements* (Baltimore: Genealogical Publishing Company, 1987), 91. Four years later, that number had surged: "Schedule of the Whole Number of Persons in the Territory of the United States of America, South of the River Ohio," in William Blount to Thomas Jefferson, September 19, 1791, in *TPUS* 4: 81. Davidson County, including Nashville, had 639 white adult men and 659 slaves; in the poor area south of the French Broad River, in east Tennessee, 681 adult white men owned just 163 slaves. Davidson's total population was 3,459, for an enslaved percentage of 19%. South of the French Broad, the total population was 3,619, or an enslaved percentage of 4.5%. For a prediction of Cumberland statehood, see Imlay, *Topographical Description*, 14.

15 Entry for March 16, 1790, in *Natchez Court Records*, Book D, 146–47; J. C. Mountfleurence to Andrew Jackson, July 23, 1790, box 18, Provine Papers, TSLA; Buchanan, *Jackson's Way*, 118; *PAJ* 1: 432–33.

16 Ramsey, *Annals of Tennessee*, 457 ("watching"), 345–46 (Indian reactions to Donelson murder); Entry for August 11, 1792, in *Natchez Court Records*, Book D, 149 ("guard of men" on boat); Entry for John Donelson, in Fulcher, *1770–1790 Census* (buffalo tongue story); Letter of Stockley Donelson, March 12, 1884, box 17, Provine Papers, TSLA (grandson of John Donelson describing the seventy to eighty pages of surveys that John carried); Original Land Entries, Western Lands, 1783–1784, NCSA.

17 Andrew Jackson to Rachel Jackson, May 9, 1796, in *PAJ* 1: 92 and 91–92; Buchanan, *Jackson's Way*, 108–10; James Curtis, *Andrew Jackson and the Search for Vindication*, ed. Oscar Handlin (Boston: Little, Brown and Company, 1976), 25; *Encyclopedia of Women in American History*, ed. Joyce Appleby, Eileen K. Cheng, and Joanne L. Goodwin (3 vols., New York: Taylor and Francis, 2002), 1: 124–25. For the location of the Donelson compound, see *PAJ* 1: 386–87.

18 Buchanan, *Jackson's Way*, 108–10 and 117–19. Relevant studies of eighteenth-century divorce include Cynthia Cumfer, *Separate Peoples, One Land: The Minds of Cherokees, Blacks, and Whites on the Tennessee Frontier* (Chapel Hill: University of North Carolina Press, 2007), 168 and 155–78; Mary Beth Norton, *Liberty's Daughters: The Revolutionary Experience of American Women, 1750–1800* (Boston: Little, Brown and Company, 1980), 47–50.

19 Andrew Burstein, *The Passions of Andrew Jackson* (New York: Alfred A. Knopf, 2003), 29–33; Melissa J. Gismondi, "The Character of a Wife: Rachel Jackson and the Search for Zion, 1760s–1820s" (PhD dissertation, University of Virginia, forthcoming).

20 Sharon Block, *Rape and Sexual Power in Early America* (Chapel Hill: University of North Carolina Press, 2006), 78–80; Sarah Nott, "Female Liberty?: Sentimental Gallantry, Republican Womanhood, and Rights Feminism in the Age of Revolutions," *WMQ* 71 (July 2014): 425–56; Bertram Wyatt-Brown, *Southern Honor: Ethics and Behavior in the Old South* (New York: Oxford University Press, 1982).

21 Carole Shammas, *A History of Household Government in America* (Charlottesville: University of Virginia Press, 2002); Marylynn Salmon, "Women and Property in South Carolina: The Evidence from Marriage Settlements, 1730 to 1830," *WMQ* 39 (October 1982): 655–85; Jay Fliegelman, *Prodigals and Pilgrims: The American Revolution Against Patriarchal Authority, 1750–1800* (New York: Cambridge University Press, 1982); "Inhabitants of Record of Sumner County," in Fulcher, *1770–1790 Census*, 141, 145, 148, and 150 and 9; "Notice by John Smith," *KG*, March 10, 1792.

22 Matthew Bacon, *A New Abridgement of the Law . . . in Seven Volumes* (London, 1798), 1: 475; Buchanan, *Jackson's Way*, 110–11; "Petition to the United States House of Representatives," [March 6, 1792], in *PAJ* 1: 35–36 (Jackson unpaid); Jennifer Hunsicker, *Young Andrew Jackson in the Carolinas: A Revolutionary Boy* (Charleston, SC: History Press, 2014), 136–37. Bacon's first volumes were published in the 1730s, and complete editions were available by 1768.

23 Burstein, *Passions of Andrew Jackson*, 241–48, is an excellent analysis. See also Gismondi, "Character of a Wife," and Fred Anderson and Andrew Cayton, *The Dominion of War: Empire and Liberty in North America, 1500–2000* (New York: Penguin Books, 2005), 208–17. I find it significant that Jackson and Robards

never fought a duel, although Parton recounts a physical confrontation between the two men, during which Jackson threatened Robards with a knife. See Mark R. Cheathem, *Andrew Jackson, Southerner* (Baton Rouge: Louisiana State University Press, 2013), 21–23.

24 Burstein, *Passions of Andrew Jackson*, 32 and 241–48; "Inventory, Appraisal, and Division of John Donelson's Estate," January 28/April 15, 1791, *PAJ* 1: 425–27. For the enslaved couple, see Cheathem, *Andrew Jackson, Southerner*, 50–51. Examples of another Natchez marriage: "Petition of Widow Coleman, Now Wife of Emmanuel Madden," October 28, 1781, in *Natchez Court Records*, Book A, 9.

25 "Marriage License," January 18, 1794, in *PAJ* 1: 44; Deed of John Donelson to AJ, February 23, 1792, in *PAJ* 1: 434; "Public Writ Announcing Divorce Proceedings," January 24, 1792, in *PAJ* 1: 427; Cheathem, *Andrew Jackson, Southerner*, 22–23 (Overton's role). For the location of the young couple's 330-acre property, see *PAJ* 1: 386–87. For concubines, see Annette Gordon-Reed, *The Hemingses of Monticello: An American Family* (New York: W. W. Norton and Company, 2008), 106–7.

26 Henry Knox to William Blount, November 26, 1792, in *TPUS* 4: 221; Henry Knox to William Blount, April 22, 1792, in *PGW* 10: 298n ("dispassionate and enlightened"); Henry Knox to [Hostile Indians], April 4, 1792, in ibid., 10: 187n–89n; Ramsey, *Annals of Tennessee*, 484 (AJ in 1789 mission); William Blount to James Robertson, January 5, 1792, in *TPUS* 4: 110 (AJ involved in communication and planning).

27 Craig Symonds, "The Failure of America's Indian Policy on the Southwestern Frontier, 1785–1793," *THQ* 35 (Spring 1976): 29–45, esp. 30–32; "Treaty with the Cherokee, 1791," in *IT*, 30–31; William Blount to Henry Knox, January 14, 1793, *TPUS* 4: 226–34; "Extracts of Correspondence on Indian Affairs," [October 1792], in *PGW* 11: 291–316, esp. 295, and William Blount to Richard Caswell, July 19, 1787, in *JGBP* 1: 323. For continued speculation by Blount and his brother Wylie, see W[ylie] Blount to James Robertson, April 29, 1792, box 1, Robertson Papers, TSLA. See also James Seagrove to George Washington, July 27, 1792, in *PGW* 10: 577–78; Henry Knox to George Washington, August 5, 1792, in ibid., 10: 615–16; George Washington to Henry Knox, August 5, 1792, in ibid., 10: 614; William Blount to Henry Knox, May 5, 1792, in *TPUS* 4: 149; Andrew Nichols, *Red Gentlemen and White Savages: Indians, Federalists, and the Search for Order on the American Frontier* (Charlottesville: University of Virginia Press, 2008). For various business activities by Blount and his brothers, see William Blount to John Gray Blount, June 26, 1790, in *JGBP* 2: 67–72, and William Blount to John Gray Blount, March 28, 1795, in ibid., 2: 520–23.

28 "Knoxville, no. 10," *KG*, November 19, 1791 ("so terrified"); The Bloody Fellow quoted in Ramsey, *Annals of Tennessee*, 519; "A Return of the Persons Killed, Wounded, or Taken Prisoner, from the Miró District, Since the 1st of January, 1791," enclosed in Blount to Knox, November 8, 1792, in *ASP: Indian Affairs* 1: 329–32. For the 1791 count, six names are not complete, so it is not certain that they were men, and yet the record later indicates whenever a victim was a woman. Fulcher, *1770–1790 Census*, lists some 200 people killed in the Mero or Cumberland during the 1780s, with a handful of examples from the early 1790s. This number does not include the 28 members of the Stuart family, all of whom died during Donelson's initial voyage to the region. Of the identifiable victims from the 1780s, 160 were killed, and of these, 145 (91%) were men. For an excellent overview, see Tom Kanon, *Tennesseans at War, 1812–1815: Andrew Jackson,*

the Creek War, and the Battle of New Orleans (Tuscaloosa: University of Alabama Press, 2014), 8–33.

29 William Blount to Henry Knox, May 5, 1792, in *TPUS* 4: 149 ("only thing I can do . . . what they call Satisfaction"); "Knoxville," *KG*, August 27, 1793 ("by mistake"); "Knoxville," *KG*, July 13, 1793 ("by accident"). See also William Blount to Daniel Smith, April 27, 1792, in *TPUS* 4: 144, and *KG*, "Knoxville," April 21, 1792.

30 "Extracts of Correspondence on Indian Affairs," [October 1792], in *PGW* 11: 296 ("kill every white man") and 299; Andrew Pickens to the Governor of South Carolina, September 13, 1792, in *TPUS* 4: 169–70; Cumfer, *Separate Peoples, One Land*, 77–98; John Phillip Reid, "A Perilous Rule: The Law of International Homicide," in *The Cherokee Indian Nation: A Troubled History*, ed. Duane H. King (Knoxville: University of Tennessee Press, 1979), 33–45; Betty Anderson Smith, "Distribution of Eighteenth-Century Cherokee Settlements," in *Cherokee Indian Nation*, ed. King, 46–60; Deposition of Ezekiel Abel, April 16, 1792, and Deposition of Daniel Thornbury, April 10, 1792, in *ASP: Indian Affairs* 1: 274–75.

31 Robertson quote from "A Talk from the Glass to His Excellency Governor Blount, Dated at the Look-out Mountain, September 10, 1792, No. 2," in *ASP: Indian Affairs* 1: 280, and [Washington], "Extracts of Correspondence on Indian Affairs," [October 1792], in *PGW* 11: 311n. For Robertson's injuries: Ramsey, *Annals of Tennessee*, 484, and William Blount to Henry Knox, July 4, 1792, in *ASP: Indian Affairs* 1: 270. For the decision for war: "Information Given by Red Bird, a Cherokee, Respecting His Nation, September 15, 1792," in *ASP: Indian Affairs* 1: 282, and "Extracts of Correspondence on Indian Affairs," [October 1792], in *PGW* 11: 299.

32 William Blount to Henry Knox, July 4, 1792, in *ASP: Indian Affairs* 1: 270 ("great tardiness"); Haywood, *Civil and Political History*, 479 ("hair and horses"); "Governor Blount's Orders to Major Sharpe," August 10, 1792, in *ASP: Indian Affairs* 1: 279 ("cordially"); Blount to Knox, September 11, 1792, in *TPUS* 4: 167–68; Knox to Blount, November 26, 1792, ibid., 4: 220–26. For US troop numbers and movements in the 1790s, see Andrew R. L. Cayton, "'Separate Interests' and the Nation-State: The Washington Administration and the Origins of Regionalism in the Trans-Appalachian West," *JAH* 79 (June 1992): 61.

33 "Commission as Judge Advocate," September 10, 1792, in *PAJ* 1: 37–38; Blount to Knox, September 11, 1792, in *TPUS* 4: 167–68 (late night notice). Jackson's commission was for Davidson County only, but it is clear that he took part in military preparations all over the territory. For the duties of judge advocates, see Henry Campbell Black, *Black's Law Dictionary* (rev. 4th ed., St. Paul, Minnesota: West Publishing, 1968), 976, and "An Act, to Revise and Amend the Militia Laws of the State of Tennessee," November 17, 1819, *Acts of a Public or General Nature; Passed at the First Session of the Thirteenth General Assembly of the State of Tennessee* (Nashville, 1819), chapter 63, pp. 106–34.

34 "An Account of Indian Depredations in the District of Miro, and on the Kentucky Road, from the 3rd to the 14th of October, 1792," in *ASP: Indian Affairs* 1: 332 ("large quantity") and 331–32; James Robertson to William Blount, October 12, 1792, in *TPUS* 4: 198, 197–98; Symonds, "Failure of America's Indian Policy," 35–37; Haywood, *Civil and Political History*, 302–3; Buchanan, *Jackson's Way*, 127–43.

35 Deposition of John Burnett, October 31, 1791, box 1, C. Mildred Thompson Papers, 1786–1938, HRB ("late Indian war"); "Indian News," *KG*, February 23, 1793 (six attacks, seven dead from January 16 to 23 and skinless victim); *KG*, March 23, 1793; Cynthia Cumfer, "Local Origins of National Indian Policy: Cherokee and

Tennessean Ideas About Sovereignty and Nationhood, 1790–1811," *JER* 23 (Spring 2003): 21 (staged attacks) and 21–46.

36 Biographical Sketch [1860?], 7, Joseph Brown Papers, TSLA; William Blount to Henry Knox, April 11, 1793, in *TPUS* 4: 251 ("miserable manner"); Blount to Daniel Smith, June 17, 1793, in ibid., 4: 274 ("vigorous national war," emphasis in original). See also "Proclamation of Governor Blount," January 28, 1793, in *TPUS* 4: 235–36, and William Hall Memoir [1853], 19, TSLA. For the importance of salt, see "A Short Description of the State of Tenasee," in Imlay, *Topographical Description*, 519–20.

37 AJ to John McKee, January 30, 1793, in *PAJ* 1: 40 (corrections made to AJ's scribbled writing); "Knoxville," *KG*, June 15, 1793 (notice of boat owned by "Messrs. *Donelson* and *Jackson*"); *KG*, May 18, 1793 (nine attacks from April 9 to 28 and numbers of braves). On April 26, 1793, a Captain Beard was court-martialed in Knoxville for his unauthorized attack on Cherokee towns. I do not know if Jackson had a role in this. See Kanon, *Tennesseans at War*, 19.

38 "Knoxville," *KG*, September 14, 1793. This was Henry's Station, some twenty-three miles south of Knoxville. For the US Army regiment, see "Twenty Dollars Reward!" in *KG*, July 13, 1793. Blount had gone to Philadelphia at President Washington's invitation in early June. See Symonds, "Failure of America's Indian Policy," 37–38 and 43.

39 *KG*, June 1, June 29, July 13, July 27, and August 13, 1793 ("The Creek Nation must be destroyed . . . "); "Knoxville," *KG*, October 12, 1793 ("exemplary vengeance" and threats to Knoxville); "Knoxville," *KG*, November 23, 1793 (date of Sevier's departure); White, *Historical Collections of Georgia*, 476–83; James Seagrove to George Washington, July 27, 1792, in *PGW* 10: 577–78, 581n (Georgians). Blount used variations of "*Delenda est Carthage*" in private letters and probably approved its publication in the *Gazette*. See Blount to James Robertson, December 4, 1794, box 1, Robertson Papers, TSLA, and Haywood, *Civil and Political History*, 476. My thanks to Mike Fronda and Hans Beck for their generous help in understanding "*delenda est carthage*."

40 *KG*, October 12, 1793 (Blount's return); *KG*, March 13, 1794.

41 Ramsey, *Annals of Tennessee*, 424; "Knoxville," *KG*, November 23, 1793; *KG*, July 31, 1794 (Rutherford and Sevier and three others appointed as legislative councillors). For Rutherford's move to Tennessee in 1792, see Saunt, *West of the Revolution*, 27.

42 "Indian Depredations," *KG*, March 27, 1794 ("as much blood"); *KG*, October 11, 1794 (Doublehead in Philadelphia). For the relative quiet: "Knoxville," *KG*, November 23, 1793; "Knoxville," January 3, 1794; and *KG*, January 16, 1794.

43 *KG*, September 26, 1794 ("near Andrew Jackson's"); "Pittsburgh," *KG*, August 13, 1793 ("throat-cutting"); "The Memorial and Petition of the Convention of Mero District," *KG*, August 13, 1793 ("daily . . . to the Spanish government"); AJ to John McKee, May 16, 1794, in *PAJ* 1: 49 ("Discouraged," and "Declining [fast]"); Jackson on Rachel quoted in Kanon, *Tennesseans at War*, 106; Samuel C. Williams, "The South's First Cotton Factory," *THQ* 5 (September 1946): 212–21; "Cotton Manufactory," *KG*, December 17, 1791; "A List of the Names of Persons Killed, Murdered, and Captured Since the 26th of February 1794," *KG*, October 11, 1794.

44 Robertson quoted in Ramsey, *Annals of Tennessee*, 482 ("helpless woman"), 373 (sleeping child), 422 (entrails in water); Entry for Jonathan Jennings, in Fulcher, *1770–1790 Census* (scalped child). Doug Drake, *Founding of the Cumberland Settlements: The First Atlas, 1779–1804: Showing Who Came, How They Came, and*

Where They Put Down Roots (Gallatin, TN: Warioto Press, 2009) is a treasure trove of information about the early Cumberland and presents detailed evidence for 435 settler deaths between 1780 and 1795 (see page 65). These numbers accord with the periodic tallies of dead, injured, and missing settlers prepared by the territorial government. Estimates of the Mero or Cumberland population in the mid-1790s hover around 7,000.

45 [David Campbell], "The CHARGE Delivered to the Grand Jury," *KG*, December 31, 1791; *KG*, June 15, 1793 ("member of civil society"); [James Iredell], "A Charge, Delivered to the Grand Jury for the District of North Carolina," *KG*, September 6, 1794. For runaway slaves, see "Ten Dollar Reward," *KG*, October 6, 1792; "Stop the Run-Away!," *KG*, July 13, 1793; Notice by John Sharp Jr., *KG*, October 12, 1793. For Roulstone and the *Gazette:* "An Act for Appointing a Public Printer, and Directing His Duty in Office," in *Acts of Tennessee, 1794–1796* (Knoxville?, 1796), chapter 17, 102–3; Haywood, *Civil and Political History*, 476.

46 [P.Q.], "For the Knoxville Gazette," and "Knoxville," *KG*, July 13, 1793. P. Q. was writing in particular about the April 26, 1793, court-martial of Captain Beard. For Webster's use of P. Q., see Joshua Kendall, *The Forgotten Founding Father: Noah Webster's Obsession and the Creation of an American Culture* (New York: Putnam, 2010), 176, and, for his ambivalent writings about natives, Carroll Smith-Rosenberg, *This Violent Empire: The Birth of an American National Identity* (Chapel Hill: University of North Carolina Press, 2010), 234–47.

47 H. H. Brackenridge, "Further and Concluding Thoughts on the Indian War," *KG*, June 2, 1792; "From a Savannah [Georgia] Paper," *KG*, December 29, 1792 ("five hundred Creeks"); "Knoxville, Dec. 19," *KG*, December 19, 1793 ("sold from master to master").

48 "Address of the Grand Inquest of the District of Hamilton," *KG*, November 23, 1793 ("right to expect" and "immediate outrages."); *KG*, May 18, 1793 ("*philanthropic*"). See also "Grand Jury of Southern Circuit Court of United States," *KG*, July 27, 1793, which criticizes the government's "too benevolent (if not impolitic)" effort to stave off famine among Creeks.

49 "The Memorial and Petition and Convention of Mero District" and "[To] Mr. Roulston," *KG*, August 13, 1793. Jackson had referred to the "law of Nations" in his January 30, 1793, letter to John McKee. Other possible authors of the letter include David Wilson and Thomas Donnell, both mentioned in the "Memorial," and any combination of John Overton and William Blount, both of whom would have had access to Vattel and the *Gazette*.

50 "[To] Mr. Roulston," *KG*, August 13, 1793. The writer draws directly from Vattel, *Law of Nations*, Preliminaries, §6, p. 68, and Book I, chapter 17, §202, p. 212. In the former case, Vattel calls the law of nations "originally no other than the *law of nature applied* to nations" (emphasis in original) before stressing the difference between nations and individuals. In the latter case, he cites the example of the county of Zug, attacked by the Swiss in 1352 and compelled to switch allegiances from the negligent duke of Austria to the Helvetic Confederacy.

51 Leviticus 17:11 ("life of the flesh") and Hebrews 9:12 ("his own blood"); Jerome Hall, "Biblical Atonement and Modern Criminal Law," *JLR* 1 (1983): 279–95; Jill Lepore, *The Name of War: King Philip's War and the Origins of American National Identity* (New York: Alfred A. Knopf, 1998), 72–73, 79–83, 99–100; Caroline Walker Bynum, "The Blood of Christ in the Later Middle Ages," *CH* 71 (December 2002): 685–714; Peter Silver, *Our Savage Neighbors: How Indian War Transformed Early America* (New York: W. W. Norton and Company, 2008), 73–94.

52 Andrew R. Holmes, *The Shaping of Ulster Presbyterian Belief and Practice, 1770–1840* (New York: Oxford University Press, 2006), 163 ("mystical body") and 163–98; Kimberly Bracken Long, "The Communion Sermons of James McGready: Sacramental Theology and Scots-Irish Piety on the Kentucky Frontier," *JPH* 80 (Spring 2002): 10 ("hanging on the cross . . . '*great drops*,'" emphasis in original) and 3–16; John Thomas Scott, "James McGready: Son of Thunder, Father of the Great Revival," *AP* 72 (Summer 1994): 87–95. For Presbyterians' strong influence in early Tennessee, see Paul K. Conkin, "Evangelicals, Fugitives, and Hillbillies: Tennessee's Impact on American National Culture," *THQ* 54 (Fall 1995): 246–71, esp. 249–51, and James William Hagy, "Democracy Defeated: The Frankland Constitution of 1785," *THQ* 40 (Fall 1981): 239–56, esp. 241–42.

53 "[To] Mr. Roulston," *KG*, August 13, 1793; Rutherford quoted in Saunt, *West of the Revolution*, 27. See also [Washington], "Extracts of Correspondence on Indian Affairs," [October 1792], in *PGW* 11: 296, 311n.

54 William Blount to Henry Knox, November 8, 1792, in *ASP: Indian Affairs* 1: 325 ("Every Indian nation" and "'all national honors,'" latter in quotes); "Governor Blount to the Little Turkey, Chief of the Cherokees," September 13, 1792, ibid., 1: 280 ("*none* of the Indians," emphasis in original); "Governor Blount to the Bloody Fellow, a Chief of the Cherokees," September 13, 1792, in ibid., 1: 281 ("all your nation").

55 "Southwestern Frontier," June 6, 1794, in *AC: House*, 3rd Congress, 1st session, p. 774 ("offensive operations," from original bill); Remarks by Rep. Nicholas, June 6, 1794, in ibid., 775 ("*scourge*," emphasis in original); Remarks by Rep. Carnes, June 6, 1794, in ibid., 778 ("every drop" and "savage enemy") and 777 ("the line"); Remarks by Rep. McDowell, June 6, 1794, in ibid., 776 (fathers and sons). McDowell's military career from http://ncpedia.org/biography/mcdowell-joseph (accessed October 2, 2015). Matthew Carey, *Affecting History of the Dreadful Distresses of Frederic Manheim's Family* (Philadelphia, 1794) is brilliantly discussed in Smith-Rosenberg, *This Violent Empire*, 223–33.

56 "Treaty with the Cherokee, 1794," in *IT*, 33; "Southwestern Frontier," June 6, 1794, in *AC: House*, 3rd Congress, 1st session, p. 779 (vote); "A List of the Names of the Persons Killed, Murdered, and Captured Since the 26th of February 1794," *KG*, Sept. 26, 1794. I took the names of the twenty-six members who voted to send the US soldiers (against forty-two opposed) and compared them with David Hackett Fischer, *The Revolution of American Conservatism* (New York: Harper and Row, 1965), appendix, and *Biographical Directory of the United States Congress, 1774–Present*, http://bioguide.congress.gov/biosearch/biosearch.asp (accessed August 26, 2013). The only three whom I could not confirm as consistently Federalist were John Van Allen, John Watts, and Peter Van Gausbeck of New York. The only four votes from south of the Mason-Dixon line came from Maryland. See also "Report of Committee of Congress: Territorial Defense," April 8, 1794, in *TPUS* 4: 335–36.

57 Andrew Jackson to John McKee, May 16, 1794, in *PAJ* 1: 49 (corrections made to scribbled writing); Conkin, "Evangelicals, Fugitives, and Hillbillies." Archibald Roane was the attorney general of the Hamilton District and had been educated by his uncle, a Presbyterian minister. See *PAJ* 1: 83n.

58 William Blount to James Robertson, April 14, 1793, box 1, Robertson Papers, TSLA; Blount to Robertson, November 29, 1793, ibid.; Buchanan, *Jackson's Way*, 141–43; Kanon, *Tennesseans at War*, 9–10.

59 Robertson's orders quoted in Ramsey, *Annals of Tennessee*, 610, and see generally 610–14 and Buchanan, *Jackson's Way*, 142 (number of log houses). Other accounts

include Jonathan McDonald to the Baron de Carondelet, September 20, 1794, in *Spain in the Mississippi Valley*, ed. Kinnaird, 3: 344–45; and *KG*, September 26, 1794. For possible origins of the name, "Nickajack," see Vicki Rozema, *Footsteps of the Cherokees: A Guide to the Eastern Homelands of the Cherokee Nation* (Winston-Salem, NC: John F. Blair, 2007), 78.

60 Peter Luna to James K. Polk, December 12, 1832, in *CJP* 1: 566; Andrew Jackson to James Robertson,? 1796, box 2, Robertson Papers, TSLA; Ramsey, *Annals of Tennessee*, 614–15. Although this letter from Jackson is filed in Robertson's papers as being from 1796, I strongly suspect that it dates from 1806. For one thing, the letter makes no reference to the particulars of the 1792–94 carnage, or of Nickajack. It focuses on Robertson's recent offer of further service, not on his resignation. This probably refers to the fall of 1806, when Robertson and other aged veterans offered to form a group called the "Invincible Grays" to save the Union from the Burr conspiracy. This would explain Jackson's use of the term "Corps of Invincibles." Besides, the language of republicanism is much more characteristic of Jackson in 1806 than in 1796. Finally, the letter is signed (with a ~~strikethrough~~), "Andrew Jackson [Major] General 2nd Division," a title that he did not hold until 1803–4. My thanks to Tom Kanon and Daniel Feller for their advice on this source. For the "Invincible Grays," see William A. Walker Jr., "Martial Sons: Tennessee Enthusiasm for the War of 1812," *THQ* 20 (March 1961): 21.

61 Proceedings with the Cherokee, Tellico Blockhouse, December 1794–January 1795, box 2, Robertson Papers, TSLA; "Treaty with the Cherokee, 1794," in *IT*, 34. For recovered horses, see *KG*, November 28, 1796, and April 3, 1797. The records of the conference note that "many of the frontier Citizens" were present along with territorial and federal officials.

62 [John McNairy to Grand Jury of Hamilton District], "Charge," *KG*, May 2, 1796; [William C. C. Claiborne to Grand Jury of Mero District], "Charge," *KG*, December 12, 1796; Imlay, *Topographical Description*, 75 (benefits of federal government); "A Short Description of the State of Tenasee," in Imlay, *Topographical Description*, 520n (benefits of Pinckney's treaty with Spain).

63 "A Short Description of the South-Western Territory," [July 1795], in Imlay, *Topographical Description*, 525; William Blount to Thomas Jefferson, September 19, 1791, introductory letter to "Schedule of the Whole Number of Persons in the Territory of the United States of America, South of the River Ohio," September 19, 1791, in *TPUS* 4: 80 ("very generally"); Memorial to Congress by Citizens of the Territory, December 6, 1800, in *TPUS* 5: 110–17; Memorial to Congress by Citizens of the Territory, November 25, 1803, in ibid., 5: 279–87. Figures from poll in Robert E. Corlew, *Tennessee: A Short History* (1969; 2nd ed., Knoxville: University of Tennessee Press, 1981), 96 and 86. See also Andrew R. L. Cayton, "When Shall We Cease to Have Judases?: The Blount Conspiracy and the Limits of the 'Extended Republic,'" in *Launching the "Extended Republic": The Federalist Era*, ed. Ronald Hoffman and Peter J. Albert (Charlottesville: University of Virginia Press, 1996), 156–89; Peter Onuf, *Jefferson's Empire: The Language of American Nationalism* (Charlottesville: University of Virginia Press, 2000); Bethel Saler, *The Settlers' Empire: Colonialism and State Formation in America's Old Northwest* (Philadelphia: University of Pennsylvania Press, 2014).

64 In the 1795 census, Davidson counted 728 free white males aged sixteen and over, of whom 613 (84%) responded to the question "Is it your wish if, on taking the enumeration there should prove to be less than sixty thousand inhabitants, that the territory shall be admitted as a State in the Federal Union with such a number or not?" Of the respondents, 517 (84%) replied no, while 96 (16%) supported

statehood. Results were similar in Tennessee County, where 289 of 380 free white men (76%) responded to the question, voting 231 to 58 (80%) against statehood. In the eastern counties, the yes votes won overwhelmingly but often with smaller participation rates. See Corlew, *Tennessee*, 96, and Kanon, *Tennesseans at War*, 16.

65 Corlew, *Tennessee*, 95–99; "Journal of the Proceedings of a Convention Begun and Held at Knoxville, January 11, 1796," in *Journal of the Proceedings of the Legislative Council of the Territory of the United States of America, South of the River Ohio, Begun and Held at Knoxville, the 25th Day of August, 1794* (Nashville, 1852).

66 Tennessee Constitution, 1796, Tennessee Founding and Landmark Documents, TSLA, Article X, section 4 ("excepted out" and "pretence"); Article XI, section 17 ("bringing suit") and section 20 ("impairing contracts"); Article VII (militia) at http://teva.contentdm.oclc.org/cdm/ref/collection/tfd/id/90 (accessed October 14, 2015); Eric Foner, *Tom Paine and Revolutionary America* (1976; rev. ed., New York: Oxford University Press, 2005), 62–66; Corlew, *Tennessee*, 95–99. The surviving records of the Constitutional Convention do not include the records of the drafting committee.

67 AJ to William Blount, February 29, 1796, in *PAJ* 1: 82; Tennessee Constitution, Article V, section 5. Jackson empowered Blount to sell twenty-six thousand acres of land inside Indian country along with four thousand acres inside the Mero District to James Stuart, to pay some of Jackson's creditors in Philadelphia. Blount made good on this deal in April 1796. See *PAJ* 1: 441. For impatience with federal treaties, see also "A Short Description of the State of Tenasee," in Imlay, *Topographical Description*, 521.

68 William Blount to AJ, September 2, 1795, in *PAJ* 1: 70 ("best Friends"); "Agreements with John Overton," May 12, 1794, in *PAJ* 1: 46 ("without as within") and 1: 436–37; AJ to William Blount, February 29, 1796, in *PAJ* 1: 83 ("good Judiciary"); *The Political Club of Danville, Kentucky, 1786–1790* (Louisville, 1894), 130–31 (debates of May 5, 1787); Article V, section 5 of the 1796 constitution gave judges the power to "state the testimony and declare the law," although not to "charge juries with respect to matters of fact." For his appointment as supervisor of revenue, see Theodore Brown Jr., "John Overton," *Tennessee Encyclopedia of History and Culture*, at http://tennesseeencyclopedia.net/index.php (accessed June 7, 2016). In May 1794, Jackson and Overton bought two tracts, one fifteen thousand acres and the other ten thousand, in the "Western District." They purchased thirty thousand more acres on July 26th.

69 "Journal of the Proceedings of a Convention Begun and Held at Knoxville, January 11, 1796," 8–9; Stuart Banner, *How the Indians Lost Their Land: Law and Power on the Frontier* (Cambridge, MA: Harvard University Press, 2005), 112–49; Samuel Cole Williams, *The Admission of Tennessee into the Union* (1945; Johnson City, TN: Overmountain Press, 1994).

70 "Memorial of Legislative Council and House of Representatives, to the Congress of the United States," September 18, 1794, in *Journal of the Proceedings of the Legislative Council of the Territory of the United States of America*; Journal of the Senate, August 9, 1796, in ibid.; "Message from the Governor to Legislative Council, June 30, 1795," in ibid.; Elizabeth H. Peeler, "The Policies of Willie Blount as Governor of Tennessee, 1809–1815," *THQ* 1 (December 1942): 312.

71 James Grant to AJ, November 16, 1795, in *PAJ* 1: 77 ("hold a pole"); Joseph Anderson to AJ, August 4, 1796, in *PAJ* 1: 97 ("most certainly"); "Election Returns for Representative to Congress," in *PAJ* 1: 98–99. Grant acted as an attorney for Jackson and Overton in Philadelphia, and Anderson was US judge of the territory south of the Ohio River. See *PAJ* 1: 58n and 1: 78n.

72 Calhoun in 1811 speech quoted in Merrill D. Peterson, *The Great Triumvirate: Webster, Clay, and Calhoun* (New York: Oxford University Press, 1987), 26. Henry Adams reproduced this quote with slight variation and trenchant criticism of how prior Republican policy had inhibited just that kind of nationhood. See Adams, *History of the United States of America During the Administrations of James Madison* (1889–91; New York: Library of America, 1986), 394.

73 AJ to Nathaniel Macon, October 4, 1795, in *PAJ* 1: 74; William E. Dodd, "The Place of Nathaniel Macon in Southern History," *AHR* 7 (July 1902): 663–75.

CHAPTER 4

1 John Overton to Andrew Jackson, March 8, 1795, in *PAJ* 1: 54 ("likely Negroe"), xxxvii–xxxviii (Philadelphia trips); "A Short Description of the South-Western Territory," [July 1795], in Gilbert Imlay, *A Topographical Description of the Western Territory of North America* (1797; New York: A. M. Kelley, 1969), 527; "Agreements with John Overton," May 12, 1794, in *PAJ* 1: 46; Lewis L. Laska, "'The Dam'st Situation Ever Man Was Placed In': Andrew Jackson, David Allison, and the Frontier Economy of 1795–96," *THQ* 54 (Winter 1995): 336–47; Stuart Banner, *How the Indians Lost Their Land: Law and Power on the Frontier* (Cambridge, MA: Harvard University Press, 2005), 161–63; Thomas P. Abernethy, "The Early Development of Commerce and Banking in Tennessee," *MVHR* 14 (December 1927): 311–25; Katherine Anne St.-Louis, "St. Domingue Refugees and Their Enslaved Property: Abolition Societies and the Enforcement of Gradual Emancipation in Pennsylvania and New York" (MA thesis, Université de Montréal, 2015), 25–26; Carol Wilson, *Freedom at Risk: The Kidnapping of Free Blacks in America, 1780–1865* (Lexington: University Press of Kentucky, 1994).

2 [Andrew Jackson], "Speech Before the United States House of Representatives," December 29, 1796, in *PAJ* 1: 107; [George Washington], "Extracts of Correspondence on Indian Affairs," [October 1792], in *PGW* 11: 293 (regarding such speculation in the Northwest); William C. C. Claiborne to AJ, July 20, 1797, in *PAJ* 1: 148. For Overton's speculation in military pay: John Overton to AJ, December 18, 1796, in *PAJ* 1: 105, 105n, and Overton to AJ, December 20, 1796, in *PAJ* 1: 106. For reimbursement: "Report of House Select Committee on Claims," January 17, 1797, in *PAJ* 1: 113–14 and 114n; AJ to David Henley, February 17, 1797, in *PAJ* 1: 124–25; William C. C. Claiborne to AJ, April 30, 1798, in *PAJ* 1: 195–96; "Andrew Jackson in the United States Congress," in *PAJ* 1: 480. The roughly $23,000 that Congress recommended in early 1797 compares with the more than $130,000 just spent to build coastal forts. See Lawrence A. Peskin, *Captives and Countrymen: Barbary Slavery and the American Public, 1785–1816* (Baltimore: Johns Hopkins University Press, 2009), 128–29.

3 *KG*, October 12, 1793 ("surrendered to the Indians"); AJ to John Sevier, February 24, 1797, in *PAJ* 1: 126; John Sevier to AJ, November 26, 1797, in *PAJ* 1: 155; "Andrew Jackson in the United States Congress," in *PAJ* 1: 484; AJ to David Campbell, December 29, 1797, in *PAJ* 1: 159. For complaints on federal policy: "To the People of America," *KG*, March 6, 1797; "For the Knoxville Gazette," *KG*, January 30, 1797. See also AJ to Willie Blount, February 21, 1798, in *PAJ* 1: 183, and Cynthia Cumfer, *Separate Peoples, One Land: The Minds of Cherokees, Blacks, and Whites on the Tennessee Frontier* (Chapel Hill: University of North Carolina Press, 1997), 84–85.

4 Laska, "'The Dam'st Situation'"; Robert Remini, *Andrew Jackson and the Course of American Empire, 1767–1821* (New York: Harper and Row, 1977), 129–33;

Proceedings on the Impeachment of William Blount (Philadelphia, 1799); Andrew R. L. Cayton, "When Shall We Cease to Have Judases?: The Blount Conspiracy and the Limits of the 'Extended Republic,'" in *Launching the "Extended Republic": The Federalist Era*, ed. Ronald Hoffman and Peter J. Albert (Charlottesville: University of Virginia Press, 1996), 156–89; Bruce H. Mann, *Republic of Debtors: Bankruptcy in the Age of American Independence* (Cambridge, MA: Harvard University Press, 2002), 96–99.

5 Adams quoted in John Ferling, *John Adams: A Life* (New York: Oxford University Press, 1992), 357; AJ in 1807 letter quoted in William A. Walker Jr., "Martial Sons: Tennessee Enthusiasm for the War of 1812," *THQ* 20 (March 1961): 22 ("energy"); AJ to John Adams, March 5, 1798, in *PAJ* 1: 186 ("Military Tyranny" and "Sovereignty"); "Andrew Jackson in the United States Congress," in *PAJ* 1: 485 and 488; AJ to Willie Blount, February 21, 1798, in *PAJ* 1: 183. For earlier praise of Napoleon: AJ to James Robertson, January 11, 1798, in *PAJ* 1: 165. Jackson briefly served in the US Senate and asked for a leave of absence to begin on April 16, 1798. For the XYZ affair, see Stanley Elkins and Eric McKitrick, *The Age of Federalism: The Early American Republic, 1788–1800* (New York: Oxford University Press, 1993), 588–89.

6 Thomas Jefferson, "Second Inaugural Address, March 4, 1805," in *The Life and Selected Writings of Thomas Jefferson*, ed. Adrienne Koch and William Peden (1944; New York: Modern Library, 2004), 314; Jefferson, "Summary View of the Rights of British America," [1774], in ibid., 287–88; Jefferson, "Autobiography," [1821], in ibid., 50, 38; Jefferson, "To Mssrs. Nehemiah Dodge et als.," [1802], in ibid., 307. Relevant studies of Jefferson include Holly Brewer, "Entailing Aristocracy in Colonial Virginia: 'Ancient Feudal Restraints' and Revolutionary Reform," *WMQ* 54 (April 1997): 307–46; Johann N. Neem, "Developing Freedom: Thomas Jefferson, the State, and Human Capacity," *SAPD* 27 (April 2013): 36–50; Brian Steele, *Thomas Jefferson and American Nationhood* (New York: Cambridge University Press, 2012); John Lauritz Larson, "'Bind the Republic Together': The National Union and the Struggle for a System of Internal Improvements," *JAH* 74 (September 1987): 370–72; Merrill D. Peterson, *Thomas Jefferson and the New Nation: A Biography* (New York: Oxford University Press, 1970), 97–158; Joseph J. Ellis, *American Sphinx: The Character of Thomas Jefferson* (New York: Alfred A. Knopf, 1997), 32–42; Gordon S. Wood, "The Trials and Tribulations of Thomas Jefferson," in *Jeffersonian Legacies*, ed. Peter S. Onuf (Charlottesville: University of Virginia Press, 1993), 395–417; Seth Cotlar, "'Every Man Should Have Property': Robert Coram and the American Revolution's Legacy of Economic Populism," in *Revolutionary Founders: Rebels, Radicals, and Reformers in the Making of the Nation*, ed. Alfred F. Young, Gary B. Nash, and Ray Raphael (New York: Alfred A. Knopf, 2011), 337–53.

7 Peter S. Onuf, *Jefferson's Empire: The Language of American Nationhood* (Charlottesville: University of Virginia Press, 2000); Gordon S. Wood, *Empire of Liberty: A History of the Early Republic, 1789–1815* (New York: Oxford University Press 2009), 620–58; Joyce Appleby, *Capitalism and a New Social Order: The Republican Vision of the 1790s* (New York: New York University Press, 1984).

8 AJ to John Sevier, May 8, 1797, in *PAJ* 1: 136; Thomas Johnson to John Sevier, January 28, 1797, filed in "Robertson County Election Protest, 1797," box 1, Military Elections, 1796–1862, Record Group 131, State Records, TSLA; "Knox County Election Protest, 1796," in ibid.; "Sumner County Election Protest," in ibid.; "Washington County Election Protest, 1796," in ibid.; "Davidson County

Election Protest, 1797," in ibid.; "Grainger County Election Protest, 1797," in ibid.; "Robertson County Election Protest, 1797," in ibid.; Remini, *Andrew Jackson and the Course of American Empire*, 100–102.

9 AJ to John McNairy, May 12, 1797, in *PAJ* 1: 144; AJ to John Sevier, May 8, 1797, in *PAJ* 1: 136 (Jackson reproduced what Sevier had written about him). Andrew Burstein, *The Passions of Andrew Jackson* (New York: Alfred A. Knopf, 2003), 37–38 and 41–49, offers an insightful study of AJ's 1797 conflicts. Burstein notes that Sevier was staying with McNairy in Nashville as of May 1797.

10 AJ to John Sevier, May 8, 1797, in *PAJ* 1: 136, 137; Joanne B. Freeman, *Affairs of Honor: National Politics in the New Republic* (New Haven, CT: Yale University Press, 2001), esp. 159–98; Richard Bell, "The Double Guilt of Dueling: The Stain of Suicide in Anti-Dueling Rhetoric in the Early Republic," *JER* 29 (Fall 2009): 383–410.

11 John Sevier to AJ, May 8, 1797, in *PAJ* 1: 137, 138; John Sevier to AJ, May 11, 1797, in *PAJ* 1: 142 ("friendship"); AJ to John Sevier, May 10, 1797, in *PAJ* 1: 141; Freeman, *Affairs of Honor*; Nicole Eustace, *Passion Is the Gale: Emotion, Power, and the Coming of the American Revolution* (Chapel Hill: University of North Carolina Press, 2008), 385–438.

12 "Statement Regarding Land Frauds," December 6, 1797, in *PAJ* 1: 157–58 and 158n; Remini, *Andrew Jackson and the Course of American Empire*, 117–19; Robert E. Corlew, *Tennessee: A Short History* (2nd ed., Knoxville: University of Tennessee Press, 1981), 133–34.

13 Stockley Donelson to AJ, August 3, 1792, in *PAJ* 1: 37; AJ to John Overton, January 22, 1798, in *PAJ* 1: 169; Indenture Between Andrew Jackson and Edward Ward, July 6, 1804, ser. 1, reel 3, AJPLC (initial grant was from a pre-emption to "Lewis Roberts" and given by North Carolina in July 1788); Remini, *Andrew Jackson and the Course of American Empire*, 117–19. For relations between Stockley, Rachel, and AJ, see *PAJ* 1: 432 and 442.

14 AJ to Rachel Jackson, September 17, 1799, in *PAJ* 1: 223–24 and xxxviii; Laska, "'The Dam'st Situation,'" 344 (salary). Relevant treatments of the "country" tradition include Isaac Kramnick, *Bolingbroke and His Circle: The Politics of Nostalgia in the Age of Walpole* (Cambridge, MA: Harvard University Press, 1968) and Lance Banning, *The Jeffersonian Persuasion: Evolution of a Party Ideology* (Ithaca, NY: Cornell University Press, 1978). The Jacksons began taking on wards in the late 1790s and eventually had partial or full custody of fifteen relatives and friends. See Rachel Meredith, "'There Was Somebody Always Dying and Leaving Jackson as Guardian': The Wards of Andrew Jackson" (MA thesis, Middle Tennessee State University, 2013).

15 Cumfer, *Separate Peoples, One Land*, 171–73; Corlew, *Tennessee*, 119–24 and 237–38; "Masonic Minutes," in *PAJ* 1: 253 and 254n; Thomas B. Craighead to AJ, January 14, 1803, in *PAJ* 1: 321–22 and 322n; "Account Book, Jackson's Nashville Store, 1795," in ibid., 1: 469 (Craighead buys paper, ink powder, and other items). For religious ferment, see Melissa J. Gismondi, "The Character of a Wife: Rachel Jackson and the Search for Zion, 1760s–1820s" (PhD dissertation, University of Virginia, forthcoming), chapter 2; Ronald P. Byars, "Cane Ridge: A Presbyterian Perspective," *AP* 70 (Fall 1992): 141–50; John Opie Jr., "James McGready: Theologian of Frontier Revivalism," *CH* 34 (December 1965): 445–56; and David J. Voelker, "Church Building and Social Class on the Urban Frontier: The Refinement of Lexington, 1784–1830," *RKHS* 106 (Spring 2008): 191–229. For Blount's last years and death by illness: Michael Toomey, "William Blount," *North Carolina History Project*, http://northcarolinahistory.org/encyclopedia/

william-blount-1749–1800/ (accessed July 28, 2016). For the concept of "deep Christianity," or a set of meta-narratives that run through fundamentalist traditions, see Marlene Winnell, "Trump's Worldview Mirrors the Most Archaic and Apocalyptic of Christian Beliefs," October 15, 2016, at www.alternet.org/election-2016/trumps-worldview-mirrors-most-archaic-and-apocalyptic-christian-beliefs (accessed October 21, 2016).

16 AJ to John Sevier, March 27, 1802, in *PAJ* 1: 291; Tom Kanon, *Tennesseans at War, 1812–1815: Andrew Jackson, the Creek War, and the Battle of New Orleans* (Tuscaloosa: University of Alabama Press, 2014); Saul Cornell, *A Well-Regulated Militia: The Founding Fathers and the Origins of Gun Control* (New York: Oxford University Press, 2006).

17 AJ to Henry Dearborn, November 12, 1803, in *PAJ* 1: 396 and 396n; "Election Returns of Mero District for Major General of the Tennessee Militia," February 5, 1802, in *PAJ* 1: 277 and 277n; Archibald Roane to AJ, July 10, 1803, in *PAJ* 1: 334–35; AJ to Benjamin J. Bradford, July 19, 1803, in *PAJ* 1: 337–45. Roane was the incoming governor who passed the deciding vote for AJ, and Bradford was the editor of the *Tennessee Gazette*.

18 Remini, *Andrew Jackson and the Course of American Empire*, 121; "Documents Relating to the Jackson-Sevier Controversy, October–December 1803," in *PAJ* 1: 489–506.

19 Anti-dueling critics quoted in Bell, "The Double Guilt of Dueling," 396 and 404; AJ to John Sevier, October 2, 1803, in *PAJ* 1: 367; Sevier to AJ, October 2, 1803, in *PAJ* 1: 368.

20 "An Act to Prevent the Evil Practice of Dueling," November 10, 1801, *Acts Passed at the First Session of the Fourth General Assembly of the State of Tennessee* (Knoxville, 1801), chapter 32, pp. 102–3; John Sevier to AJ, October 9, 1803, in *PAJ* 1: 377; AJ to Sevier, October 3, 1803, in *PAJ* 1: 369. Sevier originally told AJ that they should duel out of state in his October 2 letter. See also C. A. Harwell Wells, "The End of the Affair? Anti-Dueling Laws and Social Norms in Antebellum America," *VLR* 54 (May 2001): 1805–47, esp. 1825–30.

21 "Knox County Citizen to *Knoxville Gazette* Printer," November 10, 1803, in *PAJ* 1: 495 ("head of a faction" and "assassinate") and 496n; Affidavit of Howell Tatum, November 8, 1803, in *PAJ* 1: 491–92; Remini, *Andrew Jackson and the Course of American Empire*, 122–23. See also Nancy Isenberg, "The 'Little Emperor': Aaron Burr, Dandyism, and the Sexual Politics of Treason," in *Beyond the Founders: New Approaches to the Political History of the Early American Republic*, ed. Jeffrey L. Pasley, Andrew W. Robertson, and David Waldstreicher (Chapel Hill: University of North Carolina Press, 2004), 137 ("assassin") and 129–58.

22 "Address of His Excellency John Sevier, to Both Houses of the Legislature," *Tennessee Gazette* (Nashville), October 28, 1801; Ron Simbeck, *Tennessee State Symbols* (2nd ed., Knoxville: University of Tennessee Press, 2002), 129–33.

23 July 13, 1802, sale in *PAJ* 1: 452; "Memorandum for Payment of Debt Owed by John Overton," May 27, 1802, in *PAJ* 1: 296–98 and 298n and also 283n–284n; Frances Clifton, "John Overton as Andrew Jackson's Friend," *THQ* 11 (March 1952): 24–25; Laska, "'The Dam'st Situation.'" Jackson bought seventy-five thousand acres in two pieces on behalf of one of Allison's creditors. Of the ten thousand acres he bought for himself, he gave Overton a thousand acres as payment for legal services and sold four thousand additional acres to his friend. True to form, Remini, *Andrew Jackson and the Course of American Empire*, 129–31, offers a thorough look at the Allison affair. I differ only in Remini's presentation of a

continuous headache for Jackson. Between 1802 and 1810 or 1811, when the legitimacy of the titles he had acquired came under question, the Allison notes do not seem to have hurt Jackson.

24 John Overton to John Sevier, February 13, 1804, in Murdock Collection: Overton Papers, box 3, TSLA ("land business" and "extremely laborious"); Opinion of J. Overton, "Philip's Lessee vs. Robertson," August 1815, in *TR* 2: 405; Thomas Overton to John Overton, April 24, 1802, box 3, Overton Papers (thirty-one slaves to Nashville); Moses Fisk to John Overton, January 29, 1798, box 4, Overton Papers; Fletch Coke, "Profiles of John Overton: Judge, Friend, Family Man, and Master of Traveller's Rest," *THQ* 37 (Winter 1978): 393–409; Mary T. Orr, "John Overton and Traveler's Rest," *THQ* 15 (September 1956): 216–23.

25 John Overton to [? Dickson], February 3, 1803, box 3, Overton Papers ("out of doors," "appearances," and "every principle"); John Overton to [? Dickson], January 24, 1804, box 3, Overton Papers ("I am not aware"). In an 1808 case, Overton strenuously defended the right of some Virginia heirs to recover property from their widowed mother, who had remarried and moved to Tennessee. Other justices argued that the plaintiffs' remedy was in Virginia, where the will had been written. Overton replied: "[It] would be derogatory from every idea of justice to exempt the citizens of this State from their contracts abroad, by throwing their burdens on the shoulders of innocent men, their securities there." See Comments by J. Overton, "Caldwell and Wife, vs. Maxwell and Wife," September 1808, *TR* 2: 107.

26 Comments by J. Overton, "Sevier and Anderson's Lessee vs. Hill," April 1809, in *TR* 2: 37 ("ordinary principles of contracts"); Overton, "Philips's Lessee vs. Robertson," August 1815, in *TR* 2: 411 ("strict adherence") and 412 ("fluctuating passions"); John Overton to? Dickinson, Feb. 3, 1803, box 3, Overton Papers; Overton to?, Jan. 24, 1804, in box 3, Overton Papers. See also "John Smith and Others vs. The Lessee of Craig," August 1814, in *TR* 2: 290–92. For the 1806 Compact see "Claim of the United States to Lands in Tennessee," January 8, 1805, in *ASP: Public Lands* 1: 193–96; Corlew, *Tennessee*, 154–57; Thomas Perkins Abernathy, *From Frontier to Plantation in Tennessee: A Study in Frontier Democracy* (1932; rev. ed., Tuscaloosa: University of Alabama Press, 1967), 182–93. The most important land laws for Virginia and Kentucky reflected a 1779 statue and subsequent "occupant claimant laws" from 1790 and 1812. See Humphrey Marshall, *The History of Kentucky* (Frankfort, 1812), 100–113; *Green v. Biddle*, 21 U.S. 8 Wheat.1.1 (1823); Stephen Aron, "Pioneers and Profiteers: Land Speculation and the Homestead Ethic in Frontier Kentucky," *WHQ* 23 (May 1992): 179–98; Peterson, *Thomas Jefferson and the New Nation*, 113–24.

27 Overton, "Sevier and Anderson's Lessee vs. Hill," April 1809, in *TR* 2: 38 ("bare possessor" and "any title"); "Bacon, Assignee, vs. Parker," September 1809, in *TR* 2: 58 (debt actions "particularly" the province of courts); Overton, "Philips's Lessee vs. Robertson," August 1815, in *TR* 2: 418 ("exemption from restraint" and "law of nature"), 419 ("freedom"), 420 ("manifestly repugnant").

28 "John Smith and Others vs. the Lessee of Craig," August 1814, in *TR* 2: 298; John Overton to [? Dickson], February 3, 1803, Overton Papers, box 3 ("obvious principles"); Overton to [? Dickson], January 24, 1804, Overton Papers, box 3 ("safe in pre-emptions"); Abernathy, *From Frontier to Plantation*, 190–93; Wood, *Empire of Liberty*, 400–432; Christopher Doyle, "Judge St. George Tucker and the Case of *Tom v. Roberts*: Blunting the Revolution's Radicalism from Virginia's District Courts," *VMHB* 106 (Autumn 1998): 419–42; John Radabaugh, "Spencer Roane

and the Genesis of Virginia Judicial Review," *AJLH* 6 (January 1962): 63–70. For settlers and squatters, see Reeve Huston, "Land Conflict and Labor Policy in the United States, 1785–1841," in *The World of the Revolutionary American Republic: Land, Labor, and the Conflict for a Continent*, ed. Andrew Shankman (New York: Routledge, 2014), 324–45.

29 John Overton to? Dickinson, February 3, 1803, box 3, Overton Papers; Robert Williams to John Overton, June 22, 1805, in box 3, ibid. From a sample of household heads in Davidson County as of 1805 (n = 100), I found that 35% owned at least one slave, with the largest owner having sixty human chattels. John and Thomas Overton were together listed as having twenty-seven taxable slaves. See Davidson County Tax List, 1805, Early Tax Lists Collection, TSLA. For a later view of Overton's wealth, see "Lands of John Overton," [1833], box 6, Overton Papers.

30 James Parton, *Life of Andrew Jackson* (New York, 1863), 78 (emphasis in original) and 77–81. And see Preface: "It is proper to state, that a great part of the information given in these pages respecting the childhood, the youth, the frontier experiences, the White House life, and the last years of General Jackson, was derived by the author, in the course of an extensive tour in the Southern States, from the general's surviving relations, comrades, and political associates" (5–6).

31 "Articles of Agreement," AJ and John Hutchings, August 23, 1803, ser. 1, reel 3, AJPLC ("Mercantile Business"); Tax Receipt, April 19, 1804, in ibid. ($25 annual tax on "Merchants, Peddlars, and Hawkers"). For Jackson's partnerships in this period, see *PAJ* 2: 6. His first partners were Thomas Watson and John Hutchings. From 1802 to 1803, they had stores at Lebanon and on Watson's property; after Watson left the partnership, Jackson also opened a store at his plantation. He and Hutchings also acquired a store at Gallatin. Then, with Hutchings and John Coffee, Jackson operated a store and tavern at Clover Bottom on Stone's River. Apparently he also sold goods at a military cantonment on the Tennessee River. For examples of what they were selling: John Coffee to AJ, April 23, 1804, ser. 1, reel 3, AJPLC, and Andrew Jackson Account Book Collection, 1804–1806, TSLA.

32 "Resolutions of Cotton Gin Committee," July 13, 1802, in *PAJ* 1: 304 and 303–4; Samuel Jackson to AJ, June 9, 1802, in *PAJ* 1: 298 and also 223n ("Prime" slaves sought); Mark Mitchell to AJ, November 21, 1795, in *PAJ* 1: 77 ("Put your Negros"); *PAJ* 1: 450 (February 16, 1802, agreement to use a cotton gin) and 1: 452 (September? 1802 purchase by promissory note of $9.664.77 in goods). "Articles of Agreement," AJ and John Hutchings, August 23, 1803, ser. 1, reel 3, AJPLC, indicates that Jackson had paid for half of the goods on credits for cotton already sent to New Orleans. During 1801, Jackson sold land twenty-three times, totalling 14,250.5 acres. In 1802, he sold land thirteen times, totalling 4,801 acres. Together this makes 19,051.5 acres, mostly in Knox County and often for the nominal sum of $1. During this period he purchased 20,622 acres in eight transactions; of this, 10,000 acres came from the marshals' sale of Allison's land, another 5,000 acres from a sheriff's sale, and 960 acres from two other sheriff's sales. I did not count copurchases. Counting Allison's land, all but 5,000 of these acres (from a sheriff's sale for Knox County land) were in mid-Tennessee, that is, in Davidson, Wilson, Robertson, or Sumner Counties or along the Duck River. See "Calendar of Transactions and Agreements," *PAJ* 1: 447–52. See also Petition of the Inhabitants of Mero District, September 25, 1801, Tennessee Legislative Petitions, 1799–1801, reel 1, TSLA; Samuel C. Williams, "The South's First Cotton Factory," *THQ* 5 (September 1946): 212–21; "List of Cotton Gins for the years 1804, 1805, 1806, and 1807," [Montgomery County], Cotton Gins, Owners'

Tax, 1804–1807, box 1, Secretary of State Records, 1796–1865, TSLA; Mark R. Cheathem, *Andrew Jackson, Southerner* (Baton Rouge: Louisiana State University Press, 2013), 25.

33 Thomas Watson to AJ, March 27, 1803, in *PAJ* 1: 327; "A Short Description of the State of Tenasee," [March 1796], in Imlay, *Topographical Description*, 519, and see also 403; Nathan Davidson to AJ, June 3, 1803, in *PAJ* 1: 332; Boggs and Davidson to AJ, August 2, 1803, in *PAJ* 1: 350 (40,332 lb. shipped); Boggs and Davidson to AJ, October 7, 1803, in *PAJ* 1: 370 (prices from $0.16 to $0.14). For hoped-for prices: William C. C. Claiborne to AJ, January 20, 1802, in *PAJ* 1: 272, and William C. C. Claiborne to AJ, March 20, 1802, in *PAJ* 1: 284–86. For river conditions: W. A. Provine, "Bedford's Tour in 1807 down the Cumberland, Ohio, and Mississippi Rivers," *THM* 5 (April 1919): 40–69; Claudio Saunt, *West of the Revolution: An Uncommon History of 1776* (New York: W. W. Norton and Company, 2014), 173–74; Walter Johnson, *River of Dark Dreams: Slavery and Empire in the Cotton Kingdom* (Cambridge, MA: Harvard University Press, 2012), 244–79.

34 John Ryerson to AJ, October 11, 1803, in *PAJ* 1: 382 ("alledging"); Seth Lewis to AJ, November 11, 1803, in *PAJ* 1: 394 ("in the Spanish Territory"); AJ to John Hutchings, March 17, 1804, in *PAJ* 2: 10 ("sell at any market" and pelts). AJ contracted with a manufacturer in Abingdon, Virginia, for his iron: see *PAJ* 2: 12n.

35 John Hutchings to AJ, March 30, 1804, in *PAJ* 2: 12; William Stothart to AJ, July 15, 1804, in *PAJ* 2: 26 ("very bad order" and cotton prices); AJ to John Hutchings, March 17, 1804, in *PAJ* 2: 11. Stothart wrote from Philadelphia, but indicated that the damage had occurred during the trip to New Orleans. For overland costs: Receipt, May 14, 1804, for Benjamin Hoover; Receipt, May 12, for George Gelson [?]; Receipt, May 11, 1804, for Jacob Grace; Receipt, May 8, 1804, for John Daily; Receipt, May 9, 1804, for Hayes Irvin, all in ser. 1, reel 3, AJPLC. Jackson agreed to pay these drivers around $7 per one hundred pounds of cargo upon delivery in Pittsburgh.

36 AJ to Rachel Jackson, April 6, 1804, in *PAJ* 2: 13; AJ to Thomas and John Clifford, July 24, 1804, in *PAJ* 2: 28. For sale of Hunter's Hill: Indenture between Andrew Jackson and Edward Ward, July 6, 1804, ser. 1, reel 3, AJPLC, and *PAJ* 2: 27n. For subsequent trips to market: John Williamson to AJ, December 12, 1805, in *PAJ* 2: 75. For cotton production on their farms: John Hutchings to AJ, March 30, 1804, *PAJ* 2: 12. For examples of Jackson buying or accepting cotton from other planters, see "Agreement with John and Robert Allen," February 28, 1803, in *PAJ* 1: 325–26, and Thomas Watson to AJ, March 27, 1803, in *PAJ* 1: 327. On the names "Rural Retreat" and "Hermitage," see Meredith, "'There Was Somebody Always Dying,'" 27–28, and Burstein, *Passions of Andrew Jackson*, 49–50.

37 AJ to John Hutchings, March 17, 1804, in *PAJ* 2: 11; Johnson, *River of Dark Dreams*, 8–9, 151–52; Robert H. Gudmestad, *Steamboats and the Rise of the Cotton Kingdom* (Baton Rouge: Louisiana State University Press, 2011).

38 Matthew Rainbow Hale, *The French Revolution and the Forging of American Democracy* (Charlottesville: University of Virginia Press, forthcoming); Rachel Hope Cleves, "On Writing the History of Violence," *JER* 24 (Winter 2004): 641–65; Richard S. Chew, "Certain Victims of an International Contagion: The Panic of 1797 and the Hard Times of the Late 1790s in Baltimore," *JER* 25 (Winter 2005): 565–613; Jane Kamensky, *The Exchange Artist: A Story of High-Flying Speculation and America's First Banking Collapse* (New York: Penguin Books, 2008), 30–59. For confiscations: Albert Mathiez, "La Révolution Française," *AHRF* 55 (janvier–février 1933): 12.

39 William C. C. Claiborne to AJ, March 20, 1802, in *PAJ* 1: 284 ("quite low"); Boggs and Davidson to AJ, October 7, 1803, in *PAJ* 1: 370 ("most gloomy"); Samuel Meeker to AJ, October 10, 1803, in *PAJ* 1: 378 ("desperate"); William C. C. Claiborne to AJ, January 20, 1802, in *PAJ* 1: 272; Adam Rothman, *Slave Country: American Expansion and the Origins of the Deep South* (Cambridge, MA: Harvard University Press, 2005), 46–47 (1798 peak price). See also Martin Öhman, "Perfecting Independence: Tench Coxe and the Political Economy of Western Development," *JER* 31 (Fall 2011): 410–11.

40 AJ to Boggs and Davidson, September 2, 1803, in *PAJ* 1: 357; [AJ], "Toasts for Independence Day Celebration," July? 1805, in *PAJ* 2: 64; AJ to Thomas Jefferson, August 18, 1802, in *PAJ* 1: 308–9 (salt making). On the importance of toasts, see Jeffrey L. Pasley, "The Cheese and the Words: Popular Political Culture and Participatory Democracy in the Early American Republic," in *Beyond the Founders*, ed. Pasley, Robertson, and Waldstreicher, 40–41.

41 AJ to Boggs and Davidson, September 2, 1803, in *PAJ* 1: 357 ("truly sorry"); AJ to Nathan Davidson, August 25, 1804, in *PAJ* 2: 40 ("equal Justice"); AJ to Boggs and Davidson, July 31, 1804, in *PAJ* 2: 32 ("principals of Justice"); AJ to Edward Ward, June 10, 1805, in *PAJ* 2: 60; AJ [and Hutchings] to George Bullitt, August 6, 1808, in *PAJ* 2: 199. In September 1808 alone, Jackson and Hutchings received word of two judgments, obtained a writ to revive a judgment (*scire facias*) on two others, dismissed a case, and obtained an action on still another. See *PAJ* 2: 553 and 2: 181–82.

42 AJ to Nathan Davidson, August 25, 1804, in *PAJ* 2: 40; *PAJ* 1: 454; Cheathem, *Andrew Jackson, Southerner*, 50–51. See also Walter Johnson, *Soul by Soul: Inside the Antebellum Slave Market* (Cambridge, MA: Harvard University Press, 2001), and Robert H. Gudmestad, *A Troublesome Commerce: The Transformation of the Interstate Slave Trade* (Baton Rouge: Louisiana State University Press, 2003). For the arrival of merchants from western Pennsylvania, see Gabriel Hawkins Golden, "William Carroll and His Administration," *THM* 9 (April 1925): 11n and 12n, and advertisements in *Impartial Review* (Nashville), August 16, 1806.

43 "Advertisement for Runaway Slave," [September 26, 1804], in *PAJ* 2: 40–41; Thomas Terry Davis to AJ, February 20, 1805, in *PAJ* 2: 51; AJ to John Hutchings, April 7, 1806, in *PAJ* 2: 94–95 and 95n and *PAJ* 2: 528; James W. Ely Jr., "Andrew Jackson as Tennessee State Court Judge, 1798–1804," *THQ* 40 (Summer 1981): 148 (thirty-lash judgement). Jackson returned home from his Pennsylvania trip on June 19 and reported in his advertisement that the slave escaped on June 25. I am unable to identify the date of George's escape. The slave who ran away with George was quickly recaptured, while George seems to have disappeared in New Orleans. See Cheathem, *Andrew Jackson, Southerner*, 50–51; Robert P. Hay, "'And Ten Dollars Extra, for Every Hundred Lashes Any Person Will Give Him, to the Amount of Three Hundred': A Note on Andrew Jackson's Runaway Slave Ad of 1804 and on the Historian's Use of Evidence," *THQ* 36 (Winter 1977): 468–78. For more on AJ's disciplining of slaves, see AJ to James Craine Bronough, July 3, 1821, in *PAJ* 5: 66; AJ to Andrew Jackson Donelson, July 3, 1821, in *PAJ* 5: 66n–67n; AJ to Hardy Murfee Cryer, July 12, 1823, in *PAJ* 5: 284–85; and Remini, *Andrew Jackson and the Course of American Empire*, 133–34. For an excellent analysis and discussion of a possible sexual relationship between AJ and one slave, see Mark R. Cheathem, "Hannah, Andrew Jackson's Slave," *Humanities* 35 (March/April 2014), at https://www.neh.gov/humanities/author/mark-r-cheathem (accessed July 28, 2016).

44 "An Act to Amend the Law in Force and Use Concerning Free Negroes, Mulattoes, and Slaves," September 13, 1806, *Acts Passed at the Second Session of the Sixth General Assembly of the State of Tennessee* (Knoxville, 1806), chapter 32, p. 136 and pp. 135–38; "State vs. Thompson," November 1807, in *TR* 2: 97, 98, and 96–99; also in abbreviated form in *Judicial Cases Concerning American Slavery and the Negro*, ed. Helen Tunnicliff Catterall (5 vols., New York, 1968), 2: 483; Sally E. Hadden, *Slave Patrols: Law and Violence in Virginia and the Carolinas* (Cambridge, MA: Harvard University Press, 2003). The woman was described as "coming from the spring," and the defendant was fined. The year before, Overton had offered a "handsome reward" for a runaway slave: *Impartial Review* (Nashville), August 16, 1806.

45 "Advertisement for Runaway Slave," [September 26, 1804], in *PAJ* 2: 41; "Toasts for Independence Day Celebration," July 1 [?], 1805, in *PAJ* 2: 63 ("blood") and 64 (other quotes). For Overton and out-of-state contracts and wills: John Overton to Henry Clay, May 3, 1805, in *PHC* 1: 185–86; Henry Clay to John Overton, December 10, 1799, in *PHC* 1: 19–20; "Caldwell and Wife vs. Maxwell and Wife," September 1808, in *TR* 2: 106–7. Praise of the judiciary: William C. C. Claiborne to AJ, March 20, 1802, in *PAJ* 1: 286, and James Robertson to AJ, September 7, 1803, ser. 1, reel 3, AJPLC.

46 AJ to Henry Dearborn, November 12, 1803, ser. 1, reel 3, AJPLC (also in *PAJ* 1: 395–96). Here Jackson denounces Sevier's appointments of militia officers, arguing that such "usurpation" would dampen the people's "ardor" and "Spirit of Patriotism." A demoralized militia, Jackson suggested, would ultimately help the Federalists.

47 "Philips's Lessee vs. Robertson," August 1815, in *TR* 2: 406 ("latitude") and 420 ("contest for first choice"); "John Smith and Others vs. the Lessee of Craig," August 1814, in *TR* 2: 299–300 ("infested" and "extermination"). Banner, *How the Indians Lost Their Land*, 150–90, identifies *Marshall v. Clark*, 8 Va. 268, 273 (1791), as the seminal case regarding pre-emptions in Indian land, followed by *Weiser's Lessee v. Moody*, 2 Yeates 127 (Pa. 1796), and *Glasgow's Lessee v. Smith*, 1 Tenn. 144, 167 (1805). See Banner, *How the Indians Lost Their Land*, 160–62 and 321n. An 1813 case before the Pennsylvania Supreme Court is also interesting given the role played by Justice Hugh Henry Brackenridge. Reprising his arguments from the early 1790s, Brackenridge insisted that "these Aborigines were not considered as having any right [to the land], not being Christians, but mere heathens and unworthy of the earth." See Banner, *How the Indians Lost Their Land*, 176.

48 AJ quoted in 1810 letter in Elizabeth H. Peeler, "The Policies of Willie Blount as Governor of Tennessee, 1809–1815," *THQ* 1 (December 1942): 319 ("knowledge and art"); AJ to Henry McKinney, May 10, 1802, in *PAJ* 1: 295; AJ to James Winchester, May 10, 1802, in *PAJ* 1: 296. The incident occurred northeast of Nashville. For his observation of US Army units in the Mississippi Territory, see "General Jackson a Negro Trader," *Scioto Gazette* (Chillicothe, Ohio), July 3, 1828.

49 AJ to Thomas Jefferson, August 7, 1803, in *PAJ* 1: 354; Thomas Jefferson to AJ, September 19, 1803, in *PAJ* 1: 365; AJ to Norton Pryor, December 12, 1805, in *PAJ* 2: 74–75. For the 1805–6 cessions see "Treaty with the Chickasaw, 1805," "Treaty with the Cherokee, 1805," and "Treaty with the Cherokee, 1806," in *IT*, 79–80, 82–83, and 90–92; Corlew, *Tennessee*, 148.

50 Matthew L. Davis, *Memoirs of Aaron Burr, with Miscellaneous Selections from His Correspondence* (2 vols., New York, 1836–37), 1: 182 ("inconceivably") and 2: 359 ("mere curiosity"); Freeman, *Affairs of Honor*, 159–98; Nancy Isenberg, *Fallen*

Founder: The Life of Aaron Burr (New York: Viking, 2007); Ron Chernow, *Alexander Hamilton* (New York: Penguin Press, 2004), 714–17.

51 Burr quoted in Davis, *Memoirs of Aaron Burr,* 2: 372; David S. Heidler and Jeanne T. Heidler, *Old Hickory's War: Andrew Jackson and the Quest for Empire* (Baton Rouge: Louisiana State University Press, 2003), 1–5; Nathan Schachner, *Aaron Burr: A Biography* (New York: A. S. Barnes, 1937), 300–301 and 303–4.

52 [J. B. Provenchere?], A Private Memorial, [?] 1807, in *TPUS* 14: 156 ("hard Conditions"), 157 ("Spanish generosity"); Petition to Congress by Citizens of the Territory, January 2, 1808, in *TPUS* 14: 158–61; Aaron Burr to AJ, March 24, 1806, in *PAJ* 2: 91–92. On fears of Haiti-inspired slaves, see Kanon, *Tennesseans at War*, 136–37.

53 Aaron Burr to AJ, March 24, 1806, in *PAJ* 2: 91–92. On gunboats: *PAJ* 1: xxx–viii. Quarrel with Erwin and Swann: *PAJ* 2: xxiii–xxiv and 77–78; Thomas Swann to AJ, January 3 and January 12, 1806, in *PAJ* 2: 78 and 82–83, 83n; Remini, *Andrew Jackson and the Course of American Empire,* 136–43. On horse racing, see Rhys Isaac, *The Transformation of Virginia, 1740–1790* (Chapel Hill: University of North Carolina Press, 1982), 98–101, 118–19, and 132.

54 Charles Henry Dickinson to AJ, January 10, 1806, in *PAJ* 2: 81–82; "Court Minutes in *State vs. Andrew Jackson*," November 9, 1807, in *PAJ* 2: 173–74; Bell, "Double Guilt of Dueling." The origin of Jackson's hatred for Dickinson is mysterious, although most historians argue that Dickinson had slandered Rachel. See *PAJ* 2: 77–78.

55 James Robertson to AJ, February 1, 1806, in *PAJ* 2: 84 and 83–84. Robertson did not mention the Hiwassee missionary school, opened by the Reverend Gideon Blackburn in 1803. For the school and its influence over Sevier and others, see Gismondi, "The Character of a Wife," chapter 2.

56 "Arrangements of Thomas Overton and Hanson Catlet for Duel," in *PAJ* 2: 99–100; Parton, *Life of Andrew Jackson*, 84–95; Z. F. Smith, "Dueling, and Some Noted Duels by Kentuckians," *RKSHS* 8 (September 1910): 77–87; Wells, "The End of the Affair?," 1825–26 and 1834. Details of the duel remain at issue, but everyone agrees that Dickinson fired first and that Jackson's first effort "clicked" but did not discharge. See Andrew Burstein, *The Passions of Andrew Jackson* (New York: Alfred A. Knopf, 2003), 56–61; Parton, *Life of Andrew Jackson*, 92–93 (Dickinson's agony and wife's arrival). I thank Dr. Steven Opal of the Brown University School of Medicine for explaining the anatomical dimensions of the injuries sustained.

57 John Overton to AJ, June 1, 1806, in *PAJ* 2: 100; Bell, "Double Guilt of Dueling"; *PAJ* 2: xxiv (record of violence in early 1806); Freeman, *Affairs of Honor*, 190–96.

58 AJ to Thomas Eastin, June? 1806, in *PAJ* 2: 106 ("private dispute," "Publick feeling," and "humane persuit"), 107 ("esential service") and 107n; see also AJ to Thomas Eastin, June 6, 1806, in *PAJ* 2: 101, and AJ to Thomas Gassaway Watkins, June 15 [?], 1806, in *PAJ* 2: 102–3. The June 7 editions of both the *Tennessee Gazette* and *Impartial Review* are either nonextant or badly damaged. In 1828, twenty-two years after the fact, the anti-Jackson *Truth's Advocate* claimed that forty-six Nashville citizens had signed a petition to the editors, asking for the mourning border, and that another twenty-six had signed and then asked that their names be removed once Jackson threatened them. See *PAJ* 2: 101.

59 John Overton to AJ, September 12, 1806, in *PAJ* 2: 109, 108. The next time Jackson and Overton exchanged letters seems to have been March 1808, when either Overton or John Coffee wrote to Jackson.

60 AJ to James Winchester, October 4, 1806, in *PAJ* 2: 111 ("not only the Floridas," "freedom and commerce," and "Should there be a war"); [AJ], "Order to Brigadier Generals of the Second Division," October 4, 1806, in *PAJ* 2: 112 ("laudable ambition"); AJ to Thomas Jefferson, November 5, 1806, in *PAJ* 2: 114 ("one moments"). Judging by the October 4 letter to Winchester, Burr was at the Hermitage as of October 3 and did not leave Nashville until October 6. See Schachner, *Aaron Burr*, 329, and [AJ], "Testimony Before the Grand Jury in the Case of Aaron Burr," June 25, 1807, in *PAJ* 2: 168; Isenberg, *Fallen Founder*, 279–82; Davis, *Memoir of Aaron Burr*, 2: 377–91.

61 Isenberg, *Fallen Founder*, 217–36.

62 AJ to William C. C. Claiborne, November 12, 1806, in *PAJ* 2: 116; AJ to Daniel Smith, November 12, 1806, in *PAJ* 2: 117; Peterson, *Thomas Jefferson and the New Nation*, 849 ("daring" and "criminal") and 841–74; Dumas Malone, *Jefferson the President: Second Term, 1805–1809* (Boston: Little, Brown and Company, 1974), 260. At this time Claiborne was the governor of Orleans Territory and Smith was the US senator from Tennessee.

63 Thomas Jefferson to AJ, December 3, 1806, in *PAJ* 2: 121; Abernathy, *From Frontier to Plantation*, 181. Abernathy notes that the unspoken target of the demonstration may have been Jackson himself, although he bases this on A. C. Buell, *History of Andrew Jackson* (2 vols., New York: Charles Scribner's Sons, 1904), 1: 198. Buell was the source of many falsehoods regarding Jackson. See Hendrik Booraem, *Young Hickory: The Making of Andrew Jackson* (Dallas: Taylor Trade, 2001), 201–4. For the Jefferson administration and Florida, see J. C. A. Stagg, *Borderlines in Borderlands: James Madison and the Spanish-American Frontier, 1776–1821* (New Haven, CT: Yale University Press, 2009). Burr returned to Nashville on December 14, 1806, and apparently went on preparing his boats with no interference from the locals or from Jackson. According to Henry Adams, Jackson simply asked Burr to disavow any designs against the Union, which Burr did "with his usual dignified courtesy." See Henry Adams, *History of the United States of America during the Administrations of Thomas Jefferson* (1889–91; New York: Library of America, 1986), 801.

64 [AJ], "Testimony Before the Grand Jury in the Case of Aaron Burr," June 25, 1807, in *PAJ* 2: 168; Adams, *History of the United States of America*, 920 ("blackguard"); see also AJ to Daniel Smith, November 28, 1807, in *PAJ* 2: 174–76 and *PAJ* 2: 164n–66n. In 1810, Jackson bitterly recalled that three years earlier many honest patriots were "branded with the apethet of *Traitor Burrite etc*." See AJ to Jenkin Whiteside, February 10, 1810, in *PAJ* 2: 231, and also William Preston Anderson to AJ, May 10, 1807, in *PAJ* 2: 166. On the trial: Isenberg, "The 'Little Emperor,'" 145–46; Peterson, *Thomas Jefferson and the New Nation*, 850–74; Remini, *Andrew Jackson and the Course of American Empire*, 144–64. Jackson tried to redirect blame toward General James Wilkinson, whom he already despised and correctly suspected of double-dealing with the Spanish.

65 Peskin, *Captives and Countrymen*, 150 and 137–62; Walter LaFeber, "Jefferson and an American Foreign Policy," in *Jeffersonian Legacies*, ed. Onuf, 370–91; J. M. Opal, "The Republic in the World, 1783–1801," in *The Oxford Handbook of the American Revolution*, ed. Edward G. Gray and Jane Kamensky (New York: Oxford University Press, 2012), 595–611. For a Federalist view of the North African states, see "Barbary Powers," *United States Oracle of the Day* (Portsmouth, NH), July 11, 1801.

66 Jon Latimer, *1812: War with America* (Cambridge, MA: Harvard University Press, 2007), 15–18; Alan Taylor, *The Civil War of 1812: American Citizens, British Subjects, Irish Rebels, and Indian Allies* (New York: Vintage Books, 2010), 102–6; Paul A. Gilje, "'Free Trade and Sailors' Rights': The Rhetoric of the War of 1812," *JER* 30 (Spring 2010): 1–23.

67 "Washington City," *National Intelligencer*, December 28, 1807; Michigan chief justice from 1811 quoted in Taylor, *Civil War of 1812*, 153–54; Emmanuel Eyre to Jonathan Roberts, January 24, 1813, box 2, Jonathan Roberts Papers, 1780–1930, HSP; Peterson, *Thomas Jefferson and the New Nation*, 874–921 (New England plot and British squadron).

68 Robert E. Cray Jr., "Remembering the USS *Chesapeake*: The Politics of Maritime Death and Impressment," *JER* 25 (Fall 2005): 445–74; Richard R. Beeman, *The Old Dominion and the New Nation, 1788–1801* (Lexington: University Press of Kentucky, 1972), 125n, 125–26, 137, 174n, 174–76; Taylor, *Civil War of 1812*, 111–12; Malone, *Jefferson the President*, 426–28 and 430.

69 Alexander McRae to Jefferson quoted in Malone, *Jefferson the President*, 425; AJ to Thomas Monteagl Bayly, June 27, 1807, in *PAJ* 2: 170 and 170n; *Impartial Review*, July 29, 1807, quoted in *PAJ* 2: 194n. Jackson apparently left Richmond on June 27 after writing the letter to Bayly.

70 Jefferson quoted in Forrest McDonald, *The Presidency of Thomas Jefferson* (Lawrence: University of Kansas Press, 1976), 142 ("unfriendly") and 142–52; Jefferson quoted in Malone, *Jefferson the President*, 483 ("we keep") and 469–90; Jabez D. Hammond, *An Oration, Delivered on the Glorious Tenth of June, 1809* (Otsego, NY, 1809), 8 ("venerable fabric") and 23 ("philosophic calmness"). See also "National Intelligencer," *National Intelligencer*, January 18, 1808, and Steele, *Thomas Jefferson and American Nationhood*.

71 Peterson, *Thomas Jefferson and the New Nation*, 876 and 892–94; Richard Buel Jr., *America on the Brink: How the Political Struggle over the War of 1812 Almost Destroyed the Young Republic* (New York: Palgrave Macmillan, 2005); Brian Schoen, "Calculating the Price of Union: Republican Economic Nationalism and the Origins of Southern Sectionalism, 1790–1828," *JER* 23 (Summer 2003): 173–206; Adams, *History of the United States of America During the Administrations of Thomas Jefferson*, 1119–21.

72 Thomas Jefferson to Thomas Leiper, January 21, 1809, in *Life and Selected Writings*, ed. Koch and Peden, 543 ("lately inculcated") and Jefferson to John Melish, January 13, 1813, in ibid., 568–69; "Washington City," *National Intelligencer*, December 28, 1807 ("internal sufficiency"), and "Petersburg, March 5," *National Intelligencer*, March 18, 1808. The 1820 US Census counted agriculture, commerce, and manufactures while categorizing heads of households. In Pennsylvania, 60,215 heads were listed as manufacturers among 208,099 total (29%), and in New York, the numbers were 60,038 out of 316,799 (19%). The national numbers were 349,247 out of 2,487,143 (14%). See also Lawrence A. Peskin, "How the Republicans Learned to Love Manufacturing: The First Parties and the 'New Economy,'" *JER* 22 (Summer 2002): 235–62, and Andrew Shankman, "'A New Thing on Earth': Alexander Hamilton, Pro-Manufacturing Republicans, and the Democratization of American Political Economy," *JER* 23 (Autumn 2003): 323–52.

73 Nicole Eustace, *1812: War and the Passions of Patriotism* (Philadelphia: University of Pennsylvania Press, 2012).

74 George Michael Deadrick to AJ, January 15, 1808, ser. 1, reel 4, AJPLC; Burr quoted in Davis, *Memoirs of Aaron Burr*, 2: 434; Sampson Williams to AJ, April 25, 1808, in *PAJ* 2: 195. See also Dumas Malone, *Jefferson the President: First Term, 1801–1805* (Boston: Little, Brown and Company, 1970), 269–70 and 306–8; Malone, *Jefferson the President: Second Term*, 49–53, 149–53; Adams, *History of the United States of America During the Administrations of Thomas Jefferson*, 886–87. Monroe mostly attracted the support of the "Old Republicans" of Virginia, who criticized the administration for drifting from the opposition principles of the 1790s. Monroe even proposed repealing the Judiciary Acts of 1789 and 1801. But he also favored a larger military, anathema to the "Old Republicans." See McDonald, *Presidency of Thomas Jefferson*, 51, and Banning, *The Jeffersonian Persuasion*, 192–96 and 282–83. For early opposition to the caucus, see Thomas Coens, "The Early Jackson Party: A Force for Democratization?," *A Companion to the Era of Andrew Jackson*, ed. Sean Patrick Adams (Malden, MA: Blackwell Publishing, 2013), *Blackwell Reference Online*.

75 AJ to Thomas Jefferson, April 20, 1808, in *PAJ* 2: 192; AJ to Officers of the Second Division, April 20, 1808, in *PAJ* 2: 191; AJ to Thomas Jefferson, May 14, 1808, in *PAJ* 2: 196–97. See also Sarah J. Purcell, *Sealed with Blood: War, Sacrifice, and Memory in Revolutionary America* (Philadelphia: University of Pennsylvania Press, 2002).

76 John Sevier to AJ, January 12, 1809, in *PAJ* 2: 206, 205–7, and 207n; AJ to the Brigadier Generals of the Second Division, December 19, 1808, in *PAJ* 2: 203–4; Kristofer Ray, "New Directions in Early Tennessee History, 1540–1815," *THQ* 69 (Fall 2010): 217–18.

77 [AJ], "Resolutions of the Second Division Officers," January 16, 1809, in *PAJ* 2: 208, 208–9.

78 Petition of the People South of French Broad and Holston, Petition #36, [?] 1809, ser. 1, reel 3, TLP; Petition of the Inhabitants of Cock[e] County, Petition #6, March 6, 1809, ser. 1, reel 3, TLP; Petition of Sundry Good Citizens of Bledsoe County, Petitions #14-15, 1809, ser. 1, reel 3. In 1806, the Tennessee legislature enabled settlers south of the French Broad to pay less than the federal minimum price per acre and also to do so in ten yearly installments. See Abernathy, *From Frontier to Plantation*, 190–93. For AJ and the Bank of Nashville, also called the Nashville Bank, see "Receipt for Fifty Shares of Bank Stock," October 24, 1808, in *PAJ* 2: 200, and Corlew, *Tennessee: A Short History*, 142.

79 Petition of the People South of French Broad and Holston, Petition #36, [?] 1809, ser. 1, reel 3, TLP; Abernathy, *From Frontier to Plantation*, 182–93, 227–49.

80 "Committee Report on Sundry Petitions," December 16, 1808, in *PHC* 1: 390 (quote), and [Henry Clay], "Speech on Domestic Manufactures," March 26, 1810, in *PHC* 1: 459–63; "Assize of Bread," *National Intelligencer*, January 4, 1808 (commenting on Maryland's proposed stay law); *A Compilation of the Laws of the State of Georgia*, comp. Augustin Smith Clayton (1812), 447–48, 426–27, 448, and 534–35; "For the Carthage Gazette, etc.," *Carthage Gazette* (Carthage, TN), February 13, 1809 ("public acts" and "barbarous cupidity"); Peterson, *Thomas Jefferson and the New Nation*, 894 (Virginia stay law).

81 AJ to Thomas Jefferson, May 14, 1808, in *PAJ* 2: 197; [AJ], "Address to Citizens of Nashville," January 16, 1809, in *PAJ* 2: 210; *PAJ* 2: 207n–208n.

82 "For the Carthage Gazette, etc.," *Carthage Gazette*, February 13, 1809 ("A Friend of the People" and call for petitions and meetings); "Circular," *Carthage Gazette*, December 15, 1809 (lawmaker Thomas K. Harris quoted); "Argument on the Execution law," *The Enquirer* (Richmond), January 31, 1809 (Federalist Daniel

Sheffey condemning relief); *A Fair and Just Comparison of the Lives of the Two Candidates, Andrew Jackson and John Quincy Adams, Part I, From Their Birth to the Year 1814* (1828?), 6, available at LCP (Judge Nathan Williams, recalling his time in Nashville in 1804); Stockley Donelson Hays to AJ, June 17, 1809, ser. 1, reel 4, AJPLC ("secure from the grasp"). For AJ's collection efforts see also *PAJ* 2: 555–57, and John Hutchings to AJ, May 28, 1810, ser. 1, reel 4, AJPLC. John Bach McMaster, *A History of the People of the United States: From the Revolution to the Civil War* (8 vols., New York, 1883–1919), 3: 416 and 416n, notes that the legislature passed a stay law late in November 1809, offering a grace period of between sixty days and nine months for debts of value up to $50. On Sheffey, the anti-relief Virginian, see "Biographical Sketch of Daniel Sheffey," *Southern Literary Messenger* 4 (June 1838): 346–47; Ronald L. Hatzenbuehler, "Party Unity and the Decision for War in the House of Representatives, 1812," *WMQ* 29 (July 1972): 378, 385; Norman K. Risjord, "The Virginia Federalists," *JSH* 33 (November 1967): 486–517.

CHAPTER 5

1 AJ to William Henry Harrison, November 28, 1811, in *PAJ* 2: 270 ("imperious"); AJ to Thomas Eastin, June? 1806, in *PAJ* 2: 106 ("humane persuit"); AJ to Rachel Jackson, December 17, 1811, in *PAJ* 2: 273. For more on this encounter, see Bette B. Tilley, "The Jackson-Dinsmoor Feud: A Paradox in a Minor Key," *JMH* 39 (May 1977): 117–32, and AJ to Willie Blount, January 25, 1812, in *PAJ* 2: 277–79. For Choctaws and the cotton economy, see Daniel H. Usner Jr., "American Indians on the Cotton Frontier: Changing Economic Relations with Citizens and Slaves in the Mississippi Territory," *JAH* 72 (September 1985): 297–317.

2 "An Act to Regulate Trade and Intercourse with the Indian Tribes, and to Preserve Peace on the Frontiers," May 19, 1796, 1 *SL* 469–74; William C. C. Claiborne to James Madison, May 24, 1804, in *Official Letter Books of William C.C. Claiborne, 1801–1816*, ed. Dunbar Rowland (6 vols., Jackson: Mississippi Department of Archives and History, 1917), 2: 165; Claiborne to Madison, June 22, 1804, ibid., 2: 216–17; Mary Givens Bryan, *Passports Issued by Governors of Georgia, 1785 to 1809, 1810 to 1820* (Washington, DC: National Genealogical Society, 1959); Silas Dinsmoor to Secretary of War [William Eustis], November 13, 1811 (25 of 212 stopped), in "Passports Through Indian Country," *NWR*, April 12, 1828, 110; Angela Pulley Hudson, *Creek Paths and Federal Roads: Indians, Settlers, Slaves and the Making of the South* (Chapel Hill: University of North Carolina Press, 2010), 53–55 and 69–73 (passports) and 34–35; Cletus Francis Joseph Fortwendel Jr., "Federal Agent Silas Dinsmoor and the Cherokee: A Study in Frontier Policies, Politics, and Personalities" (MA thesis, Western Carolina University, 1996). See also "General Jackson a Negro Trader," *Scioto Gazette*, July 3, 1828.

3 AJ to Willie Blount, January 25, 1812, in *PAJ* 2: 277 ("good Citizens" and "honest face"); "General Jackson a Negro Trader" ("*These are General Jackson's*"); "Narrative of a Trip Made by Gen. Andrew Jackson in the Winter of 1811 from Nashville Tenn. to Natchez, Mississippi Territory," [1843?], in *Passports of Southeastern Pioneers, 1770–1823*, ed. Dorothy Williams Potter (Baltimore: Genealogical Publishing Company, 1982), 80; AJ to Willie Blount, January 25, 1812, in *PAJ* 2: 277 and 277–79; James Parton, *Life of Andrew Jackson* (3 vols., New York, 1861), 1: 349–60; John Frost, *Pictorial Life of Andrew Jackson* (Philadelphia, 1846), 42–44; Tilley, "The Jackson-Dinsmoor Duel." See also J. M. Opal, "General Jackson's Passports: Natural Rights and Sovereign Citizens in the Political Thought of Andrew Jackson, 1780s–1820s," *SAPD* 27 (October 2013): 69–85.

4 AJ to Willie Blount, January 25, 1812, in *PAJ* 2: 279 ("That citizens are to be"); AJ to George W. Campbell, October 15, 1812, in *PAJ* 2: 334 ("*my god,*" emphasis in original), 335 ("our Citizens" and "wrath and indignation"), 336; Col. Stamp [?] to Silas Dinsmoor, September 15, 1812, ser. 1, reel 5, AJPLC. Stamp, a licensed trader in the Choctaw nation, reported that Jackson had repeatedly said "in Public Company" that he wished to burn down the agency house with Dinsmoor inside. Jackson and others also charged Dinsmoor with intoxication.

5 AJ to George W. Campbell, October 15, 1812, in *PAJ* 2: 334 ("our rights"), 335 (variations of "invader"), 336 ("burst forth"). For efforts to return Crawley: AJ to the Second Division, July 9, 1812, in *PAJ* 2: 314 and 315n, and Tom Kanon, "The Kidnapping of Martha Crawley and Settler-Indian Relations Prior to the War of 1812," *THQ* 64 (Spring 2005): 3–23. Among the many new studies of the War of 1812 that inform this chapter, see especially Pietro S. Nivola, "The 'Party War' of 1812: Yesterday's Lessons for Today's Partisan Politics," in *What So Proudly We Hailed: Essays on the Contemporary Meaning of the War of 1812,* ed. Pietro S. Nivola and Peter J. Kastor (Washington, DC: Brookings Institute, 2012), 18–35; Nicole Eustace, *1812: War and the Passions of Patriotism* (Philadelphia: University of Pennsylvania Press, 2012); and Alan Taylor, *The Civil War of 1812: American Citizens, British Subjects, Irish Rebels, and Indian Allies* (New York: Vintage Books, 2010).

6 Tecumseh quoted in Jon Latimer, *1812: War with America* (Cambridge, MA: Harvard University Press, 2007), 174; Taylor, *Civil War of 1812*, 126–27; Hudson, *Creek Paths and Federal Roads*, 87–89, and Kathryn E. Holland Braund, *Deerskins and Duffels: The Creek Indian Trade with Anglo-America, 1685–1815* (Lincoln: University of Nebraska Press, 1993), 164–88.

7 "Imposing Attitude," *Columbian Centinel* (Boston), January 13, 1813; Stephen Budiansky, "The War of 1812 and the Rise of American Military Power," in *What So Proudly We Hailed*, ed. Nivola and Kastor, 37 (ships seized since 1807); J. MacKay Hitsman, *The Incredible War of 1812: A Military History*, updated by Donald E. Graves (1965; Toronto: University of Toronto Press, 1999), 25–48; Latimer, *1812*, 24–25; Richard Buel Jr., *America on the Brink: How the Political Struggle over the War of 1812 Almost Destroyed the Young Republic* (New York: Palgrave, 2005); Henry Adams, *History of the United States of America During the Administrations of James Madison* (1889–91; New York: Library of America, 1986), 15–16.

8 "From the Inhabitants of Northampton, Massachusetts," July 1, 1812, in *PJM* 4: 529 ("protection . . . National Union"), 529–35 and 535n (the nearby town of Deerfield adopted the same letter and sent it to Madison on July 9); "Prize Money," *Columbian Centinel*, January 13, 1813 ("English and Irish"); "An Address of the Minority to Their Constituents, on the Subject of War with Great-Britain," [June? 1812], in *The War of 1812: Writings from America's Second War of Independence*, ed. Donald R. Hickey (New York: Library of America, 2013), 51 ("rage" and "vengeance") and 46–53. See also Taylor, *Civil War of 1812*, 182, and Lawrence Delbert Cress, "'Cool and Serious Reflection': Federalist Attitudes Toward War in 1812," *JER* 7 (Summer 1987): 123–45.

9 Andrew Shankman, "'A New Thing on Earth': Alexander Hamilton, Pro-Manufacturing Republicans, and the Democratization of American Political Economy," *JER* 23 (Autumn 2003): 323–52; Raymond W. Champagne Jr. and Thomas J. Rueter, "Jonathan Roberts and the 'War Hawk' Congress of 1811–1812," *PMHB* 104 (October 1980): 434–49; Paul A. Gilje, *Free Trade and Sailors' Rights in the War of 1812* (New York: Cambridge University Press, 2013).

10 "Address . . . in Support of the Nomination of the Hon. DeWitt Clinton," August 17, 1812, in *War of 1812*, ed. Hickey, 132; Taylor, *Civil War of 1812*, 15–43; Gordon S. Wood, *Empire of Liberty: A History of the Early Republic, 1789–1815* (New York: Oxford University Press, 2010), 660–62; Andrew R. L. Cayton, "When Shall We Cease to Have Judases?: The Blount Conspiracy and the Limits of the 'Extended Republic,'" in *Launching the "Extended Republic": The Federalist Era*, ed. Ronald Hoffman and Peter J. Albert (Charlottesville: University of Virginia Press, 1996), 156–89; Norman K. Risjord, "1812: Conservatives, War Hawks, and the Nation's Honor," *WMQ* 18 (April 1961): 196–210.

11 "Anglo-Savage Affairs," *The Reporter* (Lexington), September 19, 1812; Richard M. Johnson to James Madison, September 18, 1812, in James A. Padgett, ed., "The Letters of Colonel Richard M. Johnson of Kentucky," *RKSHS* 38 (July 1940): 194 ("drive the Savages"); Johnson to Madison, July 24, 1812, in ibid., 193; John H. Barnhill, "Pigeon Roost Massacre," *The Encyclopedia of the War of 1812: A Political, Social, and Military History*, ed. Spencer C. Tucker (3 vols., Santa Barbara, CA: ABC-CLIO, 2012), 2: 575. Johnson was later celebrated as the man who killed Tecumseh at the Battle of the Thames (or Moraviantown) in October 1813. See Daniel K. Richter, *Facing East from Indian Country: A Native History of Early America* (Cambridge, MA: Harvard University Press, 2001), 236.

12 Willie Blount to Return J. Meigs, May 26, 1811, in box 3, George Edward Matthew Collection, TSLA; Newspaper quoted in Kanon, "Kidnapping of Martha Crawley," 9, 10–11. The attack took place in Humphreys County, established in 1809. See also Willie Blount to James Madison, November 23, 1811, in *PJM* 4: 33–34. For counties bordering Indian or territorial land, I used the county maps available at http://www.mapsofus.org/tennessee and http://www.mapsofus.org/georgia; the 1818 map of Tennessee by John Melish, included and cited in Kanon, *Tennesseans at War*; and the 1814 atlas map of Georgia from the David Rumsey Historical Maps Collection. For Tennessee, I find twelve of thirty-seven (32%) counties bordering Cherokee, Chickasaw, or territorial land. In Georgia, using 1812 lines, I count fifteen of thirty-nine counties (38%) bordering Creek or Cherokee land.

13 George Michael Deadrick to AJ, January 15, 1808, ser. 1, reel 4, AJPLC; Adam Rothman, *Slave Country: American Expansion and the Origins of the Deep South* (Cambridge, MA: Harvard University Press, 2005), 120; Reginald Horsman, "Western War Aims, 1811–1812," *IMH* 53 (March 1957): 1–18. On War Hawks: Risjord, "1812"; Robert V. Haynes, "The Southwest and the War of 1812," *LH* 5 (Winter 1964): 41–51.

14 John Clopton quoted in Risjord, "1812," 205; Thomas Jefferson to James Maury, April 25, 1812, in *The Life and Selected Writings of Thomas Jefferson*, ed. Adrienne Koch and William Peden (New York: Modern Library, 2004), 567; J. C. A. Stagg, *Mr. Madison's War: Politics, Diplomacy, and Warfare in the Early American Republic, 1783–1830* (Princeton, NJ: Princeton University Press, 1983), 61 (Jefferson's use of republican "nation"). See also Benjamin Wittes and Ritika Singh, "James Madison, Presidential Power, and Civil Liberties in the War of 1812," in *What So Proudly We Hailed*, ed. Nivola and Kastor, 97–121; Wood, *Empire of Liberty*, 620–58.

15 [U.S. House of Representatives, Committee on Foreign Relations], "Report on the Causes and Reasons for War," June 3, 1812, in *War of 1812*, ed. Hickey, 10 ("long forbearance"); "Message from the Governor of Georgia," *NWR*, November 28, 1812; "From the General Assembly of the State of Ohio," December 26, 1811 [enclosure], in *PJM* 4: 114; "From the Citizens of Lexington, Kentucky," June 26,

1812, in ibid., 4: 512; "From the Citizens of Charleston, South Carolina," June 27, 1812, in ibid., 4: 515; "From the Citizens of New York," June 24, 1812, in ibid., 4: 506. See also François Furstenberg, *In the Name of the Father: Washington's Legacy, Slavery, and the Making of a Nation* (New York: Penguin, 2006), 43–44 and 50–64.

16 "From the Tennessee Congressional Delegation," March 1, 1810, in *PJM* 4: 615 ("our population"), 613 ("self-preservation"), and 612–16; Willie Blount to AJ, November 24, 1813, in *PAJ* 2: 461; AJ to the Tennessee Volunteers, November 14, 1812, in *PAJ* 2: 341. See also Elizabeth H. Peeler, "The Policies of Willie Blount as Governor of Tennessee, 1809–1815," *THQ* 1 (December 1942): 309–27.

17 AJ to Second Division, March 7, 1812, in *PAJ* 2: 290 ("hour of vengeance"); *PAJ* 2: 296n–297n; Mark R. Cheathem, *Andrew Jackson, Southerner* (Baton Rouge: Louisiana State University Press, 2013), 93–94.

18 AJ to Willie Blount, June 5, 1812, in *PAJ* 2: 301 ("cruel outrage" and "punishd"); AJ to Willie Blount, June 4, 1812, in *PAJ* 2: 300 ("lay their Towns"); AJ to the Second Division, July 9, 1812, in *PAJ* 2: 314 ("He that . . . *not my son*," emphasis in original); Peeler, "Policies of Willie Blount," 317–18 (Tennessee Senate tables resolution).

19 [AJ], "The Massacre at the Mouth of the Duck River," *Democratic Clarion*, July 7, 1812, in *PAJ* 2: 311, 310; "Extract of a Letter to the Editor of the Enquirer, from West Tennessee, Dated July 31, 1812," *The Reporter* (Lexington), September 19, 1812; "Extract of a Letter from an Officer in West-Tennessee to General Winchester," *The Reporter*, September 19, 1812. The content of these anonymous letters strongly suggests that Jackson was the author. For one thing, they refer to plans to raise three thousand volunteers "in my division" from West Tennessee. For another, they use several phrases and themes that were characteristic of Jackson, including grandiose promises to "make the American Eagle wave over the walls of Pensacola." Finally, these letters appeared along with another, "Extract of a Letter from Lieutenant A. Kingsley to General Andrew Jackson."

20 For troop numbers: Budiansky, "War of 1812," in *What So Proudly We Hailed*, ed. Nivola and Kastor, 38 and 43–44; C. Edward Skeen, "Mr. Madison's Secretary of War," *PMHB* 100 (July 1976): 342 and 336–55; Hitsman, *Incredible War of 1812*, 88 (land bounty); J. C. A. Stagg, *The War of 1812: Conflict for a Continent* (New York: Cambridge University Press, 2012), 110–12 (conscription plan). See also J. C. A. Stagg, "Enlisted Men in the United States Army, 1812–1815: A Preliminary Survey," *WMQ* 43 (October 1986): 615–45; Donald R. Hickey, *The War of 1812: A Forgotten Conflict* (Urbana: University of Illinois Press, 1989), 302; and Eustace, *1812*, ix–x.

21 Thomas Hart Benton to AJ, January 30, 1812, in *PAJ* 2: 280; Latimer, *1812*, 9–10 (three years in British Army); Hitsman, *Incredible War of 1812*, 25–48 and 88–89; Taylor, *Civil War of 1812*, 192; Kanon, *Tennesseans at War*; John F. Kutolowski and Kathleen Smith Kutolowski, "Commissions and Canvasses: The Militia and Politics in Western New York, 1800–1845," *NYH* 63 (January 1982): 4–38, and John C. Fredriksen, "The Pittsburgh Blues and the War of 1812: The Memoir of Private Nathaniel Vernon," *PH* 56 (July 1989): 196–212. For commissions and terms of service under Jackson in 1812, see "A Master Roll of the Volunteers from the 2nd Division of the Militia of Tennessee Who Have Tendered Their Services to the President of the United States," ser. 5, reel 65, AJPLC. Jackson estimated the number of military-age men in the state at 40,000, but a state tally of militia members in 1812 counted 29,183. See AJ to the Second Division, September

8, 1812, in *PAJ* 2: 320; Kanon, *Tennesseans at War*, 39; "Annual Return of the Militia of the State of Tennessee for the Year 1812," box 1, Governor Willie Blount Papers, 1809–1815, Governors' Papers Collection, TSLA.

22 Samuel H. Williams to AJ, July 27, 1812, ser. 1, reel 5, AJPLC; AJ to William C. C. Claiborne, January 5, 1813, in *PAJ* 2: 352 ("choice citizens"); John Coffee to AJ, August 24, 1812, ser. 1, reel 5, AJPLC. For disappointing mobilizations, see Thomas Williamson to AJ, March 19, 1812, ser. 1, reel 5, AJPLC, and William Carroll to AJ, December 15, 1813, ser. 1, reel 7, AJPLC. For social differences among volunteers, see Willie Blount to John Armstrong, December 10, 1813, box 1, Governor Willie Blount Papers, 1809–1815, Governors' Papers Collection, TSLA. After receiving word from Secretary of War William Eustis in late October, the governor told Jackson that New Orleans was the destination: Willie Blount to AJ, November 11, 1812, in *PAJ* 2: 338–40 and 340n.

23 AJ to Tennessee Volunteers, December 31, 1812, in *PAJ* 2: 349 ("Let it be"); AJ to the Tennessee Volunteers, November 14, 1812, in *PAJ* 2: 341 ("rights and liberties," and "blood of heroes"); AJ to William Berkeley Lewis, March 4, 1813, in *PAJ* 2: 378 ("Canedy"); AJ to the Second Division, September 8, 1812, in *PAJ* 2: 320–21 (various preferences to march north or south); AJ to James Monroe, January 4, 1813, in *PAJ* 2: 351 (figure of 2,070). For volunteers wanting to go to Creek country, see Thomas Hart Benton to AJ, July 4, 1812, ser. 1, reel 5, AJPLC. For others wanting to go north, see Richard M. Johnson to James Madison, July 24, 1812, in Padgett, ed., "Letters of Colonel Richard M. Johnson," 193. On fiscal problems and the Nashville Bank, see Peeler, "Policies of Willie Blount," 322–23. For the Bank of Nashville, also called the Nashville Bank, see "Receipt for Fifty Shares of Bank Stock," October 24, 1808, in *PAJ* 2: 200. For Jackson and the Nashville Bank: "Cashier of the Nashville Bank," February 19, 1812, sum of $1,350, ser. 1, reel 5, AJPLC; "Cashier of the Nashville Bank," July 21, 1813, sum of $750, ser. 1, reel 6, AJPLC.

24 Thomas Hart Benton to AJ, January 9, 1813, in *PAJ* 2: 355 ("joy"); AJ to William Berkeley Lewis, March 4, 1813, in *PAJ* 2: 378 ("without advice"); AJ to Felix Grundy, March 15, 1813, in *PAJ* 2: 385 ("must have been drunk"); AJ to Rachel Jackson, February 15, 1813, in *PAJ* 2: 364 (arrival and weather); John Armstrong to AJ, February 6, 1813, in *PAJ* 2: 361. For early problems of planning and strategy, see Alan Taylor, "Dual Nationalisms: Legacies of the War of 1812," in *What So Proudly We Hailed*, ed. Nivola and Kastor, 75–83; Budiansky, "War of 1812," 40–44; William B. Skelton, "High Army Leadership in the Era of the War of 1812: The Making and Remaking of the Officer Corps," *WMQ* 51 (April 1994): 253–74.

25 Thomas Hart Benton, Broadside, September 10, 1813, in *War of 1812*, ed. Hickey, 300 ("outrageous"), 301 ("So little"); Andrew Burstein, *The Passions of Andrew Jackson* (New York: Alfred A. Knopf, 2003), 93–97. See also AJ to Thomas Hart Benton, August 4, 1813, in *PAJ* 2: 418–22 and *PAJ* 2: 408n–409n. For his injuries: Reda C. Goff, "A Physical Profile of Andrew Jackson," *THQ* 28 (Fall 1969): 307–8. There is some confusion as to whether Jackson became "Old Hickory" in late 1813 or early 1814.

26 Claudio Saunt, "Domestick . . . Quiet Being Broke: Gender Conflict Among Creek Indians in the Eighteenth Century," in *Contact Points: American Frontiers from the Mohawk Valley to the Mississippi, 1750–1820*, ed. Andrew R. L. Cayton and Fredrika J. Teute (Chapel Hill: University of North Carolina Press, 1998), 151–74; Braund, *Deerskins and Duffels*, 3–25; Joshua Piker, *Okfuskee: A Creek Indian Town in Colonial*

America (Cambridge, MA: Harvard University Press, 2004), esp. 111–34; Hudson, *Creek Paths and Federal Roads*, 98–99 and 108.

27 "Extract of a Letter from an Officer in West-Tennessee to General Winchester," *The Reporter*, September 19, 1812 ("in their bosoms"); Nathaniel Millett, *The Maroons of Prospect Bluff and Their Quest for Freedom in the Atlantic World* (Gainesville: University of Florida Press, 2013), 31–47; Daniel Rasmussen, *American Uprising: The Untold Story of America's Largest Slave Revolt* (New York: Harper Collins, 2011), 167–72.

28 Kanon, *Tennesseans at War*, 68 (Craighead quote) and 194 ("extensive inland," from Rev. Charles Coffin); John Catron to AJ, June 8, 1836, in *CAJ* 5: 402 ("fever" over the Alamo in 1836 compared to response to Fort Mims); Karl Davis, "'Remember Fort Mims': Reinterpreting the Origins of the Creek War," *JER* 22 (Winter 2002): 630 (Mississippi forts), 631–32 (casualties), and 611–36; David S. Heidler and Jeanne T. Heidler, *Old Hickory's War: Andrew Jackson and the Quest for Empire* (Baton Rouge: Louisiana State University Press, 1996), 7–28.

29 AJ to Robert Grierson, November 17, 1813, in *PAJ* 2: 457 ("war of destruction"); AJ to Willie Blount, July 31, 1813, in *PAJ* 2: 417 ("drive the Indians"); AJ to Tennessee Volunteers, September 24, 1813, in *PAJ* 2: 428. See also James Robertson to AJ, March 15, 1813, ser. 1, reel 6, AJPLC.

30 AJ to John Cocke, December 28, 1813, in *PAJ* 2: 511; AJ to Leroy Pope, October 31, 1813, in *PAJ* 2: 443 ("for a wife" and Cotalla slaves); AJ to John Coffee, October 7, 1813, in *PAJ* 2: 436. See also Claudio Saunt, "Taking Account of Property: Stratification Among the Creek Indians in the Early Nineteenth Century," *WMQ* 57 (October 2000): 733–60.

31 John Coffee to AJ, October 22, 1813, in *PAJ* 2: 438 ("no pilot"); Coffee quoted in Hickey, *War of 1812: A Forgotten Conflict*, 148 ("savage fury . . . to be spared"); AJ to Thomas Pinckney, December 3, 1813, in *PAJ* 2: 465–67. For Jackson's supply problems: AJ to Thomas Flournoy, October 24, 1813, in *PAJ* 2: 441, and AJ to Gideon Blackburn, December 3, 1813, in *PAJ* 2: 465. For starvation, scarcity, and mourning among the Creeks: Robert Grierson to AJ, November 13, 1813, in *PAJ* 2: 451; Millett, *Maroons of Prospect Heights*, 38; Hudson, *Creek Paths and Federal Roads*, 87–88; Braund, *Deerskins and Duffels*, 3–25; Hobohoilthle Micco to James Madison, September 29, 1809, in *PJM* 4: 607.

32 C? Simpson to AJ, October 6, 1813, ser. 1, reel 6, AJPLC ("previously engaged"); Joshua B. Hobson to AJ, October 7, 1813, in ibid. ("some occurrences"); AJ to Second Division, March 7, 1812, in *PAJ* 2: 291 ("free born").

33 Benjamin Bradford to AJ, August 7, 1812, ser. 1, reel 5, AJPLC ("against the Villians" and "they do not like"); Robert B. Harney et al. to AJ, December 16, 1813, ser. 1, reel 7, AJPLC ("great personal," "avenge the blood," and "bare of clothing"); Ezekiel Polk to AJ, September 2, 1813, ser. 1, reel 6, AJPLC ("local principles"; Polk was denying that his men were governed by such principles); John Overton to AJ, May 8, 1814, in *PAJ* 3: 72 and 71–72. See also William Martin to AJ, November 14, 1813, ser. 1, reel 7, AJPLC.

34 AJ to John Coffee, December 9, 1813, in *CAJ* 1: 378 ("strings" and "fire"); AJ to Rachel Jackson, December 14, 1813, in *PAJ* 2: 487. See also AJ to Willie Blount, November 14, 1813, in *CAJ* 1: 345, and John Coffee to AJ, December?, 1813, ser. 1, reel 8, AJPLC, and AJ to Thomas Pinckney, December 13, 1813, in *PAJ* 2: 484–86.

35 Taylor, *Civil War of 1812*, 260 (Federalist quote) and 210–12 (Raisin River); John Lathrop, *A Discourse on the Law of Retaliation* (Boston, 1814), 14; Latimer, *1812*,

120 and 185–89 ("Remember the Raisin" and Tecumseh); Alexander Cochrane to Commanding Officers of the North American Station, July 18, 1814, in *War of 1812*, ed. Hickey, 483n ("Remember Black Rock and Buffalo!").

36 "P" [Richard E. Parker] to *Richmond Enquirer*, July 16, 1813, in *War of 1812*, ed. Hickey, 274 ("Virginian!" and "thirst"), 271 ("feelingly alive"), 275 ("irrepressible desire"); *Barbarities of the Enemy, Exposed in a Report of the Committee of the House of Representatives of the United States* (Worcester, MA, 1814), 10 ("shrieks") and 111 ("blacks"); Motion by Sen. Campbell (TN) in *AC: Senate*, 12th Congress, 2nd Session, pp. 70–71, and "Proceedings of Congress," *NWR*, February 6, 1813; Ralph Robinson, "Retaliation for the Treatment of Prisoners in the War of 1812," *AHR* 49 (October 1943): 65–70; Wittes and Singh, "James Madison, Presidential Power, and Civil Liberties," 97–121. See also "Retaliation," *The Investigator* (Charleston, SC), November 30, 1813.

37 AJ to William Carroll, February 17, 1814, in *PAJ* 3: 31 ("religiously") and 32n (eight others); George Doherty to AJ, March 2, 1814, in *PAJ* 3: 38; Thomas Pinckney to AJ, January 9, 1814, in *PAJ* 3: 13; AJ to Pinckney, March 23, 1814, in *PAJ* 3: 50. For the importance of the Thirty-Ninth, see Thomas Kanon, "'A Slow, Laborious Slaughter': The Battle of Horseshoe Bend," *THQ* 58 (Spring 1999): 2–15.

38 AJ to Rachel Jackson, January 28, 1814, in *PAJ* 3: 19 ("slaughter"); "Jesse Denson Address to the Company under Major General Andrew Jackson . . . [Dec. 9, 1813]," ser. 1, reel 7, AJPLC; Kanon, *Tennesseans at War*, 76–77. My thanks to Margaret Carlyle for her help with Denson's speech. The minister who read Coffee's report was the Reverend Thomas Nelson. See Kate White, "Knoxville's Old Educational Institutions," *THM* 8 (April 1924): 6. For the Reverend Gideon Blackburn's role, see AJ to Gideon Blackburn, December 3, 1813, in *PAJ* 2: 465, and William B. Sprague, *Annals of the American Pulpit* (9 vols., New York, 1857–69), 4: 49–50 and 43–58.

39 Jesse Denson, *The Chronicles of Andrew . . . With a Biographical Sketch of His Life* (Lexington, 1815), 6 ("mighty man" and "transgressing heathens"), 19–20 ("sweareth by the eternal"), 5 ("Ethiopians"), 17 ("all sexes and sizes"), 8 ("spareth"); Joshua 6:21, 7:24, and 11:11; Karen Armstrong, *Fields of Blood: Religion and the History of Violence* (New York: Alfred A. Knopf, 2014), 103–27.

40 AJ to Rachel Jackson, February 1, 1814, in *PAJ* 3: 23–24 ("put an end"); AJ to Rachel Jackson, January 28, 1814, in *PAJ* 3: 19 ("all things cautiously" and "my march") and 18 ("providential"); Rachel Jackson to AJ, April 7, 1814, in *PAJ* 3: 59; Kanon, "'A Slow, Laborious Slaughter,'" 4–5; Piker, *Okfuskee*, 196–204.

41 AJ to Rachel Jackson, February 21, 1814, in *PAJ* 3: 34 ("*died*," emphasis in original, and "usual firmness"); AJ to Robert Hays, January 4, 1814, in *PAJ* 3: 7 ("disgrace"); AJ to John Wood, March 14, 1814, in *PAJ* 3: 49 ("rebelious and obstinate"); Kanon, "'A Slow, Laborious Slaughter,'" 5. Executions were far more common in the regular forces. See Budiansky, "War of 1812 and the Rise of American Military Power," 44.

42 AJ to Thomas Pinckney, March 28, 1814, in *PAJ* 3: 52–53; Piker, *Okfuskee*, 196–204.

43 John Coffee to AJ, April 1, 1814, in *PAJ* 3: 56 ("squaws and Children") and 57 ("much execution"); AJ to Thomas Pinckney, March 28, 1814, in *PAJ* 3: 52 ("history of warfare") and 53 ("most tremendous"); Kanon, "'A Slow, Laborious Slaughter.'"

44 AJ to Rachel Jackson, April 1, 1814, in *PAJ* 3: 54 ("*carnage* was *dreadfull*," emphasis in original); Kanon, "'A Slow, Laborious Slaughter.'" Jackson initially reported

106 wounded and 26 killed among his white forces. See AJ to Thomas Pinckney, March 28, 1814, in *PAJ* 3: 53.

45 AJ to Rachel Jackson, December 29, 1813, in *PAJ* 2: 516 ("He is a Savage"); AJ to Rachel Jackson, February 1, 1814, in *PAJ* 3: 24 ("like an orphan"); AJ to Rachel Jackson, February 21, 1814, in *PAJ* 3: 35 ("sweet kisses"); Dawn Peterson, "Domestic Fronts in the Era of 1812: Slavery, Expansion, and Familial Struggles for Sovereignty in the Early Nineteenth-Century Choctaw South," in *Warring for America, 1803–1818*, ed. Nicole Eustace, Robert Parkinson, and Fredrika J. Teute (Chapel Hill: University of North Carolina Press, forthcoming); Rachel Meredith, "'There Was Somebody Always Dying and Leaving Jackson as Guardian': The Wards of Andrew Jackson" (MA thesis, Middle Tennessee State University, 2013), 32–41 and 77.

46 *The Life of Andrew Jackson, by John Reid and John Henry Eaton*, ed. Frank Lawrence Owsley Jr. (Tuscaloosa: University of Alabama Press, 1974), 50–51. In "civilized" war, such mercy had its equivalent in the belief that civilians should provide occupying troops with food and supplies as a reward for the army's "forbearance." See Henry, Earl Bathurst to Sir Thomas Sidney Beckwith, March 20, 1813, in *War of 1812*, ed. Hickey, 212.

47 AJ to Tennessee Troops in Mississippi Territory, April 2, 1814, in *PAJ* 3: 58 ("fiends," "orgies," and "made to atone . . . general good"); AJ to Tennessee Troops in Mississippi Territory, April 28, 1814, in *PAJ* 3: 65 ("*twenty years*," emphasis in original; "retaliatory vengeance" and "We have seen them"); Eustace, *1812*, 36–75.

48 "St. Louis," *Missouri Gazette and Illinois Advertiser*, May 28, 1814 (also cited in Kanon, *Tennesseans at War*, 106); Skelton, "High Army Leadership in the Era of the War of 1812," 267–68; [Andrew Jackson], "Address to the Cherokee and Creek Nations," August 5, 1814, in *War of 1812*, ed. Hickey, 476–78; *PAJ* 3: 67–68n; Hitsman, *Incredible War of 1812*, 206–7. The call for more regions to be "Jacksonised" was reprinted in "St. Louis, May 28," *American Commercial Daily Advertiser* (Baltimore), June 22, 1814.

49 "Treaty with the Creeks, 1814," in *IT*, 107 and 107–10; Kanon, *Tennesseans at War*, 112; Hudson, *Creek Paths and Federal Roads*, 122–23.

50 AJ to John Williams, May 18, 1814, in *PAJ* 3: 75 ("wealthy inhabitants"); Big Warrior quoted in Hudson, *Creek Paths and Federal Roads*, 120; AJ to James Monroe, November 20, 1814, in *PAJ* 3: 191–93. See also Walter Johnson, *River of Dark Dreams: Slavery and Empire in the Cotton Kingdom* (Cambridge, MA: Harvard University Press, 2013), 25–34, and Fred Anderson and Andrew Cayton, *The Dominion of War: Empire and Liberty in North America, 1500–2000* (New York: Penguin, 2005), 232–33.

51 AJ to Rachel Jackson, May 8, 1814, in *PAJ* 3: 71 ("I intend"); "Treaty with the Creeks, 1814," in *IT*, 107–10; AJ to Leroy Pope, October 31, 1813, in *PAJ* 2: 443; AJ to John Cocke, December 28, 1813, in *PAJ* 2: 511 and 512n; AJ to William Berkeley Lewis, May 20, 1814, in *PAJ* 3: 437 (letter summary; order to apply proceeds of sales of captured property to widows and orphans); AJ to John Pryor Hickman, July 16, 1814, in *PAJ* 3: 442 (letter summary; orders rations for Indians); William M. Wynne to AJ, July 17, 1814, in *PAJ* 3: 442 (letter summary; report on orphaned native). In her brilliant biography of her maternal grandparents, Pauli Murray notes that native women were sometimes sold as "mulattos." See Murray, *Proud Shoes: The Story of an American Family* (1956; Boston: Beacon Press, 1999), 38.

52 John Strachan to John Richardson, September 30, 1812, in *War of 1812*, ed. Hickey, 156 ("forbearance"); George Prevost, "A Proclamation," January 12,

1814, in ibid., 385 ("full measure") and 386 ("that system"); Alexander Cochrane to Commanding Officers of the North American Station, July 18, 1814, in ibid., 483 ("lay waste"); Henry, Earl Bathurst to Sir Thomas Sidney Beckwith, March 20, 1813, in ibid., 212 ("atrocities"); Alexander Cochrane, "A Proclamation," April 2, 1814, in ibid., 424–25 (offer); Millett, *Maroons of Prospect Bluff*, 43 and 31–47. See also Elsbeth Heaman, "Constructing Innocence: Representations of Sexual Violence in Upper Canada's War of 1812," *JCHA* 24 (2013): 114–55. My thanks to Professor Heaman for showing me an earlier version of this essay.

53 1814 quotes in Millett, *Maroons of Prospect Bluff*, 69 ("infernal combination") and 70 ("horde") and 12–30 and 48–73; [John Overton], *A Vindication of the Measures of the President and His Commanding Generals, in the Commencement and Termination of the Seminole War* (Washington, DC, 1819), 5 ("renedago").

54 Thomas Hart Benton to Thomas Flournoy, July 5, 1814, in *PAJ* 3: 84–85; AJ quoted in Millett, *Maroons of Prospect Bluff*, 57 ("exciting") and 66 ("the Colonel"); AJ to Mateo Gonzáles Manrique, August 24, 1814, in *PAJ* 3: 120 ("day of retribution"; "Matricidal"; "*Our* Christianity," emphasis in original; and "Banditti"), 121 ("Eye for an Eye"); AJ to Mateo Gonzáles Manrique, September 9, 1814, in *CAJ* 2: 45 (law of nations). See also Anderson and Cayton, *Dominion of War*, 234–36.

55 AJ quoted in Robert C. Vogel, "Jean Laffite, the Baratarians, and the Battle of New Orleans: A Reappraisal," *LH* 41 (Summer 2000): 264; Millett, *Maroons of Prospect Bluff*, 71–73; Latimer, *1812*, 369–88; Matthew Warshauer, "The Battle of New Orleans Reconsidered: Andrew Jackson and Martial Law," *LH* 39 (Summer 1998): 261–91; Douglas R. Egerton, *Death or Liberty: African Americans and Revolutionary America* (New York: Oxford University Press, 2009), 276–79.

56 Hickey, *War of 1812: A Forgotten Conflict*, 206–14; Kanon, *Tennesseans at War*, 141–42; Rasmussen, *American Uprising*, 179–82; Latimer, *1812*, 369–88; Usner Jr., "American Indians on the Cotton Frontier," 313–14; Vogel, "Jean Laffite, the Baratarians, and the Battle of New Orleans," 268n (figure of 5,200) and 261–76.

57 Kanon, *Tennesseans at War*, 166 ("evil foreboding") and 150–76; "A Kentucky Soldier's Account of the Battle of New Orleans," in *War of 1812*, ed. Hickey, 670–71.

58 Kanon, *Tennesseans at War*, 172–73 (casualties and divine intervention); Eustace, *1812*, 211–35 (alleged threat of rape). For postwar settlements, see Nivola, "The 'Party War' of 1812," 20; Taylor, *Civil War of 1812*, 409–39.

59 AJ quoted in Warshauer, "Battle of New Orleans Reconsidered," 282 ("lurking traitor") and 286–91; William H. Crawford to AJ, May 20, 1816, in *PAJ* 4: 32; "Treaty with the Cherokee, 1816," in *IT*, 125–26; Hudson, *Creek Paths and Federal Roads*, 122–23; Matthew Warshauer, *Andrew Jackson and the Politics of Martial Law: Nationalism, Civil Liberties, and Partisanship* (Knoxville: University of Tennessee Press, 2006). For the Jackson–Crawford quarrel, see also *PAJ* 4: 24n–25n.

60 William H. Crawford to AJ, May 20, 1816, in *PAJ* 4: 33 ("no great" and "act of injustice"); Crawford to AJ, June 19, 1816, in *PAJ* 4: 36n ("submission to the laws," in letter summary); Nivola, "The 'Party War' of 1812," 18; AJ to John Williams, May 18, 1814, in *PAJ* 3: 75; Frank Lawrence Owsley and Gene A. Smith, *Filibusters and Expansionists: Jeffersonian Manifest Destiny, 1800–21* (Tuscaloosa: University of Alabama Press, 1997), 80; Jane Twitty Shelton, *Pines and Pioneers: A History of Lowndes County, Georgia 1825–1900* (Atlanta: Cherokee Publishing Company, 1976), 19, 30–35, 47–53; Kenneth Coleman, "The Expanding Frontier Economy,

1782–1820," in *A History of Georgia*, ed. Coleman (2nd ed., Athens: University of Georgia Press, 1991), 105–15.

61 AJ to William H. Crawford, April 24, 1816, in *PAJ* 4: 26 ("*Land Pirates*," emphasis in original); "General Edmund P. Gaines's Official Report of the Battle of Fort Erie," August 15, 1814, in Notes and Queries, *PMHB* 21 (1897): 264 ("*majestically* splendid," emphasis in original); AJ to Edmund P. Gaines, April 8, 1816, in *CAJ* 2: 239 ("restore the stolen negroes"); Joshua R. Giddings, *The Exiles of Florida* (Columbus, 1858), 36–38. On Gaines's early career: "The Capture of Aaron Burr," *AHM* 1 (April 1896), 140–53. Crawford and Hawkins agreed with Jackson about the Negro Fort: William H. Crawford to AJ, March 15, 1816, in *PAJ* 4: 16, and Millett, *Maroons of Prospect Bluff*, 214–30. See also Edmund P. Gaines to AJ, December 2, 1817, in *PAJ* 4: 154; Parton, *Life of Andrew Jackson*, 2: 397–407; and "Apalachicola," *NWR*, September 14, 1816.

62 Millett, *The Maroons of Prospect Bluff*, 227–28 and 214–30 generally; Benjamin W. Crowinshield to Daniel T. Patterson, January 22, 1816, in *Letter from the Secretary of the Navy . . . Sundry Documents Relating to the Destruction of the Negro Fort* (Washington, DC, 1819); Patterson to Crowinshield, August 15, 1816, in ibid.; Owsley and Smith, *Filibusters and Expansionists*, 103–17. After the Battle of Fort Erie in August 1814, some soldiers wondered if their commanders had used a "train" to ignite the British magazine. Gaines made no mention of this in his report, and it is hard to imagine how he could have rigged anything outside the well-guarded Negro Fort. Then again, it is hard to imagine how such an (un)lucky shot could have demolished the fort. See Jarvis Hanks: Memoir [1831], in *War of 1812*, ed. Hickey, 474–75, and Taylor, *Civil War of 1812*, 396–99.

63 "From General Gaines to the Seminoly Chief," in "Trial of Arbuthnot and Ambrister," *NWR*, December 12, 1818, 272; Edmund P. Gaines to AJ, November 21, 1817, in *PAJ* 4: 150 ("deep regret"); Gaines to AJ, December 2, 1817, in *PAJ* 4: 154 ("pale of natural law") and 155n; "From King Hatchy to General Gaines, in Answer to the Foregoing," in "Trial of Arbuthnot and Ambrister," *NWR*, December 12, 1818, 272; John K. Mahon, "The First Seminole War, November 21, 1817–May 24, 1818," *FHQ* 77 (Summer 1998): 62–67; Alcione M. Amos, "Captain Hugh Young's Map of Jackson's 1818 Seminole Campaign in Florida," *FHQ* 55 (January 1977): 336–46; Millett, *Maroons of Prospect Bluff*, 144 and 231–49.

64 James Monroe to John Taylor, June 13, 1812, in *War of 1812*, ed. Hickey, 35; AJ to James Monroe, January 6, 1818, in *PAJ* 4: 167, 165–66n; Daniel Feller, "The Seminole Controversy Revisited: A New Look at Andrew Jackson's 1818 Florida Campaign," *FHQ* 88 (Winter 2010): 316 ("preserve with care") and 309–25. For AJ's concern about enemy ships moving up Florida rivers, see Entry of February 3, 1819, in *MJQA* 4: 239.

65 "A Short biographical Sketch of the Undersigned by Himself," John Banks Diary, HRB; Mahon, "First Seminole War," 62–67; "Indian War," *NWR*, July 11, 1818. Banks says that volunteers were pressed into service from among the militia.

66 [Andrew Jackson], "Address to the Cherokee and Creek Nations," August 5, 1814, in *War of 1812*, ed. Hickey, 478; Alexander Arbuthnot to Officer Commanding at Ft. Gaines, March 3, 1817, in Letters Received by the Office of the Secretary of War Relating to Indian Affairs, roll 2, 1817–19, NA ("infortunate"); Testimony of John [?] Arbuthnot, April 27, 1818, in "Trial of Arbuthnot and Ambrister," *NWR*, December 12, 1818, 279 ("righted"). See also Owsley and Smith, *Filibusters and Expansionists*, 141–63. Ambrister's father stated that Robert had been born in New Providence in 1797; American witnesses called him "young, not exceeding

25." See Memorial of James Ambrister, in "Arbuthnot and Ambrister," *NWR*, October 3, 1818, 84 and "Milledgeville, Ga., May 26," *NWR*, June 13, 1818. See also Millett, *Maroons of Prospect Bluff*, 237–38 and 193, and Hudson, *Creek Paths and Federal Roads*, 117.

67 "Trial of Arbuthnot and Ambrister," *NWR*, December 12, 1818, 270 ("special court") and 270–78; Remarks of Rep. Mercer (VA), January 26, 1819, in *AC: House*, January 26, 1819, 15th Congress, 2nd Session, p. 807 (description of St. Marks and vicinity). See also Owsley and Smith, *Filibusters and Expansionists*, 111–12 and 141–63; Frank L. Owsley Jr., "Ambrister and Arbuthnot: Adventurers or Martyrs for British Honor?," *JER* 5 (Autumn 1985): 289–308; and Deborah A. Rosen, "Wartime Prisoners and the Rule of Law: Andrew Jackson's Military Tribunals During the First Seminole War," *JER* 28 (Winter 2008): 559–95.

68 "Trial of Arbuthnot and Ambrister," *NWR*, December 12, 1818, 278 ("negroes and Indians"), 281 ("established principle"); "Milledgeville, Ga., May 26," in *NWR*, June 13, 1818, 269 ("more like a woman"); AJ letter to Secretary of War, May 5, 1818 ("certain, if slow retribution") quoted in Remarks of Rep. Sawyer (NC) in *AC: House*, January 25, 1819, 15th Congress, 2nd Session, p. 784; AJ letter to Rachel from June 2, 1818, quoted in Burstein, *Passions of Andrew Jackson*, 218–19; Rosen, "Wartime Prisoners and the Rule of Law," 563 and 563n.

69 Andrew Jackson to Governor Rabun, May 7, 1818, in "Gov. Rabun and Gen. Jackson," *NWR*, December 5, 1818, 254 ("monster" and "*bleeding scalps*," emphasis in original); "The Chehaw Village," *NWR*, June 20, 1818, 292 ("take any satisfaction," paraphrase of Jackson's message of May 7). For various accounts, see "Destruction of the Chehaw Village," *NWR*, June 13, 1818, 267–68 and Obed Wright to Gov. Rabun, April 25, 1818, in "Expedition Against the Chehaws," *NWR*, May 23, 1818, 218; "Short Biographical Sketch," Banks Diary, 30. For Jackson's poor health, see Mahon, "First Seminole War," 66.

70 Entry of June 25, 1818, in *MJQA* 4: 103 ("unexpected" and British and Spanish protests); Entries of July 7 and 8, in *MJQA* 4: 105 (French reaction); Entries of July 13 and 15, in *MJQA* 4: 107–9 (Calhoun and Monroe reactions); Entry of February 3, 1819, in *MJQA* 4: 239–40 (Crawford motives according to AJ). See also Lynn Hudson Parsons, "'A Perpetual Harrow upon My Feelings': John Quincy Adams and the American Indian," *NEQ* 46 (September 1973): 339–79; Greg Russell, "John Quincy Adams and the Ethics of America's National Interest," *RIS* 19 (January 1993): 23–38; William B. Skelton, "The Commanding General and the Problem of Command in the United States Army, 1821–1841," *MA* 34 (December 1970): 117–22, and Skelton, "High Army Leadership in the Era of the War of 1812," 267–68; Feller, "The Seminole Controversy Revisited," 314. For Crawford and the caucus: Thomas Coens, "The Early Jackson Party: A Force for Democratization?," *A Companion to the Era of Andrew Jackson*, ed. Sean Patrick Adams (Malden, MA: Blackwell Publishing, 2013), *Blackwell Reference Online*.

71 Adams quoted in Robert R. Thompson, "John Quincy Adams, Apostate: From 'Outrageous Federalist' to 'Republican Exile,' 1801–1809," *JER* 11 (Summer 1991): 176 ("British piratical"), and see 161–83; Entry for July 21, 1818, in *MJQA* 4: 115 ("shock"); "Indian War," *NWR*, July 11, 1818; Eunice Barber, *Narrative of the Tragical Death of Darius Barber and His Seven Children* (Boston, 1818), front matter (quote) and 5. See also Lynn Hudson Parsons, *The Birth of Modern Politics: Andrew Jackson, John Quincy Adams, and the Election of 1828* (New York: Oxford University Press, 2009), 56, and for other postwar atrocity stories, *Narrative of*

the Captivity and Sufferings of Mrs. Hannah Lewis and Her Three Children (Boston, 1817), 3, and *The Indian Captive; Or a Narrative of the Captivity and Sufferings of Zadock Steele* (Montpelier, 1818), 6–10.

72 Entry for November 8, 1818, in *MJQA* 4: 168 ("highest order"); John Quincy Adams to George William Erving, November 28, 1818, in *WJQA* 6: 480 ("receptacle" and "nuisance"), 482 ("mingled horde"), 495 ("exterminating war"). On the "necessary" law of nations, see David Armitage, "The Declaration of Independence and International Law," *WMQ* 59 (January 2002): 39–64. On nuisances, see William J. Novak, *The People's Welfare: Law and Regulation in Nineteenth-Century America* (Chapel Hill: University of North Carolina Press, 1996).

73 John Quincy Adams to Erving, November 28, 1818, in *WJQA* 6: 481–82 ("No sooner . . . all the horrors of savage war"), 487 ("written in every page"), 486 ("purest patriotism"), 497–98 (graphic details). For the importance of Psalm 137, which anticipates the day when the Israelites' enemies will see their infants' heads dashed against rocks, see Melissa J. Gismondi, "The Character of a Wife: Rachel Jackson and the Search for Zion, 1760s–1820s" (PhD dissertation, University of Virginia, forthcoming).

74 Report cited in "Congress," *NWR*, January 16, 1819; Remarks by Rep. Poindexter (Miss.), January 12, 1819, in *AC: House*, 15th Congress, 2nd Session, p. 528 ("forget the wrongs") and 517–28 (first exchanges); Remarks by Rep. Tallmadge (NY), January 22, 1819, in *AC: House*, 15th Congress, 2nd Session, p. 711 ("great national question"). The *Supplement to Volume XV of Niles Weekly Register* reproduces the full text of eight speeches (Cobb, Holmes, Clay, Johnson-KY, Smyth, Mercer, Tallmadge, and Rhea). Discussions include Rosen, "Wartime Prisoners and the Rule of Law," and Rosen, *Border Law: The First Seminole War and American Nationhood* (Cambridge, MA: Harvard University Press, 2015); David S. Heidler, "The Politics of National Aggression: Congress and the First Seminole War," *JER* 13 (Winter 1993): 501–30; Anderson and Cayton, *Dominion of War*, 238–46; Stephen Skowronek, *The Politics Presidents Make: Leadership from John Adams to George Bush* (Cambridge, MA: Harvard University Press, 1993), 94–98. The line "Whenever severity is not an absolute necessity, mercy becomes a duty" is from Vattel, *Law of Nations,* Book III, chapter 8, §141, p. 544, with slight variations in phrasing.

75 Remarks by Rep. Tyler (VA), February 1, 1819, in *AC: House*, 15th Congress, 2nd Session, p. 928 ("desolating"); Entry for December 25, 1818, in *MJQA* 4: 198 ("high sticklers" and "all Virginia"); Remarks by Rep. Colston (VA), January 26, 1819, in *AC: House*, 15th Congress, 2nd Session, p. 824 ("degradation"); Remarks of Rep. Clay, January 20, 1819, in ibid., p. 644 ("attribute"); Remarks by Rep. Cobb, January 18, 1819, in ibid., p. 587 ("placed upon"). The anti-Jackson speakers from Virginia were Tyler, Colston, James Johnson, and Charles F. Mercer. See also Heidler, "The Politics of National Aggression." Jonathan Booth categorized the congressmen by region, age, and political affiliation, and found that the clearly anti-Jackson delegates were effectively the same age as the clearly pro-Jackson ones (44.5 years vs. 46.1 years). Here again I thank Booth for his fine research. Five anti-Jackson speakers were under the age of 40: Thomas Cobb (GA), Henry Storrs (NY), Edward Colston (VA), William Lowndes (SC), and John Tyler (VA). James Johnson's (VA) age is unknown. The anti-Jackson speakers Henry Clay and Charles Fenton Mercer were under 45. In a subsequent letter, Adams noted that Virginia was "divided against herself." See John Quincy Adams to John Adams, February 14, 1819, in *WJQA* 6: 530 and 528–32.

76 See Remarks of Rep. Mercer, January 26, 1819, in *AC: House*, 15th Congress, 2nd Session, pp. 808–11; Millett, *Maroons of Prospect Bluff*, 229.

77 Remarks by Rep. Clay, January 20, 1819, in *AC: House*, 15th Congress, 2nd Session, p. 634 ("wretched" and "miserable") and 634–35 ("*their* prophets," emphasis in original); Remarks by Rep. Hopkinson, January 29, 1819, in ibid., 877 ("beggarly"); Merrill D. Peterson, *The Great Triumvirate: Webster, Clay, and Calhoun* (New York: Oxford University Press, 1987), 11 and 55–56.

78 Remarks by Rep. Cobb, January 18, 1819, in *AC: House*, 15th Congress, 2nd Session, p. 588 ("In one day"); Remarks by Rep. Mercer, January 26, 1819, in ibid., p. 823; Douglas R. Egerton, "To the Tombs of the Capulets: Charles Fenton Mercer and Public Education in Virginia, 1816–1817," *VMHB* 93 (April 1985): 155–74.

79 Remarks by Rep. Hopkinson, January 29, 1819, in *AC: House*, 15th Congress, 2nd Session, p. 873; Francis Hopkinson, "On Duelling," in *The Miscellaneous Essays and Occasional Writings of Francis Hopkinson* (3 vols., Philadelphia, 1792), 2: 24–33.

80 Remarks by Rep. Baldwin (Pa.), February 5, 1819, in *AC: House*, 15th Congress, 2nd Session, p. 1041 ("beyond protection"); Remarks by Rep. Tallmadge, January 23, 1819, in ibid., p. 729 ("a prophet"); Remarks by Rep. Strother (VA), January 27, 1819, in ibid., p. 839 ("forbearance" and "rose in majesty"); Remarks by Rep. Smyth, January 21, 1819, in ibid., p. 697 ("are we alone") and pp. 674–703 (Vattel citations throughout speech).

81 Remarks by Rep. Tallmadge, January 22, 1819, in *AC: House*, 15th Congress, 2nd Session, p. 716; Remarks by Rep. Holmes, January 19, 1819, in ibid., p. 615. Holmes had voiced some of these themes before: John Holmes, *An Oration, Pronounced at Alfred, on the Fourth of July, 1815* (Boston, 1815). See also Rosen, *Border Law*, and Robert Pierce Forbes, *The Missouri Compromise and Its Aftermath: Slavery and the Meaning of America* (Chapel Hill: University of North Carolina Press, 2007).

82 Remarks by Rep. Barbour, January 25, 1819, in *AC: House*, 15th Congress, 2nd Session, p. 777 ("scene of innocence" and "family group"); Remarks by Rep. Smyth, January 21, 1819, in ibid., 702 ("great and fundamental"). See also Remarks by Rep. Rhea (TN), January 27, 1819, in ibid., 862, in which Rhea cites "The *salus populi* . . . the supreme, irrevocable law of nations."

83 Remarks by Rep. Ervin (SC), February 8, 1819, in *AC: House*, 15th Congress, 2nd Session, p. 1121 ("characters of blood"); Remarks by Rep. Poindexter, February 2, 1819, in ibid., p. 955 ("all occasions"); Remarks by Rep. Smyth, January 21, 1819, in ibid., 702 ("appointed by Heaven").

84 Jonathan Roberts and Philip S. Klein, "Notes and Documents: Memoirs of a Senator from Pennsylvania: Jonathan Roberts, 1771–1854," *PMHB* 62 (July 1938): 403 ("ruffians"), and see also Jonathan Roberts to Nathan Roberts, January 24, 1819, and February 10, 1819, box 3, Jonathan Roberts Papers, 1780–1930, HSP; Parton, *Life of Andrew Jackson*, 2: 561–62 and 570; Goff, "Physical Profile of Andrew Jackson," 297–99; Burstein, *Passions of Andrew Jackson*, 138–39 (portraits); *PAJ* 4: xxxvi (purchases Sally). I cannot confirm or disprove the rumor about AJ and the ears of his critics, but he definitely considered a duel with Senator Eppes. See Entry for November 5, 1819, in *MJQA* 4: 433–34.

85 Remarks by Rep. Smyth, January 21, 1819, in *AC: House*, 15th Congress, 2nd Session, p. 702 ("great avenger"). Smyth specifically asked the Pennsylvania delegates to "remember Wyoming" and other atrocities from the Revolutionary War. For the votes: February 8, 1819, in *AC: House*, 15th Congress, 2nd Session, pp. 1132–38. For state legislatures' approval of Jackson: Rosen, "Wartime Prisoners and the Rule of Law," 576n–577n. The House took a number of votes on separate resolutions from individual members and the Committee on Military Affairs. The most telling: Did the House disapprove of the trial and execution of

Ambrister and Arbuthnot? No, 50–94. (Subsequent votes by the entire House, not just the Committee of the Whole, were similar, 62–108 refusing to condemn Arbuthnot's execution and 63–107 refusing to condemn Ambrister's death.) And: Was the seizure of Pensacola and St. Carlos de Barrancas unconstitutional? No, 65–91 (70–100 for the entire House). See also Parton, *Life of Andrew Jackson,* 2: 549–50, and Remini, *Andrew Jackson and the Course of American Empire,* 374–75.

86 [Overton], *A Vindication of the Measures of the President and His Commanding Generals,* 50 ("Indian wars," original in quotes), 27 ("*natural . . . perfect,*" emphases in original), 94 ("*golden age,*" emphasis in original); John Overton to AJ, February 12, 1814, in *PAJ*, 3: 29; Overton to AJ, May 8, 1814, in *PAJ*, 3: 72 and 71–72. For Overton's 1818 defense of Jackson in the *Nashville Whig*, see *PAJ* 9: 54n.

CHAPTER 6

1 AJ [and other Indian Commissioners] to William H. Crawford, September 20, 1816, in *PAJ* 4: 66 ("alarmed" and bribes); AJ to John Coffee, September 19, 1816, in *PAJ* 4: 63 ("firm and decided") and 64 ("no reservation"); William H. Crawford to the Senate, March 14, 1816, *ASP: Indian Affairs* 2: 28; AJ to John Coffee, December 26, 1816, in *PAJ* 4: 77; Alan Taylor, *The Civil War of 1812: American Citizens, British Subjects, Irish Rebels, and Indian Allies* (New York: Vintage Books, 2010), 429 (Crawford on Ohio and Michigan). See also "Treaty with the Chickasaw, 1816" and "Treaty with the Chickasaw, 1818," in *IT*, 135–37 and 174–77, and Walter Johnson, *River of Dark Dreams: Slavery and Empire in the Cotton Kingdom* (Cambridge, MA: Harvard University Press, 2013), 25–34.

2 AJ to John Coffee, February 13, 1816, in *PAJ* 4: 12 ("bring into" and permission to begin surveying), and AJ to Coffee, December 26, 1816, *PAJ* 4: 77; AJ to James Monroe, November 12, 1816, in *PAJ* 4: 74 ("deeply impressed"); AJ to Monroe, October 23, 1816, *PAJ* 4: 69–70; Giles County, Petition #140, October 15, 1819, ser. 3, roll 6, TLP ("heathen lands"); [Sundry inhabitants to General Assembly], September 11, 1819, in ibid. ("more Equal" and "all the wars"). See also Petition of a Number of Inhabitants of Blount County, Petition #32, 1813, ser. 2, roll 4, TLP; and Hiawassee Settlement, Petition #8, 1821, ser. 4, roll 7, TLP; Robert E. Corlew, *Tennessee: A Short History* (2nd ed., Knoxville: University of Tennessee Press, 1981), 154–58.

3 AJ to John Hutchings, April 22, 1816, in *CAJ* 2: 241 ("conditional contracts" and sugar estates); AJ to Francis Smith, March 29, 1817, in *PAJ* 4: 105 ("to the capitalist"); "Application of Alabama for the Relief of Certain Purchasers of Public Lands," January 10, 1835, in *ASP: Public Lands* 7: 655 ("extravagant" and "unreal," referring to 1818). For Jackson's modest role in the Marathon and Cypress Land Companies, see *PAJ* 4: 176n–177n. See also AJ to John Coffee, February 2, 1816, in *PAJ* 4: 6–7, and Arthur Peronneau Hayne to AJ, August 5, 1817, in *PAJ* 4: 131; S. F. Horn, *The Hermitage: Home of Old Hickory* (Nashville, 1950), 18–23; Mark R. Cheathem, *Andrew Jackson, Southerner* (Baton Rouge: Louisiana State University Press, 2013), 91. There is no direct evidence that the wallpaper was manufactured in France, but French producers and styles were pre-eminent in the early nineteenth century. See Ada K. Longfield, "History of the Dublin Wall-Paper Industry in the 18th Century," *JRSAI* 77 (December 1947): 104–5, and Longfield, "Old Wall-Papers and Wall-Paintings in Ireland, III: Some More Chinese, French, and English Examples," *JRSAI* 80 (July 1950): 187–92. AJ made a point of replacing the wallpaper after a major fire at the Hermitage in 1834. See "Bill for Furnishing the Hermitage," January 2, 1836, in *CAJ* 5: 382–83. My thanks to Marsha Mullin for her help here.

4 AJ to Isaac Shelby, November 24, 1818, in *PAJ* 4: 250, 250n; Daniel Feller, *The Public Lands in Jacksonian Politics, 1815–1840* (Madison: University of Wisconsin Press, 1984), 18 ($4 million); Robert M. Blackson, "Pennsylvania Banks and the Panic of 1819: A Reinterpretation," *JER* 9 (Autumn 1989): 338; Andrew Shankman, "'A New Thing on Earth': Alexander Hamilton, Pro-Manufacturing Republicans, and the Democratization of American Political Economy," *JER* 23 (Autumn 2003): 344–45; Sandra F. VanBurkleo, "'The Paws of Banks': The Origins and Significance of Kentucky's Decision to Tax Federal Bankers, 1818–1820," *JER* 9 (Winter 1989): 457–87. For Tennessee and Virginia see Murray N. Rothbard, *The Panic of 1819: Reactions and Policies* (New York: Columbia University Press, 1962), 90–97, and Harry Ammon, "The Richmond Junto, 1800–1824," *VMHB* 61 (October 1953): 395–418. See also Reeve Huston, "Land Conflict and Labor Policy in the United States, 1785–1841," in *The World of the Revolutionary American Republic: Land, Labor, and the Conflict for a Continent*, ed. Andrew Shankman (New York: Routledge, 2014), 334.

5 Tench Coxe quoted in Martin Öhman, "Perfecting Independence: Tench Coxe and the Political Economy of Western Development," *JER* 31 (Fall 2011): 432 (emphasis in original), and see 397–433; Robert Conrad, *The Destruction of Brazilian Slavery, 1850–1888* (Berkeley: University of California Press, 1972), 283 (figure of two million); Edwin J. Perkins, "Langdon Cheves and the Panic of 1819: A Reassessment," *JEH* 44 (June 1984): 455–61. For cotton competitors and prices: Matthew Carey, *Address to Congress: Being a View of the Ruinous Consequences of a Dependence on Foreign Markets* (Philadelphia, 1820), 391, and Carey, *The Crisis: A Solemn Appeal . . . on the Destructive Tendency of the Present Policy of this Country* (Philadelphia, 1823), 25–26. See also Cathy Matson, "Matthew Carey's Learning Experience: Commerce, Manufacturing, and the Panic of 1819," *EAS* 11 (Fall 2013): 455–85. For earlier "panics," see Richard S. Chew, "Certain Victims of an International Contagion: The Panic of 1797 and the Hard Times of the Late 1790s in Baltimore," *JER* 25 (Winter 2005): 565–613, and Jane Kamensky, *The Exchange Artist: A Tale of High-Flying Speculation and America's First Banking Collapse* (New York: Penguin, 2008).

6 Tennessee newspaper from April 1820 as quoted in Charles G. Sellers Jr., "Banking and Politics in Jackson's Tennessee, 1817–1827," *MVHR* 41 (June 1954): 69 ("horse-leeches"), and see 61–84; Matthew Carey, *Essays on Political Economy* (Philadelphia, 1822), 259 ("radically wrong," from his 1821 essay, "The New Olive Branch"); Report by Felix Grundy, September 21, 1821, in *Journal of the House of Representatives at the First Session of the Fourteenth General Assembly of the State of Tennessee* (Nashville, 1821), 50. See also Petition #36, June 15, 1820, ser. 3, roll 6, TLP and Farmers' and Mechanics' Bank of Indiana to William H. Crawford, June 14, 1820, in *ASP: Finances* 3: 739–41. Number of failed banks from Thomas H. Greer, "Economic and Social Effects of the Depression of 1819 in the Old Northwest," *IMH* 44 (September 1948): 230.

7 James Monroe, "Fourth Annual Message," November 14, 1820, in *CMP* 2: 74; Calhoun quoted in Daniel Peart, *Era of Experimentation: American Political Practices in the Early Republic* (Charlottesville: University of Virginia Press, 2014), 137; Charles Sellers, *The Market Revolution: Jacksonian America, 1815–1846* (New York: Oxford University Press, 1991), 163–71; Sean Wilentz, *The Rise of American Democracy: From Jefferson to Lincoln* (New York: W. W. Norton and Company, 2005), 181–217; Priscilla Ferguson Clement, "The Philadelphia Welfare Crisis of the 1820s," *PMHB* 105 (April 1981): 150–65; Samuel Rezneck,

"The Depression of 1819–22, A Social History," *AHR* 39 (October 1933): 28–47; Andrew R. L. Cayton, "The Fragmentation of 'A Great Family': The Panic of 1819 and the Rise of the Middling Interest in Boston, 1818–1822," *JER* 2 (Summer 1982): 143–67; Janet A. Riesman, "Republican Revisions: Political Economy in New York After the Panic of 1819," in *New York and the Rise of American Capitalism*, ed. William Pencak and Conrad E. Wright (New York: New York Historical Society, 1989), 1–44.

8 Carey, *Essays on Political Economy*, 320 ("noble") and 319–21; Banker quoted in Donald F. Carmony and Sam K. Swope, "From Lycoming County, Pennsylvania, to Parke County, Indiana: Recollections of Andrew TenBrook, 1786–1823," *IMH* 61 (March 1965): 4; Feller, *Public Lands*, 8–9 (payment terms).

9 Feller, *Public Lands*, 18–27; William H. Crawford to the several receivers of public money in Ohio, Indiana, Illinois, Missouri, and Michigan, August 1, 1820, in *ASP: Finances* 3: 728; Crawford, "State of the Finances, Communicated to the Senate," December 5, 1820, in ibid., 3: 547–53. On Crawford's career, see also Philip J. Green, "William H. Crawford and the Bank of the United States," *GHQ* 23 (December 1939): 337–50; Green, "William H. Crawford and the War of 1812," *GHQ* 26 (March 1942): 16–39; Lawrence S. Kaplan, "The Paris Mission of William Harris Crawford, 1813–1815," *GHQ* 60 (Spring 1976): 9–22; Peart, *Era of Experimentation*, 111–12; Brian Schoen, "Calculating the Price of Union: Republican Economic Nationalism and the Origins of Southern Sectionalism, 1790–1828," *JER* 23 (Summer 2003): 173–206, esp. 194; George R. Lamplugh, "'Oh the Colossus! The Colossus!': James Jackson and the Jeffersonian Republican Party in Georgia, 1796–1806," *JER* 9 (Autumn 1989): 315–34.

10 James Hall, *Notes on the Western States* (Philadelphia, 1838), 174 ("rigid creditor"), 175 ("whole population"); Remarks by Sen. Johnson (Ky.), January 22, 1821, *AC: Senate*, 16th Congress, 2nd Session, p. 218 ("awful suspense"); Crawford, "State of the Finances, Communicated to the Senate," in *ASP: Finances* 3: 551; Merrill D. Peterson, *The Great Triumvirate: Webster, Clay, and Calhoun* (New York: Oxford University Press, 1987), 67 (Clay casework as of February 1821); Feller, *Public Lands*, 10 (repayment and forfeiture).

11 Crawford, "State of the Finances, Communicated to the Senate," in *ASP: Finances* 3: 551; Monroe, "Fourth Annual Message," in *CMP* 2: 78; "An Act for the Relief of the Purchasers of Public Lands Prior to the First Day of July, Eighteen Hundred and Twenty," March 2, 1821, 3 *SL* 612–14; "Acts Which Have Been Passed for the Relief of Purchasers of Public Lands," in *The Public Statutes of the United States: Volume IV*, ed. Richard Peters (Boston, 1846), 259n. Thirteen separate statutes are listed, one a supplemental bill and the other prescribing how lands that revert to the public were to be resold. For Georgia land laws see Lamplugh, "'Oh the Colossus!"; for Spanish comparison, see Remarks by Rep. Metcalf (Ky.), February 26, 1821, in *AC: House*, 16th Congress, 2nd Session, pp. 1231–32. Consult also Feller, *Public Lands*, 35–38; Hugh C. Bailey, "John W. Walker and the Land Laws of the 1820s," *AH* 32 (April 1958): 120–26; and Paul W. Gates, "Tenants of the Log Cabin," *MVHR* 49 (June 1962): 3–31.

12 "The Augusta Address," *St. Louis Enquirer*, May 31, 1823 ("judicious"); Hall, *Notes on the Western States*, 175 ("not easy to imagine"); William E. Bartelt, "The Land Dealings of Spencer County, Indiana, Pioneer Thomas Lincoln," *IMH* 87 (September 1991): 215 (debt figures) and 211–23. For the achievements of the Sixteenth Congress: Feller, *Public Lands*, 36. For votes in Congress: February 10, 1821, in *AC: Senate*, 16th Congress, 2nd Session, p. 333, and February 28, 1821,

in *AC: House*, 16th Congress, 2nd Session, p. 1249. See also Michael Burlingame, *Abraham Lincoln: A Life* (2 vols., Baltimore: Johns Hopkins University Press, 2008), 1: 22–51. Jonathan Roberts of Pennsylvania, an eccentric Jeffersonian who was horrified by Andrew Jackson's violence and was one of the five nays in the Senate's 1821 vote, was in contact with Crawford at this time. Roberts stressed the need to avoid new debts and taxes. See Jonathan Roberts to Nathan Roberts, January 12, 1821, and February 12, 1821, in Jonathan Roberts Papers, 1780–1920, box 3, HSP.

13 AJ to John Coffee, December 31, 1823, in *PAJ* 5: 333 ("great curse"); AJ to Andrew Jackson Donelson, January 21, 1824, in *PAJ* 5: 343 (sales of relinquished land in northern Alabama too slow); AJ to John Coffee, July 26, 1821, in *PAJ* 5: 83 (relinquishment for himself and for Andrew Hutchings); AJ to James Jackson, August 2, 1821, in *PAJ* 5: 92. The very bad feelings between AJ and Crawford were mutual. See Entry of March 13, 1820, in *MJQA* 5: 22. In June 1820, Jackson's friend Arthur Peronneau Hayne had written from Alabama, reporting, "We find ourselves very much in debt in this Country to the United States, for land." He wanted to know AJ's thoughts on "the plan, which in your opinion the Govt ought to adopt and extend." I cannot determine if AJ offered his thoughts, but in Hayne's next letter there is no mention of the subject. See Hayne to AJ, June 10, 1820, ser. 1, reel 29, AJPLC, and Hayne to AJ, August 6, 1820, in ibid.

14 "Public Meeting," *St. Louis Enquirer*, June 9, 1819 ("numerous" and "general welfare"). Grundy outlined his proposals on September 21, 1819, and they dominated the session. On November 2, eleven members voted to enable holders of bank notes to sue for the property of bank stockholders. Grundy opposed this. See *Journal of the House of Representatives at the First Session of the Thirteenth General Assembly of the State of Tennessee* (Murfreesborough, 1819), 22–23, 131–33, and 236, and *Nashville Gazette*, November 10, 1819. For the stay law: "An Act Regulating Proceedings on Judgements and for Other Purposes," in *Acts of a Public or General Nature, Passed at the First Session of the Thirteenth General Assembly of the State of Tennessee* (Nashville, 1819), 44–45. Pleasant M. Miller of Knox County was a hold-out against relief of all kinds. On November 30, 1819, however, he introduced a Pennsylvania proposal that would have kept Congress from forming any bank outside of the District of Columbia, a clear attack on the BUS branch offices. See *Journal of the House . . . of the Thirteenth General Assembly*, 112, 236, and 298–99. The total number of votes cast for state representative in Davidson County jumped from 2,179 (1,339 vs. 840) in 1817 to 3,082 (1,163 vs. 991 vs. 928) in 1819. Although population increase in Davidson (some 29% between 1810 and 1820) accounts for some of this jump, voter turnout was volatile in the county, surging during the War of 1812 before actually declining in 1817. From 1819 to 1821, voter turnout again jumped 31% before stabilizing. See "Tennessee 1817 House of Representatives, Davidson County" and "Tennessee 1819 House of Representatives, Davidson County," in *A New Nation Votes: American Election Returns, 1787–1825*, dl.tufts.edu/about/a_new_nation_votes (accessed October 15, 2016). The panic played havoc with county politics all over Tennessee, sometimes multiplying the number of candidates and sometimes consolidating a single leader's hold on power.

15 Governor's Address to Special Session of General Assembly, June 26, 1820, in box 1, Governor's Papers: Joseph McMinn, 1815–1821, TSLA; William G. Leger, "The Administration of John Adair" (MA thesis, University of Kentucky, 1951), 21–35; Message from Lt. Governor and Acting Governor, December 8, 1818, *Journal of*

the House of Representatives of the Commonwealth of Kentucky (Frankfort, 1819), 16–18; Rothbard, *Panic of 1819*, 42–45; VanBurkleo, "'The Paws of Banks'"; Harry R. Stevens, "Henry Clay, the Bank, and the West in 1824," *AHR* 60 (July 1955): 843–48; Perry McCandless, *A History of Missouri, Volume II: 1820 to 1860* (Columbia: University of Missouri Press, 1972), 2: 23–30.

16 "A Friend of the People," *Carthage Gazette and Friend of the People*, February 13, 1809 ("in force every day"); [McMinn], Address to Fellow-Citizens, September 18, 1821, in *Journal of the House of Representatives at the . . . Fourteenth General Assembly*, 17 ("happiest"); Address by Gabriel Slaughter, Lt. Governor, December 8, 1818, in *Journal of the House of Representatives of the Commonwealth of Kentucky* (Frankfort, 1818), 19 ("visitorial" and "safety,"); Adair quoted in Leger, "Administration of John Adair," 39 ("fatal tendency"); "Public Meeting," *St. Louis Enquirer*, June 9, 1819 ("merciful forbearance" and "*general* calamity," emphasis in original); "Execution Law," *The Enquirer* (Richmond), February 1, 1820 ("*legal process*," emphasis in original, and "Creditors must take"); Sandra Frances VanBurkleo, "'That Our Pure Republican Principles Might Not Wither': Kentucky's Relief Crisis and the Pursuit of 'Moral Justice,' 1818–1826" (PhD dissertation, University of Minnesota, 1988).

17 [McMinn], Governor's Address to Special Session of General Assembly, June 26, 1820; Nashville supporters quoted in John Wooldridge, *History of Nashville, Tenn.* (Nashville, 1890), 266 ("New Bank"); Grand Jury quoted in William Graham Sumner et al., *A History of Banking in all the Leading Nations: The United States* (4 vols., New York, 1896), 1: 149 ("barely tolerated"); Kentucky supporter quoted in VanBurkleo, "'The Paws of Banks,'" 485 ("republican bank"); Rothbard, *Panic of 1819*, 57–111. McMinn's 1820 speech is also in *Journal of the House of Representatives at the Second Session of the Thirteenth General Assembly of the State of Tennessee* (Murfreesborough, 1820), 6–17.

18 [McMinn], Address to Fellow-Citizens, September 18, 1821, in *Journal of the House of Representatives at the . . . Fourteenth General Assembly*, 8 ("economical"); [McMinn], Governor's Address to Special Session of General Assembly, June 26, 1820 ("common destinies" and "schemes of national prosperity"). For the bank charter: "An Act to Establish a Bank of the State of Tennessee," in *Acts of a Public or General Nature, Passed at the Second Session of the Thirteenth General Assembly of the State of Tennessee* (Nashville, 1820), 9–16. See also W. J. Hamilton, "The Relief Movement in Missouri, 1820–1822," *MHR* 22 (October 1927): 69–72 and 51–94, and Patrick Bolton and Howard Rosenthal, "Political Intervention in Debt Contracts," *JPE* 110 (October 2002): 1103–34.

19 Henry Clay to Langdon Cheves, November 14, 1819, in *PHC* 2: 722 ("Our Legislature"); Henry Clay to Langdon Cheves, November 20, 1820, in *PHC* 2: 903 ("unfavorable laws"); Stevens, "Henry Clay, the Bank, and the West."

20 Carey quoted in Matson, "Matthew Carey's Learning Experience," 474 ("paralysis"); [Matthew Carey and others], "Protection to Printers of Books," January 10, 1820, reported to Senate January 26, in *ASP: Finances* 3: 461–62; [Joseph Heister], "Inaugural Address to the Assembly," December 19, 1820, in *Pennsylvania Archives: Papers of the Pennsylvania Governors* (12 vols., Harrisburg: State of Pennsylvania, 1900), 5: 247; James L. Huston, "Virtue Besieged: Virtue, Equality, and the General Welfare in the Tariff Debates of the 1820s," *JER* 14 (Winter 1994): 523–47; Daniel Peart, "Looking Beyond Parties and Elections: The Making of United States Tariff Policy during the Early 1820s," *JER* 33 (Spring 2013): 87–108; Peart, *Era of Experimentation*, 73–107.

21 Remarks by Sampson David, July 11, 1820, in *Journal of the House of Representatives at the . . . Thirteenth General Assembly*, 72 ("demoralizing") and 72–73; Carey, *Essays on Political Economy*, 318 ("*acts of legislature*"); Carey in 1794 *History of Algiers*, quoted in Lawrence A. Peskin, *Captives and Countrymen: Barbary Slavery and the American Public, 1785–1816* (Baltimore: Johns Hopkins University Press, 2009), 167 ("fully avenge"). On David see "Will of Sampson David, April 26, 1826," and "Inventory of Estate of Sampson David, September 13, 1826," in *Records of Campbell County, Tennessee: Wills, Bonds, Inventories, 1806–1841* (Nashville, 1936), 82 (wish to free slaves), 87–90 (wealth), both at TSLA; *Records of the 1820 Census of Manufactures, Schedules for the Eastern District of Tennessee*, Document #100 (David listed as whiskey distiller and, with a partner, a tanner), microfilm at TSLA.

22 AJ to AJ Donelson, September 17, 1819, in *PAJ* 4: 323 ("distressed") and 322 (palsy); AJ to James Gadsden, August 1, 1819, in *PAJ* 4: 307 ("foreign notes"); "Tennessee Bank and Relief Law," *NWR*, September 2, 1820 (full text of June 22, 1820, motion by Andrew Jackson, Edward Ward, et al., including call for "industry and simplicity"); for Jackson's high hopes for Andrew Jackson Donelson, see Rachel Meredith, "'There Was Somebody Always Dying and Leaving Jackson as Guardian': The Wards of Andrew Jackson" (MA thesis, Middle Tennessee State University, 2013), 49–55. Jackson's disgust at relief measures may well have been intensified by repayment demands made by the US government on him for earlier military and treaty expenditures. See William Lee to AJ, David Meriwether, and Jesse Franklin, May 10, 1820, ser. 1, reel 29, AJPLC. For a superb discussion of "foreign bills of exchange," see Jessica M. Lepler, *The Many Panics of 1837: People, Politics, and the Creation of a Transatlantic Financial Crisis* (New York: Cambridge University Press, 2013), 17–18.

23 AJ to William Berkeley Lewis, July 16, 1820, in *PAJ* 4: 378 ("principles of general Justice") and 380 ("as long as I live"); AJ to Andrew Jackson Donelson, February 8, 1823, in *CAJ* 3: 187 ("not voidable" and "social compact"), 186 ("independent government"); "Tennessee Bank and Relief Law," *NWR*, September 2, 1820. "General Jackson," *Alexandria Gazette*, April 27, 1827, quotes the outraged legislators who felt threatened by Jackson's personal intervention, and the paper stresses that Jackson presented himself as "a *major general in the United States army*!" For AJ's anti-relief efforts in Wilson and Sumner, as well as Davidson, in July 1820, see Rothbard, *Panic of 1819*, 95–96. For his presence at the opening of the 1819 assembly, see *PAJ* 4: xxxi–xxxvii. See also Sellers, "Banking and Politics in Jackson's Tennessee," and William M. Gouge, *A Short History of Paper Money and Banking in the United States*, ed. Joseph Dorfman (1833; New York: A. M. Kelley, 1968), 133–39.

24 Davidson County Circuit Court Minute Books: First Circuit, Minutes Civil and Criminal, roll 522, Volume C, 1817–1820, pp. 137–93 (November 1818) and 243–302 (November 1819), mass deposition by Nashville Bank on page 268; Davidson County Circuit Court Minute Books, Volume D, 1820–24, pp. 1–50 (November 1820), TSLA. The records of these circuit courts, created in 1809 as a level between the common pleas courts and the Supreme Court of Errors and Appeals (formerly the Superior Court of Law and Equity), are messy and ambiguous. I counted all cases that were categorized as "ejectment" and "debt" matters and that clearly concerned such actions. But other cases that were categorized differently also dealt with sums owed. Therefore, I made the most conservative counts possible and offer the figures cautiously. Further study of the common pleas courts might yield more information. In the case of Greene County,

ejectments seem to have been categorized as *scire facias* cases. I found eight cases for debt and ejectment in September 1818, nineteen in September 1819 (fourteen categorized as *scire facias*), and just two *scire facias* in March 1820. See Greene County Circuit Court Minute Book, Civil, roll 36, Volume 1, November 1809 to May 1820, pp. 341–74, 378–438, and 439–483, TSLA. Of the thirteen no votes for the Bank of the State of Tennessee (against twenty-six yes votes), nine had supported Grundy's legal residence laws the year before. They came from the counties of Giles/Lawrence, Overton, Campbell, Sullivan, Claiborne, Washington, White, Davidson, and Anderson. Six of these are in the northeastern part of the state. See also William O. Lynch, "An Early Crisis in Indiana History," *IMH* 43 (June 1947): 105–24, and Sellers, "Banking and Politics in Jackson's Tennessee."

25 "The Bank of the State of Tennessee, No. 1," *Nashville Gazette,* September 16, 1820; "The Bank of the State of Tennessee, No. 6," *Nashville Gazette*, October 21, 1820; Petition #62, June 30, 1820, ser. 3, roll 6, TLP. For Overton's connection to the *Gazette*, see Charles Grier Sellers Jr., *James K. Polk, Jacksonian, 1795–1843* (Princeton, NJ: Princeton University Press, 1957), 501. For anti-relief conservatism in Virginia and the Carolinas, see also Michael O'Brien, *Conjectures of Order: Intellectual Life and the American South, 1810–1860* (2 vols., Chapel Hill: University of North Carolina Press, 2004), 2: 799–816.

26 Jackson and Smith Counties, Petition #18, June 20, 1820, ser. 3, roll 6, TLP. These two documents were very similar and probably coordinated between these adjacent counties. They were signed by forty-three and forty-eight people. Proceedings of July 11, 1820, *Journal of the House of Representatives at the Second Session of Thirteenth General Assembly of the State of Tennessee* (Murfreesboro, 1820), 65–73. A second June 1820 petition from Smith County was signed by thirty-three people and objected to the stay law but not to the state bank or loan office. I cross-checked these names with *Tennessee Records of Smith County: Will Book 4, Smith County, 1820–1823* (Nashville, 1936) and *Transcriptions of the County Archives of Tennessee: Minutes of the Court of Smith County, 1820–22* (Nashville, 1941) but could only find definite information on fourteen of the men. Abner Luck and James Alexander had been granted licenses to keep taverns, and Daniel Ford seems to have been a cabinet maker. Judging by William William's will (he died in 1822) he was quite prosperous, with thirteen slaves, about a hundred cattle and hogs, and a well-furnished home.

27 "An Act, Supplemental to an Act, Entitled, 'An Act to Establish a Bank of the State of Tennessee,'" July 29, 1820, in *Acts of a Public or General Nature Passed at the Second Session of the Thirteenth Assembly*, 17 ("faith"); Pleasant M. Miller to AJ, August 9, 1820, ser. 1, reel 29, AJPLC (AJ had written to Miller on August 3, but I cannot find this letter). Miller was either the lawyer or security for Taylor Townsend, the East Tennessee man who brought his long-standing dispute over how his sons should pay him for lands to the courts. See Bond agreement, May 28, 1819, Taylor Townsend and Pleasant M. Miller, in "James Townsend et als. vs. Taylor Townsend," Supreme Court Records, East Tennessee, box 58, TSLA. For Missouri terms: Hamilton, "Relief Movement in Missouri," 63, 75, and also 79n for merchant opposition. See, too, Sellers, "Banking and Politics in Jackson's Tennessee, 1817–27"; Lewis E. Atherton, "The Services of the Frontier Merchant," *MVHR* 24 (September 1937): 165, 167, and 153–70. Condemning the "private Banks" of Tennessee, Governor McMinn noted that the more clever stockholders would "readily assent" to laws that might bring about "an immediate closing

of the concern." They had no interest in maintaining banks for their own sake, given "the unproductive state of the capitol." See [McMinn], "Address to Fellow-Citizens," September 18, 1821, in *Journal of the House of Representatives at the . . . Fourteenth General Assembly,* 10.

28 *Townsend vs. Townsend and Others*, Peck 1, 7 Tenn. 1, 1821 ("personal exertion," "unconscionable," and "extraordinary"), original available at TJM; 1822 newspaper quoted in Hamilton, "Relief Movement in Missouri," 80. Early uses of the contracts clause: Saul Cornell and Gerald Leonard, "The Consolidation of the Early Federal System, 1791–1812," in *The Cambridge History of Law in America: Volume I, Early America (1580–1815)*, ed. Michael Grossberg and Christopher Tomlins (New York: Cambridge University Press, 2008), 1: 541–42. Judge Haywood wrote the *Townsend* opinion, and all four of his colleagues more or less consented, although not with his admonition to creditors. My thanks to Trent Hanner and Tom Kanon for helping me with this case. See also Rothbard, *Panic of 1819*, 92–96; McCandless, *History of Missouri*, 26–28; Gouge, *Short History of Paper Money and Banking*, 133–39. For a discussion of *Townsend*, see also Sumner et al., *A History of Banking in All the Advanced Nations,* 1: 149–50.

29 [McMinn], "Address to Fellow-Citizens," September 18, 1821, in *Journal of the House of Representatives at the . . . Fourteenth General Assembly,* 7–8; *Lapsley vs. Brashears and Barr*, 4 Litt. 61 (1823), Court of Appeals of Kentucky ("international law . . . civilized states"); "Opinion of Judge Mills, in the Two Proceeding Cases," [October 11, 1823], in *Lapsley vs. Brashears and Barr*, 4 Litt. 102, 84 ("international principle" and "free course to the coercion"); John Boyle, William Owsley, and B[enjamin] Mills to Honorable Representatives, December 9, 1824, in *Journal of the House of Representatives of the Commonwealth of Kentucky* (Frankfort, 1824), 326 ("social justice") and 311–48; Rothbard, *Panic of 1819*, 109 (bonfires). Sellers, *The Market Revolution*, 163–64, notes that the courts never challenged the "patently illegal" practice of private banks suspending their specie payments.

30 *Argus of Western America* (Frankfort, Ky.), October 22, 1823 ("Is there an Englishman?" and "sovereignty"); "The Appeal of 'Common Sense' . . . No. V," *Argus of Western America*, March 24, 1824 ("man is a social being" and "*justice* and *mercy*," emphasis in original); "Speech of Samuel Daveiss," *Kentucky Gazette*, May 13, 1824 ("*grind to death,*" emphasis in original, and "feelings"), and also "Speech of Samuel Daveiss," *Kentucky Gazette*, May 20, 1824; Report by Felix Grundy, September 21, 1821, in *Journal of the House of Representatives at the . . . Fourteenth General Assembly*, 49–53. See also Donald B. Cole, *A Jackson Man: Amos Kendall and the Rise of American Democracy* (Baton Rouge: Louisiana State University Press, 2004), 67–94.

31 *Providence Gazette*, "By the Mails," August 17, 1822, reprinted this praise of Ohio from a Kentucky paper, where it was originally titled "Manufactures of Ohio"; Timothy Flint, "A Condensed Geography and History of the Western States, or the Mississippi Valley," [1828], in *Indiana as Seen by Early Travelers*, ed. Harlow Lindley (Indianapolis: Indiana Historical Commission, 1916), 462 ("spurious banks" and "ridiculous," spelling corrected); AJ to Andrew Jackson Donelson, February 8, 1823, in *CAJ* 3: 187. On Flint, see Terry A. Barnhart, "'A Common Feeling': Regional Identity and Historical Consciousness in the Old Northwest, 1820–1860," *Michigan Historical Review* 29 (Spring 2003): 39–70. The pro-Ohio article subsequently appeared in *Boston Weekly Messenger*, August 22, 1822, and *Berks and Schuylkill Journal* (Reading, Pa.), August 24, 1822. For Ohio's replevin law, see Greer, "Economic and Social Effects," 238. On the fall-out from other state banks: Robert P. Howard, *Illinois: A History of the Prairie State* (Grand Rapids,

MI: William B. Eerdmans Publishing Company, 1972), 120–25, and McCandless, *History of Missouri*, 27–28.

32 *Green vs. Biddle*, 21 U.S. 92 (1823); Van Burkleo, "'The Paws of Banks'"; Peterson, *Great Triumvirate*, 67; Cornell and Leonard, "Consolidation of the Early Federal System," in *Cambridge History of Law in America*, ed. Grossberg and Tomlins, 539–45.

33 "The Judiciary, no. IV," *St. Louis Enquirer*, June 7, 1823 ("must yet remain" and "Radical"); *Richmond Enquirer*, "The Times," January 6, 1821 ("warring"); "Agricultural," *American Beacon and Norfolk and Portsmouth Daily* (Norfolk, VA), January 28, 1820 ("experimental"); "On Manufacturers," *Charleston Courier* (Charleston, SC), September 14, 1820 ("charity"). See also Gates, "Tenants of the Log Cabin," and John Phillip Reid, *Legislating the Courts: Judicial Dependence in Early National New Hampshire* (DeKalb: Northern Illinois University Press, 2009), 110–21.

34 AJ to John Coffee, February 2, 1816, in *PAJ* 4: 7; Report by Felix Grundy, October 7, 1819, in *Journal of the House of Representatives at the . . . Thirteenth General Assembly*, 84 ("entirely safe"); Farmers' and Mechanics' Bank of Nashville, Petition #19, July 12, 1820, ser. 3, roll 6, TLP; Leger, "Administration of John Adair," 23, 39–40. According to the July 1820 petition, the Farmers' and Mechanics' Bank had sixty-six shareholders, including William Carroll, who had paid $1,040 for stocks and who owed $1,340.

35 Carroll address of June 21, 1821, in *Nashville Clarion*, June 27, 1821; "An Act Prescribing the Mode by Which the Holders of the Notes of the Farmers' and Mechanics' Bank at Nashville . . . May Receive Payments," November 15, 1821, *Acts Passed at the First Session of the Fourteenth General Assembly of the State of Tennessee* (Knoxville, 1821), 186–90; "Dinner to George W. Campbell, Esq.," *Nashville Gazette*, January 20, 1821; Jonathan M. Atkins, "William Carroll," *Tennessee Encyclopedia of History and Culture*, http://tennesseeencyclopedia.net (accessed October 12, 2015); Corlew, *Tennessee*, 159–68; Gabriel Hawkins Golden, "William Carroll and His Administration," *THM* 9 (April 1925): 9–30.

36 Ward quoted in "Fellow Citizens," *Nashville Gazette*, June 2, 1821; "A Gentleman," *Nashville Clarion*, February 6, 1821 (anti-Ward accusations); Golden, "William Carroll and His Administration," 17–18; Ruth Hiltenbrand Hall, "Colonel Edward Ward: The Life and Death of a Tennessee Senator," *WTHSP* 64 (December 2010): 45–89; [A]? Anderson to William H. Crawford, August 27, 1821, William Harris Crawford Papers, DL (my thanks to Melissa Gismondi for this source).

37 AJ to Choctaw Indians, October 17, 1820, in *PAJ* 4: 394 ("you are advised," during talks for Treaty of Doak's Stand); AJ to Secretary of State, October 6, 1821, in *TPUS* 22: 237 ("by far"); AJ to the Officers and Soldiers Composing the Division of the South, May 31, 1821, in *PAJ* 5: 76 ("thrown upon"); AJ to John Coffee, July 26, 1821, in *PAJ* 5: 83. For the reduction of the US Army in 1821, see Francis Paul Prucha, "Distribution of Regular Army Troops Before the Civil War," *MA* 16 (Winter 1952): 169–73. For Doak's Stand see "Treaty with the Choctaw, 1820," in *IT*, 191–95.

38 [William Carroll], "To Fellow-Citizens of the Senate, and of the House of Representatives," October 1, 1821, in *Journal of the House of Representatives at the . . . Fourteenth General Assembly*, 109 ("every feeling" and "unfortunate"), 114 ("*domestic or household*," emphasis in original), 121 ("Citizens of the same"). Carroll won 79.6% of the 54,392 votes cast, and every county but Hamilton and Cocke. See "Complete Returns," *Nashville Clarion*, August 22, 1821, and Michael J. Dubin, *United States Gubernatorial Elections, 1776–1860: The Official Results*

by State and County (Jefferson, NC: McFarland and Company, 2003), 242–43. For Carroll's ongoing enthusiasm for public education and penal reforms, see Governor's Address, September 17, 1827, in Governor's Papers: William Carroll, 1821–27, box 1, TSLA.

39 Overton quoted in Frances Clifton, "John Overton as Andrew Jackson's Friend," *THQ* 11 (March 1952): 28 ("forcibly struck" and "leading member"), 29 ("gave into"); "Sentiments of Tennessee," *Daily National Intelligencer* (Washington, DC), December 15, 1821 (toasts from November 23 public dinner, with Jackson attending and Overton presiding). Grundy was on a four-man committee in 1819 to review Jackson's conduct in Florida. See Proceedings of October 15, 1819, *Journal of the House of Representatives at the . . . Thirteenth General Assembly*, 116–17, September 21, 1819, in ibid., 20, and September 23, 1819, in ibid., 37. For Miller's role, see Cheathem, *Andrew Jackson, Southerner*, 99–100.

40 "Hero of New Orleans," *NWR*, August 3, 1822 (from July celebration; "*holy* zeal" and "*zeal alone*," emphasis in original); AJ to AJ Donelson, July 25, 1822, in *PAJ* 5: 206. Jackson also referred to "the late British and Indian wars," as well as the singular, "the whole British and Indian war." For the belated financing and construction of the sword, see Joseph McMinn, "Address to Fellow-Citizens of the Senate and House of Representatives," September 18, 1821, in *Journal of the House of Representatives . . . of the Fourteenth General Assembly of the State of Tennessee* (Nashville, 1821), 24. The Tennessee House and Senate caucuses issued separate nominations of Jackson in late July and early August 1822. See *PAJ* 5: xxix.

41 John Overton to AJ, May 8, 1814, in *PAJ* 2: 72; John Henry Eaton to AJ, March 20, 1817, in *PAJ* 4: 104; AJ to John Reid, January 15, 1816, in *PAJ* 4: 3–4; Frank Lawrence Owsley Jr., "Editor's Introduction," in *The Life of Andrew Jackson, by John Reid and John Henry Eaton*, ed. Owsley Jr. (Tuscaloosa: University of Alabama Press, 1974), v–xv, esp. viii.

42 *American Monthly Magazine and Critical Review* (New York), July 1817; John Eaton, *The Life of Andrew Jackson, Major-General in the Service of the United States, Comprising a History of the War in the South, from the Commencement of the Creek Campaign, to the Termination of Hostilities before New Orleans* (Philadelphia, 1817). The volume edited by Oswley Jr. reproduces this text.

43 *Life of Andrew Jackson*, ed. Owsley Jr., 14 ("pulpit"), 17 ("elegant farm" and "all the comforts"), 396 ("great parties" and "blind infatuated"). For a contemporary review see "General Jackson," *Weekly Recorder* (Chillicothe, Ohio), September 18, 1817. My thanks to Katherine Wilson for her help in tracking down reviews and excerpts of this biography.

44 *Life of Andrew Jackson*, ed. Owsley Jr., 393 ("nothing repulsive," "honest," and "titled"), 395 ("seen acting . . . woes"). For Jackson as Cincinnatus, see "General Jackson," *The Pennsylvanian* (Columbia), November 15, 1822, and "Reception of General Jackson," *Nashville Gazette*, April 22, 1825. For reprints of the Lyncoya story: "Anecdote of General Jackson," *Vermont Intelligencer and Bellow's Falls Advocate* (Bellows Falls, Vt.), December 15, 1817; *New York Evening-Post*, February 2, 1818; *American Mercury* (Hartford), February 10, 1818. On Washington's legend: Scott E. Casper, *Constructing American Lives: Biography and Culture in Nineteenth-Century America* (Chapel Hill: University of North Carolina Press, 1999), 68–76; François Furstenberg, *In the Name of the Father: Washington's Legacy, Slavery, and the Making of a Nation* (New York: Penguin, 2006), 123–29.

45 *Life of Andrew Jackson*, ed. Owsley Jr., 395 ("gratitude" and "ambition"), 399 ("confusion" and "forbearance"), 180 ("whilst the tomahawk"). For the problem

of ambition: J. M. Opal, *Beyond the Farm: National Ambitions in Rural New England* (Philadelphia: University of Pennsylvania Press, 2008); William Casey King, *Ambition, A History: From Vice to Virtue* (New Haven, CT: Yale University Press, 2013).

46 "Jackson and Adams," *City Gazette and Commercial Daily Advertiser* (Charleston, SC), November 5, 1824 ("fierce vindictive" from a pro-Adams delegation from Maryland); 1822 commendation quoted in Corlew, *Tennessee*, 170; "The Presidency," *Nashville Gazette*, July 25, 1823 ("employed on his farm," signed by Overton and five others). For Jackson's makeover, see also Henry Clay to Benjamin W. Leigh, October 20, 1823, in *PHC* 3: 501.

47 James Gadsden to AJ, May 3, 1819, in *PAJ* 4: 294; David Brion Davis, *From Homicide to Slavery: Studies in American Culture* (New York: Oxford University Press, 1986), 129 (demographic figures); Peart, *Era of Experimentation*, 130. The Jackson biography might also be compared to William Wirt, *Sketches of the Life and Character of Patrick Henry* (Philadelphia, 1817). On Gadsden: *PAJ* 4: 12n and 177n.

48 "Reception of General Jackson," *Nashville Gazette*, April 22, 1825 ("firm and inflexible," from Overton's reception speech); John Eaton, *The Life of Andrew Jackson* (Philadelphia, 1824), 432 and 432–33; Quotes from June 25, 1819, toasts and July 19, 1819, *National Intelligencer* in *PAJ* 4: 537; "Tennessee Bank and Relief Law," *NWR*, September 2, 1820. Besides Overton, William B. Lewis was a key member of the so-called Nashville Junto, which later became the Nashville Committee for Jackson's campaign. Pleasant M. Miller had helped nominate Jackson for president on behalf of the Tennessee assembly in 1822. Jackson had written to both Lewis and Miller about relief and banking in 1820. For various accounts of the "Junto" and the informal "Nashville Committee" that succeeded it before the 1828 election, see *PAJ* 6: 14n, 15n; Cheathem, *Andrew Jackson, Southerner*, 99–100; Donald B. Cole, *Vindicating Andrew Jackson: The 1828 Election and the Rise of the Two-Party System* (Lawrence: University of Kansas Press, 2009), 79–80; Lynn Hudson Parsons, *The Birth of Modern Politics: Andrew Jackson, John Quincy Adams, and the Election of 1828* (New York: Oxford University Press, 2009), 139.

49 "Abridged from *The Telegraph*," *Frankfort Argus and Western Reporter*, July 14, 1824; "Jackson Dinner," *Kentucky Gazette* (Lexington), July 27, 1827; Squire Turner to Henry Clay, January 7, 1827, in *PHC* 6: 25 ("Military chieftain" and "Jackson was the man"). Turner was paraphrasing John Pope's rant against the "old court" party; Pope was one of eight signatories of a set of resolutions adopted for relief in Frankfort, Kentucky, in June 1819. See "Public Meeting," *St. Louis Enquirer*, June 9, 1819. In a series of articles under the name "Patrick Henry," a relief party supporter attacked the "Court Party" as latter-day Federalists and traitors. Besides *NWR*, which published Jackson's June 1820 rant against relief, the only direct mention of the general's fierce opposition to relief that I have found is "General Jackson," *Alexandria Gazette*, April 27, 1827. For the movement of Kentucky relief leaders and strongholds to Jackson, see Lynn L. Marshall, "The Genesis of Grass-Roots Democracy in Kentucky," *Mid-America*, 47 (1965): 273–81, and Cole, *Vindicating Andrew Jackson*, 190 and 120–29.

50 AJ to John Coffee, April 15, 1823, in *PAJ* 5: 271 ("verry corrupt") and 271–72n; AJ to John Overton, November 8, 1823, in *PAJ* 5: 316 ("Dear Sir"); AJ to John Overton, December 5, 1823, in *PAJ* 5: 321 (new judgeship); AJ to John Overton, December 19, 1824, in *PAJ* 5: 455 ("My Dear friend"); Abernathy, "Early

Development of Commerce and Banking," 311–25; AJ to Coffee, August 15, 1823, in *PAJ* 5: 289–90.

51 AJ to John Overton, January 10, 1825, in *PAJ* 6: 14 ("*great whore*," emphasis in original); AJ to John Coffee, October 5, 1823, in *PAJ* 5: 302 ("astonished" and vote); AJ to Rachel Jackson, November 28, 1823, in *PAJ* 5: 320 ("tiresome" and "gratifying"); AJ to John Overton, November 8, 1823, in *PAJ* 5: 316 (Rachel disconsolate); Corlew, *Tennessee*, 170–75. Earlier in the year, Pleasant M. Miller had wanted to run for Senate, telling supporters that his creed was "decidedly Republican" and that his top goal was to help Jackson become president. See Miller to James K. Polk, August 18, 1823, in *CJP* 1: 19 and 19–20. Apparently Jackson's friends turned to him when they realized that neither Miller nor John Rhea would be able to beat the incumbent, John Williams.

52 John H. Eaton to Rachel Jackson, December 18, 1823, in *PAJ* 5: 327 ("constantly") and P.S. by Jackson, *PAJ* 5: 328 ("all the world"). For his fall 1823 settlement of the long dispute with Andrew Erwin, see *PAJ* 5: 307n.

53 AJ to AJ Donelson, January 18, 1824, in *PAJ* 5: 340 ("great leading state" in P.S.); AJ to John Coffee, June 18, 1824, in *PAJ* 5: 417 ("cotton growers"); AJ to AJ Donelson, April 11, 1824, in *PAJ* 5: 391 ("President of the nation"); "Jackson's Recorded Votes in the United States Senate, 1823–25," in *PAJ* 5: 463–67; Cheathem, *Andrew Jackson, Southerner*, 101–2; Huston, "Virtue Besieged," and Peart, "Looking Beyond Parties and Elections." For AJ's views on the tariff, see also AJ to Littleton H. Coleman, April 26, 1824, in *PAJ* 5: 398–400.

54 Remarks by Robert Y. Hayne (SC), April 6, 1824, "Imprisonment for Debt," *AC: Senate*, 18th Congress, 1st Session, p. 485; Remarks by James Noble (IN), January 10, 1825, "Imprisonment for Debt," *RD: Senate*, 18th Congress, 2nd Session, p. 163; Remarks by Richard M. Johnson, February 16, 1824, "Imprisonment for Debt," *AC: Senate*, 18th Congress, 1st Session, p. 259. For anti-relief support for abolishing debt imprisonment, see "On Imprisonment for Debt, from the *St. Genevieve* (Mo.) *Correspondent*," *Palladium of Liberty* (Morristown, NJ), December 19, 1822.

55 Objections and remarks by Richard M. Johnson et al., April 9, 1824, "Imprisonment for Debt," *AC: Senate*, 18th Congress, 1st Session, p. 505 ("sweet belief") and 504 (first vote); Vote of January 17, 1825, "Imprisonment for Debt," in *RD: Senate*, 18th Congress, 2nd Session, p. 230; James W. Ely Jr., "Andrew Jackson as Tennessee State Court Judge, 1798–1804," *THQ* 40 (Summer 1981): 152 and 144–57; Stephen Mihm, *A Nation of Counterfeiters: Capitalists, Con Men, and the Making of the United States* (Cambridge, MA: Harvard University Press, 2007). In the final vote, the bill received the unanimous (both senators) support of Tennessee, Kentucky, Louisiana, North Carolina, and Pennsylvania. Mississippi and Alabama also gave their support. For revisions to the Tennessee penal code in 1829, see Corlew, *Tennessee*, 163–64. For constitutional restrictions on debt imprisonments, see Constitution of North Carolina [1776], art. II, sec. 39; Tennessee Constitution [1796], art. I, sec. 18; Alabama Constitution [1819], art. I, sec. 18; and Mississippi Constitution [1817], art. I, sec. 18.

56 "The International Significance of the Jones and Immell Massacre and of the Aricara Outbreak in 1823," ed. Abraham S. Nasantir et al., *PNQ* 30 (January 1939): 91 ("continue to forbear"), 94 ("lucrative adventures"), and 98–99 (Gaines); Ted Binnema and William A. Dobak, "'Like the Greedy Wolf': The Blackfeet, the St. Louis Fur Trade, and War Fever, 1807–1831," *JER* 29 (Fall 2009): 412 (body count), 430–31 and 411–40.

57 Porter quoted in "Shameful Aggression," *Connecticut Mirror* (Hartford), December 27, 1824 ("American property" and "atonement"); David Porter, *An Exposition of the Facts and Circumstances, Which Justified the Expedition to Foxardo* (Washington, DC, 1825), 59 ("supposed will"), 58–61, and 14–17; David F. Long, *Nothing Too Daring: A Biography of Commodore David Porter, 1780–1843* (Annapolis: United States Naval Institute, 1970); Allan B. Cole, "Captain David Porter's Proposed Expedition to the Pacific and Japan, 1815," *PHR* 9 (March 1940): 61–65. For South American privateers or pirates in southern ports: Entry of March 13, 1820, in *MJQA* 5: 19–20.

58 Thomas Jefferson to James Monroe, October 24, 1823, in *The Life and Selected Writings of Thomas Jefferson*, ed. Adrienne Koch and William Peden (1944; New York: Modern Library 2004), 646; Remarks by Mahlon Dickerson (NJ), March 31, 1824, "Indian Fur Trade," *AC: Senate*, 18th Congress, 1st Session, p. 452 ("ought to be"), 454 ("name of humanity"); Vote on section 5 of the proposed bill, April 9, 1824, in *AC: Senate*, 18th Congress, 1st Session, p. 507; Binnema and Dobak, "'Like the Greedy Wolf,'" 431–35; Ernest R. May, *The Making of the Monroe Doctrine* (Cambridge, MA: Belknap Press of Harvard University Press, 1975); Don E. Fehrenbacher, *The Slaveholding Republic: An Account of the United States Government's Relations to Slavery*, ed. Ward M. McAfee (New York: Oxford University Press, 2001), 93–98; Howard Jones and Donald A. Rakestraw, *Prologue to Manifest Destiny: Anglo-American Relations in the 1840s* (Wilmington, DE: Scholarly Resources, 1997); Duncan Andrew Campbell, *Unlikely Allies: Britain, America, and the Victorian Beginnings of the Special Relationship* (New York: Continuum, 2007).

59 "Shameful Aggression," *Connecticut Mirror* (Hartford), December 27, 1824 and *Saratoga Sentinel* (Saratoga Springs, NY), January 5, 1825; Remarks by Littleton Tazewell (VA), January 21, 1825, "Suppression of Piracy," *RD: Senate*, 18th Congress, 2nd Session, p. 308 ("establish the reputation"), 305 ("high law" and "whole civilized"), 307 ("come again within the pale"); Vote for striking out section 3 of proposed bill, February 1, 1825, in ibid., p. 407. For concerns about presidential powers over war, see especially Remarks by Samuel Smith (Md.), February 1, 1825, "Suppression of Piracy," in ibid., p. 404. On Tazewell: Hugh Blair Grigsby, *Discourse on the Life and Character of the Hon. Littleton Waller Tazewell* (Norfolk, 1860), esp. 58 and 77.

60 Remarks by Philip Barbour, "Suppression of Piracy," *RD: Senate*, January 21, 1825, 18th Congress, 2nd Session, p. 315 ("idolatrous," "latitude," and "self-preservation"), p. 317 ("demons"), p. 318 ("blood of our people"); Remarks by Sen. Barbour, "Suppression of Piracy," January 20, 1825, in ibid, p. 276 ("*too* far," emphasis in original), p. 278 ("contaminated" and "must cause vengeance"). See also "Horrible," *East Florida Herald* (St. Augustine), April 26, 1823.

61 "Commerce with Asia," *St. Louis Enquirer*, November 3, 1819 ("take its course"); Remarks by Philip Barbour, "Suppression of Piracy," January 20, 1825, in *RD: Senate*, 18th Congress, 2nd Session, p. 281 ("will of the nation" and "sovereign capacity"); Remarks by Sen. Benton, March 29, 1824, in *AC: Senate*, 18th Congress, 1st Session, pp. 432–33 (Florida). Benton was editor of the *Enquirer* when "Commerce with Asia" was published from September to November 1819.

62 South Carolina Senate quoted in Jon Meacham, *American Lion: Andrew Jackson in the White House* (New York: Random House, 2008), 53; "Planters in Christ Church Parish Summarize the Problems with Maroons," [1829], in *Maroon Communities in South Carolina: A Documentary Record*, ed. Timothy James Lockley (Columbia:

University of South Carolina Press, 2009), 124 (quotes) and 122–27; Alan Taylor, *The Internal Enemy: Slavery and War in Virginia, 1772–1832* (New York: W. W. Norton and Company, 2013); Philip M. Hamer, "Great Britain, the United States, and the Negro Seamen Acts, 1822–1848," *JSH* 1 (February 1935): 3–28. The events of 1822 in Charleston remain the subject of intense controversy. See David Brion Davis, *Inhuman Bondage: The Rise and Fall of Slavery in the New World* (New York: Oxford University Press, 2006), 222–26. The six senators to vote for both militant measures were Jackson and John Eaton of Tennessee, Richard Johnson of Kentucky, Robert Hayne of South Carolina, William Kelly of Alabama, and J. S. Johnston of Louisiana, a Connecticut native who later supported Adams and Clay.

63 [Brutus], *The Crisis: Or, Essays on the Usurpations of the Federal Government* (Charleston, 1827), 13 ("insurrectionary"), 87 ("*national welfare*," emphasis in original), 125 ("walking pestilence"); Michael Schoeppner, "Peculiar Quarantines: The Seamen Acts and Regulatory Authority in the Antebellum South," *LHR* 31 (August 2013): 565 ("*moral contagion*," emphasis in original) and 559–86; Taney quoted in Mark H. Haller, "The Rise of the Jackson Party in Maryland, 1820–1829," *JSH* 28 (August 1962): 312 and 307–26; Timothy S. Huebner, "Roger B. Taney and the Slavery Issue: Looking Beyond—and Before—Dred Scott," *JAH* 97 (June 2010): 17–38; Michael Schoeppner, "Navigating the Dangerous Atlantic: Racial Quarantines, Black Sailors, and United States Constitutionalism" (PhD dissertation, University of Florida, 2010); Robert Pierce Forbes, *The Missouri Compromise and Its Aftermath: Slavery and the Meaning of America* (Chapel Hill: University of North Carolina Press, 2007).

64 AJ to William Berkeley Lewis, February 20, 1825, in *PAJ* 6: 37; Donald J. Ratcliffe, "Popular Preferences in the Presidential Election of 1824," *JER* 34 (Spring 2014): 71, 73, and 45–78; Jabez Z. Rabun and James Harvey Young, "William H. Crawford on the Election of 1828: Two Letters," *GHQ* 37 (December 1953): 340–45; Michael J. Dubin, *United States Presidential Elections, 1788–1860: The Official Results by County and State* (Jefferson, NC: McFarland and Company, 2002), 31–42. Jackson also received some or all of the electors from Illinois, Louisiana, and South Carolina (and one from New York). The most meticulous study of party organization in the period is Thomas Coens, "The Formation of the Jackson Party, 1822–1825" (PhD dissertation, Harvard University, 2004).

65 David Holmes to AJ, June 19, 1814, in *PAJ* 3: 82; [untitled], *City Gazette and Commercial Daily Advertiser* (Charleston), September 14, 1822 ("Every honest"), and see also "General Jackson's Prospects," *City Gazette and Commercial Daily Advertiser*, September 24, 1822; James K. Polk to William Polk, December 14, 1826, in *CJP* 1: 59 ("sovereignty . . . as expressed"); William C. Cross to Polk, January 23, 1828, in *CJP* 1: 130 ("god on earth"); Parsons, *Birth of Modern Politics*, 121.

66 AJ to James K. Polk, December [2]4, 1826, in *PAJ* 6: 246; George W. Ewing to William H. Crawford, January 28, 1826, in William Harris Crawford Papers, DL; Crawford to Jesse B. Thomas, January 9, 1829, in Rabun and Young, "William H. Crawford on the Election of 1828," 344 ("compelled"). In 1828, Jackson supporters ran two slates of electors, and voters cast their ballots for electors instead of candidates, muddling the results somewhat. Still, Jackson electors received 96.7% of the votes, higher even than the 95.1% that the general won in Tennessee. See Dubin, *United States Presidential Elections*, 43, 49, and 42–51. My thanks to Tom Coens for his help with the 1828 results. For the Treaty of Indian Springs: "Treaty with the Creeks, 1825," in *IT*, 214–17.

67 *The Crisis*, 122 ("exquisite"), 97 ("*one great*," emphasis in original), 64 ("State Sovereignties"), 26 ("*vital* sovereignty," emphasis in original), 163 ("*outraged sovereignty*," emphasis in original); John Quincy Adams, "First Annual Message, December 6, 1825," in *CMP* 2: 311; Andrew Shankman, "John Quincy Adams and National Republicanism," in *A Companion to John Adams and John Quincy Adams*, ed. David Waldstreicher (Malden, MA: Wiley-Blackwell, 2013), 263–80; Sean Patrick Adams, "John Quincy Adams, Internal Improvements, and the Nation State," in ibid., 348–66.

68 *The Crisis*, 118 ("without a noise"), and see also 6; Pennsylvania legislator quoted in Thomas Coens, "The Early Jackson Party: A Force for Democratization?," *A Companion to the Era of Andrew Jackson*, ed. Sean Patrick Adams (Malden, MA: Blackwell Publishing, 2013), *Blackwell Reference Online*; Ratcliffe, "Popular Preferences," 67 (turnout figures); Richard I. Shelling, "Philadelphia and the Agitation in 1825 for the Pennsylvania Canal," *PMHB* 62 (April 1938): 175–204; Cole, *Vindicating Andrew Jackson*, 98–108; Peart, *Era of Experimentation*, 151 and 154–55; Philip Shriver Klein, *Pennsylvania Politics, 1817–1832: A Game Without Rules* (Philadelphia: Historical Society of Pennsylvania, 1940), 150–66; Herman Hailperin, "Pro-Jackson Sentiment in Pennsylvania, 1820–1828," *PMHB* 50 (1926): 193–240. For fears of "Jacksonism," see George Poindexter to Henry Clay, December 1, 1826, in *PHC* 5: 969, and Jonathan Roberts and Philip S. Klein, "Notes and Documents: Memoirs of a Senator from Pennsylvania: Jonathan Roberts, 1771–1854," *PMHB* 62 (July 1938): 408.

69 [John A. Shulze], "Inaugural Address to the Assembly," December 16, 1823, in *Pennsylvania Archives: Papers of the Pennsylvania Governors* (12 vols., Harrisburg: State of Pennsylvania, 1900), 5: 495; *Communications from the Governor, Accompanied with a Report of the Board of Canal Commissioners of Pennsylvania . . . No. 2* (Harrisburg, 1827), 13 ("dissipated"), 8–10 (costs); Shelling, "Philadelphia and the Agitation," 199–200. In 1827, the government of Pennsylvania formally thanked Carroll for his services in the War of 1812, and he responded by praising his native state. See William Carroll to John A. Shulze, June 15, 1827, in *Papers of the Pennsylvania Governors*, 5: 757.

70 William J. Duane, *Letters, Addressed to the People of Pennsylvania Respecting the Internal Improvements of the Commonwealth* (1811; New York: B. Franklin, 1967), 8 ("well-regulated"), 2 ("bound to promote"); [Shulze], "Inaugural Address," December 16, 1823, in *Papers of the Pennsylvania Governors*, 5: 495 ("completely protect"), 496 ("nations of Europe"); *Biographical Directory of the Governors of the United States, 1788–1917*, ed. Robert Sobel and John Raimo (Westport, CT: Meckler Books 1978), 3: 1299–1301. For the election results in 1823 and 1827: Dubin, *United States Gubernatorial Elections*, 220–21.

71 *Address of the Democratic Republican Committee of Allegheny County Friendly to the Election of General Andrew Jackson* (Pittsburgh, 1823), 3–4 ("*We were all*," emphasis in original), 1 ("land mark"), 17 ("real resources"); available LCP; Melissa J. Gismondi, "Rachel's 'Jackson Flat': Gender, Political Economy, and the Politics of Representation in the Lead-Up to the 1824 Presidential Election," unpublished essay in author's possession (quotes on pp. 1 and 9); *Proceedings of a Meeting of the Democratic Citizens of the County of York* (Pennsylvania?, 1827), 6, available LCP. For the 1827 vote on the Woolens' Bill in Pennsylvania, in which all seven of the Pennsylvania nays were Jackson men, see Klein, *Pennsylvania Politics*, 240–41.

72 *Address of the Democratic Republican Committee of Allegheny County*, 1–2; preacher quoted in Hailperin, "Pro-Jackson Sentiment in Pennsylvania," 201

("Saviour"); James Buchanan to AJ, May 29, 1825, in *PAJ* 6: 77 ("chiefly"); *The Letters of Wyoming, to the People of the United States, on the Presidential Election* (Philadelphia, 1824), 28 ("stands aloof" and "no parasite"), 19 ("Holy Bible"), and 57–66; Robert P. Hay, "The Case for Andrew Jackson in 1824: Eaton's *Wyoming Letters*," *THQ* 29 (Summer 1970): 139–51; Parsons, *Birth of Modern Politics*, 92–95. The word "Wyoming" to refer to the bloodshed in that valley in 1778 was familiar to Pennsylvanians during the 1820s: "Wyoming Massacre," *National Gazette and Literary Register* (Philadelphia), December 9, 1820; Remarks by Rep. Smyth, January 21, 1819, in *AC: House*, 15th Congress, 2nd Session, p. 702.

73 "Democratic Meeting," *Oracle of Dauphin* (Harrisburg), February 28, 1824 ("governmental munificence" and "diplomatic refinements"); "A Few Facts, Which Demonstrate That Mr. Adams Ought Not to Be Re-Elected," *Kentucky Gazette* (Lexington), June 13, 1827 ("affected to become"); *Letters of Wyoming*, 88 ("*father's son*," emphasis in original); *Proceedings of a Meeting of the Democratic Citizens of the County of York*, 3 ("*favorite* of the rulers," emphasis in original); Klein, *Pennsylvania Politics*, 229 ("John the Second" and "Palace"). This focus on Adams as a Federalist made the revelation that Jackson had recommended William H. Drayton, a South Carolina Federalist, for secretary of war back in 1816 a potential bombshell. Jackson's supporters claimed that it revealed his extrapartisan patriotism. See AJ to James Monroe, October 23, 1816, in *PAJ* 4: 69–71, 68n–69n, and 70n.

74 AJ to Samuel Houston, December 15, 1826, in *PAJ* 6: 243 ("secrete"); AJ to James K. Polk, December [2]4, 1826, in *PAJ* 6: 246 ("old republican"); Harrisburg paper from August 1828 quoted in Hailperin, "Pro-Jackson Sentiment," 225 ("all the measures"). See also *Address of the Democratic Republican Committee of Allegheny County* and John Sergeant to Henry Clay, October 2, 1826, in *PHC* 5: 744–45. For the long memory of Fries's Rebellion in eastern Pennsylvania, see Paul Douglas Newman, *Fries's Rebellion: The Enduring Struggle for the American Revolution* (Philadelphia: University of Pennsylvania Press, 2004), 189–92.

75 *Address of the Democratic Republican Committee of Allegheny County*, 13 ("race" and "avenge the wrongs"), 12 ("reeking with the blood").

76 [John A. Shulze], "Annual Message to the Assembly—1827," December 5, 1827, in *Papers of the Pennsylvania Governors*, 5: 747; Louis H. Arky, "The Mechanics' Union of Trade Associations and the Formation of the Philadelphia Workingmen's Movement," *PMHB* 76 (April 1952): 142–76, esp. 170–71; Shankman, "John Quincy Adams and National Republicanism."

77 Pittsburgh speaker quoted in Hailperin, "Pro-Jackson Sentiment," 212 and 228 (attack on Binns's home); Philadelphia committee quoted in Cole, *Vindicating Andrew Jackson*, 106–7, and see 32–33 and 179–203. Story from Juniata River Valley from A. K. McClure, *Old Time Notes of Pennsylvania* (Philadelphia: John C. Winston Company, 1905), 26. Jackson carried forty-five of fifty counties in Pennsylvania, taking 66.8% of the total vote and receiving overwhelming (80% or more) support in thirteen counties. Among these strongholds was Perry County in the Juniata River Valley, where bullet-marked log houses were still standing: Sherman Day, *Historical Collections of the State of Pennsylvania* (Philadelphia, 1843), 537–42, esp. 538–40. Jackson also did exceptionally well in remote parts of the Poconos and the north-central border with New York (Pike, Venango, and Tioga), in the southwestern corner of the state (Somerset and Westmoreland), and in German-dominated farming areas (Northampton and Northumberland). On the other hand, Luzerne County, home of the Wyoming Valley, favored Jackson only by 53% to 47%. See Dubin, *United States Presidential Elections*, 48.

See also Robert Moore to Henry Clay, February 10, 1827, in *PHC* 6: 181–82; Peter Paul Francis Degrand to Clay, February 8, 1827, in ibid., 6: 177; Thomas Smith to Clay, August 1, 1827, in ibid., 6: 840, 840n.

78 Rachel Jackson quoted in Meacham, *American Lion*, 5. This is not to suggest that the general's friends were above sexual innuendo. In 1828, for example, Jacksonian editor Isaac Hill of New Hampshire began a scurrilous rumor about John Quincy Adams acting as a kind of pimp for the Russian czar. For Rachel in New Orleans, see Tom Kanon, *Tennesseans at War, 1812–1815: Andrew Jackson, the Creek War, and the Battle of New Orleans* (Tuscaloosa: University of Alabama Press, 2014), 178.

79 AJ to Samuel Houston, December 15, 1826, in *PAJ* 6: 243 ("*you know me . . . Justice will vissit him*," emphasis in original); Cole, *Vindicating Andrew Jackson*, 50–51 (AJ waiting for mail) and 194–95 (Jackson issues addresses); Parsons, *Birth of Modern Politics*, 144. For AJ's paternalistic posture toward his slaves in this period, see AJ to William Donelson, October 8, 1829, in *PAJ* 7: 480–82.

80 Andrew Burstein, *The Passions of Andrew Jackson* (New York: Alfred A. Knopf, 2003), 172–73; Daniel Walker Howe, *What Hath God Wrought: The Transformation of America, 1815–1848* (New York: Oxford University Press, 2007), 328–29. An enlarged tomb with the inscription was added between 1831 and 1833: Patricia Brady, *A Being So Gentle: The Frontier Love Story* of *Rachel and Andrew Jackson* (New York: St. Martin's Press, 2001), 229; email correspondence with Melissa Gismondi, July 4, 2016; email correspondence with Marsha Mullin, July 28, 2016.

CONCLUSION

1 Jon Meacham, *American Lion: Andrew Jackson in the White House* (New York: Random House, 2008), 64 and 62–65; Reda C. Goff, "A Physical Profile of Andrew Jackson," *THQ* 28 (Fall 1969): 297–309, esp. 307–9. See also Andrew Burstein, *The Passions of Andrew Jackson* (New York: Alfred A. Knopf, 2003), 172–73, and Daniel Walker Howe, *What Hath God Wrought: The Transformation of America, 1815–1848* (New York: Oxford University Press, 2007), 328–29.

2 AJ to John Coffee, June 18, 1824, in *PAJ* 5: 417 ("monied aristocracy"); AJ, "Inaugural Address," March 4, 1829, in *CMP* 2: 436–38. Important overviews include Daniel Feller, *The Public Lands in Jacksonian Politics, 1815–1840* (Madison: University of Wisconsin Press, 1984); Feller, "Politics and Society: Toward a Jacksonian Synthesis," *JER* 10 (Summer 1990): 135–61; Donald B. Cole, *The Presidency of Andrew Jackson* (Lawrence: University of Kansas Press, 1993), 54–61; Seth Rockman, "Jacksonian America," in *American History Now*, ed. Eric Foner and Lisa McGirr (Philadelphia: Temple University Press, 2011), 52–74; Sean Wilentz, "Society, Politics, and the Market Revolution," in *The New American History*, ed. Eric Foner (Philadelphia: Temple University Press, 1997), 61–84; Harry L. Watson, *Liberty and Power: The Politics of Jacksonian America* (New York: Noonday, 1990); Richard J. Moss, "Jacksonian Democracy: A Note on the Origins and Growth of the Term," *THQ* 34 (Summer 1975): 145–53.

3 Lynn L. Marshall, "The Authorship of Jackson's Bank Veto Message," *MVHR* 50 (December 1963): 469 (quote as rendered by Amos Kendall) and 466–77; AJ to Hardy Murfee Cryer, August 18, 1831, in *PAJ* 9: 507 (disgust with cabinet members); AJ to Andrew Jackson Jr., August 20, 1829, in *PAJ* 7: 386 (tomb). See also AJ to Anthony Bledsoe Shelby, April 23, 1832, in *PAJ* 10: 250. For the Eaton affair, see Meacham, *American Lion*, 66–68 and 70–85, and Howe, *What Hath God Wrought*, 335–42.

4 AJ to John Christmas McLemore, April 26, 1829, in *PAJ* 7: 184; John M. Belohlavek, *"Let the Eagle Soar!": The Foreign Policy of Andrew Jackson* (Lincoln:

University of Nebraska Press, 1985), 9 ("Ask nothing . . . submit to nothing"). In the letter to McLemore, AJ also denounced Pleasant M. Miller, the Tennessee arch-conservative with whom he had allied to fight relief in 1820 and 1822. Miller remained one of AJ's supporters until 1829. See *PAJ* 7: 140n.

5 "Constitution of the Cherokee Nation, 1827," in *Indian Removal: A Norton Casebook*, ed. David S. Heidler and Jeanne T. Heidler (New York: W. W. Norton and Company, 2007), 103 ("African race"), 102 ("prevent the citizens"); "John Eaton and the Cherokees, 1829," letter of April 18, 1829, in ibid., 127 ("original Sovereignty" and "waged war"), 128 ("mildness"), 130 ("Sovereign States"). See also AJ to John Coffee, October 4, 1829, in *PAJ* 7: 477–78.

6 See especially Mary Hershberger, "Mobilizing Women, Anticipating Abolition: The Struggle Against Indian Removal in the 1830s," *JAH* 86 (June 1999): 15–40, and Howe, *What Hath God Wrought*, 342–57 and 331–34. For accounts more sympathetic to Jackson, see Sean Wilentz, *The Rise of American Democracy: From Jefferson to Lincoln* (New York: W. W. Norton and Company, 2005), 322–29; Andrew V. Remini, *Andrew Jackson and the Course of American Democracy, 1833–1845* (New York: Harper and Row, 1984); and F. P. Prucha, "Andrew Jackson's Indian Policy: A Reassessment," *JAH* 56 (December 1969): 527–39.

7 Eaton and Coffee quoted in Ethan Davis, "An Administrative Trail of Tears: Indian Removal," *AJLH* 50 (January 2008–2010): 67, and see 49–100; Mary Young, "The Exercise of Sovereignty in Cherokee Georgia," *JER* 10 (1990): 56–57 and 43–63; Hershberger, "Mobilizing Women, Anticipating Abolition," 15–16; Louis Assier-Andrieu, *L'autorité du passé: Essai anthropologique sur la Common Law* (Paris: Dalloz, 2011), 152 (discussion of Supreme Court of Tennessee ruling on natives in 1826). For Jackson's disgust with wealthy chiefs, see AJ to Secretary of State, October 6, 1821, in *TPUS* 22: 233.

8 Wilson Lumpkin, *The Removal of the Cherokee Indians from Georgia* (2 vols., New York: Dodd, Mead, and Company, 1907), 1: 11 ("unwavering"); Lumpkin, "Inaugural Address," [November 9, 1831], in ibid., 1: 91 ("unofficial"); AJ to John Coffee, April 7, 1832, in *PAJ* 10: 226 ("arm of the Government"). See also AJ to Robert Love, December 10, 1831, in *PAJ* 9: 768; Wilson Lumpkin to AJ, July 12, 1832, in *PAJ* 10: 412–14; and Young, "Exercise of Sovereignty," 46–47 and 62. Lumpkin beat Gilmer, 51.4% to 48.6%, in 1831: Michael J. Dubin, *United States Gubernatorial Elections, 1776–1860: The Official Results by State and County* (Jefferson, NC: McFarland and Company, 2003), 32–33.

9 ["William Penn"], "A Brief View of the Present Relations Between the Government and the People of the United States and the Indians Within Our National Limits," November 1829, in *Discovering the American Past: A Look at the Evidence: Volume I: to 1877*, ed. William Bruce Wheeler, Susan Becker, and Lorri Glover (7th ed., Boston: Cengage Learning, 2012), 193 ("great end"); James Booker Gardiner to AJ, April 2, 1831, in *PAJ* 9: 161; Alfred A. Cave, "Abuse of Power: Andrew Jackson and the Indian Removal Act of 1830," *Historian* 65 (Winter 2003): 1330–53; Howe, *What Hath God Wrought*, 350 (Pittsburgh petition); Davis, "Administrative Trail of Tears," 52–60. See also "Removal of the Indians," *North American Review*, 31 (October 1830): 423 and 396–442; and *The Cherokee Removal: A Brief History with Documents*, ed. Theda Perdue and Michael D. Green (Boston: St. Martin's Press, 1995), 1–21, esp. 13–14.

10 "Speech of the Hon. Wilson Lumpkin of Georgia," [May 1830], in Lumpkin, *Removal of the Cherokee Indians*, 1: 69 ("Yes, sir," "for so many years," and "perplexities"), 1: 74 ("No man" and "times that are gone by"); "Henry G. Lamar Supports Indian Removal, 1830," in *Indian Removal*, ed. Heidler and Heidler, 141

and 140–43; Fred S. Rolater, "The American Indian and the Origin of the Second Party System," *WMH* 76 (1993): 180–203.

11 AJ to William Berkeley Lewis, August 25, 1830, in *PAJ* 8: 501; AJ to John Pitchlynn, August 5, 1830, in *PAJ* 8: 466 (also quoted in Cave, "Abuse of Power," 1340); Davis, "Administrative Trail of Tears," 77–85; George E. Lankford, "Trouble at Dancing Rabbit Creek: Missionaries and Choctaw Removal," *JPH* 62 (Spring 1984): 51–66; Greg O'Brien, "Treaty of Dancing Rabbit Creek [1830]," *Encyclopedia of Alabama* online, at http://encyclopediaofalabama.org/article/h-3426 (accessed October 21, 2016).

12 AJ to Anthony Bledsoe Shelby, April 23, 1832, in *PAJ* 10: 250 ("get clear of," referring to Indians in Mississippi); Marshall quoted in Howe, *What Hath God Wrought*, 355; "First Blood Shed by the Georgians, 1830," in *Indian Removal*, ed. Heidler and Heidler, 119; Davis, "Administrative Trail of Tears," 86–90.

13 AJ to John Coffee, April 7, 1832, in *PAJ* 10: 226 ("still born"); Tim Alan Garrison, "Beyond *Worcester*: The Alabama Supreme Court and the Sovereignty of the Creek Nation," *JER* 19 (Autumn 1999): 439 ("pretension"), 442 ("the beast"), 428 (Lumpkin quote), 435 (two of three judges), and 423–50 generally; Mary E. Young, "The Creek Frauds: A Study in Conscience and Corruption," *MVHR* 42 (December 1955): 411–37; Steven Inskeep, *Jacksonland: President Andrew Jackson, Cherokee Chief John Ross, and a Great American Land Grab* (New York: Penguin, 2015), 242–54.

14 Wilson Lumpkin to AJ, May 20, 1835, in *CAJ* 5: 351; W. J. Beattie to Margaret Beattie, April 29, 1833, in Brett E. Whalen, comp., "A Vermonter on the Trial of Tears," *VH* 66 (Winter/Spring 1998): 34 ("emigrating"); J. McNab to W. J. Beattie, July 2, 1834, in ibid., 36; Jane Beattie to W. J. Beattie, July 15, 1835, in ibid., 37 ("kill her" and family dislike of slavery); W. J. Beattie to Jacob Covert, June 25, 1830, in ibid., 33 (profits); James Beattie to W. J. Beattie, February 16, 1831, in ibid., 34. On steamboats and removal, see Robert H. Gudmestad, *Steamboats and the Rise of the Cotton Kingdom* (Baton Rouge: Louisiana State University Press, 2011), and Davis, "Administrative Trial of Tears," 95. See also Young, "The Creek Frauds," and Cole, *Presidency of Andrew Jackson*, 54–61.

15 Young, "Creek Frauds," 427–28; Matthew T. Pearcy, "'The Ruthless Hand of War': Andrew A. Humphreys in the Second Seminole War," *FHQ* 85 (Fall 2006): 123–53; Albert Hubbard Roberts, "The Dade Massacre," *FHQ* 5 (January 1927): 123–38; John K. Mahon, *History of the Second Seminole War, 1835–1842* (Gainesville: University of Florida Press, 1967).

16 J. McNab to W. J. Beattie, July 14, 1836, in "Vermonter on the Trail of Tears," 37; Inskeep, *Jacksonland*, 335 ("for the payment") and 312–36; Davis, "Administrative Trail of Tears," 89 (regulations about horses and luggage); Katherine DuVal, *The Native Ground: Indians and Colonists in the Heart of the Continent* (Philadelphia: University of Pennsylvania Press, 2006), 227–44; Gaston Litton, "The Journal of a Party of Emigrating Creek Indians, 1835–36," *JSH* 7 (May 1941): 225–42.

17 Pearcy, "'Ruthless Hand of War,'" 138 ("Indian in every bush") and 152–53; Edward C. Coker and Daniel L. Schafer, "A West Point Graduate in the Second Seminole War: William Warren Chapman and the View from Fort Foster," *FHQ* 68 (April 1990): 470 (1838 letter); Michael G. Schene, "Ballooning in the Second Seminole War," *FHQ* 55 (April 1977): 480–82; Remini, *Andrew Jackson and the Course of American Democracy*, 306–12. The bounty plan was ignored and the balloon plan rejected, but the War Department did pay for bloodhounds. These dogs

never made it into the field, but they did provoke much disgust among the war's critics. See Mahon, *History of the Second Seminole War*, 265–67.

18 Cass quoted in Alan Taylor, *The Civil War of 1812: American Citizens, British Subjects, Irish Rebels, and Indian Allies* (New York: Vintage Books, 2010), 433 ("Sovereignty") and 430–35; Belohlavek, *"Let the Eagle Soar,"* 41 (naval budget and Jackson quote) and 43; Pearcy, "'Ruthless Hand of War,'" 153 ($30 million); Davis, "Administrative Trial of Tears," 96–97 ($5 million); William Savin Fulton to AJ, April 25, 1832, in *PAJ* 10: 253–54. On the importance of the navy, see also AJ, "Seventh Annual Message," December 7, 1835, in *CMP* 3: 173.

19 David F. Long, "'Martial Thunder': The First Official American Armed Intervention in Asia," *PHR* 42 (May 1973): 148 ("Who great man") and 143–49; AJ, "Fourth Annual Message," December 4, 1832, in *CMP* 2: 596 ("lawless pirates"); AJ, "Sixth Annual Message to Congress," December 1, 1834, in *CMP* 3: 106 ("take redress"), 107 ("just censure"); Belohlavek, *"Let the Eagle Soar!,"* 90–126 and 152–62.

20 Daniel Parker to AJ, February 10, 1817, in *PAJ* 4: 90 ("money changers" and "*great* bank," emphasis in original); AJ to AJ Donelson, January 21, 1824, in *PAJ* 5: 343 ("u states"); Cheathem, *Andrew Jackson, Southerner*, 160–71.

21 James Houston to James K. Polk, February 4, 1827, in *CJP* 1: 82; Robert V. Remini, *Andrew Jackson and the Bank War* (New York: W. W. Norton and Company, 1967), 36–39; Howe, *What Hath God Wrought*, 373–77. Houston was a former representative of Blount County, and as of 1827 a farmer in Maury County.

22 AJ to John Overton, June 8, 1829, in *PAJ* 7: 271 ("*curbed*," emphasis in original); AJ to Moses Dawson, July 17, 1830, in *PAJ* 8: 431 ("intirely national"); Worden Pope to AJ, June 19, 1831, in *PAJ* 9: 317 ("great majority") and 318 ("effigy Banks"); James Booker Gardiner to AJ [summary of conversation with Samuel D. Ingham], April 2, 1831, in *PAJ* 9: 163 ("*hard battle*," emphasis in original); Howe, *What Hath God Wrought*, 375 (Biddle vote); Marshall, "Authorship of Jackson's Bank Veto Message." For Biddle's 1829 offer, see *PAJ* 7: 568n–69n. For Tennessee support for the BUS: "From [Grand Jury of Maury County]," April 26, 1832, in *CJP* 1: 466–67.

23 AJ to Hardy Murfee Cryer, April 25, 1831, in *PAJ* 9: 214 ("*monster*," emphasis in original); Felix Grundy to AJ, October 22, 1829, in *PAJ* 7: 505 ("National Bank"); "Alexis de Sarcy" to Henry Clay, February 11, 1830, in *PHC* 8: 176 ("cannot satisfy"), 175 ("system"); William Branch Giles to AJ, October 22, 1829, in *PAJ* 7: 504 ("individual owners"); AJ to William Branch Giles, November 21, 1829, in *PAJ* 7: 566; Kevin R. Gutzman, "Preserving the Patrimony: William Branch Giles and Virginia Versus the Federal Tariff," *VMHB* 104 (Summer 1996): 341–72. See also John Lauritz Larson, "'Bind the Republic Together': The National Union and the Struggle for a System of Internal Improvements," *JAH* 74 (September 1987): 363–87; Carlton Jackson, "The Internal Improvement Vetoes of Andrew Jackson," *THQ* 25 (Fall 1966): 261–79; Lacy K. Ford, "Republican Ideology in a Slave Society: The Political Economy of John C. Calhoun," *JSH* 54 (August 1988): 405–24, and AJ to John Kintzing Kane, Robert M. Lewis, and William Platt, October 2, 1829, in *PAJ* 7: 476.

24 AJ to Allan Ditchfield Campbell, May 13, 1832, in *PAJ* 10: 270 ("Mamoths of corruption") and 266n; Remini, *Andrew Jackson and the Bank War*, 67–87; AJ to James Alexander Hamilton, December 12, 1831, in *PAJ* 9: 769; AJ to John Randolph, December 22, 1831, in *PAJ* 9: 782; Donald B. Cole, *A Jackson Man: Amos Kendall and the Rise of American Democracy* (Baton Rouge: Louisiana State University Press, 2004), 9–30, 120–29, 163–70; Marshall, "Authorship of Jackson's Bank Veto Message"; Wilentz, *Rise of American Democracy*, 288–91.

25 "Draft by Amos Kendall," in *PAJ* 10: 390 ("Generals . . . of a hostile") and 379–410; AJ, "Veto Message," July 10, 1832, in *CMP* 2: 578 ("subjects"), 590 (conclusion); Marshall, "Authorship of Jackson's Bank Veto Message." See also Howe, *What Hath God Wrought*, 331–34, and Watson, *Liberty and Power*, 132–71. Here again, my thanks to Dan Feller for his help with this source.

26 Remini, *Andrew Jackson and the Bank War*, 98 (thirty thousand copies); Wilentz, *Rise of American Democracy*, 367–74; Robert V. Remini, "Election of 1832," in *History of American Presidential Elections, 1789–1968*, ed. Arthur M. Schlesinger Jr. et al. (4 vols., New York: Chelsea House, 1971), 1: 494–516. For a fresh look at the political alliances around and against Jackson, see Jeffrey S. Selinger, *Embracing Dissent: Political Violence and Party Development in the United States* (Philadelphia: University of Pennsylvania Press, 2016), 83–108, esp. 97–101.

27 AJ, "Second Inaugural Address," March 1, 1833, in *CAJ* 5: 27 ("let all alone," rough draft in AJ's writing, not in final text); [AJ], "Paper Read to the Cabinet," September 18, 1833, in *CAJ* 5: 194 ("misnamed," "British system," "system of bargaining," "system of favoritism," and "monied classes"); AJ to Joel R. Poinsett, February 7, 1833, in *CAJ* 5: 15 ("Repleven laws"), and see also AJ to Martin Van Buren, January 25, 1833, in *CAJ* 5: 13.

28 Taney quoted in Howe, *What Hath God Wrought*, 442 ("sovereignty of any state") and 387–89; Roger B. Taney to AJ, August 5, 1833, in *CAJ* 5: 148 ("My mind"); Taney to AJ, March?, 1833, in *CAJ* 5: 35–40; Taney to AJ, April 29, 1833, in *CAJ* 5: 67–71; Taney to AJ, September 17, 1833, in *CAJ* 5: 191–92. For Jackson's thinking about the BUS and other banks in this period, see also AJ to William J. Duane, June 26, 1833, in *CAJ* 5: 113–28.

29 James K. Polk to AJ, December 23, 1833, in *CAJ* 5: 236 ("nay all Banks," in AJ reply on backside); AJ to Martin Van Buren, September 19, 1833, in *CAJ* 5: 204 ("sterling man"); Remini, *Andrew Jackson and the Bank War*, 41–42 and 88–108; AJ to William J. Duane, June 26, 1833, in *CAJ* 5: 113–28, esp. 125 (BUS and panic of 1819). See also "Removal of Federal Deposits," in *Historical Dictionary of the Jacksonian Era and Manifest Destiny*, ed. Terry Corps (Lanham, MD: Scarecrow Press, 2006), 253–55; Michael F. Holt, *The Rise and Fall of the American Whig Party: Jacksonian Politics and the Onset of the Civil War* (New York: Oxford University Press, 1999).

30 AJ to William Findlay, August 20, 1834, in *CAJ* 5: 285–86 (credits Benton along with Taney and Polk for policy shift to hard money); "Commerce with Asia," *St. Louis Enquirer*, September to November 1819; William Gouge, *A Short History of Paper Money and Banking in the United States* (Philadelphia, 1833), Part II, 135; Watson, *Liberty and Power,* 140; Bray Hammond, *Banks and Politics in America: From the Revolution to the Civil War* (Princeton, NJ: Princeton University Press, 1957), 176–77, 493–99; Stephen Mihm, *A Nation of Counterfeiters: Capitalists, Con Men, and the Making of the United States* (Cambridge, MA: Harvard University Press, 2007). The literature on the social changes overtaking northern artisans and farmers is vast. See Sean Wilentz, *Chants Democratic: New York City and the Rise of the American Working Class* (New York: Oxford University Press, 1984); Paul E. Johnson, *Sam Patch, the Famous Jumper* (New York: Hill and Wang, 2003); Christopher Clark, *The Roots of Rural Capitalism: Western Massachusetts, 1790–1860* (Ithaca, NY: Cornell University Press, 1990); and Mary Babson Fuhrer, *A Crisis of Community: The Trials and Transformation of a New England Town, 1815–1848* (Chapel Hill: University of North Carolina Press, 2014). For the Workingmen's parties see especially Wilentz, *Rise of American Democracy*, 282–87, and Louis H. Arky, "The Mechanics' Union

of Trade Associations and the Formation of the Philadelphia Workingman's Movement," *PMHB* 76 (April 1952): 142–76.

31 AJ to Martin Van Buren, August 8, 1834, in *CAJ* 5: 281 ("many had not" and "prosperity"); AJ to Van Buren, August 16, 1834, in *CAJ* 5: 283 ("as well dug"); *Morning Post* from 1837 quoted in Leland Hamilton Jenks, *The Migration of British Capital to 1875* (1927; London: Nelson, 1963), 365n ("law of debtor and creditor"); Alexander Trotter, *Observations on the Financial Position and Credit of Such of the States of the North American Union as Have Contracted Public Debts* (London, 1839), 1 ("national credit") and 41–42 ("British sovereign" made legal tender); Felix Grundy to AJ, October 22, 1829, in *PAJ* 7: 505. For the statutes, both dated June 28, 1834, and titled "An Act concerning the gold coins of the United States, and for other purposes" and "An act regulating the value of certain foreign gold coins within the United States": 4 *SL* 699–700 and 4 *SL* 700–701. For the dramatic shift by British investors from South America to the United States in the 1830s, see Peter Temin, "The Economic Consequences of the Bank War," *JPE* 76 (March–April 1968): 263 and 257–74; Temin, "The Anglo-American Business Cycle, 1820–60," *ECHR* 27 (March 1974): 207–21; Namsuk Kim and John Joseph Wallis, "The Market for American State Government Bonds in Britain and the United States, 1830–43," *ECHR* 58 (November 2005): 736–54; J. Fred Rippy, "Latin America and the British Investment 'Boom' of the 1820s," *JMH* 19 (June 1947): 122–29.

32 Dorothy R. Adler, *British Investment in American Railways, 1834–1898*, ed. Muriel E. Hidy (Charlottesville: University of Virginia Press, 1970), 8–9 (total state debts from \$26 million to \$172 million, 1830–38), 9–11 (Alabama, Mississippi, Arkansas, and Florida have \$22.3 million in debts by 1838, of which \$19.3 million in banking, or 86.5% and foreign holdings); Remini, *Andrew Jackson and the Bank War*, 125 (number of deposit banks).

33 "List of the Purchases of Land at Columbus and Chocchuma in Mississippi in 1833 and 1834," in *ASP: Public Lands* 7: 377–447, summary on 447 (totals from these years including two other land offices in the state came to over seven million acres); Trotter, *Observations on the Financial Position and Credit*, 377 (land sales); Jenks, *Migration of British Capital*, 65–98 (trade from 1832 to 1836). See also Howe, *What Hath God Wrought*, 363; Major L. Wilson, *The Presidency of Martin Van Buren* (Lawrence: University of Kansas Press, 1984), 45–46; and Joshua D. Rothman, *Flush Times and Fever Dreams: A Story of Capitalism and Slavery in the Age of Jackson* (Athens: University of Georgia Press, 2012).

34 Trotter, *Observations on the Financial Position and Credit*, 36; AJ to Andrew Jackson Jr., February 12, 1834, in *CAJ* 5: 247 ("farmer" in singular and "must go"); Jackson quoted in Donald B. Cole, *Martin Van Buren and the American Political System* (Princeton, NJ: Princeton University Press, 1984), 277; Feller, *Public Lands in Jacksonian Politics*, 129–31 and 184–86; Cole, *Presidency of Andrew Jackson*, 59–61 and 234–36. See also "Memorand[u]m for Andrew Jackson jnr.," [March 1832], in *PAJ* 10: 215–18; AJ to Andrew Jackson Jr., December 22, 1833, in *CAJ* 5: 234–35, and AJ to Andrew Jackson Jr., February 16, 1834, in *CAJ* 5: 248–49.

35 Martin Van Buren to AJ, April 24, 1837, in *CAJ* 5: 479; Peter L. Rousseau, "Jacksonian Monetary Policy, Specie Flows, and the Panic of 1837," *JEH* 62 (June 2002): 457–59; Jessica M. Lepler, *The Many Panics of 1837: People, Politics, and the Creation of a Transatlantic Financial Crisis* (New York: Cambridge University Press, 2013); Alastair Roberts, *America's First Great Depression: Economic Crisis and Political Disorder After the Panic of 1837* (Ithaca, NY: Cornell University Press, 2012).

36 AJ to Martin Van Buren, June 6, 1837, in *CAJ* 5: 487 ("drain us"); AJ to Van Buren, July 6, 1838, in *CAJ* 5: 555 ("own sovereign"); AJ to Van Buren, May 12, 1837, in *CAJ* 5: 483 ("produce good . . . sweeps off"); Martin Van Buren, "Special Session Message," September 4, 1837, in *CMP* 3: 344 ("All communities") and 324–45; Henry Clay, "Speech in Senate, January 20, 1840," in *PHC* 9: 378; James Roger Sharp, *The Jacksonians Versus the Banks: Politics in the States After the Panic of 1837* (New York: Columbia University Press, 1970), 79; Wilson, *Presidency of Martin Van Buren*, 72–74 and 143–44. For the Tennessee Whigs in the late 1830s, see Thomas P. Abernathy, "The Origin of the Whig Party in Tennessee," *MVHR 12* (March 1926), 504–22, and Carroll Van West, "The Democratic and Whig Political Activists of Middle Tennessee," *THQ* 42 (Spring 1983): 3–17.

37 Paul Goodman, "The Emergence of Homestead Exemption in the United States: Accommodation and Resistance to the Market Revolution, 1840–1880," *JAH* 80 (September 1993): 470 ("sound" and "wholesome"), 472 and 470–98; Lena London, "The Initial Homestead Exemption in Texas," *SWHQ* 57 (April 1954): 443 (terms of 1839 law), 440n (Spanish origins), 432 (number of states), and 432–53; London, "Homestead Exemption in the Indiana Constitution of 1851," *IMH* 44 (September 1948): 267–80; J. F. D, "The Homestead Exemption," *American Law Register* 10 (September 1862): 641–56. Taney ruled against two Illinois statutes for protecting mortgaged estates from auctions: Howe, *What Hath God Wrought*, 441–45. See also Alison D. Morantz, "There's No Place Like Home: Homestead Exemption and Judicial Constructions of Family in Nineteenth-Century America," *LHR* 24 (Summer 2006): 245–95; David E. Narrett, "A Choice of Destiny: Immigration Policy, Slavery, and the Annexation of Texas," *SWHQ* 100 (January 1997): 271–302; and Brian Delay, *War of a Thousand Deserts: Indian Raids and the U.S.-Mexican War* (New Haven, CT: Yale University Press, 2008).

38 AJ to the Senate and House of Representatives of the United States, February 6, 1837, in *CMP* 3: 278; AJ in interview quoted in James E. Arnold, "The Hermitage Church," *THQ* 28 (Summer 1969): 117. The story comes from James Parton's 1860 biography. For these last messages, see Wilson, *Presidency of Martin Van Buren*, 147–49; AJ to Roger B. Taney, October 13, 1836, in *CAJ* 5: 429–30; and AJ, "Farewell Address," March 4, 1837, in *CMP* 3: 292–308.

39 AJ to Francis P. Blair, May 23, 1842, in *CAJ* 6: 153; William M. Wiecek, "'A Peculiar Conservatism' and the Dorr Rebellion: Constitutional Clash in Jacksonian America," *AJLH* 22 (July 1978): 237–53; Cheathem, *Andrew Jackson, Southerner*, 189–99 (Texas) and 182–88 (firewood and plantation management).

40 Goff, "A Physical Profile of Andrew Jackson," 300 (quote and daguerreotype); John Catron to AJ, June 8, 1836, in *CAJ* 5: 401 ("great Slave"); Cheathem, *Andrew Jackson, Southerner*, 200–205 (deathbed) and 150–51 (Andrew Jackson Jr.).

41 Adams quoted in Lynn Hudson Parsons, "In Which the Political Becomes the Personal, and Vice Versa: The Last Ten Years of John Quincy Adams and Andrew Jackson," *JER* 23 (Autumn 2003): 443, and see 421–43; Cheathem, *Andrew Jackson, Southerner*, 202 ("I was very proud").

42 James K. Polk, "Inaugural Address," March 4, 1845, in *CMP* 4: 379 ("merge"), 380 ("can not be" and "dominions"), 376 ("swarming millions"); Walter Nugent, "The American Habit of Empire, and the Cases of Polk and Bush," *WHQ* 38 (Spring 2007): 4–24, esp. 13–14; Amy S. Greenberg, *A Wicked War: Polk, Clay, Lincoln, and the 1846 U.S. Invasion of Mexico* (New York: Vintage Books, 2012); Michael Scott Van Wagenen, *Remembering the Forgotten War: The Enduring Legacies of the*

U.S.-Mexican War (Amherst: University of Massachusetts Press, 2012); Robert W. Merry, *A Country of Vast Designs: James K. Polk, the Mexican War, and the Conquest of the American Continent* (New York: Simon and Schuster, 2010).

43 Polk quoted in Howe, *What Hath God Wrought*, 741, and see 740–43; Bill Groneman, *Alamo Defenders, A Genealogy: The People and Their Words* (Fort Worth: Eakin Press, 1990); Robert W. Ikard, "The Walker Boys: Were Maury Countians at the Alamo?," *THQ* 51 (Winter 1992): 191–96; Delay, *War of a Thousand Deserts*, 194–225. American newspapers closely followed news from Texas. See "Disastrous Intelligence," *National Banner and Nashville Whig* (Nashville), April 8, 1836, and "Highly Important from Texas," *New York Spectator*, April 11, 1836.

44 Howe, *What Hath God Wrought*, 756 ("New Orleans!") and 744–91; "Our Relations with Mexico," *The North American* (Philadelphia), May 11, 1846; Benton quotes from "Missouri on Annexation," *Alexandria Gazette* (Alexandria, VA), January 22, 1845.

45 "Missouri on Annexation," *Alexandria Gazette*, January 22, 1845; Lacy K. Ford Jr., "Making the 'White Man's Country' White: Race, Slavery, and State-Building in the Jacksonian South," *JER* 19 (Winter 1999): 713–37, quote from 1834 Tennessee convention ("social compact") on 731 and from 1835 North Carolina convention ("nation of white people") on 732; Winbourne Magruder Drake, "The Mississippi Constitutional Convention of 1832," *JSH* 23 (August 1957): 368 ("*democracy*," emphasis in original) and 354–70; Democrats quoted in Eric Ledell Smith, "The End of Black Voting Rights in Pennsylvania: African Americans and the Pennsylvania Constitutional Convention of 1837–1838," *PH* 65 (Summer 1998): 289–90. See also Chase C. Mooney, "The Question of Slavery and the Free Negro in the Tennessee Constitutional Convention of 1834," *JSH* 12 (November 1946): 487–509; James T. Currie, "From Slavery to Freedom in Mississippi's Legal System," *JNH* 65 (Spring 1980): 112–25, esp. 116–17. For white supremacy overseas, see Brian Rouleau, "How Honolulu Almost Burned and Why Sailors Matter to Early American Foreign Relations," *DH* 38 (June 2014), 501–25.

46 David Grimsted, "Rioting in Its Jacksonian Setting," *AHR* 77 (April 1972): 361–97; Michael J. Pfeifer, *The Roots of Rough Justice: Origins of American Lynching* (Urbana: University of Illinois Press, 2011), 15–21; Walter Johnson, *River of Dark Dreams: Slavery and Empire in the Cotton Kingdom* (Cambridge, MA: Harvard University Press, 2013), 46–72; Alan Taylor, *The Internal Enemy: Slavery and War in Virginia, 1772–1832* (New York: W. W. Norton and Company, 2013); Carl E. Prince, "The Great 'Riot Year': Jacksonian Democracy and Patterns of Violence in 1834," *JER* 5 (Spring 1985): 18–19. For relevant treatments of abolitionists, see Hershberger, "Mobilizing Women, Anticipating Abolition"; David Brion Davis, *Inhuman Bondage: The Rise and Fall of Slavery in the New World* (New York: Oxford University Press, 2006), 250–96; John Demos, "The Antislavery Movement and the Problem of Violent 'Means,'" *NEQ* 37 (December 1964): 501–26. On the death penalty, see Stuart Banner, *The Death Penalty in America: An American History* (Cambridge, MA: Harvard University Press, 2002), 112–43; Louis P. Masur, *Rites of Execution: Capital Punishment and the Transformation of American Culture, 1776–1865* (New York: Oxford University Press, 1989), 119–21 and 141–53; Alan Rodgers, "'Under Sentence of Death': The Movement to Abolish Capital Punishment in Massachusetts, 1835–1848," *NEQ* 66 (March 1993): 27–46. For violence in antebellum culture, see also Lisa Arellano, *Vigilantes and Lynch Mobs: Narratives of Community and Nation* (Philadelphia: University of Pennsylvania

Press, 2012); Richard Slotkin, *Regeneration Through Violence: The Mythology of the American Frontier, 1600–1860* (Middletown, CT: Wesleyan University Press, 1973), and Amy Greenberg, *Manifest Manhood and the Antebellum American Empire* (New York: Cambridge University Press, 2005).

47 John Quincy Adams famously declared that the United States did not—or should not—go abroad "in search of monsters to destroy" in an Independence Day address in Washington in 1821. See Greg Russell, "John Quincy Adams and the Ethics of America's National Interest," *RIS* 17 (January 1993): 23–38, esp. 37–38.

INDEX

Note: The initials AJ refer to Andrew Jackson. References to figures are denoted by an italic *f* following the page number.